Making **Jews** Modern

THE MODERN JEWISH EXPERIENCE

Making **Jews** Modern

The Yiddish and Ladino Press in the
Russian and Ottoman Empires

Sarah Abrevaya Stein

INDIANA UNIVERSITY PRESS
BLOOMINGTON AND INDIANAPOLIS

PUBLICATION OF THIS BOOK IS MADE POSSIBLE IN PART BY GENEROUS SUPPORT
FROM THE KORET FOUNDATION.

THIS BOOK IS A PUBLICATION OF

INDIANA UNIVERSITY PRESS
601 NORTH MORTON STREET
BLOOMINGTON, INDIANA 47404-3797 USA

HTTP://IUPRESS.INDIANA.EDU
Telephone orders   800-842-6796
Fax orders   812-855-7931
Orders by e-mail   IUPORDER@INDIANA.EDU

MANUFACTURED IN THE UNITED STATES OF AMERICA

LIBRARY OF CONGRESS CATALOGING-IN-PUBLICATION DATA

STEIN, SARAH ABREVAYA.
MAKING JEWS MODERN : THE YIDDISH AND LADINO PRESS IN THE RUSSIAN AND OTTOMAN
EMPIRES / SARAH ABREVAYA STEIN.
P. CM. — (THE MODERN JEWISH EXPERIENCE)
INCLUDES BIBLIOGRAPHICAL REFERENCES AND INDEX.
ISBN: 978-0-253-21893-3
1. YIDDISH NEWSPAPERS — RUSSIA — HISTORY. 2. LADINO NEWSPAPERS — BALKAN PENINSULA —
HISTORY. 3. JEWS — CIVILIZATION — PRESS COVERAGE — RUSSIA. 4. JEWS — CIVILIZATION —
PRESS COVERAGE — BALKAN PENINSULA. 5. FRAYND. 6. TIEMPO.
I. TITLE.
PN5274.S786 2004
077'.089'924 — DC21   2003010922

1   2   3   4   5   09 08 07 06 05 04

LIST OF FIGURES

ACKNOWLEDGMENTS

There are many institutions, colleagues, and friends who shaped this book during its long gestation. It began as a doctoral dissertation written for Stanford University's Department of History under the guidance of Steven Zipperstein and Aron Rodrigue, indefatigable advisors, teachers, colleagues, and friends. In different ways, Steve and Aron taught me that good scholarship is, above all else, the expression of passion, compassion, and joy. This book might have been written without this knowledge, but the process of writing it — and, no doubt, the results — would have been far less rewarding.

As a graduate student at Stanford University I benefited immeasurably from the intelligence, generosity, and friendship of peers engaged in the study of Jewish history and culture, in particular Cecile Kuznits, Tony Michels, Ken Moss, Steve Rappaport, and Greg Kaplan. Mary Louise Roberts, Joel Beinin, Martin Jay, Arnold Eisen, Norman Naimark, Amir Weiner, and Keith Baker were also influential in shaping my thinking and my sense of myself as a scholar.

While writing the dissertation from which this book grew, I received support from Stanford's Department of History, Program in Jewish Studies, Center for Russian and East European Studies, and School of Humanities and Sciences. Outside help came from the American Council of Learned Societies, The Andrew W. Mellon Foundation, the Newhouse Foundation, and the Maurice Amado Scholarship Fund of Temple Tifereth Israel, Los Angeles. Finally, during 1997–98, I was coddled with good conversation and company as a dissertation fellow of Stanford's Humanities Center.

Accessing and reading thousands of pages of turn-of-the-century Yiddish and Ladino periodicals has been an exciting but occasionally frustrating task. I offer my thanks to the staff of the Stanford Libraries for facilitating this process with humor, especially Roger Kohn, Sonia Moss, and Heidi Lerner (who knew me long before I set out to make myself into a scholar).

Gratitude is also due to Zachary Baker, who generously helped me make use of the collection of the Jewish Institute for Scientific Research (YIVO) and, subsequently, Stanford University Libraries from afar. In addition to the YIVO Institute, this research has relied on the collections and staffs of the Ben Zvi Institute, the Hoover Institution Library and Archives, Harvard's Widener Library, the New York Public Library, the Jewish National and University Library, and the University of Washington Libraries.

Since joining the University of Washington's faculty in the autumn of 1999, I have been supported by remarkable colleagues. Thanks are due to the various chairs of the Department of History, the Jackson School of International Studies, and the Jewish Studies Program under whose tenure I have served. All of them managed to offer a magical combination of freedom and support: Robert Stacey, Jere Bacharach, Martin Jaffee, Resat Kasaba, Naomi Sokoloff, Joel Migdal, Kathie Friedman, John Findlay, and Anand Yang. Uta Poiger, Lynn Thomas, Glennys Young, and Reşat Kasaba were kind enough to read and comment on my work in progress, as did the members of the History Reading Group and the fellows of the 2001–2002 Society of Scholars of the Walter Chapin Simpson Center for the Humanities. In addition to reading my work in progress, Susan Glenn helped craft the title of this work: I thank her for leaving so memorable a mark. Critical support has also been offered by the University of Washington's Royalty Research Fund, Keller Fund in History, Graduate School Fund, Walter Chapin Simpson Center for the Humanities, and School of Arts and Sciences.

Colleagues further from home have been rewarding interlocutors, among them Jonathan Frankel, Vicki Caron, Derek Penslar, and Mitchell Cohen. Matthias Lehmann, Michelle Campos, Eyal Ginio, and Scott Ury have been kind enough to share their research and insights. Intimate conferences organized by Mark Steinberg, Michael Geyer, and Joel Migdal proved stimulating intellectual forums in which to share my ideas.

Jordanna Bailkin and Kalman Weiser read portions of this manuscript before it went to press and Mark Von Hagen read the completed version with amazing kindness and speed: all offered pivotal final suggestions. Edward Portnoy has been something of a research soul mate and deserves immeasurable praise for so skillfully preparing a portion of the illustrations from the Yiddish press that accompany this volume.

Others helped ensure that this book would be beautifully illustrated. Warm thanks to Olga Akunevich, Director of the Vitebsk Regional Museum, for permitting me to reproduce Yehuda Pen's arresting "Reading a Newspaper" (1910), a copy of which appears on this book's jacket. The Jewish Museum (New York) facilitated my use of Pen's work by leading me to Ms. Akunevich and by allowing me to duplicate their copy of the painting. In addition to Edward Portnoy, Laura Todd helped "neaten" illustrations derived from very untidy microfilm originals. Marian Morgan Ezzell and

Daniel Leathersich, both of Indiana University Press, displayed great patience in guiding my illustrations through publication.

I thank Jackie Marquez and Ronald Kim for helping me standardize my Ladino transliterations and Kalman Weiser for his assistance with those in Yiddish and Hebrew. Ali Igmen and Elizabeth Angell performed wonders as research assistants: Ali facilitated my exploration of Turkish-language sources and Elizabeth edited my notes and bibliography, thereby preventing untold agony.

Indiana University Press's anonymous readers took great care in reviewing my manuscript. Their comments, and those of my copyeditor, Joyce Rappaport, helped me develop and polish this project. I am honored that *Making Jews Modern* joins Indiana University Press's series on "The Modern Jewish Experience" and am grateful to Paula Hyman and Deborah Dash Moore for their support in this regard. It has been a great pleasure working with Janet Rabinowitch, who has offered perceptive and influential commentary. I thank her especially for her confidence in the ambitious scope of this project.

The completion of this project would have been far more trying had I not shared innumerable laps in the pool with Ali Igmen, runs with Lynn Thomas, hometowns with Jordanna Bailkin and Chris Johnson, dinners with Danielle Zerr and Dimitri Christakis, and neighborhood adventures with Uta Poiger and Kyriacos Markianos.

Finally, gratitude must be expressed to my family. To my extraordinary grandparents, Jay and Lorayne Stein and Victor and Sally (née Sarah) Abbey (Abrevaya): cultural pioneers all, and none afraid to cross borders. To Joan Abrevaya, host, neighbor, and aunt extraordinaire. To my parents, Richard and Carole Stein, lovers of print culture and newspapers, for providing a model of how to live ethically and fully. To my sister, Rebecca Luna Stein, confidante, companion, and colleague, who fills my life with levity and depth. To Fred Zimmerman, who not only read and commented on every page of this book, but whose unstinting curiosity, integrity, and affection makes life a pleasure. And finally, to Ira Jacob Zimmerman, who arrived shortly before this book was completed but who has already brought more happiness and pride than it could.

NOTE ON TRANSLITERATIONS, DATES, AND TERMS

In transliterating Yiddish I have utilized the system of the YIVO Institute for Jewish Research. In transliterating Ladino I have relied on the system employed by the journal *Aki Yerushalayim*. In transliterating Russian and Hebrew I have followed the Library of Congress rules. In all cases, I have eliminated most diacritical marks (including those used to distinguish the letters het and hei and alef from ayin). In transliterating names, I have preserved conventional spellings of names widely used in scholarly and popular writing (e.g., Sholem Aleichem) but transliterated names less familiar to the reader. Because the scripts employed by Hebrew, Yiddish, and Ladino periodicals of the turn of the century did not make use of capitalization, my transliterations of journal and article names capitalize first words only.

When referencing articles published in the Yiddish, Hebrew, Russian, Ladino, or French press, I have used the dates employed by the press in question. In the turn-of-the-century Russian setting, Jewish newspapers often utilized both the Julian (or Old Style) calendar and the Gregorian calendar, in that order, with the Gregorian date in parenthesis; I have reproduced this style in the endnotes. In some cases, the Hebrew calendar was used to date newspapers and periodicals; I have reproduced this style, too, in the endnotes, but have added the Gregorian year in parenthesis for clarification.

The language of Sephardi Jewries is referred to by a variety of names, including Ladino, Judezmo, and Judeo-Spanish. Many scholars employ the terms "Judeo-Spanish" or "Judezmo" to refer to the vernacular language that was spoken and printed by the Sephardim of Southeastern Europe, reserving the term "Ladino" for the highly literal calque of Hebrew used primarily in religious study and prayer. Though I recognize this linguistic distinction, I have chosen to refer to spoken and printed Judeo-Spanish as "Ladino" simply because the latter term is widely recognizable.

Making **Jews** Modern

INTRODUCTION: MAKING JEWS MODERN

On the eve of the twentieth century, European Jewish culture was in a state of dramatic flux. Though never rigid, some of the most important emblems and agents of Jewish identity were now being reconsidered as cultural norms. The language one spoke, the food one ate, where one lived, how one dressed or self-identified, the class or professional status one might attain, the influence of communal loci of power, the importance of religious practice: all these were increasingly matters of choice rather than convention. These choices arose out of and helped define the major social and cultural transformations that historians associate with the European Jewish experience of modernity: acculturation, embourgeoisement, politicization, secularization, and urbanization.

The Jewish populations of the Russian and Ottoman Empires were caught up in these upheavals. But in Eastern and Southeastern Europe, the experience of modernity assumed forms that were markedly different than one found in Western or Central Europe and from one another. This book explores myriad ways in which modernity was discussed and defined by Jews in the European regions of the Russian and Ottoman Empires in one of the most influential and modern of printed sources: the vernacular popular

1

press. Newspapers and journals illustrated the extent to which turn-of-the-century Jews' experiences of change varied across the European continent, suggesting that there was not one but many European Jewish modernities.

In a number of important respects, turn-of-the-century Russian and Ottoman Jewries resembled one another (and the Jews of the Austro-Hungarian Empire) more than they did their peers in the nation-states of Western and Central Europe.[1] The empires where they lived did not emancipate their subjects, nor did they consistently attempt to absorb them into a coherent body politic. This in turn had powerful implications for the shaping of Jewish politics and culture. For example, one finds forms of Jewish political expression in Eastern and Southeastern Europe — such as loyalty to the structure of empire and fear of the nation-state — that were all but absent in the states of Western and Central Europe. In the Russian and Ottoman contexts, one also finds cultural movements that attracted little attention elsewhere in Europe, such as the creation of modernizing movements in Yiddish and Ladino, the vernacular languages of the vast majority of Russian and Ottoman Jews. Russian and Ottoman Jews were likely to be more multi-lingual than were the Jews of Western or Central Europe, and the societies in which they lived were more multi-ethnic and multi-sectarian than most European states. Paradoxically, Russian and Ottoman Jewish women and girls were traditionally and increasingly better educated and less confined to private spheres than their Western European peers.[2] Yet Russian and Ottoman Jews experienced embourgeoisement and abandoned traditional practices at a slower pace than did Jews in Western and Central Europe.

Russian and Ottoman Jews were nonetheless distinct from each other in how they chose to redefine themselves at the turn of the twentieth century. While for Jews of the Russian Empire embourgeoisement often fostered absorption into the Russian cultural landscape, for Ottoman Jews the same process tended to mean Westernization. And while both Russian and Ottoman Jewries became politicized in the late nineteenth century, the politics of Jewish nationalism proved popular in the Russian setting but by and large lacked a popular following in the Ottoman lands. Russian Jewish intellectuals typically defended Yiddish as a political and literary tool and language of every-day life, whereas Ottoman Jewish intellectuals mostly belittled Ladino even when they employed it. And while both Russian and Ottoman Jewries were physically mobile populations on the eve of the twentieth century, they tended to move toward different destinations at different moments and for different reasons. On the whole, Jews' ability to enter the middle class, their interest in the politics of Jewish nationalism, their support for the creation of nation-states or irredentism, their relationship to the empires in which they lived, to the majority culture and minority cultures that surrounded them, or to the Jewish vernaculars and languages of their region or regime: all this unfolded asymmetrically in the Russian and Ottoman settings.

Few scholars have reckoned with the similarities and differences in the panoply of European Jewish cultures at the turn of the twentieth century. Histories of European Jews have tended to be delineated by the borders of nation-states and empires; it is the rare scholarly work that crosses political boundaries in order to consider the far more fluid boundaries of Jewish culture. In particular, studies rarely cross sub-ethnic boundaries considered internal to Jewish culture: the boundary, for example, that divides the Ashkenazim (who constituted the vast majority of Russian Jews) from the Sephardim (who constituted the vast majority of Ottoman Jews), and these from other Jewish sub-groups. This book offers the first in-depth comparison of Jewish culture under the rule of the Russian and Ottoman Empires and the first comparative study of modern Yiddish and Ladino — and thus Ashkenazi and Sephardi — cultures. By scrutinizing the very different historical landscapes of Russian and Ottoman Jewries, it reflects on the complex meaning of modernity for Jews in *fin-de-siècle* Europe.

Similarities in the histories of these empires suggest one reason to compare them. In the nineteenth- and early-twentieth-century Russian and Ottoman settings, one finds a multitude of common processes: the centralization and rationalization of high politics under the influence of Western European models; revolutions and the creation of constitutional regimes; the breakdown of imperial systems and the emergence of successor states; the weakening of certain political, ethnic, and religious ties and the strengthening of others; the development of nationalist sentiments; and finally, the undermining of multi-ethnicity as a lived reality and political ambition. Yet the differences remain decisive. By the late nineteenth century, the Ottoman Empire found itself in a state of semi-colonial dependency on Western Europe while the Russian Empire remained (for the most part) economically independent. The Ottoman regime was losing control over its territories and subject peoples precisely as the Russian imperial regime was consolidating its power. Finally, these empires had very different historical relationships with their multi-ethnic populations: while in the Ottoman Empire, ethnic and religious difference had a tradition of being juridically protected (or, at least, benignly neglected), in the Russian setting, the empire's multi-national nature was never truly recognized by the regime, which tended instead to support the ethnic, religious, and linguistic homogenization of its subjects.

Neither the Russian nor the Ottoman Empires treated all of their subject peoples or territories the same. Imperial policies varied according to whim and design and over time and space. Partly as a result, modernity was a complex and multi-faceted phenomenon within the boundaries of these empires. To make matters more complicated, cultural, ethnic, and religious groups were themselves internally diverse in both settings. The Jews of Salonika, Constantinople, and Sofia, for example, though all subjects of the Ottoman Empire, faced very different constraints and developed very different aspirations at the turn of the twentieth century. How much more so for Jews in Russia, as the tsarist regime employed "selective integration" to welcome certain Jews to Russian society?[3] Russian and Ottoman Jewries (like other ethnic and religious groups of these empires) were further varied by class, gender, age, and political leaning: and these are only a few lines of division among many. This astonishing array of institutional and cultural variation makes it difficult to speak of Russian and Ottoman Jewries as wholes. Certainly it renders a comparison of their histories challenging. And yet one need not deny the differences *among* Russian and Ottoman Jewries in order to focus on the differences *between* them. As the following chapters argue, major differences between the Russian and Ottoman legal, political, and economic landscapes contributed to major differences in the shape of local Jewish modernities.

To compare Russian and Ottoman Jews' experiences of modernity, this book considers the creation of secular print culture in Yiddish and Ladino, the vernacular languages of the vast majority of Russian and Ottoman Jews (respectively). At the turn of the twentieth century, 97 percent of Russian Jews declared Yiddish their mother tongue while as late as the Second World War, 85 percent of Turkish Jewry and the vast majority of Jews in the empire's other successor states (in Bulgaria, Yugoslavia, Serbia, and Greece) identified Ladino as their native language. In both contexts, Jewish rates of literacy in these vernacular languages were extraordinarily high.[4] By the late nineteenth century, Yiddish and Ladino were being used to produce new genres of Jewish culture, resulting in original works of poetry; drama; fiction; scholarly essays; dictionaries and encyclopedias; translations of world literature; and daily, weekly, and monthly periodicals. In these media, readers and writers of Yiddish and Ladino debated and displayed what it meant to be modern and Jewish.

Without a doubt, the single most prolific genre of Yiddish and Ladino print culture was the popular press. Yiddish and Ladino periodicals emerged within twenty years of each other: the first Ladino periodical, *La buena esperansa* (Izmir [Smyrna], 1842, 1871–1911), was published in 1842, and the first Yiddish periodical, *Kol mevaser* (Odessa, 1862–70), twenty years later. Over the course of the next century, Jewish periodicals in Yiddish and Ladino (and, to a lesser extent, in Hebrew, Russian, Polish, French, and Turkish) blossomed in the Russian and Ottoman Empires and in their successor states. By 1913, there were no less than 389 Jewish periodicals published in Turkey and the Balkans, while the number of Yiddish periodicals in Eastern Europe exceeded the thousands.[5] Despite the enormous popularity of Yiddish and Ladino newspapers at the turn of the twentieth century, the genre remains one of the least-explored facets of Russian and Ottoman Jewish culture. Indeed, despite the wealth of literature on popular presses in other historical fields, scholarship on Russian and Ottoman presses in general is young and sparse.[6] Scholars have turned to popular newspapers in Jewish vernaculars for the events they chronicled, but have virtually ignored the press as an agent of historical change. Yet it is precisely in newspapers, with their plurality of subject matter and authors, their immediate reactions to cultural and political events, their need to appeal to many kinds of readers, and — not least — the responses provided by their readerships, that emerging Jewish modernities may be read most vividly. This book redirects attention toward the Jewish popular press not only because it chronicled the transformation of Russian and Ottoman Jewish cultures, but also because it had a rich culture all its own.

Among the hundreds of Yiddish and Ladino periodicals published in the Russian and Ottoman Empires were scores of daily newspapers. The introduction of daily newspapers represented an important step in the history of Yiddish and Ladino publishing. These were by and large more accessible, affordable, and comprehensible than the weeklies and monthlies that preceded them. Further, not only did daily newspapers report on change, but they also served as barometers of the interests and predilections of readers. While the earliest producers of periodicals designed for Jews shared the didactic goal of educating readers in an Enlightened or *maskilic* tradition, the first Jewish dailies published in Yiddish and Ladino tended to draw a distinction between the "traditional" need to educate and the "modern" need to inform (a "traditional" need that was, to be sure, scarcely three decades old).[7] While undoubtedly didactic at times, newspapers reimagined their readerships by embracing women and men of all ages who were not necessarily well-educated, but who were interested in and who could find pragmatic benefits in the day's news. They seemed to signal a movement away from elite culture and toward a more popular culture.

At least so claimed the producers and many of the consumers of the first Yiddish and Ladino dailies. Inevitably, however, the path toward a truly popular newspaper culture was long and rocky. This study traces some of the earliest attempts at brokering this transition. To this end, this book chooses as a case study the first daily newspapers in Yiddish and Ladino published in the Russian and Ottoman Empires: *Der fraynd* (St. Petersburg, Warsaw, 1903–13) and *El tiempo* (Constantinople, 1872–1930). In many ways these were unusual newspapers, sharing neither the goals of the didactic periodicals that preceded them nor the tactics of more popular newspapers that followed. Though *Der fraynd* and *El tiempo* were theoretically designed for "common" readers, they were not terribly easy to read. Their language was often lofty, dense, and not "street" Yiddish or Ladino. These newspapers devoted little time to local or regional happenings and much to editorializing. They decried yellow journalism that catered to readers' whims. They did not clearly or consistently align themselves with Jewish party politics. Finally, the distribution of both was uneven. Neither *Der fraynd* nor *El tiempo* relied on street sales or home delivery, and neither paper attempted to target or appeal to readers in a single city or town. Partly for these reasons, their ability to survive as dailies was finite.[8]

In time and for all of these reasons, the popularity and influence of *Der fraynd* and *El tiempo* waned, but this occurred only toward the end of the first decade of the twentieth century, after viable competitors emerged and the industries of Yiddish and Ladino newspaper publishing had become firmly established. In part because state censorship limited their competition in their early years, *Der fraynd* and *El tiempo* initially maintained a kind of reign over the worlds of Yiddish and Ladino publishing. *Der fraynd* was the most widely circulated Jewish periodical in Russia in an extraordinarily influential period in Yiddish newspaper publishing, while *El tiempo* was among a handful of the longest-lived Ladino newspapers in the Ottoman lands, read, at its height, by half the Jewish adults in Constantinople. What is more, *Der fraynd* and *El tiempo* attracted some of the best young writers of Yiddish and Ladino, influenced how Jewish politics and culture were discussed and experienced, and proved that newspapers in Jewish vernaculars were viable and even potentially lucrative endeavors. To put this another way, these newspapers left a heritage and thereby exerted an impact on Jewish newspaper cultures in the Russian and Ottoman Empires even after they themselves folded. Perhaps most important of all, *Der fraynd* and *El tiempo* were among the most prolific producers of secular Jewish culture in print at a moment when this was still a new and radical phenomenon.

The editors of *El tiempo* and *Der fraynd* made grand claims for the universality of their newspapers by defending the idea that theirs were journals for "all" Jews of the Russian and Ottoman Empires. Certainly neither the circulations nor the content of these papers could substantiate such assertions. But to some extent these claims were useful fictions, valid reflections of the cultural and political environments in which these periodicals were produced. If these editors' claims of representivity did not faithfully represent the complexity of Russian and Ottoman Jewish life, it was in part because this complexity had yet to be publicly and self-consciously acknowledged. As we will see, *Der fraynd* and *El tiempo* were created just before the ideologies and political movements that would characterize twentieth-century Jewry (and, indeed, modern Russia and Turkey) had rigidified. Perhaps, indeed, the reverse holds true: these ideologies and political movements had not yet rigidified in part because the popular press — which would prove a critical space for the working out of these philosophies — had yet to emerge.

It was not only Jewish party politics that *Der fraynd* and *El tiempo* helped to define. The notion of "secular" Jewish culture, too, was worked out in their pages. Both of these periodicals strained to address secular readers and by and large limited their reporting to affairs of the secular world. Partly for this reason, members of the rabbinical elite in both contexts viewed the publications with fear and distrust, and on occasion took the dramatic step of excommunicating their editors and journalists.[9] These altercations represented a struggle over leadership; the religious authorities might not have been so wary of Jewish popular sources had not their producers proclaimed them to be "the new Bible."[10] Indeed, the editors of *Der fraynd* and *El tiempo* clearly aimed to contest and to seize some of the responsibility that the existing authorities — the rabbinical elite, *kahal* (communal leadership), and the traditional educational system — had traditionally exercised: the power to educate, to monitor communal finances, to offer moral guidance. In certain respects, as we will see, *Der fraynd* and *El tiempo* were successful in this regard. Yet this achievement did not represent a victory over the religious establishment so much as it pointed to the overlap between worlds observant and secular in Jewish Eastern and Southeastern Europe. Much to the consternation of the earliest Yiddish and Ladino newspaper editors, the distinction between secular and religious readers, on the one hand, and between secular and religious news, on the other, was difficult to define and impossible to enforce.[11] Perhaps predictably, this proved one reason the Yiddish and Ladino press was so very popular.

Though *Der fraynd* and *El tiempo* shared certain successes, tactics, and ambitions, these newspapers were in fact quite different from each other. To begin with, *El tiempo* emerged thirty years earlier than *Der fraynd*. In the Ottoman setting, Ladino editors faced few obstacles to publishing, though censorship limited expression until the Young Turk Revolt of 1908. As a result, the first popular periodicals in Ladino emerged at the same time as did the first popular periodicals in Greek, Armenian, and Turkish. Russia's Ministry of Interior, by contrast, denied dozens of requests lodged by Russian Jewish intellectuals since the 1880s for the publication of daily newspapers in Yiddish. As a result, *Der fraynd* began publication some three decades after the first dailies in Russian and Polish. *Der fraynd* and *El tiempo* differed in proclivity as well as origin. *Der fraynd* was Zionist in leaning, advocated a moderate form of cultural nationalism, supported Jews' use of Yiddish, and encouraged readers to develop a fluency in the Russian cultural milieu. *El tiempo*, by contrast, was fiercely anti-nationalist, eschewed Ladino and supported adoption of French and Turkish despite publication in Ladino, encouraged readers to become patriotic Ottomans, and simultaneously promoted the Westernization of Jewish culture. These were very different ambitions. But they were nonetheless ways of addressing the same question, the central question of this study: What did it mean to be Jewish and modern?

This term, "modern," reappeared often in the Yiddish and Ladino presses of the turn of the century. It was used to illuminate discontinuities with the past and to weave images of the future. It was used to describe an era in which Russian and Ottoman Jews were confronted with choices and challenges hitherto unknown. Perhaps most important of all, it was used to describe a world laced with possibilities. It was now possible to choose what language(s) one wished to speak, read, or write. It was possible to educate one's children in secular as well as religious schools. Possible to purchase secular reading matter in a Jewish vernacular. Possible to ally oneself with a wide spectrum of political movements (among them Jewish political parties, a once unthinkable phenomenon). Possible to imagine such a thing as leisure time, and to imagine spending it in innumerable ways. Possible for women, men, and children to assume new gender and familial roles. Possible to dress in new ways, to cook new foods, to adorn, carry, and care for one's body differently than before. It was possible to use public and private spaces in new ways. Finally, it was possible to describe oneself in new ways, and to declare and develop cultural affinities once unimaginable. Modernity made it possible not only to question but also to reject the traditions, rituals, and social and economic norms of the past.

This is not to suggest that the Russian and Ottoman Jewish past was static, nor that Russian and Ottoman Jews had hitherto lacked the agency to shape their lives. But it is to argue that the Yiddish and Ladino presses of the turn of the century acknowledged that Jewish readers were encountering a moment that was distinct and discrete and therefore understood to be modern: indeed, they promoted it. The term "modern" peppered the Ladino press more insistently than it did the Yiddish, no doubt because the world of Ladino letters was more strongly influenced by contemporary French letters. In the Ottoman Ladino press the term permitted no retort. Thus, we read, Ladino was a language in the *modern* sense of the word; Hebrew was irrelevant because it lacked terms for the *modern* world; equal pay was demanded for men and women because *modern* times rendered this a necessity; knowledge of the workings of the gastro-intestinal system was deemed obligatory for the *modern* person.[12] The contemporary Yiddish press, while more varied in terminology, nonetheless acknowledged a similar reality: that life was fundamentally different for turn-of-the-century Jews. "Jewish life has changed dramatically in the last years," *Der fraynd*'s first editorial announced: "Jewish life is no longer tied up in the old order of things. New times have awakened new desires."[13] These were florid and didactic statements. But there was a certain truth to them. Jewish life had changed and the modern press would help to change it even more.

RUSSIAN AND OTTOMAN JEWRIES ON THE
EVE OF THE TWENTIETH CENTURY

Why did change seem to accelerate for turn-of-the-century readers of Yiddish and Ladino? What conditions shaped modern Jewish culture in the Russian and Ottoman Empires? The following pages briefly sketch the contours of this dramatic period.

Jews made their way to Eastern and Southeastern Europe under similar circumstances. These populations left the German Rhine area and the Iberian Peninsula (beginning in the thirteenth and fifteenth century, respectively) in response to expulsion decrees. As a result of the Judeophobic climate of much of Christian Europe, both faced a shortage of available destinations. To the expanding Polish-Lithuanian Commonwealth and Ottoman Empire, however, Jews appeared a valuable asset and were regarded as populations that could settle new regions of the empire and serve as an urban and merchant class. At the invitation of these states, it was to Eastern and Southeastern Europe that the vast majority of Ashkenazim (in the first case) and Sephardim (in the second) moved. These Jews brought with them Judeo-Spanish and Judeo-German amalgams that would evolve into Yiddish and Ladino.[14]

Because they were valued as economic middlemen, Jews were granted a great deal of autonomy in their new homes. In both the Polish and Ottoman contexts, few restrictions were imposed on Jewish ritual practice. Jewish legal courts and decisions were by and large respected, and Jewish communities were allowed to collect and manage their own taxes. Further, in both settings Jews developed economic relations with the ruling elite that greatly benefited both parties.

Though the sizes of the Jewish populations of Poland and the Ottoman Empire were roughly comparable in the early modern period, by the modern period their numbers had diverged radically. When the Polish Commonwealth was partitioned by the Russian, Prussian, and Austro-Hungarian Empires in the last decades of the eighteenth century, nearly half a million Jews found themselves subjects of the Russian Empire. Over the next century and a half, this population expanded with astonishing rapidity such that by the eve of the twentieth century more than five million Jews lived in the Russian Empire. This population dwarfed that of Ottoman Jewry, which numbered roughly a quarter of a million at the turn of the century.[15] This demographic asymmetry is of the utmost import to the historian of Yiddish and Ladino letters; as will be explored in greater detail in the pages that follow, sheer numbers help to explain why Yiddish culture would prove more resilient than Ladino culture.

Because a majority worked as merchants and artisans, Russian and Ottoman Jews tended to cluster in towns and cities. By the nineteenth century, these populations were increasingly urban. Ottoman censuses reveal that between 1881 and 1906, the empire's cities with the highest concentration of Jews (Istanbul, Izmir [Smyrna], and Edirne) saw at least a 30 percent increase in the number of Jewish residents, and in Salonika, the Jewish population increased by nearly 40 percent.[16] Jewish concentration in Russian cities was increasing dramatically at the same time. For example, Volhynia saw a 127 percent increase in its Jewish population between 1847 and the turn of the century, while the Jewish population of Vilna tripled during the same period.[17] Strikingly, while the Jewish population of many Eastern and Southeastern European cities was numerically a minority, in others Jews constituted the majority or near-majority population.

Russian and Ottoman Jewries were not only centered in cities, but they were also largely concentrated within certain areas of their empires. At the close of the nineteenth century, 94 percent of Russian Jews lived within the confines of the Pale of Settlement, an area in the western provinces of Russia to which Jewish residency rights were by and large restricted.[18] The majority of Ottoman Jews, too, were concentrated in the European regions of the empire, in European Turkey and in the Balkans. Russia's western borderlands and the Ottoman-controlled Balkans and Turkey represented the Yiddish and Ladino heartlands of Europe. These were also the principal regions in which the Yiddish and Ladino press were consumed.

An essential fact of Jewish life in the Russian and Ottoman Empires well into the twentieth century was that the vast majority of Jews were recognizable — to themselves and to non-Jews — as Jews. Though in each context there existed growing numbers of Jews who took on the mores of the majority or hegemonic culture (including language, dress, residential patterns, and educational practices), and though Jews were increasingly varied by religious practice, politics, class, and region, by and large Russian and Ottoman Jews did not cease to be perceived and to perceive themselves as such. What complicates this fact — and what is, in some sense, the principal focus of this study — is that the meaning of the term *Jew* varied across time and space and, in the Russian and Ottoman settings, as elsewhere, was the subject of extensive debate.

Easier to pin down, perhaps, is the way in which Jews were defined by the Russian and Ottoman states. Prior to the late nineteenth century, relations between Muslims and most non-Muslims in the Ottoman Empire were technically regulated by a pact called *dhimma* (*zimmet* in Turkish), but in fact were conditioned by a complex web of social, religious, and economic practices that undermined — or at least provided alternatives to the strict observance of — Islamic law.[19] Indeed, though Ottoman society was technically ordered by Islamic texts and practices, in fact much government and interpersonal business was conducted according to secular regulations. According to the traditional pact regulating relations between the *ahl al-dhimma* (people of the *dhimmi*) or *dhimmis* (*zimmi* in Turkish) and Muslims, "rights" of non-Muslims were not guaranteed. Arguably, the notion of "rights" did not exist until it was introduced by Westernizing reformers in the late nineteenth century. Before these reforms, *dhimmis* were reminded that they were inferior to Muslims by legislation that circumscribed their dress, use of animals, weapons, and places of worship, and by the threat of *sürgün* (forced migrations), which certain Muslims were subject to as well. Simultaneously, the *dhimmi* were juridically protected in ways that Jews under Christian rule were not. Certain non-Muslims were allowed to maintain their own courts and institutions and, as a result, these establishments evolved into corporate structures. In this way, ethnic and religious difference was respected and juridically sustained.[20] The success of this system — at least insofar as Jews were concerned — was reflected in the virtual absence of antisemitism from the Ottoman landscape.

The Russian state pursued no coherent policy toward its subjects, even during ongoing attempts at Russification in the late nineteenth and early twentieth centuries.[21] However, though Russia's subject populations and territories were treated differently from one another and from one moment to another, nearly all were pressured — or compelled — at one point or another to Russify: to adopt the Russian language, the Russian Orthodox religion, Russian modes of education, and so on.[22] Policies toward Russian Jewries were neither more cruel nor more calculated than were those that targeted other subjects of the empire, but were, instead, shaped haphazardly and inconsistently. Until the middle of the nineteenth century, Jewish *kehillot* (communities) were on the one hand given provisional control of all matters governed by Jewish law and recognized as separate, Jewish corporate estates. On the other hand, Jews' urban status earned many individuals the taxonomy *meschane* (members of an urban dwellers' estate).[23] Thus while the integrity of the Jewish community was legally recognized, it was simultaneously undermined, particularly when it seemed this would encourage individual Jews to shed their "particular" characteristics. Imperial policies could, in any case, almost always be challenged or undermined on the local level. In Russia's western provinces, for example, where Poles were considered the most dangerous threat to Russian dominance, officials favored lessening restrictions on Jews, in part to foil potential alliances between Jews and Poles.[24]

The regime pursued the integration of Russian Jews with fluctuating zeal. In the early nineteenth century, Russian Jewry was made subject to draconian conscription laws that were thought to facilitate homogenization. In 1844 the regime abolished the *kahal*, which had originally acted as a cultural unit invested with political power. For some time thereafter, the regime attempted to erode traditional Jewish sources of power by developing an alliance with *maskilim* (Jewish intellectuals who supported the Jewish Enlightenment movement).[25] In the wake of the Polish uprising of 1863, the governing powers saw reason to introduce softer forms of Russification.[26] Jews were now encouraged to enter the Russian middle class, adopt the Russian language, and — perhaps most significantly of all — to attend Russian universities and gymnasia, which thousands of Jewish men and women eagerly did.[27] Jewish literacy in Russian grew as a result, so that by the end of the twentieth century nearly 45 percent of Jewish men and 21 percent of Jewish women could claim literacy in Russian (and this number was as high as 51 percent for urban men and 35 percent for urban women).[28] An increase in levels of literacy and education allowed many Jews in Russia to enter the liberal professions and become increasingly affluent, producing, in the process, a generation of Russified Jewish intellectuals. Meanwhile, the quest for economic betterment led unprecedented numbers of Jews to migrate within Russia's western provinces and to emigrate from the empire.[29] Poverty remained endemic to Russian Jewry, but rising rates of migration and emigration, literacy, and educational levels indicated that many Jews were benefiting from the expansion of the Russian economy and from strategies of Russification.[30]

A very different cultural economy shaped the Ottoman landscape in the late nineteenth and early twentieth centuries. If economic expansion in Russia had the effect of benefiting a certain sector of Russian Jewry, a shifting regional economy contributed to the erosion of multi-ethnicity as a functional political and cultural reality in the Ottoman context, with attendant consequences for Jews. For Ottoman Jews, imperial policies of toleration had translated into economic success when the empire was financially at its strongest. In the sixteenth and seventeenth centuries, for example, a small Jewish elite became influential in finances and international commerce, tax collecting, and the fabulously successful production of woolen textiles based in Salonika and Safed.[31] Sales of textiles to the government linked the Jewish economy to the Ottoman regime, a relationship that the empire strove to cultivate. Salonikan cloth was designed to be consumed by the Janissary Corps (a segment of the Ottoman army dependent upon the forced conscription of conquered subjects); from the sixteenth century onward, the city's poll tax was even paid in cloth. This profitable relationship began to decay in the seventeenth century. By then, England had introduced a competitive cloth that undermined the Salonikan market, while fires and epidemics further weakened the industry. In contrast to England, the Ottoman regime did not encourage exports, rendering the textile trade even less lucrative.[32] The weakening of the Salonikan economy had reverberations throughout the Ottoman Jewish world.

Salonika's decline reflected the economic crises that the Ottoman Empire faced as a whole. Beginning in the sixteenth century, the rise of the Atlantic economy provoked the collapse of the Ottoman monetary system. By the eighteenth century, confrontations with Russia proved the Janissary Corps anemic: war, which had traditionally fueled and expanded the Ottoman economy, had become too expensive to prepare for or conduct.[33] At the same time, European trade expanded into the Ottoman territories. Partly to encourage this trade, capitulary privileges were offered to European trading partners. This, in turn, led to the establishment of European credit unions that facilitated lending to the Ottoman regime. While the Ottoman economy continued to grow, more and more economic activities moved beyond the control of the state as the empire entered into a semi-imperial relationship with Western Europe.[34] It is true that this did not prevent Ottoman industrial centers from remaining vibrant, local merchants from prospering, or the Ottoman textile industry from surviving: in the early nineteenth century, even the Ottoman monetary system remained strong.[35] But particularly from the perspective of certain non-Muslim groups in the European regions of the empire, the empire's enervated regional standing had profound implications for local practice. While Greeks and Armenians responded to these changes by diversifying their economies, Jews were unable to do the same.[36] And when the Janissary Corps was abolished in 1826, it was a final blow to an already-weak Ottoman Jewish economy.

For Jews in this context, success in the Ottoman economy increasingly depended upon ties with Western Europe rather than ties with the Ottoman authorities. To develop such ties, Ottoman Jewry turned to Western Europe for cultural and economic inspiration and for broader personal and professional possibilities. French Jewry soon offered itself as a model. In 1860, the Alliance Israélite Universelle (hereafter referred to as the AIU) was founded by the Franco-Jewish elite with the goal of educating Levantine Jewry in the French language and culture, Westernizing them and thereby readying them for success in the capitalist world economy. The AIU would educate more than three generations of Levantine Jews, and dominated secular Jewish culture in the Ottoman Empire until the Young Turk Revolt.[37] Partly as a result of the patronage of the AIU — itself a product of the declining economic strength of the empire as a whole — embourgeoisement and Westernization became inextricably linked for Ottoman Jews.

On the eve of the twentieth century, Russian Jewry, too, was undergoing processes of embourgeoisement and cultural change. But while many Jews remained deeply impoverished, they did not develop an economic or cultural subordination to Western Europe. Indeed, the influence of Western European culture upon Russian Jewish intellectuals was arguably far greater in the 1840s, '50s, and '60s than in the last decades of the nineteenth or first decades of the twentieth centuries. This was in part because of the strength of the Russian economy (relative to the Ottoman, at least) and because Russian imperial policy encouraged many of its subjects to become dependent on the culture, economy, and political leadership of the Russian hegemony.[38] This is not to say that by the late nineteenth century Western European trends had no influence upon the development of Jewish culture in Russia. But by the close of the nineteenth century, Russian Jews, if they promoted cultural change at all, tended to adopt the norms of Russian hegemonic culture, and in this they differed dramatically from many Ottoman Jews, who culturally gravitated toward an imperial French landscape. To put this another way, while both Russian and Ottoman Jewry could be said to have undergone embourgeoisement, acculturation, and Westernization on the eve of the twentieth century, the meaning of these terms differed greatly in these two very different contexts.

While the Ottoman Jewish economy suffered a decline by the nineteenth century, the overall reality and legal principle of coexistence suffered a parallel erosion through a century-long process of centralization based on European models. These reforms began in the late eighteenth century and culminated in a series of rationalizing measures known collectively as the Tanzimat reforms. In 1856, equality was granted to non-Muslims, and in 1869, a law detailed the notion of Ottoman citizenship, extending it to all subjects of the Sultan regardless of religion. This legislation had the ironic effect of eroding the autonomy of non-Muslim groups, now retroactively labeled *millets*. While these reforms emulated Western European laws that had integrated Jews into the surrounding society, in the Ottoman context, they represented a diminishment of Jewish (and of non-Muslims' and Muslim Arabs') autonomy and freedom — one reason why there was little popular support for these reforms.[39] So far as the empire's Jews were concerned, when implemented, the Tanzimat reforms often proved disadvantageous, transforming Ottoman Jewry "from a *millet* to a minority" — from a corporate body integrated into the Ottoman imperial system to a disassociated ethnic body.[40] This process intensified as Sultan Abdülhamid II abrogated the 1876 Constitution one year after it had been proclaimed (the Constitution had, among other things, recognized the equality of Jews before the law).

Russian Jews, too, faced new constraints on the eve of the twentieth century. Beginning in 1881, a wave of violence directed at Jews jeopardized not only many Jewish lives but also Jews' sense of their own security. A year later, in an ineffectual attempt to preempt further violence, the imperial regime adopted the so-called May Laws. Designed to stop the spread of violence, these regulations made it illegal for urban Jews to settle or acquire land in towns or villages, which were more likely to be sites of anti-Jewish violence than were cities. Though the government's intervention was met with a certain relief, these restrictions nonetheless represented a curtailing of rights for Russia's Jews.[41] To some extent, Russian Jewish politics and culture appear to have been refocused as a result of these events: increasingly, Jewish intellectuals directed their attention away from the pursuit of emancipation and toward the formation of Jewish political movements and parties.[42] These movements not only attracted the Jewish elite but also developed mass followings, thanks in part to the wedding of cultural production to political aims. Along with the rise of Zionism and Jewish socialism, therefore, came literary revolutions in Hebrew and Yiddish.[43] It was in this context that the various genres of modern Yiddish (and, to a lesser extent, Hebrew) culture were developed.

Revolutions of the literary variety were followed by those of the political. Within three years of each other, the Russian and Ottoman Empires were shaken by revolutions that threatened to up-end the very foundation of these empires. Although Jews in each polity initially had reasons to support revolution (though for very different motivations), Jewish support was rather quickly transformed into distrust. The Young Turk Revolt of 1908 was a largely bloodless coup d'état brought about by the Committee for Union and Progress (CUP), a group originally dominated by military officers. The Young Turks promoted Ottomanism, a philosophy that demanded loyalty to the Ottoman polity, respect for existing borders, and the maintenance of a multi-ethnic society. This movement also hoped to transform the empire into a modern state and to oppose foreign intervention. One of their first expressions of power was to force Abdülhamid to reinstate the 1876 Constitution and to permit the election of a Chamber of Deputies. Ottoman Jews at first had good reason to celebrate the new regime: five Jewish deputies were elected to the Ottoman parliament, while censorship of Zionist literature and organizing was lifted. In general, there was also widespread support among Jews for Ottomanism. Over time, however, Jews' support for Ottomanism in some sense outlived the philosophy itself, as the new Ottoman regime gradually abandoned Ottomanism in favor of the exclusivist notion of Turkism (which inextricably linked an Ottoman — and, in time, Turkish — identity to Turkish ethnicity).[44]

While many turn-of-the-century Ottoman Jews sanctioned existing (but already outdated) imperial structures, many of their Russian Jewish contemporaries sparred with the very institution of empire at a time in which the strength of the Russian Empire was being tested but would survive intact. The Russian Revolution of 1905–1907 began with a series of ambitious and sometimes bloody strikes that were the product of an unprecedented intra-ethnic push for constitutional reform. Under tremendous pressure, Tsar Nicholas II issued the October Manifesto of 1905, a document that seemed to herald the creation of a constitutional monarchy, complete with the lifting of censorship. Very quickly, however, the manifesto was recognized as a hollow attempt to deflect opposition and as a mask behind which the still-corrupt regime was attempting to hide.[45] During the ensuing months, Jewish attention was riveted on Russian domestic affairs as Jews appeared to unite behind the cause of opposition and socialist politics, exhibiting faith that the structure of empire might be reformed rather than abandoned. Influential in the production of this political mood was a wave of pogroms that psychologically devastated many Russian Jews, temporarily bolstering the popularity of the Jewish left and the radicalism of the Yiddish press.[46] And yet, if the Young Turk Revolt of 1908 pointed to the relative weakness of the Ottoman monarchist bureaucracy, the Russian Revolution of 1905–1907 proved just how strong the old regime remained. By the late summer of 1907, the Russian regime succeeded in silencing its opposition, after which the strength of the state seemed more consolidated than ever.[47]

In both the turn-of-the-century Russian and Ottoman contexts, the notion of an intra-ethnic or transnational imperial identity (e.g., Russianness or Ottomanness) was only a few decades old. Ironically, the emergence and the eventual failure of these principles were signs that multi-ethnicity was being eroded as a lived reality.[48] As Westernizing reforms divested Jewish *millets* and *kehillot* of political power, Ottoman and Russian Jews sought new vectors of cultural identification. In the Russian context, Jews shaped and joined self-consciously Jewish political parties and produced modern cultural movements in Yiddish and, to a lesser extent, in Hebrew, Russian, Polish, and other regional languages. In the Ottoman context, Jews cultivated cultural and economic relationships with the Western European Jewish elite while simultaneously evincing loyalty to the structure of the Ottoman Empire. To express and shape these affinities, Ottoman Jews produced a modernizing Ladino culture: albeit one that advocated the renunciation of this Jewish vernacular. In both the Russian and Ottoman contexts, these new vectors of cultural identification were born of constraint and of a quest for alternatives.

Though philosophies of assimilation, acculturation, and various forms of nationalism were debated by Russian and Ottoman Jews throughout the nineteenth and early twentieth centuries and on the eve of the Balkan and First World Wars, these concepts not only differed in each setting, but were also themselves eminently malleable. They could be defended, critiqued, and reshaped in the pages of a single newspaper — even in a single issue. It is this extraordinary fluidity and multi-vocality that makes the Jewish popular press a useful historical document. Yiddish and Ladino periodicals not only instruct us about the desires, concerns, and fashions of their day, but they also allow us to reflect upon the history of Jews under the rule of multi-ethnic empires and upon the experience of change for Jews in the Russian and Ottoman settings.

MAKING JEWS MODERN

Part of what distinguished turn-of-the-century Russian and Ottoman Jewish life was the fact that vast numbers of Jews had access to printed sources that allowed them to read about and respond to the many changes in their worlds. In this important sense, Jewish newspapers were both a manifestation and a mechanism of change. Though it was not novel for Russian or Ottoman Jews to raise questions about how a Jew ought to live, newspapers provided a new forum in which Jews could articulate answers and new mechanisms by which their answers could be dispersed and consumed.

This book is divided into three parts that study conceptual intersections in the histories of Yiddish and Ladino newspapers and of Russian and Ottoman Jewries. The chapters in part 1 examine the emergence and impact of the first daily newspapers published in the chief Jewish vernacular languages of Eastern and Southeastern Europe. These sources, I argue, were shaped by the existence, absence, or lifting of censorship; by the shifting economic and cultural status of readers of Yiddish and Ladino; by rates of literacy and histories of reading; by roils of local and imperial politics. So too were these newspapers influenced by readers. To understand Russian and Ottoman Jewish newspapers as experienced phenomena, part 1 considers the geography, gender, class, educational background, and political leanings of readers of Yiddish and Ladino. How, I ask, did the creation of the first Jewish vernacular dailies of the Russian and Ottoman Empires change the way in which Jews read; interacted with the day's news; and understood themselves, one another, or the meaning of Jewish, Russian, or Ottoman culture?

Recent historical scholarship has suggested that the emergence of print capitalism in ethnic vernacular languages is a necessary precursor to the development of nationalism.[49] The research presented in the first chapters of this book suggests that the converse does not hold. That is, the creation of print culture in ethnic vernacular languages does not invariably facilitate nationalism; rather, Jewish languages were used to articulate a wide array of political postures, among them anti-nationalist sentiments. What is more, literacy and reading patterns suggest that turn-of-the-century Jews in the Russian and Ottoman Empires did not necessarily read newspapers for political or ideological reasons or because they were developing a sense of camaraderie based upon shared language in print. In the extremely multilingual settings of Eastern and Southeastern Europe, it was not only unnecessary but also impractical to devote oneself to one language at the expense of others, especially before state-sponsored language policies were introduced in the wake of the First World War. Thus many Jews in Russia read newspapers in Hebrew, Yiddish, and Russian. Similarly, many Jews in Ottoman Europe read newspapers in French, Hebrew, and Ladino (among other languages). The choice to read in any one or in some combination of these languages depended on a multiplicity of factors: one's class and educational background; the permissiveness of the imperial censors; what newspaper one's library or neighbor subscribed to; what papers were sold (or read aloud) in one's town or city; whether one was interested in an emphasis on economic or literary news; how much a particular paper cost; or, finally, how clear was its prose.

While the chapters of part 1 consider the creation and impact of the institution of the Yiddish and Ladino press, the chapters that make up part 2 reflect on the very different models of cultural transformation encouraged by their pioneering dailies. For rather different reasons, chapters 3 and 4 question the usefulness of the polarity of assimilationist responses and nationalist responses that is so often used to describe and delineate European Jewries.

Chapter 3 explores the expressions of faith in the viability of a multiethnic and democratic Russia that were voiced by the Yiddish press in the early months of the Revolution of 1905–1907. During this intoxicating period, *Der fraynd* and its temporary replacement *Dos lebn* (St. Petersburg, February–July 1906) employed the genre of cartoons to articulate an affiliation with opposition and socialist politics (and hence demonstrate support for the notion of a democratic Russia) and to distance itself from Zionism, with which the newspaper was originally aligned. These aesthetic and political affinities were not to endure, at least in the pages of these periodicals. As *Der fraynd* reported on the Bialystok pogroms of 1906, it jettisoned the genre of cartoons in favor of the medium of photography. And while it lined its pages with graphic portraits of Bialystok's dead, the paper retroactively rejected the concept of Russianness, embracing in its place the politics of Jewish nationalism. Following *Der fraynd*'s meandering path offers a surprising glimpse into the porousness of early-twentieth-century Russian Jewish party politics.

Following chapter 3, which considers the fungible relationship between Yiddish sources and Russian identity, chapter 4 studies the complex cultural relationships shaped by semi-imperialism in the Ottoman setting. This chapter turns to the Ladino instructional press, a genre that sought to educate Jewish readers about the latest European trends in child-rearing, hygiene, cooking, and the natural sciences. How, I ask, did images of the moon or a treatise on clean air serve to promote intra-Jewish cultural colonialism and to subordinate Levantine Jewish culture to the French bourgeois model? At what moments did these texts—and the project of Westernization more generally—butt up against the realities of Ottoman Jewish life? Finally, to what extent did the Ladino press, although self-consciously Westernizing in orientation, promote a modern Ottoman Jewish culture that borrowed from extra-regional models while also (often inadvertently) transforming them, creating, in the process, a culture unique in texture?

By studying the genre of the advertisement, the chapters in part 3 of this book explore the economies that early Yiddish and Ladino dailies relied on and transformed. Together, these chapters demonstrate that while turn-of-the-century Russian and Ottoman Jewries were both overwhelmingly poor, Yiddish periodicals depicted and promoted commercial possibilities that were not in evidence in the Ladino press. Chapter 5 ponders the astonishing array of goods promoted in the pages of *Der fraynd*. It argues that this paper's advertising pages encouraged the economic aspiration of Jewish readers by painting a vision of social ascension and by creating a space where readers of Yiddish and merchants interacted. While *Der fraynd*'s advertisements were dominated by the sale of goods, a majority of *El tiempo*'s advertisements sold services that would alleviate insecurities born of the precariousness of economic life in the Ottoman Empire. Thus chapter 6 argues that even as *El tiempo* inflamed readers' economic aspirations, this paper simultaneously depicted Ottoman Jewries' slow and uneven climb to the middle class. Together, chapters 5 and 6 suggest that Jewish embourgeoisement was pictured and pursued very differently in Eastern and Southeastern Europe.

Following chapters that analyze the significance of popular Jewish vernacular presses to Russian and Ottoman Jews of the late nineteenth and early twentieth centuries, the epilogue pursues this story into the interwar period. The epilogue reflects upon the dramatic ways in which Russian Yiddish and Ottoman Ladino newspaper cultures—and the empires that spawned them—were transformed during and after the Balkan and First World Wars and by the eventual dismantling of the Russian and Ottoman

Empires. How, I ask, were Yiddish and Ladino cultures transformed by the end of empire? What legacies of the imperial period continued to shape Jewish culture after the structure of empire disappeared?

The three sets of paired chapters that make up the parts of this book are meant to be read in tandem, but they are not wholly symmetrical. By necessity, the primary sources on which they rely differ, and this in turn has invited different conclusions and styles of narration.[50] One is guided through the Russian and Ottoman contexts by scholarly literatures as well, and these, too, have prompted the asking of different questions.[51] And yet the following pages address a number of historiographic questions that are of equal concern to scholars of Russian and Ottoman history. There is, to begin, the question of how these empires' ethnic and religious groups responded to the official policy and reforms of the late nineteenth and early twentieth centuries, and to the gradual dissolution of the empire as a whole. Second, there exists the provocative question of when and why political or cultural nationalism emerges and when and why it does not. One faces the more general challenge, too, of reconstructing the way in which popular cultures — particularly those speaking in ethnic vernacular languages — interacted with and were shaped by the overall culture of multi-ethnic empires. Finally, this book enters into a debate about the relationship between vernacular languages and ethnic and national identities that has captivated scholars across disciplinary and regional divides.

This book also engages with historical and historiographic discussions generated by the field of Jewish Studies. One question, in particular, is central to this inquiry: How was cultural change experienced and described by Jews in Eastern and Southeastern Europe at the turn of the twentieth century? By redirecting attention to the Jewish popular press, I offer new answers to this question, thereby deepening our sense of the worlds of secular Yiddish and Ladino cultures. And by considering Russian and Ottoman Jewries alongside each other, I aim to suggest the extent to which modernity was not a single but a multiple process for European Jewries, one that assumed a different shape for Jews in different economic, cultural, and political contexts.

The differences unearthed by this comparison are fascinating. But in some sense, more exciting still is the fact that there are justifications for comparing them: justifications for questioning and transgressing the boundaries that delineate linguistic communities, so-called "nationalist" responses from so-called "acculturated" ones, Ashkenazim from Sephardim, the Russian Empire from the Ottoman, Europe from Russia and the Middle East. These acts of boundary crossing are essential to the work of the Jewish historian, who has the opportunity and, perhaps, the obligation, to write trans-national narratives.

PART ONE

THE
YIDDISH
AND
LADINO PRESS
IN THE
RUSSIAN AND
OTTOMAN
EMPIRES

1

CREATING A YIDDISH NEWSPAPER CULTURE

In 1903, Morris Shaten was a teenager living in Kutno, a small town with a sizable Jewish population located just north of Łódź, in the Polish region of the Russian Pale of Settlement.[1] Shaten considered himself Hasidic: he grew up in a Hasidic home, prayed in a Hasidic *shtibl*, and was schooled in a Hasidic house of study. Though he dreamed of becoming a bookseller, it was unthinkable that Shaten would leave his environment to attend *gymnazia* or university.

In the early years of the twentieth century, it was common for Russian soldiers to pass through Kutno. Among them were a number of Jewish soldiers from Russia's interior: worldly men, educated men, radical men, or at least so they seemed to the young Shaten. These Jewish soldiers often lingered in town, talking politics with Kutno's self-made intellectuals, flirting with local women, occasionally falling in love and making the town their home. The soldiers would gather for conversation and company in the home of one of Kutno's wealthier Jewish residents. So popular was this meeting place that it soon came to be called a *men 'hoyze*, a people's house.

In this house Shaten and his childhood friend Zundel Tsonber encountered *Der fraynd*, the only Yiddish daily newspaper either had ever seen. *Der fraynd,* Shaten recalled, "opened our eyes [and showed us] that there was a big and rich world, and that in this world people were fighting for improvements. . . . [The paper] made a strong impression on me. . . . It felt like the messiah had come."[2] Thrilled with their discovery, Shaten and Tsonber wrote to St. Petersburg to order a subscription. Soon after, they became the first residents of their town to subscribe to a Yiddish newspaper.

Shaten and Tsonber read and discussed the paper together. People soon started eavesdropping on their conversations. Friends began to borrow copies of *Der fraynd:* first a schoolmate, then his brother, then the tailor, then the sons of the town's *shoykhet* (ritual slaughterer). "People saw us reading, saw us talking. We were speaking about new things. [Thus] we created a circle of *fraynd*-readers . . . friendships based upon shared knowledge [*a gevisen frayndshaft*]."[3] The circle's appetite was whetted, and after a while, "reading *Der fraynd* was not enough." In the pages of *Der fraynd,* Shaten and his friends discovered advertisements for works of fiction by the day's leading Yiddish authors: Mendele Moykher-Sforim (pseudonym of Sh. Y. Abramovitsh), Sholem Aleichem (pseudonym of Sh. Rabinovitsh), Yitshok Leyb Peretz, Sholem Ash, and Dovid Pinsky. Pooling their rubles, they sent away for these and other books with topics as varied as physics, chemistry, and astronomy, and new writings by Tolstoy translated into German. In time they built up an informal library of forty to fifty volumes. Fearing that their actions would arouse the suspicion of the authorities — according to Shaten it was forbidden to maintain either a public or a private library in Kutno — Shaten's circle stored the books in a factory in which one of their associates worked.[4] Readers would cautiously enter one at a time to borrow the books, which were stored in a glass cabinet. For further subterfuge, readers spoke of the collection as "private," though in truth it functioned as a lending library.

For Shaten and his circle, *Der fraynd* served as a gateway to a rich world of Yiddish in print. The newspaper — and the library that emerged from its pages — provided them with the secular education they were otherwise unable to acquire. According to Shaten, "it was our primary school, our high school."[5]

This story, though colorful, is not inconsistent with other reports. In the first years of the twentieth century, Jews of varied educational, social, economic, and religious backgrounds — those who lived in towns and those who lived in cities, those in the Russian Pale of Settlement and those in the Russian interior — were beginning to discover, read, and discuss a new and revolutionary medium: the Yiddish popular press. By the late nineteenth century, it was not unusual for Russia's Jews — men, women, and children — to spend time reading. Jewish literacy rates were high, and the reading of Yiddish, Hebrew, and, increasingly, Russian texts was to some extent a quotidian exercise. Still, the majority of turn-of-the-century Russian Jewish readers had access to only an extraordinarily limited variety of published material. By and large, the selections were religious in nature. Secular Yiddish publications, including romances, novellas, and adaptations of European literature, had been in print for over a century and Yiddish periodicals for some four decades. But this material was published irregularly and circulation levels tended to be low. Information about the day's news was particularly scarce; in 1903, for example, the combined circulation of secular periodicals designed for Russian Jewish readers was less than twenty thousand.[6] In the course of a scant decade, however, this number exploded, with the circulation of Yiddish periodicals in Russia reaching hundreds of thousands by the outbreak of the First World War. At the same time, there was a steep rise in the number and popularity of Jewish periodicals written in Russian, Polish, and Hebrew. By the interwar period, the number of Jewish newspapers in circulation rose further still. In Warsaw alone, the combined circulation of Yiddish newspapers exceeded 150,000.[7]

This chapter explores the tremendous expansion in Jewish newspaper publishing in the Russian Empire from the turn of the twentieth century to the First World War. It considers why the emergence of Yiddish newspapers was artificially delayed, and studies the factors that led to the rapid maturation of the Yiddish publishing industry. It contemplates the effect that Yiddish newspapers had upon readers like Morris Shaten and Zundel Tsonber: new readers of news and new readers of Yiddish newspapers. Finally, it investigates ways in which popular, affordable, and accessible Jewish newspapers changed the texture of Jewish culture and the shape of Jewish politics in the Russian Empire in the first decade of the twentieth century, not least of all by providing Russian Jewish readers with daily reading matter that was affordable, accessible, and comprehensible. Throughout, my assumption is that Yiddish newspapers like *Der fraynd* not only reported on change but also shaped it, by addressing and stimulating readers' interest in the day's news.

RUSSIAN JEWISH READING PRACTICES AND
THE RISE OF THE YIDDISH PUBLISHING INDUSTRY

Before the advent of the Yiddish daily press, Jews seeking news in print had few options. The first periodicals published exclusively for Russian Jewish readers had emerged in the 1860s in Odessa, an exceptional city that, because of imperial politics and socio-economic conditions, was at once both on the fringe and in the very center of secular Russian Jewish culture.[8] Most of these periodicals were published in Russian and in Hebrew, and, in keeping with the cultural and political orientation of the *Haskalah* (Jewish Enlightenment), their contributors tended to dismiss Yiddish as a language unsuited for "civilized" expression.[9] By the 1860s and 1870s, opposition to Yiddish cultural expression was beginning to erode, in great part because of the sway of populism over Russia's Jewish intellectuals. Nonetheless, gaining a mass readership was not a central goal of editors of early periodicals designed for Russian Jewish readers. These publications, instead, were designed for *maskilim* (proponents of the *Haskalah*) and tended to have circulations in the hundreds rather than thousands. Still, the last decades of the nineteenth century saw the emergence of the first viable (and, by some accounts, "modern") Russian Yiddish periodical: *Kol mevaser. Kol mevaser* was the only Yiddish newspaper published in Russia in the nineteenth century to receive official approval from Russia's Ministry of Interior, the imperial agency that oversaw the publication of periodicals. In getting this approval, editor Alexander Zederbaum succeeded where many others would fail, as in the 1880s, a stream of Jewish intellectuals approached the Russian Ministry of Interior to obtain permission to publish Yiddish newspapers, only to have their applications denied.[10]

As these rejections suggest, it was not simply *maskilic* (enlightened) opposition to the Yiddish language that constrained secular Yiddish print culture in the nineteenth century. Official intervention was critical in thwarting the development of Yiddish in print.[11] Officials at the Ministry of Interior, the agency that granted the required approval of would-be periodicals, were stubbornly opposed to permitting the publication of periodicals—and particularly daily newspapers—in Yiddish. They feared that Yiddish newspapers would spread revolutionary ideas and incite opposition to the state. This fear was, to some extent, well-founded; the Jewish socialist underground press, printed abroad and smuggled to Russian Jewish readers was—like the Bundist movement as a whole—swiftly gaining popularity at the turn of the century.[12] To make matters worse, officials at the ministry were aware that they lacked the means to effectively censor and control Yiddish in print. Available censors tended to be converts or Hasidic opponents of secular Jewish culture, both of whom the ministry had reason to distrust.[13]

Official fears of popular cultural forms were not, of course, directed only at the empire's Jews: on the contrary, the state was responsible for curtailing cultural activity in many other languages.[14] But opposition to and censorship of Yiddish cultural expression seems to have been particularly fierce.[15] Vyacheslav Konstantiovich von Plehve, who served (among other capacities) as Russian Minister of the Interior from 1902 to 1904, was known to be "no friend of newspapers, and especially no friend of Yiddish ones." Meanwhile Y. Feoktistov, the official in charge of press affairs at the ministry, was said to turn down applicants with the declaration that "there will never be a Yiddish [daily] newspaper in Russia."[16]

Jewish intellectuals intent on publishing secular material in Yiddish learned to bypass these obstacles in a variety of ways. Literary publications like Sholem Aleichem's *Di yidishe folksbibliotek* (Kiev, 1888); Mordechai Spektor's *Hoyzfraynt* (Warsaw, 1888–96); Yitshok Leyb Peretz's *Yidishe bibliotek* (Warsaw, 1871–95; Kracow, 1895–1904) and *Yontev bletlakh* (Warsaw, 1894–

96); and the bi-monthly *Der yud* (Warsaw, 1899–1902) provided readers with material that helped to fill the void of news in Yiddish. By and large, these periodicals were published erratically, circulated little, and were not designed to emphasize local, regional, imperial, or international happenings.[17] At the same time, a number of news-focused Yiddish periodicals were published outside the borders of the empire (in Galicia and in Prussia) with the intention of having them distributed to readers in Russia. Still others were published illegally within the boundaries of the empire.[18] Some of these experiments were quickly halted, while others succeeded for years at a time, with a literary influence that exceeded their physical reach. Until the early years of the twentieth century, then, conditions for publishing in the empire made it all but impossible for Yiddish periodicals to develop and sustain wide-reaching readerships in Russia; as a result, only a small minority of Russian Jewish readers of Yiddish were able to acquire reliable daily information about local, regional, or international news.

The near absence and limited reach of periodicals in Yiddish did not, of course, mean that turn-of-the-century Russian Jewish readers did not read. Many Jewish readers turned to Hebrew-language periodicals; indeed, at the turn of the century, the largest-circulating Russian Jewish newspaper was the Hebrew weekly *Hayom* (St. Petersburg, 1890–91), which had a run of 10,000.[19] By the year it was closed, the Hebrew weekly *Hatsefira* (Warsaw, 1862–96) printed an average of 5,000 copies: these tended to circulate in the Polish areas of the empire.[20] In the same year, 1896, the Hebrew-language monthly *Hashiloah* (Odessa, 1896–1918) circulated 1,115 copies.[21] In 1900, the Hebrew weekly-turned-daily *Hamelits* (Odessa, St. Petersburg, 1871–1904) had a circulation of about 3,000, a figure that the editor claimed was impossible for any Jewish daily to surpass.[22] Perhaps he was correct with reference to his type of newspaper. Turn-of-the-century Hebrew-language periodicals were, after all, an imperfect source of news. Their language was often lofty, abstruse, and still being formed. As a result, though publishing in Hebrew accorded with the intellectual and political goals of the *Haskalah,* Hebrew publications did not appeal to a particularly wide-reaching readership. Certainly, as we will see, they reached far smaller audiences than Yiddish sources could.

Yiddish books, novellas, and pamphlets also circulated far more widely than those published in Hebrew. After its emergence in 1853, Abraham Mapu's celebrated Hebrew novel *Ahavat tsiyon* (*Love of Zion*) sold 1,200 copies, enough to deem it an instant success, while five years later, a Hebrew adaptation of Eugène Sue's *Mystères de Paris,* itself a literary sensation, sold 2,000 copies. At the very same time, A. M. Dik's Yiddish novellas (printed, incidentally, at the same shop as *Ahavat tsiyon* and *Mystères de Paris*) were sold to hundreds of thousands of readers.[23] Perhaps more telling still, the circulation of a single text could vary dramatically depending upon the language in which it was printed. For example, in the late 1890s a pamphlet by

Theodor Herzl calling for a Jewish homeland was published in Hebrew and sold 3,000 copies; when the same article was republished in Yiddish some months later, it sold nine times as many copies.[24]

Why would readers have flocked to Yiddish sources and eschewed Hebrew ones? Simply because turn-of-the-century Russian Jewish readers were far more comfortable reading Yiddish than Hebrew. Precisely what percentage of Russian Jews was literate in Yiddish is unknown. The Russian census of 1897 claimed that 97 percent of Jews in the empire declared Yiddish to be their mother tongue. It also demonstrated that nearly 65 percent of Jewish men and over 36 percent of Jewish women over the age of ten were literate in a non-Russian language. All of these figures were underestimations.[25] Unfortunately, the census did not include Yiddish on its list of non-Russian languages, making it impossible to discern levels of Yiddish literacy from the results. Still, a great deal of evidence suggests that some degree of literacy in Yiddish was not exceptional. Certainly literacy in Yiddish was more common than literacy in Hebrew: for though a majority of Russian Jewish men claimed fluency in Hebrew, their ability to read secular (or even religious) texts in the language was limited.[26] It has been suggested — somewhat controversially — that Jewish women were more likely to be fluent in Yiddish than in Hebrew in part because they were accustomed to turning to Yiddish religious texts such as the *Tseena urena* on a regular basis. Whether or not we accept that Yiddish religious texts such as this were in fact read exclusively by women, the available evidence does seem to suggest that Yiddish literacy among women was not unusual.[27] Not only were Jewish women highly literate in Yiddish, but the available evidence suggests that they were avid readers. According to a survey of 1907, Jewish women constituted nearly half (42 percent) of the membership of a typical Russian Jewish lending library.[28]

Many Russian Jews, of course, read neither Hebrew nor Yiddish sources for their day's news, but turned, instead, to Russian-language sources. By the end of the nineteenth century, it was no longer uncommon for Russian Jews to have a reading knowledge of Russian. Nearly 50 percent of Russian Jewish men and 21 percent of Russian Jewish women between the ages of ten and fifty could claim literacy in Russian. This number was as high as 51 percent for urban males and 35 percent for urban females, and, in this case, too, the figures were significantly underestimated.[29] By 1897, nearly fifty thousand Jews residing in the Pale of Settlement alone declared Russian to be their mother tongue.[30] These Jews had access to a burgeoning number of Russian-language periodicals: by the turn of the century, approximately 125 Russian-language dailies were in circulation. *Svet* (St. Petersburg, 1877–79), *Novoe vremia* (St. Petersburg, 1876–1917), *Peterburgskii listok* (St. Petersburg, 1864–83), and *Moskovskii listok* (Moscow, 1881–1917) were among the largest, each claiming a circulation of around sixty thousand. Meanwhile, since the 1860s, Russian Jewish readers could turn to an array of Russian-language periodicals designed for Jewish readers.[31]

Russian-language sources such as these were avidly read by a segment of Russian Jewry. And yet a number of factors made it impossible for more than a small minority of Russian Jews to have been regular readers of news in Russian. Prior to 1905, when the lifting of censorship barriers permitted a dramatic rise in circulation levels for the empire's multi-lingual presses, the circulation of Russian-language newspapers (both those designed for Jews and those designed for general audiences) remained low enough that only a fraction of the empire's Jews could have read them. At the turn of the century, the largest-circulating Russian-language periodical designed for Jewish readers was *Voskhod* (St. Petersburg, 1881–1906), yet it reached no more than 3,000 readers. The circulation of Russian-language periodicals designed for general audiences was also low. Consider the case of *Novoe vremia*. At the turn of the century, this daily was likely to attract a great deal of Jewish readers. *Novoe vremia* had a large circulation, its readership was geographically broad-based, and, though politically conservative, it tended to support constitutional reform. However, even if Jewish subscribers composed 20 percent of this journals' readership — a generous figure indeed — they would total only 12,000, still a small fraction of the literate Jewish population. Further, the circulation of the most popular Russian-language newspapers was concentrated in cities where Jews did not represent a substantial portion of the population. Two of the four leading dailies of 1900 — *Peterburgskii listok* and *Moskovskii listok* — were mainly circulated in cities where a relative minority of Jews lived at the turn of the century: St. Petersburg and Moscow.[32] Finally, though many Jewish readers might have wished to turn to Russian-language sources, Jewish access to Russian-language periodicals was limited. Many Russian libraries frequented by Jews suffered from a shortage of material in Russian: the supply of Russian-language sources (and Russian newspapers, in particular) simply could not meet the demand.[33]

In 1892, ethnographer, author, and future *Der fraynd* contributor S. Ansky fictionalized these affairs in a short story entitled "Mendl Turk." The narrator of this story is a *maskilic* tutor employed in "one of the outlaying Lithuanian towns." Returning home one afternoon, this tutor is astonished to see that "a young man whom I didn't know, wearing a skullcap but no jacket, had pushed his head through the open window of my room and, with both hands on my table for support, was reading the Russian newspaper that I had left there." Caught in this theft of information, the young man stammers, "please don't get the wrong idea. . . . I didn't touch a thing in your house, God forbid. I was just passing by when I noticed the newspaper on your table and a headline caught my eye . . . I couldn't restrain myself from reading it." Engaging the young man in conversation, the narrator surmises that he is the local *heder* (religious primary school) teacher whose pupils gather in the neighboring courtyard. To the narrator's eyes, he appears to be a "young man of twenty-eight with delicate features and a short black beard . . . his velvet skullcap, the long, curled earlocks, and his short beard fram[ing] his face beautifully." Intrigued, An-sky's narrator invites the young man inside. The youth declines, but suggests returning in the evening: "It's been a long time," he muses, "since I've had the chance to speak to someone like you." This phrase, "someone like you," obliquely referred to the narrator's secular orientation, an orientation that—to his interlocutor, at least—dictated not simply what he believed or how he practiced, but what and how he read. In the eyes of this young *heder* teacher, the narrator's regular access to secular reading matter in Russian—and his linguistic abilities, which allowed him to read this material fluently, in contradistinction to the *heder* teacher who reads Russian "slowly and with difficulty"—rendered the narrator quite unlike himself. "Tell me," the religious youth asks his secularized interlocutor, "do you read the newspaper each day?"

> "Yes, every day." The teacher looked at me enviously. "Oh, I can understand that," he said with a sigh. "That kind of reading makes sense: it has meaning." "And you, what do you read?" "What do I read? I catch things in the wind; I don't read. I get the newspaper *Halevanon*[34] maybe twice a month; the rest of the time I have to depend on the 'Telegrams' which are pasted on the walls in the market—and on what people tell me, always complete with their own opinions, of course, which are never based in fact."[35]

An-sky's narrator is captivated and attempts to learn more about his new acquaintance. Seeking the confidence of a third neighbor, he is told that the young man is "[a] human being, a young man, a religious person, a Hasid, a scholar, a very learned and promising scholar, if you must know." Mendl by name, the scholar is called "Mendl Turk" because of his ardent conviction that the Turks will defeat the Russians in the ongoing Russo-Turkish war. When asked about Mendl, the narrator's informant instinctively grasps the reason for his neighbor's inquiries. Guessing that Mendl Turk was caught in an illicit pursuit of news, he crows triumphantly: "Why else would Mendl visit you? To find out what's in the papers! So he must gather his politics in the same way, in bits and pieces—like a chicken, peck, peck, peck, grain by grain until the crop is full and the egg is ready to be laid." Mendl, the narrator soon learns, is not alone in his habits. Following the young man to synagogue at the close of Sabbath afternoon prayers, the narrator discovers not the spiritual ambiance of "amity and love" that he remembers from his youth, but a group of worshipers engaged in a fiery example of what is known in Yiddish as *lezhanke politik* (stove-side politics): the "pro-Russian" side and the "pro-Turkish" side emboldened by their gleaning of the day's news.[36]

Though late-nineteenth-century Russian Jews like Mendl Turk may have read Russian with difficulty, their limited encounters with Russian-language news (and, to a lesser extent, with that in Hebrew) educated and politicized them, thereby linking the secular and religious worlds. But, if "Mendl Turk" is any indication, turn-of-the-century Russian Jews were also compelled to acquire their news in inventive and decidedly "un-Orthodox" ways. As mentioned, official intervention, literacy rates, circulation figures, and poor access prevented the vast majority from reading or securing sources in Yiddish, Russian, and Hebrew. And even those who triumphed in the hunt for printed information — individuals like Morris Shaten and Mendl Turk — were themselves quite literally news-starved, more likely to learn about the day's news between prayers in synagogue or on walls in the marketplace than from newspapers themselves. This news-poor environment explains the overwhelming popularity of *Der fraynd* and other Yiddish dailies like it, a popularity that, in some senses, may well have exceeded what was at first deserved. Into this atmosphere *Der fraynd* was dropped like a crystal into a supersaturated solution, instantly changing the fundamental character of its environment.

CREATING A READING CIRCLE: A FRIEND FOR JEWISH READERS

What, then, was the reach of this first Russian Yiddish daily? H. D. Horovits, a member of *Der fraynd*'s editorial board, has documented that the newspaper acquired a circulation of 15,000 in January 1903 (its first month of publication) and that its popularity climbed steadily thereafter.[37] Estimates of the circulation of *Der fraynd* in ensuing years vary, but it appears that the paper had somewhere between 90,000 and 100,000 subscribers at its peak in 1905.[38] This extraordinary circulation far outpaced that of any other Jewish periodical hitherto published. Indeed, for a spell it may have rendered the paper among the largest circulating newspapers in any language to be published in the empire.

Unlike the leading Russian-language dailies of St. Petersburg, *Der fraynd* did not rely on street sales, but instead sold subscriptions through numerous distributing agents who made the paper available for purchase in cities throughout the Pale of Settlement and Congress Poland, as well as in the imperial capital.[39] By 1905, the paper could be bought in St. Petersburg (through the *Der fraynd* office), Vilna (through the "Shtesel House"), Warsaw (from the agent H. D. Perlman), Odessa (from bookseller S. Hornshteyn), Kiev (through "Pedagogue" booksellers), Łódź (through *Wygoda* publishing house), Kovel (from the agent Heinrich Geller), and Riga (from bookseller Y. L. Ashkenazi).[40] Three years later, it was possible to buy the paper in dozens of cities in Russia and in numerous cities abroad.[41]

Der fraynd would remain in print for just over a decade: its first issue was published on January 1, 1903, its last on October 13, 1913. Though the paper was called a daily, it (like most Jewish periodicals of the day) never appeared seven days a week. Instead, *Der fraynd* was published five or six times a week, on average.[42] Physically, the paper was bulky: at 24 inches high and 52 inches wide, it was nearly twice the size of many other Yiddish periodicals. In shape and size, the paper closely resembled contemporary Russian-language dailies, a tactic meant to remind readers that *Der fraynd* was ushering in a new era in the world of Yiddish letters. (This tactic would be quickly mimicked by competitors: the Yiddish daily *Der tog* [St. Petersburg/Vilna, 1904–1907], which was 42 inches high and 58 inches wide, was roughly the same width as *Der fraynd* but nearly twice as long.)[43]

There were four pages in most issues of *Der fraynd*. The front page tended to feature a note *fun der redaktsya* (from the editors), the beginning of a lead story, and a column of advertisements. The second and third pages were divided between coverage of the news, serialized fiction, and the paper's regular columns; contents included Dr. Yosef Luria's popular feature on economics (signed "by a *soykher*" [merchant]), for example, or the humorous section, "Shtet un shtetlakh" [City and town]. Over time, the organization of the paper's interior pages became regularized as news was subdivided into various sections, among them "Yidishe nayes in oysland" [Jewish news from abroad], "Yidishe nayes in rusland" [Jewish news in Russia], "Rusishe nayes" [Russian news], and "Oysland" [Abroad]. These columns tended to be devoted to news of Europe's largest cities and paid less attention to the Pale of Settlement or Congress Poland, where the vast majority of Russia's Jews (and, arguably, the vast majority of the paper's readers) were concentrated. Current events were also reported in a series of telegrams culled from the privately owned Russian Telegraph Agency (RTA).[44] For some years, telegrams been a familiar feature of Russian-language newspapers, but in the first years of the twentieth century they were still an innovation to the world of Yiddish letters. According to one account, *Der fraynd* was the first Yiddish periodical to publish them and readers approached them with considerable enthusiasm.[45] Advertisements and letters to the editor were also featured in the paper, both on the back page and in the paper's interior.

Subscriptions to *Der fraynd* cost 7 rubles a year, and could also be bought by the half-year (for 3.5 rubles), quarter year (for 1.75 rubles), or month (for 60 kopecks). Compared to contemporary dailies, this was a reasonable price: prior to 1909 (when *Gazeta kopeika* became the first "kopeck daily"), a year's subscription to a daily newspaper cost anywhere from 4 to 17 rubles.[46] *Der fraynd*'s price, nonetheless, put the paper out of the reach of a significant portion of the paper's would-be consumers. It was not unusual for Jewish artisans — who, depending on region, comprised up to 90 percent of the Jewish workforce — to earn between 3 and 8 rubles a week and to receive paid employment only ten weeks a year. Weekly necessities, meanwhile, could consume up to 90 percent of a worker's salary.[47] This, no doubt, is why readers like Morris Shaten and Zundel Tsonber shared a subscription to the paper. It also explains why subscriptions to *Der fraynd* were often ordered by organizations.[48] Public and private libraries (formal and legal, or informal and underground like Shaten's) could be frequented by dozens of readers on a daily basis, allowing the reach of *Der fraynd* to extend far beyond its subscribers.

The practices of sharing papers and reading aloud suggest that *Der fraynd*'s readers — unlike the typical readers of most nineteenth-century Jewish periodicals — were a rich mixture of social and vocational classes. Readers were working-class and professional, educated and uneducated, religious and secular. Paradoxically, the available evidence suggests that many illiterate Jews could also be counted as consumers of *Der fraynd*. This newspaper, we must remember, was a novelty as it was not only the first Yiddish daily of the empire, but also the first printed source of news that many Jews encountered. Thus it is not surprising that copies of the paper were passed from hand to hand and read out loud to large groups. Editor Shoyl Ginzburg recorded in his memoirs that one of the most meaningful moments in his career was when he saw a copy of *Der fraynd* being read aloud (by "simple old Jews") in Vilna's marketplace.[49] This custom has been described from the perspective of a bystander in the marketplace, Joseph Buloff, who made a practice of listening to the town's educated recluse, "Barve's Son," summarize news of the Russo-Japanese War gleaned from the press.[50]

It is impossible to quantify with any precision the extent to which copies of *Der fraynd* were shared. Nor is it possible to determine the strength of the tradition of reading newspapers aloud. Given the absence of archival material on the topic, our sense of the practice is built mainly upon reports in memoirs and literature of the period. Some historians of Russian letters have offered approximations, suggesting that single copies of papers reached the hands of anywhere from five to fifteen "consumers."[51] Even a conservative estimate is striking: if each copy of a given paper met five "consumers" (readers or listeners of the day's news), then *Der fraynd* would have reached no fewer than 450,000 Russian Jews. This formidable reach, what Morris Shaten might call *Der fraynd*'s "reading circle" (*lezer krayz*) was the paper's greatest achievement. Though *Der fraynd* was cursed by disagreements between its contributors and editors, though it failed to articulate a coherent political agenda, though it would soon be outmoded (and outcirculated) by its successors, this paper nonetheless ushered in a new era in East European Jewish culture, an era defined by the production and consumption of news in Yiddish.

Like *Der fraynd*, the other early Yiddish newspapers not only vied for individual readers, but also aspired to cultivate a circle whose sphere of influence reached far beyond a single city, political orientation, or secular milieu. As we have seen, even by the turn of the century, the notion of a *lezer krayz* composed of Yiddish readers was novel: it was hitherto constrained by imperial censorship, *maskilic* discomfort with the notion of Jewish popular culture, and practical realities. Indeed, the phrase *lezer krayz* itself hints at all that was new about Yiddish newspapers and their readers. These were both comparatively recent words in Yiddish, borrowed from German no earlier than in the mid-eighteenth century. They were the kind of words — like *gayst* (spirit) that entered Yiddish at the same moment — that speakers of Yiddish encountered in print, and by and large in new kinds of printed texts.[52] These were also words weighted with romantic and nationalist meanings. Perhaps to belie these realities, a *lezer krayz* was immediately presented as a cultural necessity. Echoing Shaten, H. D. Horovits, who served on the editorial board of *Der fraynd*, suggested that in the early years of Yiddish publishing "it [was] not enough to have only readers, one need[ed] a reading circle [*lezer krayz*]."[53] This need, as we will see, was at once intellectual, visceral, political, and commercial. In some senses, it was also short-lived. For though the popularity and number of Yiddish periodicals in print would continue to expand long after *Der fraynd* ceased publishing, the kind of *lezer krayz* that *Der fraynd*'s successors pursued differed from that which animated the earliest readers and producers of Yiddish newspapers. We next turn to this early and transitional moment in Yiddish newspaper publishing, exploring the creation, impact, and political texture of the first Yiddish newspaper *lezer krayz,* and tracing the meteoric rise and sudden decline of *Der fraynd* and its profound influence on early-twentieth-century Russian Jewish culture.

In 1902, officials from the Ministry of Interior granted editors Shabsay Rapoport and Shoyl Ginzburg approval to publish *Der fraynd*. In his memoirs, Ginzburg speculated that one reason he received approval to publish the paper was because officials thought a Zionist newspaper "might encourage Jews to emigrate."[54] It is more likely that the ministry was interested in encouraging the editors' Russophilism rather than their Zionism. As a graduate of a Russian university and a fluent speaker of Russian, Ginzburg was no doubt less threatening than his more radical peers (particularly those from Warsaw) who were equally eager to publish Yiddish dailies. Indeed, officials of the Ministry of Interior considered *Der fraynd* a potential palliative to the growth of the Bundist underground press.[55] In this context, Ginzburg's and Rapoport's choice of St. Petersburg as the home city for their nascent periodical served as a *bona fide* for their loyalty to the empire as a whole. From the perspective of the ministry, papers printed in the capital were considered easier to censor and control.[56] Ginzburg's willingness to yield to official expectations, it should be noted, was ideological as well as tactical. As he reflected in his memoirs, St. Petersburg was for him the only logical location for *Der fraynd:* the city was the center of Russian-language publishing and in it, Russian Jews deserved some measure of visibility.[57]

Ginzburg's presentation of St. Petersburg as the natural home of *Der fraynd* was undeniably a political statement. In fact, from any but Ginzburg's or the official perspective, St. Petersburg was an inadequate home for the first Yiddish daily of the Russian Empire. A number of other cities would have been more logical choices. Warsaw, for example, was home to the empire's largest concentration of Jews; Odessa had a rich history of Jewish publishing and a large Jewish population; and Vilna was a historic center of the *Haskalah* and of Jewish religious and secular culture.[58] Indeed, many of *Der fraynd*'s would-be allies were skeptical of Ginzburg's and Rapoport's choice of St. Petersburg. They considered this a decision designed to alienate Jewish readers and writers in Congress Poland rather than to appease imperial censors. (Though such fears may have been paranoid, they were no doubt prompted by the strange ambivalence of *Der fraynd*'s project, which was always at once populist and elitist.) When Ginzburg began recruiting contributors in Warsaw, he was repeatedly greeted with the question, "Why would *Der fraynd* locate in the *goyish* [Gentile] city of St. Petersburg?"[59] The challenge reflected the relative appropriateness of Warsaw as home for the empire's first Yiddish daily. Not only was Warsaw poised to become a center of Yiddish literary activity, but it also offered editors the largest collection of potential readers in all of Europe.

Divisions between the paper's Russophilic and Russified editors and its Polonized contributors dampened the excitement that the publication of *Der fraynd* was intended to spark. Several contributors refused to participate in the celebration marking the publication of the first issue of the paper because St. Petersburg was "too far away" or (as Yankev Dineson protested) "too cold."[60] Y. L. Peretz, who traveled from Warsaw to St. Petersburg to join the paper's inaugural celebration, remained atypically quiet throughout the affair until he exploded in an outburst of anger, declaring it an outrage that the event had been conducted in Russian and not in Yiddish. Only the intervention of Peretz's childhood friend S. An-sky could soothe the disgruntled visitor and allow the event to continue.[61]

By Ginzburg's own account, the paper's founders went to extraordinary ends to ready their St. Petersburg office. Editorial board member H. D. Horovits traveled to Vilna to recruit a typesetting machine and typesetters to run it, only to encounter official resistance to granting them residency rights in St. Petersburg.[62] Meanwhile, the paper's contributors had to be recruited in Warsaw. The economic backing for the paper, too, came from afar: nearly two thirds of the advertisements appearing in the paper were for Warsaw-based establishments. And in a last-minute crisis, the publication of the first issue had to be postponed for five days while extra blocks of the letter "ayin" were imported from Warsaw. Symbolically, too, *Der fraynd* seemed ill at ease in the capital city. One account claimed that the sign outside the paper's central office was the only Yiddish sign in St. Petersburg.[63] "What a wild thing it is," penned dramatist A. Vayter to his friend Shmuel Niger, "a Yiddish newspaper published in St. Petersburg!"[64]

And yet, if discord surrounded the publication of *Der fraynd*, the dispute was initially a dimension of the paper's success. The paper's biggest feat was, in a sense, gaining official approval. For, once a daily Yiddish paper in the Russian Empire was created *de jure*, it was almost guaranteed to succeed *de facto*. Earlier Yiddish weeklies had revealed the existence both of a potential market and of a pool of talented editors and writers. Thus *Der fraynd*'s editorial board, quickly and easily assembled, was composed of Yosef Luria, H. D. Horovitz, and Shmuel Rosenfeld, all of whom were experienced in Yiddish-, Russian-, and Hebrew-language journalism. Luria was perhaps the most accomplished of all: from 1899 to 1903, he had edited the literary bimonthly *Der yud*, and under his leadership, the journal had been transformed into one of the most important Yiddish journals of the day.[65] (*Der fraynd* would eventually purchase *Der yud* and access to its subscribers for 2,000 rubles.)[66] Meanwhile, Warsaw-based contributors to the paper, as full of misgivings as they may have been, could not resist participating in the production of *Der fraynd*. Not only was this production unprecedented, but also these writers had few options but to publish in the Yiddish daily press. Most had begun to publish their work in other Yiddish periodicals: in the literary *Kol mevaser*, in Sholem Aleichem's weekly *Di yidishe folksbibliotek*, in Peretz's *Yontef bletlakh* and *Di yidishe bibliotek*, or in *Der yud*. But because it was a daily, *Der fraynd* promised to publish more material, offer writers greater visibility and, not insignificantly, provide a steadier income than other journals.[67] This was one reason, no doubt, that the paper was able to recruit so many notable contributors who (at least occasionally) called Warsaw their home. Among them were Yitshok Leyb Peretz, Yankev Dineson, Dovid Frishman, Mordkhe Spektor, Bal Makhshoves (pseudonym of Isidor Eliashev), Shimen Shmuel Frug, Chaim Nakhmen Bialik, Sholem Ash, Hersh Dovid Nomberg, and Avrom Reisen. The paper could also count two distinguished female writers from Warsaw among its contributors: Rokhl Brokhes and Rokhl Faygenberg.[68]

That *Der fraynd* managed to attract contributors in Warsaw did not mean that the dispute was over. On the contrary, divisions between the two groups, sharp to begin with, became exaggerated with time. As Yiddish publishing exploded after 1908, readers and contributors in Warsaw gained the luxury of becoming less flexible. In the beginning, however, imperial restrictions and market pressures drove the collaborators together.

Some of *Der fraynd*'s contributors would have liked the paper to be more radical, others more Zionist, and still others would have liked it to sharpen its support of Russification. But because imperial policies essentially enforced the collaboration of Yiddish writers across the political spectrum, *Der fraynd* was defined by compromise, and was thus politically more moderate than many of the writers and editors who contributed to it. To put this another way, *Der fraynd*'s political agenda reflected an unwillingness to antagonize. Although *Der fraynd* never declared itself explicitly politically neutral, in the paper's early years a tendency to conciliate was a key to the paper's success. Moreover, the fact that contributors of diverse political leanings managed to cooperate on the production of *Der fraynd* seemed to embolden the newspaper's editors to present the paper as the voice of and for "all" Russian Jews.[69] To this end, *Der fraynd* identified its readers as a coherent entity, made up of members of *di yidishe gas* (the Jewish street), *der yidishe oylem* (the Jewish public), *dos yidishe folk* (the Jewish people), or *der hamoyn* (the masses), terms that celebrated the paper's seemingly unimpeded appeal. These terms were common stylistic flourishes in Yiddish journalism of the day, but in the pages of *Der fraynd* in the paper's early years of publication, they took on a particular meaning. While in a matter of a decade these terms came to have nuanced political meanings, for the moment they (like the newspaper itself) were remarkably unpolemical. Not just political shorthand, these terms referred to a body of readers of Yiddish that the paper viewed proprietarily and somewhat monolithically.

This is not to suggest that *Der fraynd* had no political agenda. On the contrary, the newspaper quickly established positions on three intersecting issues: secularism, which the paper almost blithely took for granted; the language question, on which the paper pronounced itself pro-Yiddish (though by no means an opponent of Russian or Hebrew); and Zionism, which the paper tended to favor, though with some ambiguity.

Der fraynd rarely published outright assaults on religious observance, and only rarely drew attention to its secular posture. But secularism was nonetheless an essential characteristic of the paper, significant enough to be illuminated in *Der fraynd*'s first editorial. In recent years, this editorial explained, Jewish life had changed. It was no longer "entrenched in ancient rituals" and, partly as a result, Jews lacked a sense of cultural cohesion. Readers, the editorial continued, needed a daily newspaper that would provide information about "daily life" and answer the questions that daily life raises.[70] Traditionally, of course, it was to rabbinical authorities and courts that Jewish men and women would go with their daily queries. But now, *Der fraynd* implied, the pace of change had become too rapid for rabbinical authorities to accommodate, and the religious establishment was unable to address the sheer quantity of questions that modern Jews faced. In the pages of *Der fraynd,* information was presented as the successor to religion, and a daily newspaper its most reliable vessel.

As this suggests, the pages of *Der fraynd* were not free of references to religious life. On the contrary, remarks about the religious establishment and religious readers often served as a means of clarifying the paper's agenda. Humorous contributions to *Der fraynd* frequently parodied observant Jews and were often included in a column entitled "Shtet un shtetlakh" [Cities and towns], penned by Emes (Truth).[71] One installment described a collection of Jewish men in the *shtetl* Zhgersh, who, fearing that the imminent arrival of *Der fraynd* would corrupt their wives, declared the newspaper *treyf* (not kosher) and issued a *herem* (writ of excommunication) against the journal. "If God helped our wives to improve themselves by creating a news-paper in *taytsh yedn tog* [everyday speech]," the townsmen declare, "we will not read it: and wherever this is heard, so will it be! And further, maintained the wives of Zhgersh, '*Der fraynd* will be *treyf* for everyone.' "[72] Such hu-morous references to traditional Jewish mores were never balanced by re-porting on issues of importance to the Jewish religious world. Indeed, one could easily gain the impression from *Der fraynd* that nothing noteworthy ever happened in the worlds of the Orthodox or Hasidic. *Der fraynd*'s lack of interest in addressing observant readers was, indeed, most evident. This point was made quite clearly by Emes. "Yiddish newspapers in Russia have always had a penchant for writing more about Paris, Berlin, Madrid, or the furthest cities in Australia and Calcutta, India," reflected Emes, "than we do of the Jewish *shtetls* where one million of the five million [Jews] who reside in Russia actually live. . . . The Jewish cities and towns for which Yiddish newspapers are produced aren't even on the 'geographic map' of the Yid-dish press."[73] Thus *Der fraynd*'s supplement *Der fraynd baylage* offered read-ers the chance to explore Jewish life in New York, Bucharest, Prague, and Nagasaki before it deigned to speak of Jewish life in the Russian Pale. And when serious news of local communities did reach the pages of *Der fraynd,* it was more often than not negative. One such article disparaged the educa-tion that young men received in yeshiva. The author complained that a student could graduate from a yeshiva without knowing Russian or, in ex-treme cases, Hebrew.[74]

Not only did *Der fraynd* appear little interested in appealing to observant readers, but the editorial board may well have actively discouraged them. Ginzburg recounted in his memoirs that on one occasion, a "grey beard" (i.e., an older, observant Jew) approached him, offering to contribute a weekly article on the *parsha* (weekly Torah portion). Ginzburg's response was terse and scornful: Couldn't the reader see that *Der fraynd* was "not that kind of paper?"[75] This response may more accurately reflect the tone of the era in which Ginzburg penned his memoirs than the early years of *Der fraynd*'s publication. In truth, "that kind of paper" — that is, daily news-papers in Yiddish designed for observant readers — would not emerge until the First World War.[76] Prior to their emergence, Orthodox readers who were able to read Hebrew were more likely to turn to the Hebrew *maskilic* press than to the Yiddish. But nothing prevented them from reading Yiddish periodicals as well. Recall the wonder with which Morris Shaten received the paper; to him, "it felt as though the messiah had come."[77] That a secular Yiddish newspaper could appear to be a harbinger of a messianic age re-minds us of the fine line that divided religious Jews from secular Jews in early-twentieth-century Russia. Indeed, a profound overlap between reli-gious and secular Jews, on the one hand, and religious and secular texts, on the other, might be understood as a central feature of this terrain.

Shaten was not, of course, *Der fraynd*'s only observant reader. Others announced themselves in letters to the editor that challenged the paper's secular posture.[78] A number of observant Jews facilitated the production of *Der fraynd*. Israel Landau was a Hasid employed by the authorities as the official censor of *Der fraynd*.[79] Despite his religious leanings, he could often be found in the newspaper office as late as two in the morning, chuckling over the latest contribution by Sholem Aleichem. His friendship with editor Ginzburg developed to such an extent that the two arranged for Ginzburg to "censor the paper himself" in order to save Landau "the trouble."[80] *Der fraynd* could also count observant Jews among its staff: the paper's first typesetters were fifteen Orthodox Jews imported from Vilna for this purpose. Much to Ginzburg's chagrin, they could often be found praying in *Der fraynd*'s office, sidelocks and ritual fringes swinging.[81] Jewish censors and Yiddish typesetters were, of course, exceptional figures in turn-of-the-century Russia. And yet they were nonetheless reminders of the permeable boundary that divided religious and secular Jewish cultural productions in the first decade of the twentieth century. This line was not only blurred by necessity; the camps it divided were far from discrete.[82]

Der fraynd's secular agenda was further checked by the sobriety of the newspapers' creators. In its early years, the editors of *Der fraynd* were stubbornly unwilling to mimic the kinds of Russian "boulevard" tabloids that devoted themselves to daily news and sensationalism. In accordance with this disdain, telegrams that announced the day's news that dominated Russian-language journals like *Peterburgskii listok* were relegated to the back pages of *Der fraynd*, leaving its front pages free for verbose editorials and lead stories. Such articles, which expounded on the nature of the Austrian parliament, the state of Jewish education, or race relations in the United States, belied the *maskilic* origins and instincts of *Der fraynd*'s editors.[83] In this sense *Der fraynd* was profoundly conservative, and in many ways had not strayed far from the "European" goals of journals like *Hashiloah*, which aimed to educate readers in a didactic manner.[84] To put this another way, while *Der fraynd* eschewed religious culture, it retained a conventional sense of the *treyf* inherited from its more conservative literary predecessors. The editors of *Der fraynd* thus found a fine line for their writers to toe. They disdained the rigidities and complacencies of the old Jewish order, yet were unwilling to fully embrace the riot of rapid news and scandals espoused by their Russian counterparts. *Der fraynd*'s editors therefore showed a preference for a conservative readership over an adventurous one. This agenda was, after all, not so different than that of the Orthodox order, with the obvious difference that it should be *Der fraynd*—and not the rabbinic elite—who would educate the people and interpret events for them. This didactic tone ultimately contributed to the paper's undoing.

Der fraynd's position on language was far more lucid (and arguably more daring) than its stand on secularism. Contributors to *Der fraynd* agreed that

Russian Jews needed daily news in a language they could understand. And not just any language, but the mother tongue of the majority of Russian Jews — Yiddish, or *zhargon* as the paper called the language in its early years. Yiddish was the language that the vast majority of Russian Jews spoke at the turn of the century and in which they were most likely to be comfortably literate, even if they claimed fluency in another language (Russian, Polish, or, in time, Hebrew) on an imperial census. One article published in *Der fraynd* boasted that while 85 percent of Jews in St. Petersburg knew how to read and write in *some* language, "surely all Jews" could at least read Yiddish.[85] Elsewhere, a contributor admitted that he could not help but celebrate the "miraculous" creation of the first Yiddish daily to be published in Russia. "Tradition has it," he wrote with sarcasm,

> that before I take pen in hand and begin for the first time to write for a daily [Yiddish] newspaper in Russia, a city Jew like me should, before anything else, wash his hands and deliver an earnest prayer: "[Thank you] master of the world, for the great favor that you have granted us, small-city men and women . . . by making for us men of the world, as you did for all men of the world, a Yiddish newspaper, which speaks to us in the language which our lips have uttered from birth on, the language with which we lull our children to sleep, and in which we pronounce our joy and pain. Without this language which you, the merciful, in your favor, shaped for us, we, your slaves and servants, would be just like beasts, mute and unable to speak."[86]

This parody succeeds in part because the creation of a Yiddish daily was far from an ancient rite. Instead, a daily newspaper in Yiddish was a novelty, its publication a remarkable event. This fact was foregrounded in *Der fraynd*'s first editorial, published on January 5, 1903. "[While we do not want to] exaggerate the importance of our enterprise," it reads, "we believe that today, the first time a daily *zhargonishe* newspaper is published in Russia, will stand out in the memory of the history of *zhargon* and its literature." The article continues:

> We wholly believe in putting an end to the question of whether or not one should write in *zhargon*, whether or not there should be a literature in *zhargon*. These questions have no bearing on life. Millions of our brothers, who speak and think only in *zhargon*, who understand no other language, need neither legitimization nor support for their language and do not ask permission from authors or philosophers for its use.[87]

Zhargon in this context was not a particularly generous term for Yiddish, but it was not entirely deprecating either. Like the Ladino term *nuestra idiom*, the Yiddish word *zhargon* could — at least in 1903 — bespeak affection rather than scorn. Even strident defenders of Yiddish could use the two terms *yidish* and *zhargon* interchangeably, as did Dr. Yosef Luria in a series of articles that promoted Yiddish as the folk language of the Jews.[88] In this

Figure 1.1. *Der fraynd* masthead, 1903

significant sense, *zhargon* is not the equivalent of the English *jargon*, which has a far more pejorative connotation. Nomenclature for Yiddish was, in any case, in transition at precisely this moment. The language was undergoing a shift in status from *zhargon* to Yiddish, from a language that was derided and avoided by the intelligentsia to a language with linguistic integrity, wholly suited for scientific, philosophical, journalistic, or literary uses.[89] The fact that *Der fraynd* clung to the term *zhargon* despite its enthusiastic support for the language might suggest that the editors of and contributors to the paper were still somewhat anxious about their use of Yiddish. Indeed, as the paper's success grew, the term *zhargon* was abandoned in favor of *yidish*. From 1903 to 1904, *Der fraynd*'s masthead announced the paper as *di ershte teglikhe zhargonishe tsaytung in Rusland* (the first daily newspaper in *zhargon* in Russia). In 1904, however, overnight and without commentary, *zhargonishe* was replaced by the kinder *yidishe,* and the masthead now read *di ershte teglikhe yidishe tsaytung in rusland* (the first daily Yiddish newspaper in Russia) (figures 1.1 and 1.2).

Despite the silence with which the transition was executed, the change had enormous symbolic import. It reflected the successful reception of *Der fraynd* and, more generally, the viability of a Yiddish daily. And it demonstrated that although the existence of readers of Yiddish had justified the creation of the daily paper, the language itself needed to be reshaped to suit the new genre. *Der fraynd* actually introduced an orthography to readers of Yiddish that would — with but few variations — prevail as the common system for printed Yiddish until the First World War. In his history of Yiddish publishing written in the 1920s, Dovid Druk recalled that "a newspaper

Figure 1.2. *Der fraynd* masthead, 1904

language had to be created [by the producers of *Der fraynd*], new words had to be invented. . . . And one must not forget that this had to happen very quickly. This was not a monthly or a weekly, with which people could sit quietly, mulling over every word. With a daily one cannot think. The machine does not stop."[90]

The struggle to craft Yiddish-language news fit for daily publication immediately proved to be contentious. The first issue of *Der fraynd* was to include a poem by Chaim Nakhmen Bialik in which the poet incorrectly formed the plural of the word *taykh* (river) as *tekhter* (daughters). This was a poetic license the editors would not allow, and only after lengthy debate with the author was the poem published in its edited form.[91] Some months later, Chaim Zhitlowsky, writing under the pseudonym Dr. N. Gayderov, published a poem that poked fun at poet Shimen Frug for improperly pluralizing the word *band* (volume) as *bender* (ribbons) instead of *bend*.[92] Such assaults on sloppy grammar belied a complex political message that was central to *Der fraynd*'s platform: that Yiddish was a language with its own system, grammar, and vocabulary and that it should be defended as the "folk language" of the Jews. This position was articulated most forcefully by Yosef Luria, a frequent contributor to *Der fraynd* and a member of the paper's editorial board who published a series of articles on the subject from October 1905 to February 1906. He argued that Jews were unique in that they were bi- and often trilingual (fluent in Hebrew, Yiddish, and the language of their land), and in that each of these languages served them in unique ways. Traditionally, Luria explained, Hebrew had been considered the language of high culture, Russian the language of the land and of official and intra-ethnic communication, and Yiddish the language of the people. Because of its linguistic history, Yiddish was often dismissed as the language of diaspora, and like diaspora, was considered "bitter," "ugly," and "savage." Luria challenged this formulation, writing:

> The Yiddish language grew out of diaspora. But it isn't a foreign language
> to us. . . . When people say that *zhargon* is ugly to us, a foreign language, a
> step-daughter, they are absolutely wrong. *Zhargon* did not remain German,
> but became a truly Jewish language because it was spoken by Jews and
> because it was infused with a Jewish nature, a Jewish soul.[93]

Unlike other writers of the day, Luria did not go so far as to call Yiddish
the national language of the Jews. On the contrary, he declared unambiguously that "Yiddish, or *zhargon,* is not our national language as is Hebrew."[94] Nonetheless, he argued that Yiddish should be used to express and
develop Jews' national culture. "*Zhargon,*" he wrote, "should become a medium for the national life of the whole Jewish people. Not only should it be
the language of the masses, it should be the language of the Jewish intelligentsia."[95] Yiddish, he continued, needed to be protected: writers should
cease to rely on imported words from German and Slavic languages, and
should instead revive words from old Yiddish texts.[96]

Other contributors to the paper echoed Luria's words. Chaim Zhitlowsky
fumed: "When people accuse the Yiddish language of being only a collection of words, not a language, with no grammar, it is as foolish as when they
accuse the Jewish people of being merely a collection of people!"[97] Elsewhere, articles condemned "other" Jewish intellectuals for abandoning
readers by allowing "fashion" to turn them against Yiddish.[98] One writer
found an example of this practice in the Fourth Zionist Conference, where
participants relied upon "imported" phrases like *en bloc.* This, *Der fraynd*
argued, reflected the way in which speakers of Yiddish were taking on "foreign traditions" and thereby "condemning everything we are."[99] To prevent
such bastardizations, the paper called for a standardization of Yiddish orthography, which would ease the exercise of reading and protect the integrity of the language.[100]

Der fraynd was not alone in presenting such arguments. The question of
language choice had preoccupied Russian Jewish intellectuals since the
early nineteenth century, and these debates were beginning to gain inten-
sity in the first years of the twentieth. Though discussions over language
choice had always been heated, they became increasingly polarized after
about 1908, when the First Conference for the Yiddish Language, convened
in the Habsburg town of Czernowitz, provoked a highly publicized debate
on the topic. Participants in the conference called for Yiddish to be recognized as "a national language of the Jewish people," despite the protesta-
tions of delegates who considered Yiddish "the" Jewish national language.
Though the conference was widely viewed as farcical (at best) and a failure
(at worst), it nonetheless served to highlight the complexity and maturity of
the Yiddish press, for it provoked a cacophonous debate about language
choice that was carried on in and between the many new periodicals of the
post-1905 era. Like most other Yiddish periodicals of the day, *Der fraynd*

participated in this debate by taking sides: the paper supported the con-ference's resolution and defended the historic import of the event as a whole.[101] Ironically, even by participating in this debate, *Der fraynd* was sig-naling its own gradual demise. The polarization of the language debate and the erosion of *Der fraynd*'s reputation were intimately intertwined; both reflected and were enabled by the explosion of Yiddish publishing that allowed the language debates to enter popular discourse.[102] As we will see, *Der fraynd*— unaccustomed to competition — would prove fundamentally ill-suited to this new climate of Yiddish publishing and politics.

Der fraynd's defense of Yiddish was integrally connected to its support of the politics of Jewish nationalism. The paper had from the outset presented itself as a Zionist organ, though a moderate one. In its pages, nationalism was consistently promoted as a cultural (rather than a territorial or diplo-matic) philosophy. Though the contours of this philosophy were more often than not only vaguely defined, the newspaper did take a firm position on the need to promote Yiddish as a step toward Jewish national renewal. In *Der fraynd*'s first month of publication, an article written by Dine Tseytlin en-titled "From a Foreign Land (A Letter from a Woman)" outlined this posi-tion from what appeared to be "a woman's perspective." "The only product of the Jewish soul that we women use is Yiddish, and it alone conveys our great love for the Jewish people," the article proclaimed;

> Our language is dear to us, perhaps because for women, out of all of the richness of Jewish culture, only [Yiddish] remains our own. Perhaps the pleasure it gives us increases because of the language's natural spirituality and kinship with our true national language, Hebrew, from which it took so many words. Perhaps we love Yiddish because of its poverty, its stillness, because of the deep, heart-wrenching sadness which makes itself felt in every Yiddish word. It is, however, clear: take Yiddish literature and the Yiddish language away from Jewish women, and you take away from us the last bit of our national sentiment—and from then on you will work fruit-lessly to revive our people and their historic-national language.[103]

As this letter suggests, *Der fraynd*'s support for Yiddish was balanced with its support for Hebrew and Zionism, a synthesis that was not uncommon in 1903. Still, Tseytlin's claim to represent the deepest emotions of Jewish women was undoubtedly bombastic: not only was this premise theatrical, but Tseytlin was the pseudonym for a male member of *Der fraynd*'s staff.[104] The practice of male writers assuming female pseudonyms was often em-ployed by Yiddish journalists of the turn of the century, as was the gendering of Yiddish and Hebrew in discussions of the language question.[105] In the pages of *Der fraynd*, Tseytlin's voice was used to simplify an otherwise com-plex political negotiation involving the paper's mediation between its sup-port for Yiddish and its support for the politics of Jewish nationalism. We can find a metaphor for this relationship in the response of *Der fraynd*'s correspondent to the Fourth Zionist Party Conference, who expressed horror at the conference's willful neglect of Yiddish. When the conference speakers cried for "*silensius!* [be silent!]," wrote the correspondent with disdain, there was only chaos; only when they cried that all present should "*shvayg!* [shut up!]" was the crowd still. "I had been chosen as a delegate, and I went," concluded the journalist, "only how did I participate in the conference? I will tell you, dear reader: in . . . silence . . . silence."[106]

Der fraynd's attitude toward Zionism may fairly be described as one of modest and detached support, which was peppered by ellipsis, satire, and critique. In his reflections on the history of *Der fraynd*, H. D. Horovits described the paper's relationship with the Zionist movement as ambiguous: on the one hand, *Der fraynd* would publish the Zionist party line; on the other hand, it could break radically from it. In the wake of the Kishinev pogroms of 1903, for example, when the Zionist movement was attempting to transform Jewish grief into nationalist self-consciousness, *Der fraynd* cautioned its readers that "humanity was not like this," that they should place their trust in "humankind, democracy, rights."[107] Horovits also suggested that the paper's extensive inquiries into Russian politics — its lengthy coverage of the Russo-Japanese War, its support for a constitutional government order — diverged from the Zionist tradition of remaining aloof of *goles arbayt* (politics of the diaspora). While this distinction (between the "Zionist party line" and *goles arbayt*) may be forced, it is true that *Der fraynd* did not resist involving itself in Russian politics. This is not to say that *Der fraynd*'s investment in Russia made the paper "less" Zionist, but rather, that its relationship to Zionism was as multi-chromatic as was the movement itself.[108]

Further, as *Der fraynd*'s delegate to the Fourth Zionist Conference intimated, it was often in silence that *Der fraynd*'s affiliation with the Zionist movement was formulated. While a column describing Jewish life in South Africa written by Ben-Tsion Hersh appeared in *Der fraynd* nearly every month for more than three years, and while the paper's literary supplement *Der fraynd baylage* (St. Petersburg, 1903–1904) published long stories about life in Japan and India, the paper had no writers stationed in Palestine (though this may have been the unavoidable result of a shortage of correspondents in the region). And while *Der fraynd* offered readers regular news of events in Russia and from "the Jewish street," there was little coverage of local Zionist cultural or political work.

Silence was occasionally filled with humor. In 1903, *Der fraynd* published a single issue of the satirical supplement *Der tog* (St. Petersburg, 1903) that was devoted to mocking the divided Zionist movement. However, the paper's critique was subdued, not only by humor but also by the curious, almost careless way in which the subject was presented. Though *Der tog* had its own masthead, it appeared in the main body of *Der fraynd*, filling almost all of the paper's second page. This was unusual in a number of respects. The supplement appeared entirely unannounced and was crudely placed in the middle of an article on the Russo-Japanese War. The supplement's masthead was small and did not differ from *Der fraynd* in font or form. If one were merely to glimpse at the issue, the additional section could easily have gone unnoticed.[109]

Along with these critiques and silences, the paper offered minimal reporting about mainstream Zionist affairs. It included a flurry of coverage of the Sixth Zionist Conference in Basel and ensuing debates over "the Uganda question" (Theodor Herzl's suggestion that the movement pursue negotiations to claim Uganda as a nation-state for Jews). Herzl's position was enumerated in a letter of his own composition. In the same week, *Der fraynd baylage* printed a long, lackluster biography of Herzl, complete with childhood photographs. The tone behind this coverage was best represented by a highly stylized photograph of Herzl taken in 1897 by E. M. Lilien during the Zionist Conference; in it, Herzl is leaning out of the balcony of his hotel room, staring off in the distance, the bridges of Basel in the background.[110] The same photograph appeared in most Jewish journals of the day and would gain mystical significance with the death of Herzl some months later.[111] Such journalism, however, was remarkably dry and uninspired. Indeed, this dryness may have been part of its appeal. Printed in July 1904, the photograph of Herzl represented a politic that would be well received among readers, even if it was often rebuked by nationalist leaders.[112] Herzl was a safe icon of Zionism because he was popular, and for a still young *Der fraynd*, building popularity, even if it meant speaking in a rather vapid political voice, was the primary goal.

Der fraynd did not exploit Zionism to woo readers. What the paper did suggest was that building or being a Zionist organ was not a matter of ideological content alone. Zionism, as we well know, was not a single movement but a movement of schisms. This, paradoxically, was precisely the reason that *Der fraynd*'s brand of Zionism was only vaguely articulated. The paper strained to be as uncontroversial as possible. How else could the constituencies of Poleophile Yitshok Leyb Peretz and Russophile Shoyl Ginzburg remain satisfied with just a single source of the day's news?

Moderate Zionism did not, however, always serve as a political common denominator. During the Revolution of 1905–1907 *Der fraynd* eschewed Zionism in favor of an intra-ethnic form of radicalism for many of the same reasons that it had originally allied itself with Herzl. Here too it chose the politics of the moment, the surest way of satisfying an impossibly diverse readership.

Der fraynd's turn from Zionism was not only tactical; it was also the expression of disappointment and anger in the wake of Tsar Nicholas II's October Manifesto of 1905. While seeming to initiate new freedoms of the press, the manifesto left journalists and editors more vulnerable than ever, as it made them subject to criminal rather than civil laws. In 1906, 223 journalists and editors were accused under various articles of the criminal code, and 175 were found guilty.[113] *Der fraynd*'s editors seemed to conclude that appeasement would no longer do, and, despite the dangers, they embarked on a new and more radical course. In December 1905, for the 254th issue of *Der fraynd,* the editors published a "Financial Manifesto" that was critical of the administration. Not surprisingly, the article caught the attention of the authorities, and on December 12, the paper's editors were threatened with arrest. Not wishing to wait until *Der fraynd* was closed (which it would formally be in March of the following year), the paper's producers reissued the journal, just days later, under the name *Dos lebn.*[114] *Dos lebn* ran until July 30, 1906, when *Der fraynd* was given permission to resume publication.

Dos lebn was in many ways similar to *Der fraynd.* Serialized articles that were to have been printed in *Der fraynd* found a place in *Dos lebn,* without reference to the rupture. Columns contained their usual headings and bylines. Indeed, the paper's masthead stated that *Dos lebn* was written and published by the same journalists and editors who produced *Der fraynd,* a convenient excuse to have the words *Der fraynd* appear in large letters (even larger letters than those spelling *Dos lebn*) atop the paper. These features, however, were but superficial continuities. While *Der fraynd* had attempted to balance support of moderate Zionism with a critique of the imperial regime, and while it was slow to express original ideas or depict them in original ways, *Dos lebn* was radical and outspoken, daringly critical of Zionist leaders such as Herzl and, simultaneously, of the Russian authorities. As the paper's political allegiances shifted from moderate Zionism to radical agitation and support for Jewish socialism, its appearance changed as well, or, better put, it exploded, with a spontaneity that had political precedent but lacked an aesthetic one. Almost overnight, editorials were overshadowed by caustic political cartoons, a genre all but foreign to the previous Yiddish popular press.

That *Der fraynd* could undergo a transition from a Russian-rooted Zionism to defiant radicalism reminds us how malleable were the politics of early-twentieth-century Russian Jewry. The abrupt change shows how fine, and how permeable, were the lines dividing Zionism, Russophilism, and Bundism. The history of *Der fraynd* suggests the extent to which Russian Jewish political movements were still flexible in the first decade of the twentieth century: flexible enough to accommodate schism, avoid polemics, and be metamorphosed into other political movements entirely. By extension, *Der fraynd* reminds us that the printing of a daily press in an ethnic language cannot be assumed to be a vehicle for the expression of that group's nationalist sentiments. Though *Der fraynd* was aligned with Zionism, it successfully managed to exist in a nationalist limbo, maintaining an ambiguous political position, attempting to satisfy its factious staff, and naïvely imagining itself to be the voice of all Russian Jewry. This was not because nationalism was irrelevant to the producers of *Der fraynd,* but because other factors (among them official restrictions, economic demand, ambition, and optimism) demanded that the paper's nationalism not be known as its main concern. *Der fraynd*'s first two years of publication were not contention-free years, but they were far less polemical than the years that would follow. They were, in a sense, slender moments of possibility in which the extremes of Russian Jewish politics had not yet been identified, much less rigidified. In the years that lay ahead, *Der fraynd* would document the destruction of this short-lived moment and of the notion that a single newspaper in *zhargon* could speak to, much less satisfy, all Russian Jews (or at least all those whom it considered worth speaking to).

Der fraynd's near-monopoly over readers of the daily news in Yiddish began to erode after 1905 (and with particular speed beginning in 1908) as competitors emerged to challenge the paper's supremacy. The creation and popularity of newspapers in the post-1905 era were stimulated by several factors. First, and most importantly, the issue of the October Manifesto of 1905 made it possible to publish Yiddish serials in Warsaw and other cities in the empire that had previously been under the strict control of the Russian Ministry of Interior. Readers' interest in the day's news (in Russian as well as Yiddish) was also whetted by the Russo-Japanese War of 1904–1905, a war that was meticulously reported in both the Yiddish and Russian language presses.[115] A third cause of the rapid growth of the Yiddish press has been neglected by scholars of Jewish letters: the changing demands of readers of daily newspapers, whose desire for inexpensive and local news enabled the existence of a competitive network of newspapers.

This reading network did not emerge overnight. Beginning in 1904, dozens of Yiddish periodicals began publication only to close months later for lack of funding or readers. In describing this period, one journalist mused, "one paper dies so another can be born."[116]

Short-lived papers did not pose a real threat to the dominance of *Der fraynd*. A few periodicals did, however, manage to gather large circulations and/or remain in operation for longer periods of time. The first Yiddish daily to emerge in Warsaw was *Der veg* (1905–1907), edited by Tsvi Prilutski, who for years had lobbied the Interior Ministry to gain permission to publish a Yiddish daily in the city. *Der veg* had a rocky start. The paper had been funded with loans its founders were unable to repay; nor could they pay their typesetters and writers, who instituted a strike almost immediately after the paper was founded. After three months, the paper folded, only to reopen a few weeks later. But before it closed in 1908, the paper had gained a circulation of over 5,000, a readership primarily composed of residents of Warsaw.[117] A year after *Der veg*'s appearance, *Der yidishe togblat* emerged, a small paper devoted to daily news and scandal. *Der yidishe togblat* was the first "kopeck daily" in Yiddish: it gained a circulation of 15,000 in its first years, a number that grew to 80,000 by the time the paper closed in 1911.[118] By 1905, five Yiddish dailies were published in Warsaw, with a combined circulation of 96,000. In the same year, three Hebrew newspapers appeared in the city, with a combined circulation of 12,000. Meanwhile, the Polish-language Jewish *Ludzkósc* (Warsaw, 1906–1907) acquired a circulation of 10,000, while the three Yiddish weeklies published in Warsaw by 1906 had a combined circulation of 38,000.

The most durable and visible Yiddish dailies of the post-1905 period were *Haynt* (Warsaw, 1908–39) and *Der moment* (Warsaw, 1910–39). Though these newspapers differed in ideological orientation and in the texture of their readership, both came to provide readers with sensational stories about crime and romance (and were filled, in one writer's words, with "blood and love"), and, of course, with the day's news, which focused on local as well as international events (a practice that *Der fraynd* had long avoided). In general terms, *Haynt* and *Der moment*, like *Der fraynd*, were also nationalist in leaning and advocated Jewish civil and national-minority rights. In contradistinction to *Der fraynd*, these papers were sympathetic to Polish nationalism. *Haynt* and *Der moment* were inexpensive, fiercely competitive, and known to woo readers aggressively. And they were in great demand: *Der moment* quickly gained a circulation of nearly 40,000, while by the interwar period *Haynt* could boast 45,000 readers. These readerships are striking because they were concentrated in a single city and were in competition with dozens of new Polish, Hebrew, and especially Yiddish papers. The following joke, recounted in a memoir of the period, hints at the weighty presence of *Haynt* amid the psyches and cultural economics of Warsaw's Yiddish-reading Jews. Two men meet in a park, where they share a bench and their hunger. Both yearn for a roll and a bit of herring. One says with a sigh, "If only I had a *Haynt*." "A what?" asks his friend. "A *Haynt* . . . a newspaper." "And what would you do with your *Haynt*? Can you read?" "Who needs to read?" his friend replies. "If I had a *Haynt* I could sell it and buy myself a bit of bread!"[119]

The popularity of *Haynt* reflected more than the needs of readers. In the years after 1905, Warsaw, the city with the largest concentration of Yiddish-speaking Jews in Europe, was becoming the Yiddish literary center of Eastern Europe. Since the 1850s, Warsaw's Yiddish readers had relied upon material published elsewhere, but now they watched their city become "the metropolis of the Yiddish daily press in Eastern Europe."[120] By this time, even *Der fraynd*'s geographic balance in its circulation had shifted to privilege Warsaw. By 1908, *Der fraynd* featured nearly daily advertisements for new periodicals in Russian, Hebrew, and Yiddish, many based in Warsaw. Further, nearly all the founders and the earliest contributors had left its ranks by 1908: Horovits and Luria in 1906, Rosenfeld and Ginzburg in 1908.[121] These defections may have been a result of *Der fraynd*'s decreasing popularity or profitability, or they may have been the cause of these factors. But they also bespoke the death of a vision: that a single Yiddish daily could represent or speak to "all" readers of Yiddish, and that Yiddish culture could find a geographic and spiritual base in St. Petersburg. Many of *Der fraynd*'s contributors, too, were also shifting their allegiances. *Haynt*, for example, would soon be credited with securing Y. L. Peretz's and Sholem Aleichem's literary fame.[122] Before Peretz ceased contributing to *Der fraynd,* Ginzburg began to lose patience with Peretz's "propaganda for Yiddish-ism," and refused, as he put it, to adulate him like the "gang of young writers in Warsaw" who viewed them as their "Hasidic rebbe." Ginzburg lashed out on Peretz's writing, which he found too "symbolic impressionist" in style, and too focused upon the needs and interests of Polish Jews.[123] No doubt Ginzburg's impatience had as much to do with the increasing importance of Warsaw and Peretz's growing eminence as the leading Yiddish writer of that city than it did with Peretz's literary style. Unfortunately for the editors of *Der fraynd,* Peretz offered Warsaw precisely what a new generation of Yiddish writers sought to emulate, many of whom saw Peretz as a spiritual leader.[124] And the Warsaw paper also offered what readers seemed to want most: information focusing upon the region or city in which they lived, an emphasis on sensation and daily news, and the publication of more fiction and fewer didactic opinion-pieces.

Peretz was not the only former contributor whose political and literary evolutions seemed to render *Der fraynd* out of mode. In 1908, Bal Makhshoves (Isadore Eliashev), a contributor to *Der fraynd* who grew increasingly devoted to Warsaw's growing circle of Yiddish literary critics, published a fiery article in the journal *Kunst un lebn* criticizing *Der fraynd.* His article celebrated the emergence of Warsaw-based kopeck dailies like *Haynt* and *Unzer lebn* that, according to the author, understood the psychology of the masses more deeply than *Der fraynd* ever had. "I believe that I get more pleasure from a Warsaw kopek paper than from a 2 kopeck St. Petersburg *fraynd,*" Bal Makhshoves wrote. "Our good *fraynd* truly believes that those of us here in 'the boonies' have no other business than the *traytel-faytel-kadetishe* [higgledy-piggledy Kadet] politics[125] with which *Der fraynd* (along with its [supplement *Der*] *bezem*) is stuffed. Do the *fraynd* people truly believe that . . . all Jews wait for *fraynd*'s dramatic prophecies about events in Russia, and are so interested in its idle opinion of Russia's future?"[126] *Der fraynd,* Bal Makhshoves insisted, was out of touch with the majority of Jews in the empire and aimed, instead, to satisfy only upper-class readers in the Russian interior. According to Bal Makhshoves, *Der fraynd*'s dwindling popularity was the result of intertwining issues: Jewish readers' growing lack of interest in the politics of the Russian interior, their heightened class-consciousness, the increasing importance of Warsaw as a center of Yiddish literary and political radicalism, and the outmoded nature of *Der fraynd*'s didactic, self-confident, and preachy style. "It is well known that, according to *Der fraynd,* its level is just a bit higher than the other boulevard papers," Bal Makhshoves persisted, but "what's what and who's who doesn't depend on the idle creations of An-sky, a *shtetl* by S. Ash, a play by Pinsky, an article by Zhitlowsky, an editorial or an occasional reproachful pamphlet by S. Rosenfeld or a clear, folksy article by '*a soykher.*'[127] All in all, this is a boring paper, that can't make money from the sale of papers [and] doesn't serve the best readers."[128]

Bal Makhshoves's wrath notwithstanding, the content of Der fraynd was not impervious to the changing tastes of Jewish readers. As competition for readers grew, the paper's editorial staff tried to transform the paper in an attempt to remain competitive. While local news would never dominate Der fraynd's front page, over time the paper changed and diversified. Its cover now featured short, chatty biographies (e.g., of the Hebrew writer Abraham Mapu, the new Turkish sultan, or actress Ester Rokhl Kaminska), which replaced the paper's traditional heavy-handed opinion pieces. Photographs, previously reserved for the paper's supplement, began to appear regularly in its main section. But the pace of change in the political context, long repressed by the inconsistent policies of an imperial regime, had by the close of the first decade of the twentieth century become too rapid: its focus was too unlike Der fraynd's. It was simply not possible for the newspaper to remake itself. The new format was too sensational for the paper's original readers and not sensational enough for new readers in Warsaw.[129] "The body of the paper is a mess," playwright A. Vayter exclaimed in a letter of 1909, "a regular Jewish fair [a yarid a yidisher]."[130]

As Vayter's comment suggests, the new contents did not revive the paper; indeed, the changes might have had the opposite effect. Finally, in November 1909, in what many viewed as a desperate attempt to gain readership, Der fraynd relocated to Warsaw. The paper defended its decision to move in an editorial that it published the previous month. Its writers explained that as Der fraynd was published in the capital city, "far from the Jewish Pale of Settlement," news of "Jewish life" reached its offices "too late," and readers then received the news "too late." The editorial noted that "Yiddish readers in the past years have grown, their interests diversified, and now they live for the day . . . far more than they once did." "Faraway St. Petersburg," it continued, was simply "too far." And so the paper relocated to Warsaw, "the greatest center of Yiddish literature . . . the center of Yiddish literary creativity."[131] As this comment suggests, the editors of Der fraynd sought to renew their popularity by becoming exactly what they had once spurned. They now were willing to be economically and ideologically dependent on readers; they were guided by the cultural centrality of Warsaw; and they condescended to write about salacious news and affairs in the Pale or Congress Poland (regions they had previously refused to discuss). These phenomena, anathema in 1903, were the necessities of 1909.

The move to Warsaw did not, however, enable Der fraynd to regain control of the Yiddish reading public, a body that itself had changed. Readers of Yiddish periodicals were now younger, less likely to be acquainted with Der fraynd's historic import, and less sympathetic to its increasingly arcane content. One study of interwar Poland documented that out of 420 readers at a left-wing Jewish library, 321 (76.5 percent) were younger than age twenty.[132] And these young Polish Jews were voracious and adventurous readers, unlikely to respond to *Der fraynd*'s stodgy style.[133]

Der fraynd's readership declined steadily until the paper folded just four years after its move to Warsaw. The paper's relocation also gained *Der fraynd* enemies among Yiddish journalists and publishers in Warsaw. Though Dovid Druk admitted that *Der fraynd* had been the first Yiddish daily to gain a wide-reaching circulation (*Der fraynd*, he once wrote, "shaped readers of Yiddish, improved them"), he described the move with anger, commenting that "anyone with a sense for newspapers knew that *Der fraynd* wouldn't succeed in Warsaw."[134] Hidden behind Druk's ire seems to be the justified accusation that the move was for opportunistic and insincere reasons. But there was more to this animosity. The reason why *Der fraynd* moved, the reason why its editorial staff was changing — and with it the content of the paper — was the same reason that caused the paper to engender hostility in Warsaw's world of Yiddish letters: by 1909, competition for readers rather than the whim of imperial decree had begun to condition the production of Yiddish newspapers throughout the Russian Empire. By the time of its move, *Der fraynd* was too late, or not sincere enough, in its attempt to address the needs of its reading public.

If readers had become the engine of the Yiddish reading public by 1909, it was arguably only by this year that Yiddish-reading Jews of Russia had access to what has been called the "democratization of the printed word" that readers in Western Europe had had at their disposal for nearly a century, a process that allowed "broader social initiative and participation in the production of the printed word than ever before and, consequently, in the public exchange of ideas."[135] This temporal discrepancy reflects why the explanations offered by scholars of Western Europe and America for the emergence of the "modern" daily press (among them the rise of a consumer culture, the influence of city life, the emergence of literature aimed at the "average reader," and the newly discovered appeal of daily affairs) need to be reshaped to accommodate the nuances of Russian Jewish cultural history.[136] If *Der fraynd* initiated a popular culture negotiated through the medium of the daily press, and if it profited from the emergence of a reading public hitherto hungry for secular texts, the paper's demise was precipitated by the tactics and success of its protégés. From 1903 to 1909, *Der fraynd* tried and failed to serve a population of readers more hungry for news in a language they could understand than they were loyal to the newspaper's content, ideological mission, or editorial staff.

The case of *Der fraynd* thus poses a challenge to many theories about the role and impact of presses in popular languages upon ethnic communities. Within this body of scholarship, an inextricable link seems to bridge the publication of texts in ethnic languages and the imagining of community.[137] In some regards, studies on the imagining of community provoke insights into the cultural impact of *Der fraynd*. It was, after all, immediately obvious that the success of *Der fraynd* owed much to the language in which it was printed. And yet, though *Der fraynd*'s reading public was composed of readers of Yiddish, it was neither an ideological nor a cohesive entity. Indeed, reading *Der fraynd* did little to produce a uniformity of vision or desire among its readers: on the contrary, *Der fraynd* struggled to accommodate the changing desires of its readers and contributors. And even in its most successful years, the paper demonstrated that it was impossible to please Russian Jewish readers of Yiddish *en masse*. *Der fraynd*'s editorial board, contributors, and readers quickly realized that they were writing not for a single but for multiple communities, reading publics that could not be organized around ethnicity or language because these categories were too vague and too vast. On the simplest level, the paper could not guarantee that readers were unified in thinking about what constituted the day's news, or how it should be presented. If *Der fraynd* succeeded in creating a Yiddish *leyzer krayz*, as Morris Shaten proposed, this circle was a community of readers shaped by a common hunger for news in a familiar language. They did not form the kind of ideological or political community that scholars of nationalism, ethnicity, and print culture have been inclined to envision. Ironically, both the success and the decline of *Der fraynd*'s Yiddish reading circle demonstrated that readers of Yiddish needed the many reading circles that the numerous post-1909 (Jewish and ethnically generic) periodicals would offer: circles that, though they all counted Jews among their ranks, were fragmented along nationalist, political, geographic, linguistic, and aesthetic lines.

Arguably, scholars of modern Jewish history have been more nuanced in their approach to community than have been many theoreticians of the concept. Scholarship on modern Jewry by and large concedes that ideological consensus is not a necessary dimension of community solidarity. In the field of Jewish history, it is the scholarly exception rather than the norm that assumes community to be a homogenous entity. Perhaps this body of scholarship can be criticized for being too flexible. For though the concept of community is a leitmotif in scholarship on modern Jewry, the historical meaning of the concept remains oblique. In this regard, a study of *Der fraynd* allows us not only to reflect on the particular practices of reading among early-twentieth-century Russian Jews, but also to consider historical moments in which it was possible to imagine a singular Russian Jewish community, and to explore moments in which this imagining butted up against a far more complex reality. *Der fraynd* not only documented the newsworthy for early-twentieth-century Russian Jews. It also struggled to reflect and adapt to the way in which Russian Jews were imagining and reimagining themselves.

In this regard, it is noteworthy that *Der fraynd*'s first editorial focused on the theme of change, describing a Jewish world in transition, a world cut free from the moorings of religious and communal control. For the paper's editors, this was a moment to be celebrated. It was a moment in which readers could choose to ignore the information and guidance proffered by the religious establishment. It was a moment in which they could set aside their hostility to *zhargon*, the Jewish vernacular. It was a moment in which they could weigh the benefits of various political alternatives. Above all, it was a moment of transition. The world of Yiddish letters was expanding, but it had not yet polarized along party lines. It was still inventing itself, as were readers and writers of Yiddish.

As the Yiddish-speaking population dealt with this issue, so too did Ladino-speaking Jewry. In Constantinople, *El tiempo*'s first editorial of 1872 also promised readers that a daily newspaper in a Jewish vernacular was uniquely suited to assuage anxieties brought on by the modern world. And yet *El tiempo*'s editors understood these changes — and this world — differently than did the editors of *Der fraynd*. While *Der fraynd*'s first editorial spoke of expanding opportunities, *El tiempo*'s spoke of contracting ones, in particular Ottoman Jews' decreasing level of competitiveness in a regional economy. While *Der fraynd*'s editors described a daily newspaper in a Jewish vernacular as a symbol of cultural progress, *El tiempo*'s editors regarded a daily newspaper in a Jewish vernacular as a necessary evil. While *Der fraynd*'s editors promoted the politics of Jewish nationalism, *El tiempo*'s editors decried irredentism in general, and Zionism in particular. The different catalysts that led to these newspapers' production, and the very different postures the papers assumed, reflect the very different challenges and ambitions faced by turn-of-the-century Russian and Ottoman Jews. To understand these differences, we turn now to the city of Constantinople, to the year 1872, and to the still young world of Ladino publishing.

2

CREATING A LADINO NEWSPAPER CULTURE

In the pages of the turn-of-the-century Ottoman Ladino press, women were scolded for gossiping in Ladino and young women were told not to speak the language in public lest potential suitors hovered nearby. Readers were warned to avoid playing cards, a practice that might summon forth Ladino words of insult, triumph, or superstition even in the most "dignified" of Jews. One paper was particularly influential in shaping the assault on the Sephardi vernacular that rippled through Ottoman Ladino periodicals: *El tiempo, periodiko israelita politiko, literario, komersial i finansario* (Constantinople, 1872–1930). Due in part to its leadership in the campaign against Ladino, *El tiempo* was heralded as "the new Bible" of Ottoman Jewry; it was regarded as a source that offered readers not only coverage of current events but the ethical and political principles around which they might reshape their lives.[1]

In the pages of this and most turn-of-the-century Ottoman Ladino periodicals, a distinct linguistic caste system was created. European languages — French above all — were at the top of the order. Turkish and other regional languages were occasionally defended but rarely employed. Hebrew stood in a kind of privileged isolation, respected as a language of religion, but given little credence as a language of secular discourse. And Ladino sat at the bottom of this list, rarely defended and often derided. Indeed, that Ladino was a backward and useless language was one of few points on which virtually all contributors to the Ottoman Ladino press managed to agree. In the pages of the most popular Ladino newspapers and periodicals, the language was described as shameful (*una verguensa*), a *zhirgonza* (jargon), a bastard tongue, and a dying language.

Despite such proclamations, the vast majority of Jews in the Ottoman Empire continued to speak and read Ladino until the 1930s. Even by the interwar period, Ottoman and Balkan Jews were far more likely to be fluent in Ladino than in French, Italian, Turkish, Greek, or other regional languages. Largely for this reason, the number of Ladino newspapers in print rose steadily from the last decades of the nineteenth century to the interwar period, at which point there were nearly four hundred Ladino periodicals printed in Turkey and the Balkans.[2] On average, Jews in the Ottoman interior were far more comfortable speaking and reading Ladino than any other language. One writer reflected, "Turkish is a borrowed suit; French is gala dress; Judeo-Spanish is the worn dressing gown in which one is most at ease."[3]

As this statement so vividly suggests, though the vast majority of numbers of Ottoman Jews appeared to have felt most comfortable reading and speaking the Sephardi vernacular, there is evidence that by the late nineteenth century, many Ottoman Jews perceived Ladino to be declining in usefulness as a language of commercial exchange and social ascension. This appears to have been true even in that most Jewish of cities, Salonika, where Ladino speakers constituted a majority of the urban population. Here, as elsewhere in the empire, middle-class Ottoman Jews in general, and young Sephardim in particular, increasingly turned to other languages (to Italian and, increasingly, to French), to make and mark their new bourgeois identities.[4] In this sense, the linguistic hierarchy espoused by the Ottoman Jewish popular press was a wish rather than a utilitarian reality, an expression of ambition rather than a faithful reflection of actuality.

Both the use and abuse of Ladino in the Jewish popular press were born of pragmatic realism. For many Jews in Southeastern Europe, the Ladino press was a necessary medium of progress even as it was perceived as an impediment to social ascension.[5] This tension grew out of a complicated set of historical factors. The following pages explore the rise of popular Ladino publishing in Southeastern Europe and consider the various factors that stimulated and stymied this industry in its early years, a period stretching from the last decades of the nineteenth century roughly until the outbreak of the Balkan Wars (1912–13). There were five major catalysts to Ladino publishing during this period: the flagging Jewish economy in Southeastern Europe (and in Constantinople, in particular); the dwindling political opportunities afforded to non-Muslims in the empire and the resulting competition between *millets;* the growing importance of Western European Jewish philanthropy; the erosion of traditional forms of Jewish communal authority; and, finally, readers' demands for printed matter that would allow them to make informed choices. These dynamics catalyzed Ladino publishing, and the Ladino press in turn chronicled and influenced their unfolding. Thus Ladino presses at the turn of the century were important despite the fact that the commercial and cultural value of Ladino was being undermined by shifting urban, imperial, and international politics. Indeed, these newspapers documented this changing landscape and played an active and critical role in cultivating conversation and debate, thus transforming the Ottoman Jewish cultural landscape still further.

The following pages pay particular attention to the journal *El tiempo,* one of the longest-surviving and most influential Ladino periodicals of the Ottoman lands.[6] *El tiempo* was printed continuously from 1872 until 1930, appearing first as a daily (which, according to the reigning norms of Jewish publishing, was never published on the Sabbath), soon after as a biweekly, and, from July 1882 to 1930, three times a week. There is evidence that by the First World War, one of every two Jewish adults in the Ottoman capital subscribed to this paper. Its reach was extended further still by the practice of sharing papers.

For fifty years, *El tiempo* was edited by David Fresco, one of the dominant — and certainly one of the most intractable — forces of Ladino publishing.[7] Beginning in the 1870s, Fresco edited five Ladino periodicals and numerous supplements and published at least nineteen books in Ladino, in the process exerting considerable influence over Ottoman Sephardi culture. According to the hyperbolic words of one of Fresco's contemporaries, "from the banks of the Bosphorus to the River Danube and along the whole coastline of the Mediterranean Archipelago, there was no Jew better known in all the Orient."[8] Fresco's fame (exaggerated as the account may be) illustrates one reason why Ladino publishing varied from place to place: individual newspapers inevitably bore the imprints of their editors and readers. Conditions for Ladino publishing, too, varied dramatically from city to city. It was, for example, more difficult to produce and sustain a Ladino newspaper in Constantinople than in Salonika, where Jews at one time represented a majority of the city's multi-ethnic population. Constantinople had fewer readers of Ladino, and they represented a relatively smaller percentage of the city's total population, a fact that rendered them less visible and perhaps less confident consumers of Ladino print culture. This is one reason why Salonika maintained a passionate pro-Ladino movement while in Constantinople, secular Ladino print culture existed in the shadow of an obstreperous anti-Ladino coalition that, perhaps ironically, was championed by editors of the leading Ladino presses.

Despite these and other differences, certain factors intertwined the history of Ladino publishing throughout the European regions of the empire (and arguably in certain of the Arab provinces) in the forty years that bracketed the turn of the twentieth century. In the early years of Ladino newspaper publishing, Ladino periodicals throughout the empire were closely linked; they remained in constant contact with one another, reproduced one another's articles, and engaged in regular and often fiery dialogue.

The study of a press as influential as *El tiempo* can highlight many of the transitions and challenges faced by turn-of-the-century Ottoman Jews, particularly those in Southeastern Europe. In reconstructing the rise of the Ottoman Ladino publishing industry, this chapter examines some of the questions that were debated by turn-of-the-century readers of Ladino. What did it mean to be a Jew, an Ottoman, a participant in a cultural economy increasingly subordinate to Western Europe? Were these allegiances contradictory, and, if not, how were they to be intertwined? Finally, on the most general level, should one, and how could one, make one's self modern?

OTTOMAN JEWISH READING PRACTICES AND
THE RISE OF THE LADINO PUBLISHING INDUSTRY

Above all else, the rise of the Ladino press depended upon Ottoman Jewish readers' ability to read Ladino and their general inability to rely upon printed sources in other languages. Jewish rates of fluency in Turkish, the official language of the state, were universally low at the turn of the twentieth century.[9] At that point, Ottoman authorities were not concerned about whether or not the language was taught in non-Muslim schools. It was not until 1894 that the state began to mandate instruction in Turkish; however, this law was rarely enforced. Even the most secular of Jewish students showed little interest in learning Turkish, a language that, in any case, Jewish teachers proved unqualified to teach.[10] By one account, in 1897 it was impossible to identify even 1,000 Ottoman Jews who spoke Turkish as well as they did French and none who knew it better.[11] As late as the turn of the century, even Jewish authorities who were vested with a certain degree of authority by the state were neither required nor expected to speak Turkish.[12]

Even among the most Westernized of Ottoman Jews, Hebrew was the major language of prayer and ritual.[13] Hebrew was also taught in most Jewish schools: in traditional Talmud Torah (public Jewish primary schools) as well as in schools with a Westernizing agenda.[14] Strikingly, secular forms of Hebrew print culture rarely occurred and were met with limited popularity in the Ottoman context. By the close of the nineteenth century, Ottoman Jewish readers were gaining limited access to sources in Hebrew published outside the empire, among them periodicals from Eastern and Central Europe. Simultaneously, however, the number of books published in Hebrew inside the empire was on the decline.[15] And though a number of Hebrew language societies were created in Izmir, Salonika, and Bulgaria, no Hebrew language periodical was sustained in the European regions of the empire.[16]

Without a doubt, it was French that was acquiring ever-more importance as the language of print and public life for Ottoman Jews. French was increasingly the *lingua franca* of the Jewish bourgeoisie, and with the opening of schools sponsored by the Alliance Israélite Universelle throughout the empire, students of diverse class backgrounds gained fluency in the language.[17] According to one survey of émigrés, in the early years of the twentieth century young Ottoman Jewish readers who wished to read "serious" texts turned to French-language masterpieces or to religious works in Hebrew, while literature in Judeo-Spanish was reserved for "light reading."[18] As this suggests, a growing interest in French (and, to a lesser extent, English) literature was sustained by the availability of printed material, at least for those who could afford it.[19] A number of French-language newspapers designed for Jewish readers existed at the turn of the century, and though these could not vie with the Ladino press in number or longevity, some wielded a great deal of influence.[20] The biweekly *Journal de Salonique* (Salonika, 1895–1910) was one of the most influential French-language Jewish journals of the empire, and has been credited—by historians and former readers alike—with stimulating the increasingly French-leaning culture of Salonikan Jewry.[21] Sam Levy, who served as editor of the Ladino *La epoka* and the French *Journal de Salonique,* recalled that "the *Journal de Salonique* served as my school[,] . . . as a genuine university center and also as a traveling kaleidoscope, through whose lenses I was able to observe an intimate picture, the moral conduct, and the attitudes of my contemporaries."[22] With a young and growing reading public, the circulation of this newspaper expanded rapidly. In the last decade of the nineteenth century, approximately one thousand copies of the *Journal de Salonique* were in circulation, and this in an era in which the Jewish population of the city did not exceed 60,000.[23]

Though French texts like the *Journal de Salonique* were increasingly accessible, and though Jewish rates of fluency and literacy in French were rising, Ottoman Jewish readers did not necessarily prefer to speak or read the language in all settings. As one Jewish teacher noted with regret:

> Judeo-Spanish is the preeminent language of the people, and it will remain so for quite some time whatever we may do. . . . the lower classes, the bourgeoisie, and even the "aristocracy," as they are called here, everyone still speaks and reads Judeo-Spanish and will continue to do so. In committee meetings where all the members are well educated and everyone knows French, a discussion started in correct, even elegant, French will, often in an instant, inexplicably move into Judeo-Spanish jabbering. The most "select," dignified Jewish ladies when playing a call on a friend will be politely chitchatting in French and suddenly break into jargon.[24]

As this statement suggests, it was Ladino and not French that many Ottoman Sephardim were most comfortable speaking and reading, despite widespread bi- and multi-lingualism. In the 1890s, over 80 percent of Serbian Jews claimed Ladino as their native language, while as late as the 1930s nearly 90 percent of Greek, Bulgarian, and Turkish Jews claimed it to be their mother tongue.[25] Ladino was not only the language of the Jewish home, but it was also a language of study and scholarship. In Talmud Torah, Jewish boys received instruction in Ladino and studied Ladino translations of the Bible and the *Me'am loez* (an encyclopedic Bible commentary composed by a dozen different authors throughout the eighteenth and nineteenth centuries).[26] Until the 1840s there had been a great deal of religious and para-religious literature published in the language, including an array of vernacular rabbinic literature composed in popular Ladino and intended for average readers (who could be addressed as "ignorant" in well-meaning introductions).[27] Significantly, this type of popular religious literature was not just reserved for men or boys. It was common also for men and women to gather together to read aloud from the *Me'am loez,* a text found in most Sephardi homes. Jewish women and girls were included in these circles and were also actively encouraged to study vernacular rabbinic literature in Ladino with groups of other women, as well as with their husbands, daughters, or on their own.[28] All of this suggests that though Ladino was spoken in the home, it, like Yiddish, was never simply a language of the secular world. Better put, in the Ottoman Jewish world, as in the Russian, the realm of the secular and the realm of the religious were never entirely discrete.

While Ottoman Jews maintained the culture of reading in Ladino, before the late nineteenth century they had access to only a limited number and variety of Ladino texts, almost all of which were of a religious nature. Despite the efforts of philanthropists, Jewish libraries were scarce, and those in existence held few works in Ladino.[29] For all of these reasons, the Ladino popular press served as the first secular source that many Ottoman Jewish readers encountered. For many more, the genre gave them their first acquaintance with the day's news.

The first periodical designed for Sephardi readers had long since appeared in print (*Gazeta de Amsterdam,* Amsterdam, 1678), but it was not until the 1840s that periodicals emerged in the Ladino language. Beginning in the 1840s, a number of important Ladino periodicals were started, among them *La puertas del oriente* (Izmir, 1841–45, also known by the Hebrew name *Sha'arei mizrah*), which is often credited as the first modern Ladino newspaper. Periodicals such as these contained discussions of current and international events, but were dominated by belletristic writing: novels and novellas that were published in installments and largely adopted (or, as the Ladino verb for translation — *enladinar*— suggests, "Ladino-ized") from contemporary French and Hebrew sources.[30] By the 1850s, secular Ladino literature was also available in pamphlet form. In the 1860s and 1870s, the most influential and longest-running Ottoman Ladino newspapers emerged. The following sixty or seventy years proved the apex of the Ladino press and its heartland was undoubtedly in the European region of the Ottoman Empire.

During the century stretching from 1845 to 1945, two thirds of all Ladino periodicals in print were based in only four locations, all of them under Ottoman control: Salonika, Constantinople, Sofia, and Izmir (Smyrna).[31]

While such papers were published in the language that Ottoman Jews felt most comfortable reading, early on these periodicals were at pains to avoid seeming too linguistically populist. Ladino newspapers of the late nineteenth century (like their Yiddish and Hebrew counterparts) tended to be didactic, heavy-handed, and composed in a lofty Ladino that avoided words from everyday speech.[32] Most focused on affairs in Western Europe and eschewed local and regional news (a focus that was born of a Westernizing political posture). These norms were later defied by periodicals born in the wake of the Young Turk Revolt of 1908 and in the interwar period; the later editions were lighter on morality lessons and heavier on sensation and local news. Still, judged by the standards of their day, the Ladino periodicals of the late nineteenth century were radical documents. They spoke of women's rights, described new modes of cuisine and couture, and, not least, made available secular reading matter to audiences hitherto unacquainted with news in print.

The earliest editors of the Ladino press not only created new genres of texts, but also envisioned new kinds of Ladino readers. Editor David Fresco believed that a newspaper should appear in the hands of "the wise, the theologian, the artist, the worker, the businessman, the industrialist, the manager, the teacher and the believer, the young, the old, men and women: everyone receives an indispensable lesson from the journal."[33] At least theoretically, then, Ladino newspapers like *El tiempo* were designed to reach all readers of Ladino, regardless of age, gender, religious status, educational background, class, or professional standing. That such a diverse body of Jewish readers could all be interested in, or, indeed, benefit from the same text was an unprecedented notion. To some, the concept seemed a dangerous one. Constantinople's rabbinic leadership was initially deeply concerned with the potential effects of the popular press.[34] And after David Fresco published a series of editorials in the 1880s that exposed the irregular finances of the Grand Rabbinate, the Rabbinate sought an edict from the sultan that would silence the journalist.[35] When this failed, a *herem* (writ of excommunication) was issued against Fresco, a powerful symbolic gesture that had little concrete effect.[36]

Fresco was not the only editor who threatened to wield the Ladino press as a weapon against the religious authorities, nor was Constantinople's rabbinate the only such organization to be riled by the emergence of a popular press in the Jewish vernacular. Abraham Galanté, a long-time friend of Fresco's and editor of the Cairo-based *La vara*, was exiled from Izmir by local religious authorities in 1903, along with his journalist friend Joseph Romano. (Conflicting explanations are given for their departure. Either the men were caught breaking the Yom Kippur fast by eating in a Greek restaurant, or they were condemned for criticizing the Grand Rabbi of Izmir, Haim Palaci.) Salonika's rabbinical council, meanwhile, retained the right to shut down workshops suspected of printing antireligious material; for this reason, Sa'adi Halevy, editor of *La epoka,* was summoned before the council in 1878.[37]

By publishing the budget of the Grand Rabbinate, *El tiempo* aimed to reveal that the rabbinate was irresponsible in its use of funds ("tyrannical" and "abusive of the poor," in the words of Fresco). Implicitly, the paper was doing much more. Fresco was demonstrating that the leadership of the Jewish community was accountable to individual Jews rather than individual Jews being subordinate to the leadership. He was intimating that traditional Jewish leadership could not be trusted either as a purveyor of information or as a moral or fiscal authority. And he was quietly asserting that the Ladino press was poised to take its place. The centuries-old monopoly on the means of preaching to the community was being tested.

This encounter offers a hint as to why the Ladino newspaper was a radical genre. But why was it needed and why did it succeed? Over the course of the late nineteenth century, a series of changes had rocked the Ottoman Jewish cultural, social, economic, and political landscape — changes that both stimulated and stymied the institution of the Ladino press. These changes instilled in readers a fear of falling behind and a desire to progress. These were virulent emotions that drove readers to the press and shaped Jewish modernity in the Ottoman setting.

THE NEED FOR NEWS IN AN EMPIRE IN FLUX

The success of the Jewish *millet* had for centuries depended upon an Ottoman economic, social, and juridical system that was becoming antiquated by the mid-nineteenth — and certainly by the early twentieth — century. Certain Jewish communities proved more adaptable to these circumstances than others. While the Jewish populations of Constantinople, Izmir (Smyrna), and Edirne witnessed gradual (though certainly not complete) economic decline, the Jewish bourgeoisie of Salonika proved resilient. Partly because of their success, the city of Salonika witnessed unprecedented economic growth. Arguably, however, Salonika was the exception that proved the rule. In general, the reconfigured Ottoman economy tended to punish Ottoman Jewry and to materially reward other *millets,* in particular Greeks and Armenians, who began to dominate international trade (in the case of the Greeks) and banking and money lending (in the case of the Armenians), particularly in Constantinople.[38] By 1885, there were far fewer Jews than Greeks and Armenians in the capital city, and the latter *millets* dominated the key positions in the city's economy.[39] Further, following the adoption of legislation in the nineteenth century that permitted non-Muslims to be admitted to military service to the rank of colonel and to civil service without limit of grade, Greeks and Armenians began to attain positions of high status in these fields, and to receive better salaries than Jews and other non-Muslims similarly employed (though the most prestigious and highest paying jobs would always be reserved for modernist Muslims).[40]

Encouraged, in part, by the success of the Turkish-language press, the Greek and Armenian *millets'* expressed their newfound economic security by producing newspapers in Greek, Armenian, and Turkish, the latter transliterated into the Greek and Armenian alphabets.[41] These publications quickly gained in popularity, so that by the first decade of the twentieth century, the eight leading Armenian periodicals of Constantinople reached more than 14,000 readers. These papers represented just a fraction of the 113 Armenian papers in circulation.[42] The readership of the cities' Greek-language press was higher still. In 1908, approximately 85 percent of Constantinople's Greek-speaking adults subscribed to a Greek-language newspaper, the leading titles of which had a combined circulation of 23,100. The foremost Greek-language paper, *Tachydromos* (Alexandria, 1882–present), could claim 6,000 subscribers alone.[43] And these figures are most likely conservative, for they do not assume that newspapers were shared among readers.

The production of the first Ladino daily of the empire, published some decades before these heightened circulations were attained, self-consciously responded to the growing influence of the Greek and Armenian press and the concomitant rise of the Greek and Armenian *millets*.[44] "Readers, we know well," *El tiempo*'s first editorial stated, that knowledge of "*la lingua de su patria* [the language of your country]" is necessary for survival, self-defense, and advancement. In this, it continued, "we are deficient in comparison to other *millets* that have already published journals in Turkish transliterated into the script of their *millet.*" In imitation, the editors of *El tiempo* promised to include a section written in Turkish transliterated into Hebrew letters. This would ease readers' acquisition of Turkish, the editors explained, which was necessary "because we find ourselves under the Ottoman government." This was hardly an expression of patriotism. On the contrary, it reflected a classic diasporic view of government, illustrating the extent to which the paper's producers conceived of a commitment to the Turkish language (and, by extension, Turkish culture) to be produced by physical rather than ideological conditions. In this case, knowledge of Turkish was a necessary prerequisite for entering the Ottoman civil service, and thus a necessary passport to prestigious and lucrative positions in the Ottoman bureaucracy newly open to non-Muslims and currently occupied by Greeks and Armenians.

El tiempo's promises of instruction in Turkish were never honored. Not only did the editors fail to carry through on their promise to offer Turkish text transliterated into Hebrew, but the paper also did nothing practical to promote readers' acquisition of Turkish or much to encourage them to Gallicize their speech. Nonetheless, *El tiempo*'s support of Turkish was re-animated precisely when the Greek and Armenian hold on the Ottoman bureaucracy was loosening, namely during the anti-Armenian climate of the 1890s and the Greco-Turkish War of 1901. It was precisely at these moments that Ottoman Jewish professional aspirations could grow. As the Greeks' and Armenians' hold on the civil service weakened, Jews (who were already represented in minor consular positions and as the lowest-ranked civil servants) saw the opportunity to fill the void left in their absence.[45] They would, however, need skills, among which fluency in Turkish was the most important. Thus beginning in the 1890s, *El tiempo* began a vigorous (if largely philosophical) campaign to promote Turkish among Ottoman Jews.

In sum, for the producers of *El tiempo*, Greek and Armenian language papers were competitors more than models. This was not because they vied for the same readership, but because the Greek and Armenian publications reflected the economic influence of those communities and pointed to the dwindling economic strength of Jewry in the Ottoman interior in general, and in Constantinople, in particular. When *El tiempo*'s first editorial spoke enviously of the strength of "other *millets'* newspapers," it was because by the late nineteenth century, Ottoman Jewish intellectuals had become cognizant of the growing importance of the press in general, and of ethnic presses in particular. They were aware that the production of a daily newspaper in a vernacular language could both reflect and facilitate a *millet's* economic and political security. Thus was *El tiempo* envisioned as a newspaper of commerce and finance as well as a journal of political and literary news. And thus the paper diligently published data on the arrival of ships; revealed the budgets of towns and of the Chief Rabbinate and secular organizations; announced winning lottery numbers; and updated readers on trends and technologies relevant to professional advancement. These were among the details that could turn an educated reader into an informed reader and that could make one productive as well as cultured — prerequisite qualities for the modern Ottoman Jew. These were, incidentally, among the kinds of information that would be alien to the world of Yiddish publishing for almost four decades. While in Russia such information was arguably viewed as base, in the Ottoman Empire it was considered essential if one was to be literate or competitive.

THE IMPACT OF *EL TIEMPO*

What, then, was the reach of this first Ladino daily? References to *El tiempo*'s circulation are both rare and inconsistent. One study of 1908 suggests that the paper had only 900 readers, while a more recent scholarly source identifies a circulation of 10,000.[46] In absolute terms, even the larger estimate pales relative to the circulation of *Der fraynd,* which reached ten times as many subscribers. However, given the size of the Ottoman Jewish population relative to that of the Russian, we can surmise that in the Ottoman context, the first newspaper to be published in a Jewish vernacular actually reached a larger percentage of Jewish subjects than did its contemporary in Russia.[47]

Whether *El tiempo*'s subscribers were spread throughout the empire or concentrated in Constantinople is unclear. There is some evidence to suggest that the circulation of *El tiempo* extended beyond the city in which it was produced. The newspaper published letters to the editor penned in cities far from Constantinople, and at least some readers outside of the city subscribed to the publication on a regular basis. Elias Canetti, for example, recalls in his memoir that his grandfather read *El tiempo* in Ruschuk (Rus), a town situated on the Danube some 250 miles from Constantinople.[48] Perhaps more striking still, Ladino newspapers based in Salonika, Izmir, and as far away as Jerusalem and Cairo not only reprinted articles from *El tiempo* but also engaged in active debate with it. These other papers responded to *El tiempo*'s polemical articles, challenged its editor, and queried whether or not this influential newspaper could be allowed to speak (which it often assumed it did) for all of Ottoman Jewry.[49] Notwithstanding, it is likely that *El tiempo* was consumed primarily by readers in Constantinople. Unlike *Der fraynd, El tiempo* did not make mention of distributing agents in cities other than Constantinople (though the price of circulation in various regions of the empire was made available in the pages of the paper). Further, the authors of letters to the editor from other cities in the empire may have been recruits rather than volunteers. Not only did particular authors send multiple missives, but their correspondence also has the feel of solicited news updates rather than impromptu commentary.

To suggest that *El tiempo*'s subscribers were primarily confined to Constantinople is not to diminish the paper's influence. There is, to begin with, the question of the paper's abstract influence. *El tiempo* gained a reputation for three central reasons: it was the first daily newspaper to be published in the autochthonous Jewish language of the empire; it proved to be long-lived; and it was energized by the audacity (and sometimes pomposity) of its longest-serving editor, David Fresco. *El tiempo* also developed certain journalistic standards that defined Ladino publishing for years to come. *El tiempo*'s influence was especially important in the Ottoman capital. If *El tiempo* was indeed circulated primarily in Constantinople, it is possible that by the early years of the twentieth century nearly half of the Jewish adults in the city subscribed to the paper.[50] This striking figure may actually underestimate the reach of the newspaper, for it does not assume that Ladino newspapers were passed from hand to hand or read out loud in group settings.

In fact, in the case of Southeastern Europe, as in Eastern Europe, the sharing of printed matter was a practice employed by many turn-of-the-century readers. There is even reason to believe that readers of Ladino were particularly accustomed to this practice. Speakers of Ladino often gathered together to read rabbinic literature in Ladino, including the *Me'am loez*. Ladino editors feared that this practice of reading aloud would jeopardize the commercial viability of their press. In his memoirs, editor Sam Levy reflected on the impact of this phenomenon on the commercial viability of the Salonikan *La epoka:* "I saw *La epoka* in many hands. A wide array of people from all classes spoke about it. I imagined that the whole world was subscribing to it. But after consulting the books, I was immensely surprised to learn that [the journal] had only a couple of hundred subscribers, as well as the many other readers [who shared their copies]." The problem? As Levy discovered with chagrin, *La epoka* was being purchased by families who were in the habit of passing a single copy from hand to hand during the course of the week. "In many houses," Levy notes "neighbors gathered together to hold public readings. For one subscriber, there were eight to ten readers and listeners."[51]

That *La epoka* and *El tiempo* and other Ladino newspapers like them were shared and read out loud was a sign of their vitality. But it was also a reflection of the commercial hazards of Ottoman Ladino publishing. The practice of shared reading, though important for the spread of journals' influence, simultaneously stifled circulation and limited their commercial success. Most Ladino managing editors were too poor to hire editors of their own and — according to an account of 1897 — often "furnished the entire text [of each journal], from one end to the other."[52] Levy once argued to his brothers and father that the production of *La epoka* was possible only "if we work together, we ourselves, we alone, for ourselves and our own [*les notres*], [only then] we will climb the slope, and our publications will move forward. Difficulties may arise, we will strive to surmount them. . . . The great family of readers will trust us: they are sure to be forgiving and indulgent from the very beginning and will remain faithful."[53] And it was not only Ladino editors who had difficulty making ends meet. One struggling Ladino journalist recalled rifling through the garbage of Cairo in search of food.[54]

The rupturing of the traditional Ottoman social and economic landscape was one catalyst to the creation and curtailment of the Ladino press. The emergence of Western European Jewish patronage was another. The vast majority of Ladino newspapers at the turn of the century — including *El tiempo* — were either supported by the Alliance Israélite Universelle or created by protégés (or both). Thus most turn-of-the-century Ottoman Ladino presses were, like the AIU itself, Westernizing in orientation.[55] As a result, coverage of AIU affairs was commonplace, as were detailed news reports from Paris, London, Vienna, Berlin, and Budapest. There were even advertisements for goods and stores based in these European cities. At least in the early years of

Ladino publishing, news from Ottoman urban centers was scarce. In the pages of *El tiempo,* for example, Izmir, Salonika, and Edirne — major Jewish centers of the empire — began to receive regular attention only in the mid-1880s, and even news of Constantinople was hard to come by in the paper's earliest years. In 1890, the paper instituted the column "Del mundo izraelita," which reported on affairs in major Jewish centers throughout the world. All the while, *El tiempo* obsessively reported on political and cultural affairs in France, often citing contemporary French journals as sources of information. For example, in the 1870s, *El tiempo* devoted more than thirty-three issues to a serialized article on the history of France's queens. It also religiously covered news of AIU schools throughout the empire, praising the organization, in particular, for its instruction in French.

Such adulation of Western European Jewish culture could be described as cultural, but it had a material basis too. For many Ottoman Jews in the empire's interior, Paris, London, Vienna, and Berlin had begun to eclipse Constantinople, Izmir, Edirne, and even Salonika in financial significance by the late nineteenth century. This was not because writers and readers of Ladino were intent upon betraying local cultural or commercial relationships, nor was it because they were thoughtless parrots of their Western European Jewish contemporaries. Rather, it was because the acquisition of French and the cultivation of financial relationships with Western Europe provided turn-of-the-century Ottoman Jews — especially the Jews of Constantinople — one of very few avenues for social and economic ascension.[56]

The Westernizing politics of the AIU would hold almost uncontested sway over secular-minded Ottoman Jews for nearly fifty years, from the organization's inception in 1860 until the wake of Young Turk Revolt, when the abrogation of censorship allowed Jewish politics to fragment along party lines. A sense of this early era is captured in the warring of *El tiempo* and its competitor, *El telegrafo* (Constantinople, 1886–1925). The animosity between these journals was as intense as the issues behind it were vague. *El telegrafo* was another pro-AIU paper whose political vision differed in degree rather than in substance from *El tiempo*'s. These newspapers even shared a number of founders: in cooperation with Isaac Gabay, Marco Muerkas, and Moiz Dalmediko, David Fresco helped to create *El telegrafo* in 1879, but removed himself from the editorial board a decade later (in the pages of *El tiempo,* Fresco alluded to the event vaguely, calling the split "one of the most difficult moments of my life," but not identifying its catalyst).[57] Immediately thereafter, Gabay and Fresco began a volley of personal attacks that lasted roughly until the Young Turk Revolt of 1908. Gabay and Fresco's personal attacks were often couched as political disputes. A difference of opinion over the leadership of the local hospital Or hahayim was the subject of dozens of articles in 1890, as was a debate over the success of AIU teachers in

Hasköy that dominated many pages of the paper in 1899. In retrospect, these differences seem a flimsy excuse for the vitriolic insults that the two men exchanged. What was at stake, instead, was something larger: their interaction, and the fierce competition between *El tiempo* and *El telegrafo*, reflected a jockeying for control of Constantinople's journalistic world and a struggle for the establishment of journalistic standards that would serve as a measure of this control. It also represented the twilight of a period in which personal bravado could upstage political ideology.

During its decade of contestation with *El telegrafo*, *El tiempo* proposed a number of practices that "proper" journalists should adhere to. They should not, the paper insisted, use pseudonyms, as did Victor Levy and other contributors to *El telegrafo* (Levy was accused of publishing under the names Spektator and Akel), a practice that was viewed as cowardly.[58] Fresco himself was in the habit of signing his submissions to *El tiempo* in any number of ways, a fact that contradicted but was somehow rendered irrelevant to his assault. *El tiempo* advanced a second standard that it consistently violated: that journalists should never engage in personal attacks upon one another. Frequently, long assaults on Gabay would be concluded with the preposterous claim that the preceding article contained not a personal but a political attack.[59] The flimsiness of these arguments, and the passion with which they were articulated, was captured visually in the pages of *El tiempo*. Exchanges between Gabay and Fresco were peppered with an extraordinary number of exclamation points — sometimes a single sentence could be followed by as many as a dozen.

Fresco, Gabay, and their newspapers were not fighting over readers, even though the papers were commercial competitors. Arguably, the combined circulation of both journals was hardly enough to sustain even one publication. Instead, their battle highlighted the extent to which Ottoman Ladino publishing at the turn of the twentieth century was a personal industry, dominated by indefatigable editors who, despite their avowed denials, often did write all of the articles in a single issue, many of which were penned under pseudonyms and were unabashedly self-promoting.[60] This style of interaction became arcane in the wake of the Young Turk Revolt, when *El tiempo* and *El telegrafo* were poised to face competitors far more menacing than each other.

Perhaps nothing catalogues the expansion of Ottoman Jewish publishing and politics as the debate over language choice. Deliberations over the question of language were born of concerns both abstract and concrete. There existed, on the one hand, the material questions of which language one should speak, read, or teach one's children. On the other hand, there was the analogous question of whether Jews were a religious or racial group, bearers of an Ottoman identity or proponents of a state of their own. To this debate we now turn, considering, in particular, *El tiempo*'s shifting position on the relative value of French, Turkish, and Ladino.

THE LANGUAGE OF CULTURE

Under the influence of the Alliance, support for French-language acquisition was a hallmark of *El tiempo,* as was true of most Ladino papers of the late nineteenth and early twentieth centuries. In 1891, the editors of *El tiempo* explained that to be a loyal member of the Ottoman nation, one had to be fluent in French as well as Turkish: hardly an unusual position for a pro-AIU periodical of the time.[61] The following year, an article prophesied that one day French would be the universal language because it was the most civilized.[62] All articles published in *El tiempo,* meanwhile, were composed in Gallicized Ladino, even those that promoted readers' acquisition of Turkish. In this sense, *El tiempo* was not unusual. Nearly all Ottoman Ladino journals with a Westernizing agenda (which constituted the vast majority of Ladino periodicals) were published in a linguistic style rich in international vocabulary and French syntax. Words from Hebrew, Aramaic, Turkish, and other Balkan languages were avoided.[63]

There were critics of these practices. In 1893 the journalist Nissim Yehuda Pardo of *Novelista* (Izmir, 1889–1924) suggested that *El tiempo* was corrupting Ladino with the inclusion of too many French words. Perhaps, he suggested, *El tiempo*'s writers could offer parenthetical translations into Ladino after each imported word.[64] To some extent this bit of advice was heeded, though with an unintended result. Parenthetical translations did begin to follow *El tiempo*'s "French" words (often these words were not so much French as French-inspired). The unexpected result was that journalists could include more, rather than fewer, foreign-sounding words and had even more freedom to jettison select words in Ladino, including those with Hebrew roots. *Grande miseria* now became *pauporizmo, kreasyon del mundo* became *kozmogonia,* and even the biblical *brashit* was replaced by *genesis.*[65]

Many have interpreted this process as an active erosion of Ladino. By Gallicizing the language, *El tiempo* was producing a new kind of Ladino culture in the nineteenth and early twentieth centuries. Ottoman and Turkish Jewry's acquisition of French, "far from weakening Judeo-Spanish ethnicity, simply marked it even more. French became domesticated, Judaized, Hispanicized. . . . Ethnic boundaries shifted and accommodated French and western ways, and emerged strengthened. A strong Jewish identity and ethnicity, though now secularizing, remained paramount in the self-definition of the group."[66] Arguably, this obsession with Western European culture and the advantages it availed never ceased, even after many Ladino newspapers turned to the task of nationalizing in the wake of the empire's disintegration. But over time, the Westernizing orientation of the Ladino press assumed a secondary position. Or, better put, it was simply taken for granted. By the 1890s, *El tiempo*'s opinion pieces ceased to focus on the merits of French culture. Reports on the affairs of AIU schools thinned. One can find little explicit support of the use of the French language in the pages of *El tiempo* after about 1892. Still, though *El tiempo*'s support for French culture faded, it did not disappear. The paper's advertisements sustained a vision of their readers that was self-consciously European. The fiction serialized in the paper was all European, and mostly French, in origin (much of it was translated by David Fresco, as was *Les Mystères de Paris* by Eugène Sue, a novel that was serialized for many months in the paper).[67]

Though adulation of French and Western European culture had faded from *El tiempo*'s professed goals and main articles by the 1890s, it had not disappeared but was thereafter only tacitly advanced. Yet it is precisely when cultural emulation has achieved its apogee that it can become tacit. If references to the superiority of French culture had become implicit by the 1890s, it was, after all, largely because by this time, a generation of students (and a generation of *El tiempo* readers) had graduated from AIU schools, just as a generation of teachers had completed studies at the Ecole Normale Israélite Orientale, the AIU's Paris-based teacher-training school that opened in 1867.[68] AIU graduates were fluent in French language and culture as a matter of course, and their appreciation of both was assumed. At the same time, by the 1890s not only *El tiempo* but the AIU itself had tempered its rhetoric concerning the importance of French. Though the organization had supported the use of Turkish in its schools from its inception, by 1887 its members were forced to admit it was almost impossible to teach it well given the lack of fluent instructors, a fact that coincided well with (and was, indeed, partly a result of) the AIU's sense that French was the most civilizing language.[69]

A second reason that *El tiempo* subdued its support for French in the 1890s was that by these years, the paper was beginning to develop support for Turkish language acquisition. As has already been mentioned, this was in part opportunistic. By the last decades of the nineteenth century, Turkish was required for entry in the Ottoman civil service, and the newspaper's producers hoped that readers would assume positions newly vacated by their Greek and Armenian peers. The paper's renewed support for Turkish also reflected its shifting political priorities. By the 1890s, *El tiempo* had become intent upon fashioning itself as a proponent of the imperial system and of the philosophy of Ottomanism, which the paper defined as the construction of one country made up of different religious elements.[70] In the last decade of the nineteenth century, *El tiempo* began to oppose separatist nationalism and to support the Turkicization of all Ottomans. Simultaneously, the paper was beginning to see a threat in Zionism, which was gaining a foundation in the Judeo-Spanish cultural area, and particularly in Bulgaria, where, since its independence from the Ottoman Empire in 1878, Zionism and other regional nationalisms had proved popular.[71] To respond to Zionist (and, by extension, all separatist nationalist) claims, the contributors to *El tiempo* subdued their lionization of Western Europe and began to argue that Jews were guaranteed a secure home in the Ottoman Empire. By 1899, an article spoke of the importance of the Jews' "Ottoman nationality," a notion that had been unthinkable two decades earlier.[72]

Until the 1890s, *El tiempo* had self-consciously stressed the Jewishness of its readers. The paper referred to its readers in terms that would remind them of their affiliation to one another: the *puevlo judeo* (Jewish people), *keila de mosotros* (our community), *muestra komunidad* (our community), *komunidad judia de oriente* (Jewish community of the Orient), *komunidad izraelita* (Israelite, or Jewish, community), *komunidad relijoza* (religious community), *judaizmo de turkia* (Jews of Turkey), *muestra nasyon* (our *millet*). These were terms that stressed Jewish particularism, the cohesion of the Jewish community, and a strong sense of group identification. Though they relied on phrases that would reappear in Zionist discourse, these terms did not have nationalist implications. References to Jewishness, instead, were extraordinarily flexible and not self-consciously ideological. One week, the paper might reproduce an article from a Western European newspaper on the eternal nature of the *rasa judea* (the Jewish race) and the Jewish "national spirit," and the very next week it might publish a piece decrying the politics of ethnic particularism. The fact that these positions were not seen as contradictory is not so much a sign of *El tiempo*'s disorganization as it is a hint showing how fluid the notion of identity was in the Ottoman Empire at the turn of the twentieth century.

El tiempo's many references to Jewish group cohesion were in essence reiterations of traditional Ottoman designations: synonyms for what had come to be called *millet*. This reflects the reason why the paper did not gesture toward readers' Ottomanness in its first decades. For both Jews and non-Jews there existed no sense that the borders of empire provided cohesion or an identity for its residents. This idea would emerge only at the turn of the century, when the paper began an active campaign to encourage readers to engage in a process of *turkifikasyon* (Turkicization), a noun first used in the pages of *El tiempo* in 1901.[73] There was irony in this semantic choice. Rather than emphasizing Ottomanization, this term, *turkifikasyon*, actually indicated that the salience of Ottomanness was being subdued by nationalist rhetoric. Even as *El tiempo* began to actively support the notion of Ottomanism, the integrity of this platform was being eroded.[74]

El tiempo's emerging pro-Turkish stance is exquisitely captured in the writing of Isaac Ferrara, a frequent contributor to the paper in the first years of the twentieth century. In a series of articles published in 1902, Ferrara offered readers a cultural itinerary for the process of Turkicization. He urged them to study Ottoman history and not just the history that followed the Jews' arrival in 1492.[75] He proposed that the levels of Jewish knowledge of Turkish literature be raised. His goal, he explained, was both to prove that a Turkish literary tradition existed and to help "regenerate" it.[76] He encouraged readers to explore Ottoman poetry because poetry revealed the "deepest sentiments of every nation."[77] Ferrara disparaged the idea that Jewry should strengthen their ties with Spain, telling readers that though they speak a Spanish language, it had not remained intact but had absorbed many words from Turkish and other languages.[78]

The notion that Jewish schools had an obligation to facilitate students' acquisition of Turkish emerged in the last years of the century, soon after the Ottoman state passed legislation — the first of its kind — mandating that Turkish be taught in non-Muslim schools. In the months and years that followed, the pages of *El tiempo* were filled with references to the value of learning the language. Ferrara claimed that Ladino, *muestro espanyol* (our Spanish), contained more than two thousand words of Turkish that would make the learning of Turkish easier.[79] And he reminded readers that studying Turkish was not only a patriotic act but the gateway to the speaking of a superior tongue.[80] Elsewhere, however, he cautioned readers that Turkish was difficult to learn because of the strong linguistic influence of Arabic. While European languages are based upon Latin cognates that are easy to understand, he sympathized, only "professionals" understand the "physiognomy" of Turkish. But, he argued, Arabic words are "considered distinct in Turkish, and don't amount to more than 1 percent [of the language]. Each of them is completely foreign to every Turk's mouth." As a result, he concluded, they should be purged from the language, making it more accessible to Ottoman citizens.[81]

This final suggestion is shocking in its inaccuracy and astonishing in its prescience. Far from suiting the needs of "every Turk," Ferrara's suggestion was useful only to a small minority of Ottoman citizens — those who spoke Romance languages — and, indeed, it was of great disadvantage to the many speakers of Arabic under Ottoman sovereignty. Nonetheless, some twenty years later the same motives would inform the linguistic reforms of the Kemalist Republic.[82] As this suggests, though Ferrara's many contributions to *El tiempo* provided readers with the most thorough cultural itinerary to the process of Turkicization that could be found in the paper, his articles did not provide readers with the reliable information, or practical suggestions, that they needed to embark upon this journey. Ferrara discussed the importance of Ottoman history but did not write historical essays. He described the importance of poetry but did not reproduce selections of poetry or offer reading suggestions. Again and again, he reiterated the importance of studying Turkish, but his paper did not include transliterated Turkish, as it once promised it would, did not publish articles in simple Turkish, and did not even present the alphabet for readers who wished to learn it. His articles, like so many in *El tiempo*, outlined a political vision but failed to facilitate its achievement.

As *El tiempo* built its defense of Turkish language acquisition, it began a concerted assault on Ladino. Prior to the mid-1890s, *El tiempo* had devoted little attention to Ladino. Contributors referred to the language as *muestra idioma* (our idiom), and as *el idioma espanyol* (the Spanish idiom). These were not terribly insulting terms, but not highly complimentary ones either — a reflection that "the language question," such as it existed at that time, was not as politicized as it would soon become. In 1893, *El tiempo* ran a series of anonymous articles entitled "El judeo espanyol" that expanded on the paper's opposition to Ladino. The reason *El tiempo* drew upon French phrases, the author explained, was that Ladino had no available synonyms: the language was a *jirgonza* (*zhargon*), and journalists writing in Judeo-Espanyol were simply too dignified to draw upon the available, popular terms (in Ladino, the words *popular* and *vulgar* share a root, illustrating the disdain with which "popular vocabulary" was invoked).[83] Other articles in the series suggested that journalists turned to French for inspiration because Ladino lacked words for the sentimental and the philosophical. "Spanish [*espanyol*]" one article concluded, "has no moral advantages for the Jewish people [*pueblo judeo*]."[84] Elsewhere, Ladino was labeled shameful (*una virguensa*) and a dying language.[85] These articles all reached the same conclusion: Ladino should be abandoned in favor of Turkish, which should be adopted not only as a mother tongue (*lengua maternala*) but the language of the country (*lingua de su patria*). By the turn of the century, these stances were rigidified still further. It is a matter of life and death for the Jewish people, proclaimed one contributor, to abandon Ladino; we owe it to the Sultan![86] Abandoning "this famous *patois* (*zhargon*) [*sic*] that we call Judeo-espanyol" swore another, is not simply a question to be debated in the pages of *El tiempo,* but is a pressing question for all of Turkey.[87]

Ladino had not been standardized by the turn of the century, and, partly as a result, Ladino periodicals of the late nineteenth and early twentieth centuries lacked consistency in spelling, grammar, and vocabulary. A single article could thus be borrowed from one Ladino journal and be "translated" for another: that is, writings were modified to fit local parlance and standards.[88] This helps explain the humor behind one journalist's ironic call for a Ladino–Ladino dictionary.[89] These "translations," however, reflected more than linguistic differences. Though Ladino was criticized for being a *patois,* its very flexibility allowed writers to assert their political predilections. They could, as we have seen, rely upon French words and eschew Hebrew ones. They could also spurn the influence of "provincial languages" such as Bulgarian, Greek, or Armenian. An article on Bulgarian Zionism, published in *El tiempo* in 1910, described the convening of a *suka,* a word it translated in a footnote as a "gathering of youths," and, in the same footnote, scolded Bulgarian Jews for "disfiguring" their Ladino with this and other Bulgarian imports.[90] The implication, of course, was not only that a word such as *suka* was foreign to Jewish lips, but that the phenomenon it was adopted to describe — a Zionist gathering attended by young people — was too. Opposition to Zionism was thereby articulated by the act of translation. Simultaneously, this footnote intimated that Jews in European Turkey were "purer" than their coreligionists in the provinces or neighboring states; Turkish Jews under European influences were more likely, at least, to undergo the process of "Turkicization" that the paper had so recently advocated.

Over the course of 1901, the paper's attack on Ladino was consolidated in a series of articles by David Fresco entitled "La kuestyon de la lengua" [The question of language]. The Jews of Turkey, he declared, view Ladino as a non-language: they are "a people without a language."[91] When Turkey's Jews left Spain, Fresco explained, they spoke a cultivated Spanish ("once," he wrote, "we spoke Spanish like Cervantes"). But over time, their language became corrupted, disfigured, bastardized. Today, the "idiom Judeo-Espanyol" is not a language in the modern sense of the word. It has no logic to suit the thoughts of man. It follows no grammatical rules. It lacks terms for geography, astronomy, and modern science. It cannot be used in diplomacy, for intellectual or commercial purposes. It is relied on only by the illiterate and uncultured, who are unable to prosper because of their lack of a language. Ladino, Fresco concluded, lacks utility, and since the nature of the human body is to refuse a foreign entity, it, too, should be refused, abandoned.[92]

Not all Ladino journalists echoed Fresco's hostility toward Ladino. For a variety of reasons, a small pro-Ladino coalition found voice in the pages of the Salonikan Ladino press, in particular in the newspaper *La epoka*. That Salonika proved a center of pro-Ladino writing is not surprising. At the turn of the twentieth century, Salonika was one of a handful of European cities in which Jews represented the majority population. In 1842, Jews constituted just over 51 percent of the city (36,000 of a total population of 70,000): forty years later, the percentage of Jews in the city had grown further still, to over 55 percent (50,000 of a total population of 90,000). Jews were not only a numerical majority. As a group, they were influential, visible, and well integrated into this most multi-ethnic of cities. Salonika's Sephardim were prominent in banking and international trade, two of the industries that brought economic boom to this port town in the nineteenth century. They were clustered on the city's waterfront, one of the most traversed areas of town. They were exceptionally multi-lingual, with high rates of fluency in Greek, Italian, Turkish, German, and French as well as Hebrew and Ladino. In general, they moved freely amidst a multi-ethnic population in which they constituted the numerical — if not the cultural — majority. Given the cosmopolitan nature of Salonikan Jewry, it is not surprising that the city was home to some of the most durable, prominent, and pro-Ladino periodicals of the empire.[93]

La epoka had been in existence since 1877, but had only begun to address the language question in 1901, no doubt in response to the increasingly hostile tone of *El tiempo*, to whose articles it often responded. "*El tiempo* is published two times a week, Monday and Thursday," editor Sa'adi Bezalel HaLevy complained in 1901, "and *La epoka* only once, on Wednesday: therefore everything I say is refuted not once but twice."[94] Over the course of 1901, *La epoka* published a great number of articles in defense of Ladino, all peppered with popular Ladino vocabulary that was all but absent from most Westernizing journals.[95] Despite the paper's support for the language, HaLevy conceded that Ladino was "not a language in the philological sense of the word," and called it a corrupt tongue. Nonetheless, he suggested that Jewish schools use Ladino to teach children literature and science. David Fresco, HaLevy wrote, suggests that Ladino has no utility. "Open your eyes, Signor Fresco!" he demanded, "and see how Ladino is not only not a bad influence, but is conserving the national character of Jews in the Orient."[96] To support Ladino, which he called "our fragile language *espanyol,*" HaLevy also defended the notion of multi-lingualism. Many literary figures, he pointed out, speak several languages, among them Victor Hugo, Alexander Dumas, and Leo Tolstoy. And many ethnic groups maintain several languages: Armenians speak Armenian and Turkish; Muslim Bulgarians speak Bulgarian and Turkish; Russian Jews of the Galician frontier speak Russian, Yiddish (*evraiko avlado*), and German; while Polish Jews speak Russian, Polish, Hebrew, and German. Why, he demanded of his readers, could Sephardi Jews not adopt Turkish in addition to maintaining Ladino?[97]

Prior to voicing his support of Ladino, HaLevy had established himself as a supporter of Turkish, though a hesitant one. In 1894, he encouraged Jews to study Turkish, arguing that a lack of fluency in the language would prevent the pursuit of higher education and, by extension, the defense of the nation.[98] Less than a year later, this stance was modified in an article that critically reported on a recent law requiring the use of Turkish in all schools in the capital. We can only hope, the article concluded, that this law is not applied to Ottoman Jews writ large.[99] By the turn of the century, *La epoka* published a series of articles that further modified this opinion, stressing the paper's support of democracy and Turkish (which HaLevy now called the *linguaje otomano* [Ottoman language]), concepts that by then seemed inextricably linked.[100] As this suggests, throughout his career HaLevy envisioned a brand of Ottomanism that would permit the maintenance of ethnic particularism, something Fresco's view of Ottomanism did not seem to accommodate. HaLevy's vision of Ottomanism no doubt had very much to do with the fact that its author made his home in Salonika. The Jews of Salonika had been exposed to a number of nationalist movements and were far enough away from the capital—and the Ottoman heartland—to alleviate some of the pressure of Turkicization. HaLevy's identification with Salonika not only fueled his support of Ladino, but also his resistance to David Fresco. On more than one occasion, he criticized the editor for claiming to speak for "all Ottoman Jews." A press reflects the city in which it is produced, HaLevy retorted—nothing more and nothing less.[101]

Fresco's tangles with HaLevy are reminiscent of editor Shoyl Ginzburg's struggles with Y. L. Peretz, who contributed to *Der fraynd* from Warsaw. As we have seen, from the moment Peretz joined *Der fraynd*'s staff, he was ir-ritated by *Der fraynd*'s editors' claims at representivity, their devotion to St. Petersburg, and their elitism. Ginzburg, in turn, mocked the author's folksy style, his popularism, and his devotion to Warsaw. Ginzburg's struggle with Peretz, like Fresco's with HaLevy, was personal in nature. But these conflicts were also illustrative of broader trends. These struggles were by-products of the evolution of Jewish vernacular publishing in the Russian and Ottoman contexts. In both cases, daily Jewish newspapers emerged first in the imperial center and only gradually proliferated to "provincial" cities like Warsaw and Salonika — cities that, from the Jewish perspective at least, were arguably more central than St. Petersburg or Constantinople. In the pro-cess, the Jewish popular press diversified topically and stylistically, adjusting to accommodate local conditions and readers' interests. This diversification was a sign of vivacity of the Yiddish and Ladino press, but, much to the chagrin of pioneers like Ginzburg and Fresco, it also signaled the finite influence of individuals or pioneering periodicals.

Though there is little reason to believe that Fresco spoke for all of Otto-man Jewry, there is much evidence to suggest that HaLevy was isolated in his support of Ladino. HaLevy represented no real coalition nor a threat to Fresco's more popular position. In this light, the zealousness with which Fresco attacked *La epoka* and its editor seems strangely hyperbolic. It has been suggested that the intra-communal divisions that marked Ottoman Jewry in the post-1908 period were no more than "a tempest in a teapot."[102] But in comparison to Fresco's fights with *La epoka*, the controversies that consumed the press in the wake of the Young Turk Revolt seem to have had a very sound political and material basis. As we will now see, Fresco's contest with HaLevy was soon overshadowed (and, indeed, rendered obsolete) by the events of 1908, after which debates over language choice grew more intense and evermore polarized.

LADINO JOURNALISM IN A NEW CENTURY

The Young Turks came to power through a peaceful *coup d'état* in 1908, with the goal of transforming the empire into a modern centralized state. The Committee of Union and Progress, the political body representing the largest faction of this movement, resuscitated the 1876 Constitution, which had been annulled a year after its proclamation.[103] *El tiempo* celebrated the revolution and the recognition of the constitution. Its first editorial on the topic joyously proclaimed that Turkey had, at last, entered the "civilized world" in a moment that "feels like a dream"[104] (the statement hinted at the fact that the paper had suppressed its criticisms of Abdülhamid's autocratic regime prior to 1908, no doubt out of fear of censorship. Not only did it intimate that the empire was uncivilized prior to this year but, in admitting that "the crisis is over," the paper recognized that the empire had faced a crisis in the first place). *El tiempo* was not alone in celebrating the arrival of the revolt. *La vara* (Cairo, 1906–1908), the Ladino weekly published by Fresco's long-time friend Abraham Galanté, was circulated for the last time the day the new constitution was proclaimed. Galanté saw no reason to continue publishing *La vara,* he explained, as the new administration obviated the need for opposition of any kind.[105]

Perhaps Galanté's dramatic gesture impressed the producers of *El tiempo.* Three days later, the paper published an article reminding readers that *El tiempo* relied on subscriptions for support (which it almost certainly did not), and pleading with readers to remain loyal to the periodical.[106] In the same article, Fresco articulated a new statement of purpose for the newspaper. The paper was designed to be useful to the country (*patria*) and to Judaism, and would attempt to provide readers with a "democratic education." This last phrase, unique to the post-1908 period, contains all the optimism with which *El tiempo* greeted the empire's transition to a constitutional regime. One senses that the democracy this newspaper envisioned was French in inspiration but Ottoman in implementation: one that would prize rather than fear the diversity of its constituents. And there is evidence that the paper did attempt to advance this cause — not only by defending the principles of the revolution, but also by building alliances possible only in the post-1908 period. *El tiempo* was a charter member of *Matbuat-I Osmaniye Cemiyeti,* an Ottoman publishing association founded in Constantinople shortly after the revolution. The association sought to foster financial, political, and intellectual cooperation between a number of Constantinople's multi-lingual newspapers. Abdullah Zühtü Bey represented *El tiempo* to the organization; the name was a Turkish pseudonym for one of its journalists, possibly even Fresco himself.[107]

Ottoman Jewish intellectuals seemed to have had many reasons to welcome the Young Turk regime after the revolt, though the regime by and large lacked a mass following among Jews.[108] The Constitution of 1876 promised Jews equality under the law. The new parliament included five Jewish deputies whose pictures and biographies *El tiempo* reverentially reproduced. For the first time in over two decades, a Chief Rabbi was elected to represent Ottoman Jewry, albeit not without controversy (Haim Nahum, an Alliance supporter, assumed the position in 1908).[109] In the same year, the World Zionist Organization (WZO) established its first office in Constantinople and a number of Hebrew language associations and Zionist youth groups were created.[110]

The conditions for Jewish publishing in Ladino, French, and Hebrew also changed dramatically after the Young Turk Revolt. With the lifting of censorship, dozens of new Jewish periodicals were introduced in Constantinople and other cities of the empire. Many of these were founded by the WZO, which aggressively sought to woo pre-existing presses as well.[111] Many

Ottoman Jewish periodicals did choose to evolve into Zionist organs, among them *La epoka, Journal de Salonique, La boz, El judeo, El avenir* (Salonika, 1901–13), *El pueblo* (Salonika, 1909–33), *El imparsyal* (Salonika, 1901–11), and *El telegrafo*. These newspapers were well received by Jewish readers.[112] For the first time since its inception, *El tiempo* confronted genuine economic and ideological competition. The Constantinople-based *El telegrafo* and the Salonikan *La epoka* ceased to be *El tiempo*'s primary foes, replaced now by the German- and French-language Zionist periodicals *Die Welt* (Köln, Berlin, 1897–1914) and *L'Aurore* (Constantinople, 1908–14) — and the influential coalitions that backed them. The WZO tried to woo *El tiempo*, too, and at first the journal seemed interested in a cooperative effort. Quickly, however, Fresco proved an unreliable ally of Zionism and, instead, an unwavering supporter of the anti-Zionist Chief Rabbi Nahum. By 1910, any hope of cooperation between *El tiempo* and the Zionist establishment was dashed. In this year, Fresco published several articles that his critics considered anti-semitic: one a translation of an anti-Zionist article from a contemporary Turkish paper, the other an inflammatory series, titled "Is Zionism Compatible with Ottomanism?"[113]

Fresco's answer to the latter question was resoundingly negative. Zionism, he wrote, contradicts Judaism, the mission of Israel, and the aspirations of humanity. He called it primitive, exclusivist, utopian.[114] He saw it as an exploitation of the poor, a ruse that would woo Jews away from the synagogue, a philosophy crudely imported from Russia and Galicia.[115] The Zionists, Fresco argued, call anti-Zionists assimilationists, as if this were an insult. In fact, assimilation is part of nature, a sign of progress.[116] Imagine, he continued elsewhere, if Jews, Greeks, and Armenians all retreated into isolation, speaking only the language of their *pueblo* (people)? In fact, both Greeks and Armenians have chosen to adopt the language of their country: Do we, he demanded of his readers, wish to diverge from our peers?[117] Jews, he consistently argued, are not a race, but a religion: one can be Jewish in origin and Ottoman "in spirit."[118] "I am an Ottoman," Fresco declared, "genuinely patriotic."[119] And he considered the ideal of all Ottoman Jews was to be patriotic above all else, supporters of "mak[ing] the population as homogenous as possible."[120] Elsewhere, a contributor to *El tiempo* argued that no Zionist messiah could bring about a Jewish nation in Palestine because "our fatherland, our holy land, our Jerusalem, our motherland is Turkey, a liberal and constitutional Turkey, which we should support with all our force and faith."[121]

As it defended Jews' Ottomanness, the newspaper continued to lobby for Jews to use Turkish as their language. *El tiempo* encouraged readers to study the language and it urged parents to speak it to their children. The paper also continued to insist that Jews could not be bilingual.[122] In fact, however, the process of adopting Turkish was not succeeding among Ottoman Jews, even in the Turkish-speaking regions of the empire. As late as 1927, 85 percent of the Jews in European Turkey identified Ladino as their mother tongue.[123] According to Moïse Fresco, an Alliance teacher, few students were interested in a career in the civil service, the only context in which fluency in Turkish was truly necessary.[124] *El tiempo* never recognized the unpopularity of its pro-Turkish position. In 1911, it introduced an article by Gad Franko with the concession that the author was "one of the rare [Ottoman] Jews who knows the language of his country well." (The article itself, hardly designed to promote Ottoman culture, was a Ladino translation of Franko's Turkish translation of Jean Jacques Rousseau's "On Education," originally published in the Turkish newspaper *Ikdam.*)

If *El tiempo* was overestimating the appeal of its pro-Turkish stance, it was underestimating the popularity of its critics. To a great extent, this was because Fresco's anti-Zionists tracts were blind to the originality and flexibility of Ottoman Zionism. Jewish nationalism in Turkey did not, in fact, advocate the fragmentation of the empire, and there was little outright support among Sephardi Zionists for the creation of a Jewish state in Palestine. Ottoman Jewry tended to fear nationalist claims to Palestine because the claims represented a threat to their own government. This fear shaped Ottoman Zionism into a form of nationalism with virtually no territorial dimension. Fresco's mistake, perhaps, was that he understood Zionism as a rigid institution rather than an inspiration for Ottoman Jewry and failed to anticipate that the philosophy might recast Ottoman Jews' nostalgia for the *millet* system into support for the politics of ethnic particularism. He failed to see that Ottoman Zionism was nationalist in its cultural orientation, which allowed many of its supporters (like many Arab subjects of the empire) to remain Ottomanists at least until the First World War.[125] Fresco's opposition to Ottoman Zionism prevented him from investigating Zionism's many mutations in journals such as *El telegrafo*. He preferred, instead, to meticulously critique individual Zionist thinkers from Western and Central Europe. In 1911, for example, the paper hurled a list of accusations at Max Nordau and his allies, written in a style that seemed to parody the list of plagues meted upon the Egyptians in the Book of Exodus: "False. Liar. Infamous. Traitor. Criminal. Conspirator. False to excess. Diabolical . . . Agitator . . . Disgraceful . . . Stupid."[126]

There were concrete reasons to explain why Fresco's vision of Ottomanism lacked the popularity that Zionism was gaining. Ottomanism itself was proving utopian. In the years after the Young Turk Revolt, Ottoman Jews watched as the Committee for Union and Progress's (CUP) vision of a multiethnic Ottomanism was transformed into the nationalist and increasingly racist philosophy of Turkism. Indeed, even by the time Fresco's series "Is Zionism Compatible with Ottomanism?" was published, the CUP was beginning to compromise its vision of Ottomanism, a philosophy destined to expire before it was enacted. That one of *El tiempo*'s journalists represented the newspaper to the post-revolution Ottoman publishing association with an assumed Turkish name seemed now not simply an expression of optimism but a foreshadowing of philosophical devolution. Worse still, only months before Fresco looked to the Armenians as an example of an ethnic group that had successfully assimilated, the CUP had begun its massacres of thousands of Armenians whom they regarded as political foes.[127] These were events that El tiempo reported on at some length, but with no explicit sympathy. On the contrary, the paper insisted that both ethnic nationalism and irredentism were dangerous threats. In July 1909, the paper published an article assuring readers that the empire had a strong enough army to deter hostile forces from without or within.[128] And after the issuing of the conscription law of 1909 (which required all Ottoman citizens to serve in the army), El tiempo reiterated its faith in the Ottoman military by publishing an article calling for the voluntary conscription of Jewish men, reminding readers that Jews had always been among the empire's most loyal subjects (in fact, far from supporting the conscription law, the rate of Jewish emigration increased dramatically after 1909).[129] Jews' imagined loyalty could, in any case, hardly prevent the disintegration of the empire: already by 1909, the empire had lost most of its European provinces.[130]

Throughout this massive loss of territory, El tiempo remained adamantly, even naïvely, opposed to separatism. But necessity compelled its priorities to shift. Discussions about Zionism all but disappeared from the paper by the autumn of 1911, as the issue was overshadowed by wars and internal unrest. Clearly, Fresco had misjudged the power of nationalist irredentism. Still, his trust of Ottomanism betrayed a kind of insight. Jews had indeed benefited from the Ottoman imperial system, arguably to a far greater degree than any other of the empire's non-Muslim subjects. Their cooperation with the imperial regime had allowed many Jews to thrive economically, culturally, and politically. Fresco was not alone in understanding this. The Jews of Salonika, who feared Greek antisemitism and cherished their own domination of Salonika's economy, formally protested the Greek annexation of their city in the wake of the Balkan Wars of 1912–13, proposing instead that the city exist as an international port.[131] As Fresco could not have known in 1911, Jews and many other non-Muslim groups would suffer at the hands of Balkan nation-states born of irredentism. As early as the 1890s, legislation was passed to enforce the Bulgarianization of the Jews of Bulgaria. By the 1920s and 1930s, similar laws were passed in Greece and Turkey, with the goal of Hellenizing and Turkicizing local Jews.[132] Most of the Armenian population of Turkey perished, and the Greeks of Turkey (with the exception of the Greeks of Constantinople) were forcibly transferred to Greek territory in return for the transfer of most ethnic Turks to Turkey. In Turkey and the Balkans, the construction of ethnicity, and often its wholesale creation (through population transfers or the random drawing of boundaries), was proving essential to the construction of nation-states.[133] Antisemitism, the racism of many new nation-states, and dwindling prosperity catalyzed a dramatic rise in emigration among Jews. Many moved to France — it is estimated that in 1939, as many as twenty-five thousand Sephardim lived in Paris. Between 1889 and 1924, more than twenty thousand Ottoman Jews migrated to the United States. Others left their homes for Latin America (Cuba, Mexico, and Argentina absorbed the majority) and Africa (the Belgian Congo, Rhodesia, and South Africa were favored destinations). In the late 1940s, other Sephardim fled war-torn Europe for Palestine.[134] *El tiempo* instituted a new column in 1913 entitled "Across the World," which provided readers with the financial information they needed to negotiate these changes. Here, the potential émigré could research the average cost of a home in Paris, Berlin, and London.[135]

Ironically, at the very moment that *El tiempo*'s circulation peaked — in the midst of the First World War — the paper seemed to enter a sort of ideological stasis. Arguably, it had been the paper's optimism that made it both a success and a curiosity. Its faith in the already-disintegrating imperial system, its attempt to resuscitate the flagging Ottoman Jewish economy, its persistent attack on the politics of nationalism could all be considered challenges to the onslaught of modernity. And yet, within the context of Ottoman Jewish culture, these were distinctly modern impulses. *El tiempo*'s defense of the *millet* system relied upon a modern genre, modern technologies, and modern desires. The paper was not against change. It supported the democratization of the empire, freedom of the press, and open political debate. But it imagined that the best way to achieve these goals was to tinker with, rather than dissolve, the Ottoman Empire as a whole. If the paper's circulation is any indication, these views were not just popular, but were actually gaining popularity over time.

This chapter has analyzed factors that catalyzed and shaped Ladino publishing: the erosion of traditional centers of Jewish communal control; the realignment of the Ottoman economy in general and the Ottoman Jewish economy of Constantinople in particular; the emergence of new perceptions of non-Muslims' place in Ottoman society; the growing influence of Western European Jewish patronage; and, finally, the development of a body of readers eager for reading matter in a language they could understand. Arguably, the first and last of these factors are generalizable. Elsewhere in Europe, traditional axes of Jewish control were also being challenged by intellectuals, political parties and programs, innovative religious movements, state policies, and shifting gender norms. Simultaneously, Jewish readers across the European continent — and in the Middle East and the Americas as well — were discovering new genres of secular Jewish culture printed in all of the languages Jews could or were learning to speak. Perhaps the other factors that shaped Ladino publishing in the Ottoman lands were more exceptional. After all, while elsewhere in Europe, state-sponsored liberal reforms tended to bring Jews new opportunities, in the Ottoman setting these trends seemed to pinion Jews (and other non-Muslim and Arab subjects as well). Further, while elsewhere in Europe Jews tended to support the dismantling of imperial structures, the fear of imperial disintegration was unique to Ottoman Jewry (though it was shared, perhaps, by a certain segment of Habsburg Jewry). Finally, while in Eastern, Central, and Western Europe domestic and international patronage did stimulate new forms of Jewish culture and politics on the eve of the twentieth century, in none of these settings was the imprint of philanthropy so profound and wide-reaching as in the Ottoman Empire.

This chapter also allows us to conclude that Ladino and Yiddish popular cultures charted enormously independent courses on the eve of the twentieth century. At that moment in history, both Russian Yiddish and Ottoman Ladino cultures were experiencing unprecedented expansion in form and quantity, a transformation that was signaled by the dramatic growth of the Yiddish and Ladino popular press. But while in the Russian setting Yiddish was emerging as a language of commercial possibility and cultural renewal, in the Ottoman Empire Ladino maintained a precarious standing. Ladino was, on the one hand, the language in which the vast majority of Jews in Southeastern Europe felt most at ease. On the other hand, it was a language that even the most vocal proponents of Sephardi culture (Westernizing intellectuals and the rabbinical leadership alike) were inclined to degrade. It was a language of a burgeoning cultural industry — the popular press — but an industry whose consumers, oddly enough, were unwilling or unable to pay for the print they continued to demand. These contradictory dynamics ensured that the Ottoman Ladino press would hover between success and failure, popularity and infamy, much in the same way that turn-of-the-century Ottoman Jews hovered between acceptance and marginality, rootedness and alienation. This was not a traditional balance. On the contrary, these were unprecedented dynamics that demanded innovative responses. It was an interplay that the Ladino press might describe as modern.

PART TWO

IMAGING
CULTURE

3

ICONOGRAPHIES OF AGITATION

The preceding chapters studied the historical conditions that shaped Yiddish and Ladino newspapers in the Russian and Ottoman settings and pondered the impact the newspaper publishing industry had upon Jewish readers. The pages that follow focus on the symbiotic relationship between Jewish vernacular cultures and the majority or hegemonic cultures of the Russian and Ottoman Empires. This inquiry commences with an episode that was instrumental in drawing — and also blurring — the contours of modern Russian (and modern Russian Jewish) politics: the Revolution of 1905–1907.

Historical scholarship has demonstrated that if the Revolution of 1905–1907 was waged on the street, it was also waged in print, not only in Russian, but in virtually all the languages spoken within the borders of this multilingual empire.[1] Nothing enabled the literary putsch so much as the lifting of censorship, a product of Tsar Nicholas's otherwise halfhearted October Manifesto of 1905. Hundreds of new periodicals blossomed into print, among them myriad satirical papers that vented their opposition to the old regime in visual form. Between 1905 and 1907, satirical journals featuring political cartoons, caricatures, and radical graphics were published not just in Russian but also in Polish, Ukrainian, Estonian, Latvian, Greek, and Armenian. During these years, four dozen such papers were also published in Yiddish.[2]

This chapter considers how the Jewish popular press took part in the revolution and reflects on the importance of visual texts to the articulation of political sentiment. To this end, the following pages turn to an unexamined episode in the history of early-twentieth-century Russian letters. They explore how *Dos lebn* (St. Petersburg, February–July 1906) participated in this revolution, at some moments borrowing from the Russian language press, at others presenting starkly original pictures of protest.

One of the most striking features of *Der fraynd* and *Dos lebn*—which, insofar as they shared the same editorial board, contributors, readership, and layout, were essentially one—was their reliance on visual graphics to convey the rapid shifts in political views that in abrupt succession galvanized many Russian Jews in the first decades of the twentieth century. Beginning in the early winter of 1906, cartoons, which were then a novel genre in the world of Russian Yiddish letters, were used by the editors of *Dos lebn* to remake a Zionist periodical into a socialist one in order to retain readers at a moment when Jewish popular opinion listed toward socialism, opposition politics, and intra-ethnic cooperation. In adopting a politically radical stance to pander to its readers, the paper's explicit bravado conveyed a radical message and simultaneously signaled an act of conformity.

Radicalism and conformity are rarely imagined as consistent. Certainly this mixture does not reflect the way in which Russian Jews remembered the revolutionary period. Moyshe Katz, a sometime-contributor to *Der fraynd*, reminisced about this era in his memoirs: .

> [a]s the 1905 Russian Revolution approached and after it happened, the Russian people as a whole and Jews, in particular, lost a generational fear. People suddenly lost the dread they had for the Tsar and his Cossacks, for the police, gendarmes, and spies. And at exactly the same time, they stopped fearing God and His servants on earth and fearlessly rejected the moldy traditions of the past . . . that oppressed their mothers and fathers. It was as if from the earth (truly, from under the earth) a new revolutionary generation emerged which was bold . . . because it rejected traditional values and created for itself new values, new criteria.[3]

Without gainsaying Katz's claim, one could argue that in the pages of the Yiddish press, the turn to radicalism was not always accompanied by an abandonment of fear. Sometimes, indeed, the reverse held true: radicalism could be motivated by the fear of political anachronism, the fear of being left behind. This complicated dynamic fueled *Dos lebn*'s experience and coverage of the revolution.

If shifts in content could rapidly communicate evolving political views, shifts in visual form responded to and, to some extent, promoted profound changes in the political atmosphere. One such redirection occurred when *Dos lebn* introduced the genre of cartoons; another transpired when cartoons were jettisoned from its pages and photographs—an all but novel genre of the Yiddish daily—were adopted in their place. The catalyst to the visual shift to photographs was the Bialystok pogroms of June 1906, an event, it appeared, that was too horrific to satirize. In the wake of the pogroms, *Der fraynd* employed photographs as a visual antidote to cartoons, and, simultaneously, promoted Zionism as a political antidote to socialist and opposition politics. Thus as the politics of intra-ethnic cooperation yielded to nationalism, satirical images of the Duma were replaced with the bloodied photographs of the Jewish dead.

Contemporary critics of *Der fraynd* argued that the mission of *Der fraynd*— and, ultimately, its very quality—was eventually undermined by the paper's variable political orientations. Indeed, *Der fraynd*'s second political transition (from opposition politics to Zionism) might be understood to have undermined the first (from Zionism to opposition politics). In fact, the transition between these sentiments was consistent rather than anomalous with the political paradigm of the time. Not yet polemicized or polarized, Zionism, socialism, and opposition politics were still amorphous philosophies, and popular Yiddish sources (like many Russian Jewish readers) drifted between them without taking sides.

Revisiting the genres of the Yiddish cartoon and the photograph affords a number of distinct advantages. First, this exercise permits a deeper understanding of Russian Jewish politics and culture in the first decades of the twentieth century, allowing us to reflect, in particular, on how popular Yiddish sources reflected *and* shaped evolutions in Russian Jewish popular opinion. Second, turning to Yiddish visual texts of the Revolution of 1905– 1907 provides the opportunity to reconsider the relationship between Russian and Yiddish sources and the analogous relationship between Russian and Jewish party politics. In the Yiddish press, at least, these were entities that were rendered indistinct at times and at other times were self-consciously delineated. Finally, analyzing the role of cartoons and photographs allows us to resuscitate a body of sources that has been otherwise neglected by historians of the Russian Revolution, Russian Jewish culture, and the Yiddish press.

RADICALISM *EN VOGUE*, RADICALISM INVENTED: THE
REVOLUTION OF 1905–1907 AND THE RUSSIAN YIDDISH PRESS

The popular beginnings of the Revolution of 1905–1907 date to January 1905, when strikers in St. Petersburg were fired on by troops of the tsar's Winter Palace. News of the event, subsequently labeled "Bloody Sunday," prompted a wave of strikes, revolts, and protests organized by opposition and socialist groups and reaching across religious, ethnic, and linguistic divides. By the autumn of 1905, the tsarist regime had proved itself both vulnerable and inept. Under considerable pressure, Tsar Nicholas II issued a manifesto that seemed to initiate democratic reforms. Though it fell short of popular demands for a constituent assembly, the October Manifesto promised greater participation in Duma elections, the protection of civil liberties, and freedom of speech. Quickly, however, it became apparent that the government was unwilling to support genuine change. Though Nicholas's manifesto lifted censorship, for example, it left journalists and editors more vulnerable than ever to imperial interference by making them accountable to criminal rather than civil laws. And though a new electoral system was announced some months later, only a small portion of Russia's subjects could cast direct votes. This excluded nearly all of the Jewish workers in the Pale of Settlement. (By way of protest, four Jewish socialist parties boycotted the Duma elections. Twelve Jewish deputies, of 497, were nonetheless elected, five of whom were Zionists.) Further, in the wake of the election, the powers of the Duma were considerably curtailed. A series of laws passed in April 1906 allowed the Duma no procedural way of initiating constitutional amendments and made most officials and ministers responsible only to the tsar. Three months later, the Duma was dissolved by the government and was not to be resurrected for over a year.

Notwithstanding the feebleness of tsarist-generated reforms, Tsar Nicholas's October Manifesto—and the popular outrage that defined the period—did prove a tremendous boon to publishing. In the wake of the manifesto, hundreds of periodicals were created in the empire's many languages. Countless among them acquired circulations that far exceeded those of the pre-1905 period. Many of these new periodicals were satirical and chose to vent their resistance in visual form. Between 1905 and 1907, hundreds of satirical journals featuring political cartoons, caricatures, and radical graphics were published in Russia and the empire's provinces. Approximately two hundred emerged in St. Petersburg, among them journals in Estonian, Latvian, and Armenian. In Moscow, nearly one hundred satirical journals were published, a portion of which were in Yiddish. Twenty Ukrainian satirical journals were available; Kiev itself was home to dozens. Smaller cities, too, saw the emergence of satirical sources. Tiflis could boast more than a dozen in Russian, Armenian, and Greek. More than ten were published in Odessa, including six in Yiddish. Satirical papers appeared in Saratov, Astrakhan, and Yaroslavl'. Even Siberia was home to several. And during these years, nearly fifty satirical journals were published in Yiddish, the vast majority of which were based in Warsaw.[4]

As this extraordinary figure might suggest, the Revolution of 1905–1907 rocked the Jewish street—and the world of Yiddish letters—with particular force. This was in part because Jews had multiple, deep grievances against the old regime, which had censored their publications and brought restrictions on geographic, occupational, and economic mobility, and had caused political and social disenfranchisement. Ironically, however, Jews potentially had much to lose through the dismantling of the old regime. Revolution itself seemed to leave Jews vulnerable. From 1903 to 1906, Jews witnessed an unprecedented wave of antisemitic violence as hundreds of pogroms marred the Russian landscape.[5] This in turn drove many Russian Jews toward the young socialist Bund (the General Jewish Labor Union in Lithuania, Poland, and Russia), which was gaining a reputation for its successful organization of self-defense groups. In part because of these labors, and in part because of its leadership in the general strike movement, by 1905 the Bund — an organization less than ten years old — managed to dominate Russian Jewish public opinion.[6] Not insignificant was the fact that the Zionist movement had entered 1905 in disarray; Theodor Herzl had died only a year before, leaving in his wake the messy memory of the failed Uganda proposal.[7] These factors combined ensured that Jewish popular opinion was increasingly cast in favor of socialism, and that the Zionist party was thrown on the defensive. In May 1905 the Zionist leadership in Russia issued its support for radical change, and most Russian Zionists, like most Russian Zionist institutions, began to ally themselves with opposition politics, subordinating their call for Jewish national rights to the demand for democratic reform in Russia. Inclined to adaptation rather than isolation, many Zionist institutions — newspapers among them — saw little choice but to join the fold.[8]

Among them was *Dos lebn*, a newspaper created by the editors of *Der fraynd* in December 1905 as a guard against oppression by censorship. While *Der fraynd* had built its identity on an aloofness from Russian news and politics, *Dos lebn* devoted itself to lambasting Russia's political climate. The aggressive rule of the imperial regime, the failure of the October Manifesto, the pinioning and eventual dissolution of the Duma, the corruption of tsarist ministers and appointed officials all became targets of *Dos lebn*'s artful skewering. And while *Der fraynd* had positioned itself as a moderate Zionist organ, *Dos lebn* sought to woo readers inclined toward socialism with a newly radicalized agenda. In so doing, the paper subdued its Zionist credentials in order to remain relevant to Russian Jewish readers who had new political predilections and unprecedented access to a variety of Yiddish periodicals that sought to satisfy these new political needs. *Dos lebn* now turned its focus away from affairs of the Jewish world, away from news of Berlin, London, and America, and toward the Russian regime — toward, even, affairs in Congress Poland, an area its journalistic predecessor had all but ignored.

Der fraynd had tended to placate the censors or, at least, to be Aesopian in its criticism. While the paper refrained from taking a stand on Polish independence, for example, it was outspoken in its support of the breakaway Macedonian republic; coverage of the political conflict in Macedonia served as a discreet means for commenting on Russian Imperial politics, and on Russia's control of Congress Poland, in particular.[9] Similarly, rather than analyzing relations between ethnic nationalities in Russia—or commenting on the status of its ethnic minorities—the paper explored the tempestuous relations between blacks and whites in the United States. To guarantee the success of maneuvers such as these, Der fraynd's editors personally courted the paper's censors. Recall Israel Landau, the censor assigned to the paper, who could be found on a nightly basis chatting with Der fraynd's workers and laughing out loud at Sholem Aleichem's latest installment. As a result of the paper's cautious tone and (at least outwardly) conciliatory attitude, Der fraynd experienced only minor tangles with the censor prior to its closing.[10]

That this newspaper would transform Aesopian critique into explicit oppositional sentiment in the era of the Revolution of 1905–1907 will not surprise students of Russian Jewry. As others have suggested before me, by 1905 most Zionist organizations and periodicals were inclining toward opposition and socialist politics in order to remain politically competitive. If the paper's political redirection was not surprising, however, the visual implications of this realignment were both startling and remain little understood. So dramatic was Dos lebn's change in political leaning that it seemed to require a concurrent change in format. By March 1906, each issue of Dos lebn and its satirical supplement Der bezem featured caustic political cartoons, a feature hitherto foreign to the Yiddish daily press.[11]

The vast majority of Dos lebn's cartoons were created by Aren Borisovich Lakhovski (Arnold Borisovich Liakhovskii). During Dos lebn's run, Lakhovski published dozens of cartoons in the journal. During the same period, he contributed cartoons to the Yiddish satirical journal Der sheygets (St. Petersburg, 1906) and to the Russian-language satirical journals Leshii (St. Petersburg, 1906), Piatsii (St. Petersburg, 1906), Udav (Kiev, 1906), and Serii volk (St. Petersburg, 1906–1908).[12] In 1906, Lakhovski was twenty-seven years old and had received only one year of formal training as an artist, working under Aleksandr A. Kiselev at the Academy of Arts in St. Petersburg. (With the exception of time spent in Palestine, Lakhovski would continue his studies at the academy until 1912, when he became one of several Jewish artists upon whom the title of Academician was conferred.) Like many artists of the revolutionary period, Lakhovski was inspired by and exhibited with the Mir iskusstva (World of Art) group, headed by Sergei Pavolovich Diaghilev and Alexandre Benois. Many members of this circle recorded the events of 1905 and 1906 in cartoons influenced by the style moderne.[13]

Lakhovski's cartoons immediately reflected the extent to which the boundaries of political metaphor had shifted from 1903 to 1906. The implicit now became explicit, the "accidental" brazenly intentional. Indeed, the medium of cartoons—which, after all, is a vehicle of exaggeration, sarcasm, and simplification—may have been ideally suited to the rapidly radicalizing politics of the period. While Der fraynd had turned to Macedonia to veil its commentary on Russian imperial conquests, *Dos lebn* published a political cartoon featuring a man trying to bind the territories of Finland, Poland, and the Caucuses. "The pure Russian folk," reads the caption, "you have to bind the vessel with rope and maybe it will hold tight" (figure 3.1).[14] And while references to the abuses of the old regime had been buried deep in *Der fraynd, Dos lebn* graphically depicted the hands that controlled Russian politics in the pre- and post-1905 era. A cartoon with two frames depicted a "before" in the shape of a towering Prime Minister S. Iu. Witte, author of the October Manifesto, shaking an oversized fist at a mass of people groveling at his knees. In the "after," a group of tsarist ministers, backed by a ferocious group of henchmen, intimidate an opponent who is crawling away on all fours (figure 3.2).[15]

While *Der fraynd* colluded with the imperial censors in an attempt to guarantee itself as much autonomy as possible, *Dos lebn*'s political cartoons critiqued the persistence of censorship in post-1905 Russia. One such cartoon depicted the provincial censor as a man bound to a chair and blindfolded, his hand clutching an official quill. Another featured Russia's "new cemetery," in which gravestones marked the death of "freedom of assembly," "freedom of information," "freedom of individuals," and "freedom of the press."[16] (The latter cartoon mimicked a well-known poster by Isaac Brodsky [Isaak Brodskii], in whose rendition the tombstones bore Russian rather than Yiddish epigraphs.)[17] A third cartoon pictured an angry government official trying to stamp out a cockroach labeled "the press" (figure 3.3).[18] As this last cartoon suggests, the radicalism of these images was not enabled by a loosening of imperial decree. *Dos lebn*, like all journals in the empire, was still at risk of censorship. Its contributors were accountable to Russia's criminal code, a law used to condemn, confiscate, and close many satirical journals.[19] Further, the paper violated an ineffectual but nonetheless intact ruling that forbade a suspended paper to rename itself and continue publishing.[20]

If *Dos lebn* differed from its predecessor *Der fraynd*, it also differed from contemporary Russian-language satirical journals. These differences arose partly out of differences in the sensibilities of the Yiddish and Russian press, but there were genuine stylistic differences as well. In contradistinction to many satirical journals of the 1905 era, *Dos lebn* was issued as a daily rather than a weekly and did not function exclusively as a satirical journal. Moreover, it was a journal with an established readership that its editors did not want to lose.[21] *Dos lebn*'s nervousness about retaining readers was, as has already been suggested, a plausible reason for publishing cartoons in the first place: in an era in which the popularity of Zionism was yielding to Bundism and opposition politics, and in which St. Petersburg was yielding to Warsaw as a center of the Yiddish press, the publication of cartoons allowed the *Dos lebn* to mask its conservative history behind a more daring facade. The limited circulation, regularity, and relative longevity of *Dos lebn* had a number of other more specific effects upon the physical appearance of the

די .עקמריסישעלײים: מען דאַרף דעם מאָס אײַנשנוּרעוטעע טיט דראָם. אפּשׁר וֶעם
עַ דֶ פעסטער האַלטען!..

Figure 3.1. "The pure Russian folk: you have to bind the
vessel with rope and maybe it will hold tight!" *Dos lebn* #88,
12 April 1906.

דֿעָרְנָאךֿ   פֿרִיעָר

Figure 3.2. "Before (on right) and After (on left)." *Dos lebn*
#93, 27 April 1906.

paper. While nearly all Russian-language satirical journals of this period
relied heavily on the use of color—one thinks of the brilliant images in
Burya (St. Petersburg, 1906), *Bureval* (St. Petersburg, 1906), *Kosa* (St. Petersburg, 1906), *Zhurnal zhurnalov* (St. Petersburg, 1905–1906), *Leshii,* and
Mefistofel (St. Petersburg, 1906) among other periodicals—*Dos lebn* published most of its cartoons in black and white and thus at lower cost.[22]
Perhaps for related reasons, neither *Dos lebn* nor its satirical supplement *Der
bezem* indulged in the elegant typography and graceful art-deco inserts that
could be found in many Russian-language satirical presses of the day.

But ultimately such stylistic differences arose out of cultural and political differences rather than financial concerns. The hundreds of Russian-
language satirical journals that appeared between 1905 and 1907 tended
also to focus on the depravity of the regime much more graphically than did
the cartoons of *Dos lebn.* In nearly all such journals, images of skulls litter the
terrain: they cover fields, nestle between delicacies on dinner tables, replace

93

‏– פערפאלמנו געשטאלטעניש! סימר נוטסט זיך געטאלקטען זיך און מידעס!

Figure 3.3. "Pesky creature! It's impossible to hide from!" *Dos lebn* #89, 23 April 1906.

pool balls, and decorate buildings. Skeletons, too, maintain a vivid presence. They hover over landscapes, dress as officials, peer out of windows, grip death's scythe, and fly with wings of incredible breadth. These gruesome images are joined by others: pictures of demons, goblins, enormous bats, snaking creatures with enormous claws, masses of crows. And there is blood dripping everywhere, spilling out of the earth, buildings, people, and official documents.[23] These images, so popular in Russian-language papers, were nearly entirely absent from the cartoons of *Dos lebn.* Jewish editors may have considered these images of death and evil to veer too close to the Christological. Lakhovski, the creator of most of *Dos lebn*'s cartoons, published depictions of ghoulish characters and similar imagery, but by and large was content to limit these to the Russian-language press.[24] In *Piatsii,* for example, Lakhovski published images of devils and goblins. One cartoon by the artist shows a group of devilish figures lounging about and laughing uproariously at the copy of *Piatsii* that they share.[25] Another of Lakhovski's cartoons in *Piatsii* shows a skeleton reading an official declaration, his head nearly lost amidst the clouds of smoke emanating from his pipe.[26] In the Russian-language satirical journal *Leshii,* meanwhile, one finds Lakhovski's rendering of Prime Minister Witte and Minister of Internal Affairs D. F. Trepov as small devils, huddled close to several other ghoulish figures.[27]

A selection of *Dos lebn*'s cartoons, too, lacerated individual ministers and officials (even, on occasion, the tsar himself) but they were rarely depicted as ghouls as they were in Russian-language sources. The highly unpopular P. N. Durnovo was one of Lakhovski's favorite subjects of ridicule. Durnovo was known for his reactionary politics, for his abuses of power, and for his support of the violent Black Hundreds (the bands of armed counterrevo-lutionaries responsible for much of the anti-Jewish violence of 1905 and 1906). A former policeman, Durnovo had served as minister of interior since 1899, when he had been appointed by Prime Minister Witte. By February 1906, Durnovo had nearly full control of the provincial bureaucracy and had instructed Russia's governors to prepare for a general strike and armed uprising. To this end, he urged the increase of surveillance and the arrest of all suspected radicals who were "loafing about unnecessarily."[28] Soon after, *Dos lebn* published a cartoon depicting an angry police officer confronting a group of Jewish men who are praying with exaggerated motions. "What, a rally on the street?" the officer asks; "No, we are praying, trying to keep warm," comes the answer. " — Durnovo announced — 'anyone trying to get warm, I will leave alone.' "[29] If this cartoon made a mockery of Durnovo's quest for order and control, others pictured him as a powerful force for stasis. In one such cartoon, Durnovo is depicted sharing a carriage with Tsar Nicholas and attempting to coerce two emaciated horses to pull their carriage through thick mud.[30]

Other images of Durnovo vilified him as the heartless force behind officially sponsored violence. In one cartoon, Durnovo is shown at home, his head exaggeratedly small in comparison to the grand tiger skin rug upon which his feet rest. He is chatting with his superior, the prime minister. The subject of their conversation is a controversy surrounding Witte's health that had developed over the preceding weeks. "The doctors say I have a heart murmur," Witte complains to Durnovo, "and should resign." "People say that I have no heart at all," replies Durnovo, "therefore I will never resign!"[31] Lakhovski's most lacerating depiction of Durnovo appeared soon after the dismissal of the minister was announced in April of 1906. The cartoon depicts a mass of dead bodies, several still hanging on the gallows, flanked by burning homes and a heavily guarded train departing to Siberia. Durnovo is featured walking away, his back to the gruesome scene. The caption: "I leave with a clean conscience" (figure 3.4).[32]

Cartoons such as these indicate that despite stylistic idiosyncrasies, Lakhovski and *Dos lebn* remained in animated conversation with the world of Russian letters. Perhaps the clearest indication of this was the newspaper's adulatory depiction of the Russian Duma, an institution that came to embody the paper's (fleeting) dreams of a democratic and functionally multiethnic Russia. In a number of cartoons published in *Dos lebn* shortly after the First Duma was declared dissolved, a prim aristocratic woman was presented as the embodiment of Russia and the Russian parliament.[33] In one cartoon, she is shown dressed entirely in white, grimacing as she listens to a government minister playing "the declaration" on a clarinet. "Stop your playing," she cries, "you are hitting so many false notes" (figure 3.5).[34] In another, the "Duma" looks dejectedly downward at a group of bureaucrats (rendered recognizable by their hats and uniforms) who restrict her to a circle made by

‫.אַז נשה ערק בט מיזיהקן קהוקן: כינם ראָם אָין אָנגעזאָן!‬
‫(זיריסאָם'ם הקוטער)‬

Figure 3.4. "I leave with a clean conscience!" *Dos lebn* #63, 18
March 1906.

their clenched hands. The Duma is trapped, as the caption suggests, by "a
magic ring."[35] That the woman in both of these cartoons is an ethnic Russian is irrefutable. The signs are emphatic: her tiny mouth, the shape of her
eyebrows and face, the style of her dress, the cut of her hair all point to her
ethnic origins. In every respect, she resembles the kind of female figures
that graced the Russian-language press of St. Petersburg. In *Ovod* (St. Petersburg, 1906), this figure mournfully examines her crumpled hat, labeled
"Duma."[36] In *Svoboda* (St. Petersburg, 1905–1906), she represents the press
being bullied and gouged by menacing officials.[37] In *Sekira* (St. Petersburg,
1905–1907), she is rendered as a Christ figure, complete with a crown of
thorns, struggling to keep a cross aloft on her shoulder as jeering bureaucrats look on.[38] In these journals, as in *Dos lebn,* this woman demands solidarity of her readers. But in the pages of this Yiddish journal, depictions of
this woman gained meanings of their own, partly because of her ethnicity
and partly because of her gender. For readers of Yiddish, this woman served
as a reminder that Russianness depended upon geography rather than eth-

‏— נאטאלי, הערט אויף צו שפיעלען! איהר נעהמט אזוי פיעל פאלשע נאמען!..‏

Figure 3.5. "Stop your playing! You are hitting so many false
notes!" *Dos lebn* #112, 25 May 1906.

nicity. She was a reminder that one need not be ethnically Russian (*russkii*)
to be a member of the Russian polity (*rossiiskii*). It was an awkward message,
particularly for an erstwhile Zionist journal to advance. But it was an awk-
wardness that reminds us that behind *Dos lebn*'s didactic commentary lay a
mostly wordless struggle: the struggle of a journal attempting to reinvent
itself, usually to accord with transformations in Jewish party politics and
Jewish popular opinion.

This delicate political balancing act — between *rossiiskii* activism and Jewish self-consciousness — underlay other cartoons as well. Consider the following example: in the center of one cartoon sits the "Duma," again depicted as a woman, this time with hands and feet bound (figure 3.6). Here
the Duma is presented in an ethnically generic fashion, for she wears the

טשמנהטומ רעטנה און פים.

Figure 3.6. "Bound hand and feet." *Dos lebn* #132, 17 June 1906.

long braids and modest clothing that would be common to working-class women of a variety of ethnic and religious backgrounds. Around her feet stand Russians of all ethnic and social types: a posh urban couple, he with a cane and top hat, she with a jaunty flower in her hair; a Central Asian–looking man with a wide-cuffed robe and fur hat; an Orthodox Jew with a beard and caftan; a Russian peasant couple, the man with knee-high boots, knickers, and a rope round his waist. These people, tiny in comparison with the towering Duma, have outstretched hands. They are pleading, some on their knees, for the Duma's release.[39] Sartorial and physiognomic distinctions are critical to the comprehension of this cartoon. Paradoxically, the distinctions emphasize differences in order to promote unity — a unity that is the product of (and that is intended to produce) protest. Rehabilitating the Duma, this cartoon suggests, is not an ethnic but an intra-ethnic goal. This distinction between ethnicity and politics was new. Only months earlier while defending Zionism, *Der fraynd* had drawn attention to the imbrication of the two. Now, *Dos lebn* was promoting the notion that Russia could form a single political entity made up of diverse ethnic parts. Once again, we see how *Dos lebn* used cartoons to signal that the paper was jettisoning the politics of ethnic nationalism in favor of the politics of multi-ethnicity and, at one and the same time, tending toward political accommodation at a time when Jewish socialism commanded Russian Jewish society.

Not only did this cartoon reflect shifts in Jewish party politics, like the aforementioned image of the anthropomorphized Duma, but it also looked to Russian-language sources, where images of women as victims were common. The persistent appearance of such images, it has been suggested, was born of an anxiety brought on by Russia's struggle with modernity.[40] While the same might be said of Lakhovski's cartoon, images of captive women in the Yiddish press had their own layers of meaning. At least in the Russian Jewish educated class, it was Jewish women rather than Jewish men who tended to negotiate between the Jewish and non-Jewish and between the traditional and the modern — particularly in their capacity as breadwinners and students of secular learning.[41] Thus while in the world of Russian letters a picture of a captive woman might evoke anxiety about challenges to traditional gender norms and social practices — that is, anxiety *about* change — in the world of Yiddish letters, a captive woman might evoke anxiety about the *obstruction* of change. In addition to commenting on the imperiled state of the Russian Duma, then, this cartoon may have been commenting on the rise of reactionary politics in Russia, a political development that threatened to quell the advances made by the opposition during the revolution.[42]

In *Dos lebn,* the Duma was anthropomorphized into male as well as female form. In the earliest months of *Dos lebn*'s run, cartoons frequently represented Russia and the First Duma as a male peasant engaged in rural handicrafts. This figure, too, was borrowed from Russian sources, among them the Russian satirical journal *Signal.*[43] In *Signal* and *Dos lebn,* the peasant sports a bowl-cut and knee-high boots, holds an enormous club, and scratches his head in bewilderment. In one cartoon in *Dos lebn,* his back is to the reader as he stares in dismay at a swamp, murmuring, "Everything will have to be rebuilt from scratch!" (figure 3.7).[44] Like his female counterpart, this male peasant served as a thinly veiled metaphor for the Russian Duma. Like the Duma, he is at once imbued with tremendous strength and simultaneously rendered impotent. Large and strong, he is nonetheless confronted with a decaying landscape that he is little able to revivify and is, in the process, deprived of a voice and any real autonomy. The cartoon implies that if this peasant's form and faculties are at odds with one another, so too are the Russian Parliament's. Despite appearances to the contrary, this institution continued to lack political power, autonomy, and voice.

‏– װָס װעט אַלץ דאַרפֿעט אָנהײבֿען בױעַן פֿון דאָס נײַ!‏

Figure 3.7. "Everything will have to be rebuilt from scratch!"
Dos lebn #102, 9 May 1906.

Some of Lakhovski's other cartoons exaggerated the corporeality of the Russian peasant as a means of commenting on the impotence of Russia's parliament. In one striking example, Russia as peasant appears with belt, pockets, and boots stuffed with bureaucrats straining to escape (figure 3.8). The peasant stands still, an absent expression on his face. He is towering over "Europe," a short, corpulent figure draped in fur, who muses "the Russian peasant always seems so small, so weak!"[45] Tiny, pompous, gratuitously formal Europe is clearly the butt of this joke, as are the numerous useless officials struggling to free themselves from Russia's form. It is Europe's conflation of form and function that makes this cartoon funny: he commits the naïve mistake of being impressed by the peasant's presumed

איראפאיו דער רוסישער פויער זאם זיך סיד זאָמענדיק אױפאַמערזיען פאר אזא קלײנעם, פאר
אזא שוואכען!..

Figure 3.8. "Europe: 'the Russian peasant always seems so small, so weak!' . . ." *Dos lebn* #103, 10 May 1906.

vitality. Readers were assumed to understand otherwise. They would grasp that despite the peasant's girth, he (like the Russian parliament for which he stood) was but a vehicle for the parliamentarians who gathered uselessly in his folds.

If Europe's ironic assessment of the Russian peasant served as a thinly veiled illusion to the parliament's impotency, for Jewish readers, this car-

די רעדנ֗ער אין דער סאָביאַרקסמאָנעט דיקא

Figure 3.9. "The speakers in the Russian Duma." *Dos lebn* #70, 26 March 1906.

toon offered still more. As it invited ridicule of Europe and Russia's parliamentarians, the cartoon demanded sympathy with the Russian peasant. It tempted readers to identify with Russia's mass, its as-yet unused strength, its features and garb, and even its dimwittedness. To this end, the portrayal of "Russia's" physiognomy was once again significant. As figure 3.8 reveals, his face is round, with a knobby nose, fleshy cheeks, and well-trimmed sideburns. It is not a Jewish face. Nor is his posture, or his dress, stereotypically Jewish. On the contrary, he caricatures not simply any peasant, but an ethnic Russian peasant, presented in the most exaggerated and distinct form possible. And yet, like the female aristocrat, this Russian peasant is meant to arouse the empathy of Jewish readers. The success of the satire depends upon it. Though readers could physically distinguish themselves from this Russian peasant, they were nonetheless encouraged to ally themselves with Russia's civic body. Like images of a captive female Duma, this Russian peasant invited Jewish readers to feel empathy and sympathy for the plight of Russia, reminding them that they, too, were limbs of the Russian body politic — connected to, though not the visage of, Russian society.

As with the preceding cartoon, *Dos lebn*'s cartoons identified representatives to the Duma as favored targets of sarcasm, particularly by late spring 1906. When the delegates to the First Duma were elected in April 1906, members of the liberal opposition had secured a majority of the seats. Quickly thereafter it became clear that Russian bureaucrats kept the institution in a stranglehold. *Dos lebn* represented this situation with acerbity. The paper published a cartoon depicting two Duma representatives in dialogue, both with padlocks on their mouths, a mindful bureaucrat hovering nearby (figure 3.9).[46] Other cartoons were even more explicit. One presented elected representatives of the Duma approaching the parliament in luxurious private carriages but leaving, in equal numbers, as prisoners in police carriages.[47] Lakhovski inevitably depicted representatives to the Duma as short, heavy men swaddled in elaborate layers of badges and uniforms, with the bulbous darkly colored noses of drunkards.[48] These delegates express no awareness of their impotence, a sign that *Dos lebn* had more sympathy for the socialist parties that boycotted the Duma elections than for the Zionist parties that sent delegates to serve in it. Perhaps these delegates — because of and not despite their enforced powerlessness — were perceived as no different than the officials and ministers who censored them. Indeed, officialdom in general was on several occasions the butt of Lakhovski's humor. Around the time of the holiday Sukkot, Lakhovski contributed a cartoon to the Yiddish journal *Der sheygets* depicting Russian officialdom as a hog (figure 3.10).[49] The oversized animal leans heavily against a crumbling *sukkah* (the ritual structure used in the celebration of Sukkot), representing the Russian parliament. Under the hog's weight, the structure sags dangerously, on the verge of collapse.[50]

If Russia and Russianness could be given an empathetic face in the political cartoons of *Dos lebn*, Jews and Jewishness were depicted far more ambiguously. News of "The Jewish street" (once a regular column in *Der fraynd*) faded to make room for *Dos lebn*'s new foci of political criticism. *Dos lebn* conversed far less with the Yiddish-speaking world that *Der fraynd* had engaged with. Letters from *Der fraynd*'s correspondent in South Africa disappeared, while articles on Jewish communities abroad that dotted *Der fraynd* and the weekly supplement *Der fraynd baylage* all but vanished. References to Zionism and forms of Jewish territorialism that did appear in the paper were more likely to be satirical than newsworthy, and more often appeared not in the main body of *Dos lebn* but in the satirical supplement *Der bezem*. Like *Dos lebn*, *Der bezem* featured cartoons, but rather than satirizing imperial politics, as did the cartoons of *Dos lebn*, *Der bezem*'s cartoons tended to satirize Jewish party politics.[51] Coverage of state politics — even in cartoon form — was thereby labeled "news," while coverage of Jewish politics was labeled "satire."

די סופה

Figure 3.10. "The *sukkah.*" *Der sheygets,* undated, 1906.

The cartoons, caricatures, and satirical texts that appeared in *Der bezem* suggested once again how fully this once-Zionist periodical had reoriented its political focus. The paper took particular delight in mocking territorial Zionists, as in the following selection from the day's "telephone messages":

> **London.** A telegram has been received from Mr. [Israel] Zangwill stating that the minister of the ocean has agreed to give the Jews a charter for the land that was created [by the parting of the Red Sea] when the Jews left Egypt.
> **Egypt.** 24 hours ago, [Manya] Vilbushevitsh studied the ocean-territory and reached the conclusion that it is the first spot in history where Jews laid a free foot. . . .
> **Ramses.** [Protests denounce the granting of] the "historical ground" [identified in] Vilbushevitsh's announcement.[52]

Cartoons were also used to ridicule the fissures in Jewish party politics and attempts at ideological reconciliation between Zionism, socialism, and opposition politics. Perhaps the most vivid of these was a cartoon entitled "The arrival of the *dergreykher*" (figure 3.11). The Union for the Attainment of Equal Rights for the Jewish People (known popularly as "the Attainers" [*dergreykher*]), was an organization founded in Vilna in March of 1905 by representatives of the main wings of Russian Jewish politics—the Zionists, Liberal Autonomists, and Radical-Liberals (or soon-to-be Kadets).[53] The cartoon presents three figures. Two are leaders of the Union for Equal Rights: the Zionist Shmarya Levin and the Radical Liberal Maksim Moiseevich Vinaver. The Union's goal was to promote political and national rights for Russian Jewry and to defend the restructuring of Russia as a parliamentary democracy. As the cartoon suggests, the leaders of the organization disagreed over whether to give priority to the struggle for Jewish national representation or to territorialism. Thus Levin, representing the territorialists, stretches his hand in the direction of Palestine that hovers above him, while Vinaver strains toward a ministerial seat just out of reach. Meanwhile, a third figure careens toward the two, gripping one hand into a menacing fist and holding in the other a flag that reads, "Workers, unite!" The caption relays the message of a worker frustrated by the negotiations of the Zionists and the opposition: it says, "Before you get yours, I will get mine!"[54]

In some sense, the protesting worker is the hero of this cartoon. While Levin and Vinaver reach toward unattainable goals, this worker, at least, has two prizes firmly in hand—his socialist message and his powerful fist. And yet he, too, cannot escape the cartoon's ridicule. His careening posture and exaggerated facial features render him—and the socialist cause he represents—comical and clumsy. Arguably, it is not the individuals in this cartoon who are vulnerable to satire, then, but the union of the three. *Der bezem,* it would seem, was skeptical not only of the viability of socialism, Zionism, or opposition politics, but of the possibility that political consensus could be brokered out of these warring agendas. This cartoon does not so much reject utopianisms as it mocks the attempt to reach political compromise. And this, of course, was precisely the project that *Dos lebn* was attempting.

Was *Der bezem* being used to vent some of the steam generated by *Dos lebn*'s precarious balancing act? Or was it signaling that even the editors of this journal were cognizant of the impracticality of their mission? To answer these questions, we must observe *Der bezem*'s mascot, a *bezem* (broom), shown in the hands of a comical sweeper who closely resembles the flag-waving worker in figure 3.11. The sweeper's gaze is amused and simultaneously rather fierce: his open mouth sports a wide grin exposing his teeth and lending him a slightly deranged look. From his dress, we can discern that he is working class and Orthodox. His head is covered, he wears a *kaftan* (knee-length coat) and *tallis* (prayer shawl), and has grown a beard and *peyes* (sidelocks). His pants are tucked into shiny, ankle-high workman's boots (figure 3.12).

צום צוזאַמענפּאַהר פֿון די „דערגרייכער"

אידער איהר טאָט אייערס דערגרייכט, וועל איך זיינס דערגרייכען!

Figure 3.11. "The arrival of the *dergreykher* [Congress of the
Union for Equal Rights]." *Der bezem* #42, March 1 1906.

Figure 3.12. *Der bezem* masthead, 1906

This is an image that could not have appeared in Russian Jewish periodicals of the late nineteenth century, periodicals like *Voskhod, Razsvet,* or *Hashiloah.* These were journals that prided themselves on being reading matter for educated, Russified, urban Jewish intellectuals, readers who were imagined to be clean-shaven men who would sport fashionable mustaches, waistcoats, and elegant shoes, men who would go about bareheaded, carrying books, not brooms. *Der bezem*'s logo displays a very different sense of self. By 1906, the Yiddish press was becoming confident that poor and observant Jews had a visual, if not a political, presence in Russia as warriors and custodians of revolution and as symbols of the Jewish street. At the very least, they represented a body of readers of whom Yiddish editors were increasingly compelled to be aware.[55] In this regard, there is radicalism in *Der bezem*'s picturing of *Der bezem.* This figure, after all, shows a poor man, a workingman, an angry man. In sum, he is the ultimate socialist symbol.[56]

Despite its manipulation of socialist imagery, neither *Der bezem* nor its quotidian analogue *Dos lebn* ultimately threw in its lot either with the cause of socialism or opposition politics. Instead, these journals continued to mock these political movements, Zionism, and the attempt to reconcile them. Arguably such political fungibility was less a product of a coherent (or, for that matter, fickle) political agenda than a reflection of uncertain times and, perhaps, of the very flexibility of Russian Jewish politics in the early twentieth century. *Der bezem* and *Dos lebn* used cartoons and satire to poke fun at the changes that were roiling Russian Jewish society; but this rendered neither publication immune from the challenges and confusion that change wrought.

THE "BLOODY DAYS" OF 1903–1906

The caricatures and cartoons in *Dos lebn* and *Der fraynd* gained a prominent place in the cultural landscape of Russian Jews, entertaining readers and staking out political positions for half a year. But then, almost overnight, satirical images of Jews and Jewishness ceased to appear in the pages of these publications. With these images disappeared others, among them caricatures of Russia, the Russian Duma, and Russian officialdom. In their place appeared a new genre for the Yiddish daily: the photograph. This shift to a new medium belied a political redirection, one that was in evidence in the pages of *Dos lebn* or *Der fraynd* and in Russian Jewish party politics. The cause of this political and aesthetic reorientation was the Bialystok pogrom of June 1906.

Before turning to *Der fraynd*'s rendering of the violence in Bialystok, let us consider how the paper handled the wave of anti-Jewish violence that swept Russia between 1903 and 1906. In the span of three years, somewhere between six hundred and seven hundred pogroms rocked the Russian landscape. The vast majority of these pogroms were concentrated in the Pale of Settlement and occurred directly after the issuing of the October Manifesto of 1905.[57] *Der fraynd*'s first visual documentation of pogrom violence occurred in 1903, in the wake of the Kishinev pogrom. Significantly, images of Kishinev appeared not in the main body of *Der fraynd*, but in the literary weekly *Der fraynd baylage*. This placement was not likely by design. Arguably, the Yiddish publishing industry was unprepared to document Kishinev's violence as it unfolded. Like the vast majority of Russian Jews, the producers of the paper were most likely stunned by the pogrom, which was the first major show of anti-Jewish violence in Russia since the early 1880s. Photographers intent on documenting the destruction in Kishinev may have reached the city too late to capture more timely (or more graphic) images. Those photographs that were taken, meanwhile, appear to have reached the press after a delay that rendered them less useful as documentary footage and better suited to a kind of visual retrospective. As a result of these factors, one surmises, only several pages of *Der fraynd baylage* were devoted to photographs of Kishinev's violence; several of these show evidence documenting the preparation and burial of desecrated holy books, while another captured a collection of children orphaned by the massacre.[58]

Far more extensive coverage of the 1903–1906 pogroms was presented some months later, in the photographic album *Di blutige teg* [Bloody days], published by the editors of *Der fraynd/Dos lebn* in October 1905.[59] This album was sold as a supplement for 7 kopecks, was thirteen pages long, and was printed on folio-sized paper. Unfortunately its circulation cannot be documented. Each page of *Di blutige teg* featured a cluster of photographs (ranging in number from four to a dozen per page) taken at particular pogrom sites, including Kishinev, Odessa, Kiev, Warsaw, Vilna, and Ekaterinoslav.[60]

The vast majority of *Di blutige teg*'s photographs consisted of portraits of the dead, many of which were taken at close range and that honed in on the torso and head of the victim. (This composition, as we will see, initiated a genre of pogrom photography upon which *Der fraynd* would rely heavily.) (See figure 3.13.) Other photographs depicted rows of coffins or corpses, some wrapped in prayer shawls. Additionally, *Di blutige teg* featured photographs of sites of disaster: chaotic streets, marketplaces wrecked by violence, ransacked houses and stores. These images were published without accompanying narrative, though all of the album's photographs bore captions. Most captions offered only the place of death and the names of victims. Students were also described as such, the ages of small children specified, and surviving relatives sometimes designated. In addition, the album offered several portraits of victims that had been taken prior to the pogrom. In these instances, a caption presented the name, site of death, and (less frequently) the profession of the dead.

Di blutige teg also offered viewers the chance to study photographs of corpses draped in the propagandistic banners of local socialist self-defense groups, replete with slogans in Yiddish and Russian. Such images would be absent from *Der fraynd* in the wake of the violence in Bialystok as the paper retracted its more radical stance. But as *Di blutige teg* was published in October 1905, such images served to enhance the newly radical position of *Der fraynd/Dos lebn*. Even in *Di blutige teg*, however, the potency of socialist imagery was somewhat restrained. Though the political banners depicted in these photographs were often illegible or barely legible, they were not transcribed or translated. Instead, captions ambiguously suggested that the subjects of the photographs were "members of the self-defense organization of Odessa" (and so on). This phraseology left the political substance of events somewhat vague. It implied that self-defense organizations such as these might have been overseen either by Bundist or Zionist activists. In truth, it was the Bund rather than the Zionist party that had overseen most such activities, but vagueness in this context was perhaps useful. In downplaying the competition between these movements, the significance — and perhaps, the abruptness — of *Der fraynd*'s own unfolding political reorientation was mellowed. It was not time, one gathers, for the Yiddish press to evoke political division among Jews. It was more important to emphasize burgeoning consensus, collective rage, and the point that self-defense could transcend political division.

In contrast to the aesthetic tradition that *Dos lebn* and *Der fraynd* would soon establish, *Di blutige teg* mingled cartoons and photographs. The supple-

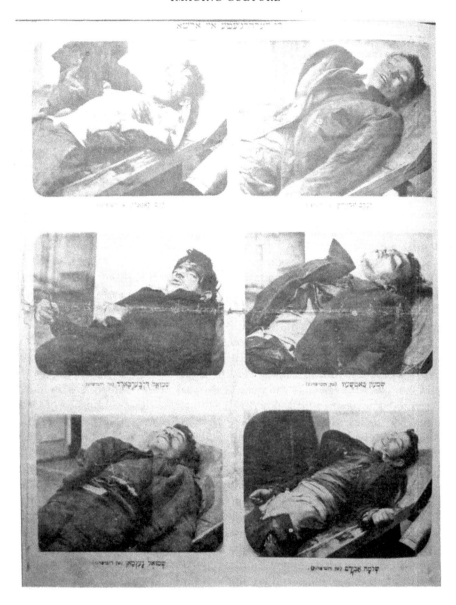

Figure 3.13. "The murdered in Warsaw." *Di blutige teg*, 1905.

ment featured a macabre title page illustrated by Lakhovski that featured what was possibly the first cartoon the artist published in the Yiddish press. The cartoon depicted serpentine creatures with human heads crawling about the ruins of the Jewish dead (see figure 3.14). Roughly a dozen corpses litter Lakhovski's scene: men and women, mothers and children, youths who died with hands clenched into fists, all tangled in thorny vines. As in the photographs that appear in the body of the album, some of these victims are wrapped in prayer shawls. Others wear tattered clothes and lie as if just fallen. One survivor is also pictured in this cartoon. Seated in the upper left-hand corner of Lakhovski's drawing and cloaked in black, this figure rests chin on hand and stares at the devastation in subdued horror. This person's posture is reminiscent of those assumed by actual survivors who were captured on film. One important detail, however, differentiates them. Clutched in the lowered hand of this mourner is an olive bough and wreath. These icons were borrowed from the art of the French Revolution and were widely reproduced in Russian art around 1905. The first represented revolution and the quest for freedom, the second martyrdom.[61] In the rendering of this compact figure, Lakhovski was helping to push *Der fraynd* to the left, toward the politics of socialism, opposition, and the spirit of revolution.

If this cartoon attempted to redirect *Der fraynd*'s political orientation, the image also maintained a perceptible Zionist mooring. While the cartoon perpetuated stylistic norms borrowed from the Russian-language press (the presence of human-headed snakes, the use of the cartoon form to document the day's news, the reliance on bold black-and-white sketches), this cartoon also clung to other sources of artistic inspiration. In particular, it was influenced by the work of Ephraim Moses Lilien, whose secessionist-style renderings were closely associated with the Zionist movement.[62] On the cover page of *Di blutige teg*, Lakhovski reproduced numerous motifs Lilien had recently canonized: the Star of David, the bodies entrapped in thorny vines, the "oriental" sandal gracing the survivor's foot, the brooding posture assumed by the seated witness, and the menacing presence of snakes. The difference between Lakhovski and Lilien's renderings is also striking. In images by Lilien, figures like these gaze not at landscapes of violence, but at utopian terrains, particularly at the cityscape of Jerusalem.[63] In Lakhovski's rendition, however, the pogrom survivor stares at a dystopian scene of destruction far closer to home. Much like *Der fraynd* itself, this witness is at once rooted in the aesthetics of Russian Zionism and radicalized by events around him. Like *Der fraynd*, he is poised to jettison a vision of Zion in favor of a less idyllic reality. At the same time, however, he (like *Der fraynd* itself) has not yet extricated himself from a Zionist landscape.[64]

If Lakhovski's cartoon for *Di blutige teg* bridged *Der fraynd*'s Zionist past and radical future, it also suggested that while visions of Zion could, at this interval, be laid aside, they were not easily extinguished. This was true (as we

Figure 3.14. *Di blutige teg* cover, 1905

will shortly see) for *Der fraynd,* and it was also true for Lakhovski personally. Just three years after Lakhovski's cartoons dominated the pages of the St. Petersburg Yiddish press, the artist left the city to assume a position at the Bezalel Academy of Arts and Design in Jerusalem, a personal and political voyage that would have seemed unimaginable but a few months earlier. Lakhovski did not, in any case, find peace in his new home. Shortly after moving to Jerusalem, Lakhovski returned to St. Petersburg to resume his engagement in the Russian art world.[65] Unlike the survivor he created for *Di blutige teg,* it would seem, Lakhovski was unable to reconcile his utopian vision of Zion with his deeply rooted commitment to the Russian cultural landscape. Or perhaps the reverse is closer to the truth. Perhaps Lakhovski's radicalism and his Zionism were seamlessly integrated rather than in contest, and perhaps the story of Lakhovski and his art reminds us how porous Russian Jewish politics were in the first decade of the twentieth century.[66] Indeed, Lakhovski's extraordinary personal transitions in many ways mimicked those of *Der fraynd.* After voyaging from Zionism to radicalism, this newspaper, too, was jolted back to a nationalist stance. And, in reinventing itself not once but thrice, it served as evidence of the fluid boundaries that defined turn-of-the-century Russian Jewish party politics.

GRIEF ON FILM, RADICALISM IN RETREAT: POGROM
PHOTOGRAPHS AND THE RUSSIAN YIDDISH PRESS REALIGNED

If signs of the persistent appeal of Zionism were embedded in *Der fraynd*'s first expressions of sympathy with socialist and opposition politics, these political sentiments became irrevocably contradictory in the wake of the Bialystok pogrom of June 1906. While there were hundreds of pogroms in Russia in the period stretching from 1903 to 1906, arguably the Bialystok pogrom was unusual in a variety of ways. First, the violence in Bialystok was particularly intense: in the course of two weeks, approximately two hundred Jews were killed and seven hundred injured.[67] Second, this outbreak of anti-Jewish violence came on the heels of a period of relative calm. From February to June 1906, there were no reported pogroms in Russia.[68] Significantly, this period overlapped almost precisely with the publication of *Dos lebn. Der fraynd* was resurrected in July 1906, just as the paper began to report on the violence in Bialystok. This synchronicity was not coincidental. *Dos lebn* had been created, after all, to reflect the growing support for revolution on the Jewish street. And, as enthusiasm for the revolutionary cause faded, the paper was poised to reclaim its original name and political posture, which is precisely what happened in the aftermath of the violence in Bialystok.

That the Bialystok pogrom inspired such political redirections points to a significant way in which this pogrom differed from its immediate predecessors. While the pogroms of the preceding years had tended to push Jews toward opposition and socialist politics, the outbreak of violence in Bialystok seemed to push Jews away from the radical cause. Since 1903, Russian Jews had tended to perceive anti-Jewish violence as an expression of the Russian right, but the violence in Bialystok challenged this reigning hypothesis.[69] Coming as it did on the heels of five months of concerted revolutionary activity and relatively subdued violence against Russia's Jews, the Bialystok pogroms seemed irrefutable evidence of how little had been (or would be) changed by intra-ethnic radicalism. The scope of the violence in Bialystok seemed to depend upon passivity at best and collusion at worst. Thus the government was accused of inaction — a charge unheard of in an era in which the ministry of war was campaigning for the expansion of repressive powers.[70] More importantly, in Russian- and Yiddish-language sources, Russian Jews accused local political parties of colluding with the ever-more organized Russian right in promoting (or at least tolerating) violence.[71] Jews' confidence in revolution was becoming tainted by suspicion: not only of the efficacy of activism, but of the resolve of non-Jewish allies. It mattered little whether these forms of collusion were imaginary or real. Both nonetheless undermined Jewish faith in the pan-ethnic struggle for Russian governmental reform, a strategy upon which the Bund's popularity had been built.

In the wake of the Bialystok pogrom *Der fraynd*, too, began to express a sense of distance from the pan-ethnic revolutionary spirit of the previous months. Once again, visual texts proved instrumental in articulating political redirection. Rather than illustrating radicalism, these texts attempted to rehabilitate a nationalist agenda. In the weeks after the Bialystok pogrom, anthropomorphic images of Russia and the Russian Duma ceased to appear in *Der fraynd*'s main pages. Cartoons directed at the illegitimacy of the regime were replaced with photographs of the distraught faces of Jewish survivors and the bloodied faces of the Jewish dead. At the same time, the paper ceased to publish Lakhovski's cartoons. The last appeared on July 6, 1906, just as the paper was presenting its most detailed coverage of events in Bialystok. The tactic of satire — its aesthetic and political power — had become outdated almost overnight. What is more, photographs of Bialystok's victims retroactively undermined the force of *Dos lebn*'s cartoons. Once the exclusive vehicle of radical critique, cartoons now seemed outdated, frivolous. *Der fraynd* seemed to be asserting the impossibility of representing deaths — Jewish deaths — through other media.[72]

The Yiddish press was not alone in representing Jewish suffering. Photographs in *Der fraynd baylage* and *Di blutige teg* participated in what has been called an aesthetic of *Judenschmerz* (Jewish suffering) that permeated the multiple media of Jewish art in the first decade of the twentieth century.[73] Lilien's drawing "Dedicated to the Martyrs of Kishinev" was perhaps the most widely viewed work of this genre, though turn-of-the-century European Jewish painters, too, looked to pogroms and pogrom victims for inspiration.[74] Nor was *Der fraynd* the only journal to publish images from pogrom-torn Bialystok. Photographic images of the event appeared in myriad journals of the day, in the socialist and Zionist-inclined Yiddish press, for example, as well as in radical Polish-language periodicals.[75] It is likely that these images migrated from the Yiddish press to the Russian- and Polish-language presses, reversing the more common flow of influence.

Photographs of the violence in Bialystok that appeared in *Der fraynd* had an emphasis and an aesthetic all their own. They tended, indeed, to be highly formulaic. Most depicted single or multiple corpses, lying alone in a coffin on the ground with others, a surviving relative nearby. These photographs are sometimes gory, but more often than not both people (living and dead) seem impassive. The faces of the dead are propped so that they stare vacantly at the camera. The living, in contrast, look at the dead, resting their elbows on coffin-edges. In these carefully arranged poses there is an eerie elegance reminiscent of the portraits favored by Russia's portrait photographers.[76] The survivors pictured are mostly women and children. They do not cry or seem to mourn. Theirs are faces of resignation, exhaustion, shock. Bialystok itself is never pictured in *Der fraynd*, though fires, bombs, and lootings are all described in accompanying articles. In previous coverage of pogrom violence that appeared in *Di blutige teg* and *Der fraynd baylage*, survival had been a central theme. In *Der fraynd*, it was death that was news. The paper's photographs, filled with empty faces, depict death itself: not the act of violence or the process of destruction, nor even the attempt to cope with the aftermath, but the intimate relationship between life and death. They convey an intimacy that bespeaks danger. The photographs hint that death hovers around life, that the living are at risk of dying, that, indeed, all Russian Jews are vulnerable. In these images, as in Bialystok, death and danger are associated with being a Russian Jew.

Thus *Der fraynd*'s photographs diverted attention from the perils of the class system and the hazards of living under an undemocratic regime, focusing attention, instead, on the rise of antisemitism and the hazards of multi-ethnic political alliances. These images did not explicitly blame revolutionaries for pogrom violence (as did an earlier generation of pogrom literature). But they nonetheless intimated that the revolutionary cause had failed to forestall bloodshed. In all of these senses, the photographs that appeared in *Der fraynd* were completely unlike Lakhovski's cartoons. They replaced a persecuted Russia with a persecuted Jew, thereby redesigning the face of protest and victimhood. In the world of Yiddish letters, the Revolution of 1905–1907 ended some months earlier than it did in the world of Russian letters, or, at the least, after the violence in Bialystok, the producers of the Yiddish press seemed inclined to differentiate these worlds after a period of unusual symbiosis.

Inevitably, the differentiation of worlds Russian and Jewish was awkward, particularly as Lakhovski's cartoons had so recently strained to emphasize their interconnectedness. It was not just the decoupling of these "bodies" that smacked of artificiality. So too did the implication that the Jews of Russia were (or were becoming) a single, discrete entity. Arguably, just as the face of Russia was invented in Lakhovski's cartoons, Jewish faces were invented by the photographs of Bialystok. This is not to say that these images did not record real deaths. It is, instead, to suggest that the Jewishness of these photographed bodies (both living and dead) was visually reiterated in ways that were previously unknown within Jewish custom. Traditionally, the practice of rapidly cleaning, shrouding, and burying the dead was of the utmost cultural and spiritual importance to Eastern European Jews. In addition, contact with the bodies of the dead was not traditionally the obligation of family members, but of the *hevra kadisha,* a burial society made up of members of the community. Finally, the Ashkenazi tradition of mourning tended to be neither subdued nor understated, as are the faces of the living in these photographs. On the contrary, the process of grieving, formalized by the ritual of *shiva* (the seven days of mourning that follow a Jewish death), was both intense and somewhat public.[77] The photographs that appeared in *Der fraynd* elided such norms. They emphasized that the shock their subjects were experiencing was political rather than cultural and presentist rather than primordial. In so doing, *Der fraynd*'s photographs conveyed sympathy at once with Bialystok's victims and the Zionist project.

If images of Bialystok's victims were parting with old Jewish traditions, names of the dead were used to mark this tragedy as unmistakably Jewish. Photographs bore captions of the names of the deceased, and by the end of the first week of violence, these names were amassed in a list, framed in a bold black rectangle and centered on the paper's first page (see figure 3.15). The list contained forty-nine names, and a caption added "in addition to the forty-nine dead listed here, there are many others—women, children, youths, old people, whose names we do not yet know."[78] Some had annotations attached: "13) Matisyohu Lapidus (a school boy from the Komertz school, seventh class)." Others list the professions of the dead or their cause of death:

> 5) Eynshteyn
> 6) his son
> Found bound together, gouges in their heads, hearts, eyes.

This graphic, like the paper's photographs, reiterated that Bialystok was a Jewish—and not a working-class or a Russian—tragedy. To this end, articles about the pogrom adopted a style of their own. Their Yiddish was seeped with *loshn koydesh* (words of Hebrew derivation). Their prose was poetic, impressionistic, often apocalyptic. They described the writer's visit to Bialystok in great detail (sometimes on an hour-to-hour basis): author and ethnographer S. An-sky, one of *Der fraynd*'s "special correspondents" to Bialystok, led readers through the ransacked city street by street.[79] Such articles were almost photographic in their detail, both in their meticulousness and insofar as they intertwined scenes real and imagined. Consider the following account:

> We don't yet know any details. But why are they important? From our vast, sad experience gained from pogroms to date we know the details with precision. It is enough to hear the word "pogrom" in order to imagine the hellish picture: rivers of blood, murdered and desecrated bodies, torn-apart children, ripped-up books, bodies intentionally destroyed: the whole of hell, with all of its suffering and anguish.[80]

This selection, like nearly all accounts of the pogroms, was written for readers who had a shared sense — or, perhaps, an emerging sense — of "our vast experience," that is, the Russian Jewish experience. As texts like An-sky's made clear, *Der fraynd* was relinquishing its willingness to speak of pan-ethnic activism in order to emphasize self-reflection, martyrdom, and national grief.

Self-reflection, martyrdom, national grief: arguably these were sentiments increasingly identified with the Zionist movement. Indeed, it was not just An-sky's words that pushed readers to new emotional heights — the style of his prose, too, was evocative of an emerging genre of pogrom literature that was affiliated with the Zionist movement. Most established, perhaps, was the genre of

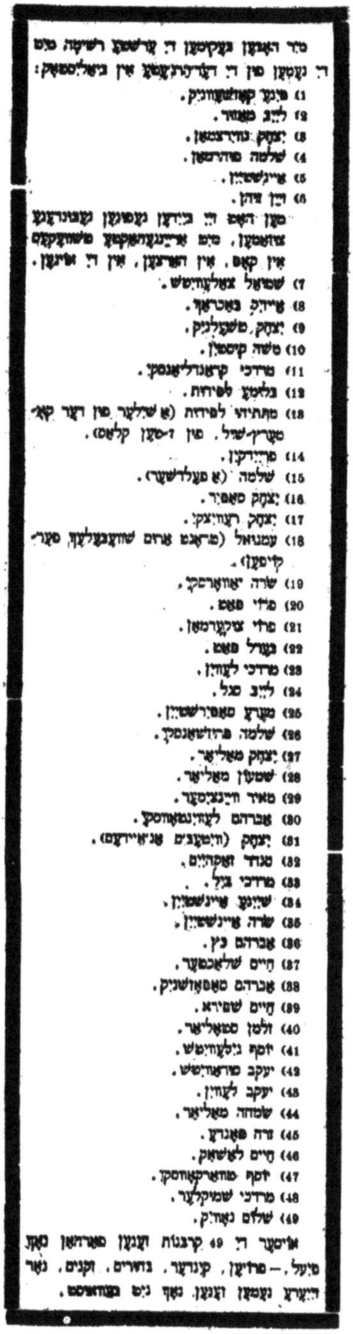

Figure 3.15. "Victims of the Bialystok pogroms." *Der fraynd* #124, 7 July 1906.

pogrom poetry, made famous by Chaim Nakhman Bialik's "In the City of Slaughter," which the poet penned in the aftermath of the Kishinev pogrom of 1903.[81] Famously, Bialik's poem condemned survivors for their assumed passivity, and, in part by so doing, "built the pogrom up into an archetype based on a support system of martyrdom, resurrection, retribution, confession, and mourning. . . . [while] sever[ing] the link to God and call[ing] for His abdication."[82] To put this in a slightly different way, Bialik's poem had not only promoted mourning, but it had also politicized it, displacing divine omnipotence in favor of human agency in the pursuit of national destinies. Though An-sky's writing is free of the condemnation that courses through Bialik's influential poem, *Der fraynd*, too, seemed to be placing the Jewish nation at the heart of its narration of destruction.[83] Thus An-sky's reports from Bialystok were *not* accompanied by photographs of survivors brandishing the banners of socialist organizations (such as readers encountered in *Di blutige teg* and in other more stubbornly socialist periodicals). Instead, they were illustrated with photographs of gruesome deaths and enervated witnesses — by the faces of Jewish martyrs.

Seen in this light, *Der fraynd*'s imaging of the Bialystok pogroms seemed evidence that the paper's support for Bundism had been conditional: evidence, indeed, of the enormously strategic use to which Lakhovski's cartoons had been put. It would, however, be misleading to suggest that the Bialystok pogroms resuscitated the "true" orientation of this once-Zionist periodical. More accurate is to assert that the paper's use of photographs in the wake of the violence in Bialystok was evidence of how smoothly the Russian Yiddish press of the early twentieth century moved between political orientations.

If *Der fraynd*'s imaging of Bialystok conveys something of the nature of early-twentieth-century Russian Jewish party politics, it also documents the evolving influence of the Yiddish press. Echoing other historical scholarship, this chapter has argued that the scope and timing of the Bialystok pogrom enervated the radical cause in the eyes of many Russian Jews and in the world of Yiddish letters. But *Der fraynd*'s coverage of the Bialystok pogrom allows us to tell a slightly different story as well. Perhaps it was not so much that the Bialystok pogrom differed from its predecessors that caused this event to take on such importance in the eyes of Jewish radicals. Perhaps, instead, it was the *coverage* of this wave of violence that so influenced Russian Jewish readers. By the summer of 1906, the Yiddish press was able to report on pogrom violence both quickly and graphically, in part because there were so many newspapers and reporters who could relay the story instantly. Thus topics and texts that might have been relegated to supplements three years earlier due to the newspapers' inability to cover them in a timely manner had, by mid-1906, become the day's news. Yiddish news sources could provide more details instantaneously and, as a result, could be far more affecting. By 1906, the Yiddish press was not so much reflecting shifts in Jewish attitudes as producing them, not so much reporting on as creating news.

This chapter has used visual texts to tell a political story, but it has, in the process, demonstrated that visual history is far from teleological in nature. Certainly in the case of *Der fraynd/Dos lebn,* visual texts do not allow us to create a story of the inevitable triumph of nationalism or any other single political ideology.[84] On the contrary, the history of *Dos lebn* suggests that the path of turn-of-the-century Russian Jewish politics was far from unidirectional. The transformations of *Dos lebn* and *Der fraynd* were in many ways unpredictable and meandering. They responded to contemporary events and shifts in popular opinion while reflecting changes in Russian Jewish cultural norms and in the wider world of the Russian Empire. At the same time, these newspapers' simultaneous affinity for the icons of Zionist and opposition politics was not extraordinary. On the contrary, this seeming contradiction was enabled by the inchoate nature of Russian Jewish party politics in the first decade of the twentieth century; it reflected that this world was neither as polemical nor as rigidified as is supposed.

REPORTAGE IN THE WAKE OF REVOLUTION

What was *Der fraynd*'s future to be in the wake of the Bialystok pogroms? The paper resumed its modestly nationalist orientation, but its own history seemed to drain this political philosophy of some of its force. After the summer of 1906, *Der fraynd*'s articles returned to themes that had been absent in the paper for over a year. Long pieces once again considered the relative value of Yiddish and Hebrew. Attention was returned to affairs abroad. Though cartoons would be published by the rehabilitated *Der fraynd* after a hiatus of about a year and a half, they would never again find their way into the main body of the paper, appearing, instead, in *Der bezem* alone. Once they reappeared, their substance had changed. Few were concerned with the illegitimacy of the Russian regime.[85] The vast majority of cartoons, instead, satirized controversies among and within the main Jewish political movements. One such cartoon satirized the political and professional struggles between Hebrew poet Chaim Nakhman Bialik and Yosef Klausner, editor of the Hebrew periodical *Hashiloah.* The two are seated on a single small table, each "editor" (as the caption reads) vying for more space.[86] A second cartoon depicts a confused Orthodox man seated in a carriage that is being pulled in opposing directions. At one end sits Yiddish activist Nathan Birnbaum, holding the reins of a horse labeled "Yiddish." At the other sits the Zionist theoretician Ahad Ha'am, holding the reins of a horse labeled "Hebrew."[87] Unlike the caustic cartoons of *Dos lebn,* these cartoons pass no judgment on their subjects. Instead, they depict individuals, or, in the first case, a journal, in flux between conflicting allegiances. Such ambiguity, such neutrality, would never have been expressed in the pages of *Dos lebn.*

Why, in the wake of 1906, had neutrality become a hallmark of *Der fraynd*? The first reason is that the political mood in Russia had shifted. This change reflected the regime's turn to the right. Soon after the dissolution of the Second Duma on June 3, 1907, opposition parties were severely hamstrung (they still sent representatives to the Third Duma and enjoyed parliamentary immunity, but the franchise made it difficult for them to be elected or to exercise power). Harsh penalties were instated for any journal or journalist perceived to harbor hostilities toward the government. Roughly one year after *Der fraynd* abandoned the cause of radicalism, nearly all of Russia's newspapers were required to follow suit. In retrospect, it seems that if discussion about the revolution had ended in the pages of *Der fraynd* earlier than it had in the pages of its Russian-language peers, this change actually presaged a return to political and literary quietude in the Russian press writ large. *Der fraynd*'s resumption of a moderate Zionist posture appears also to have been a response to shifts in Jewish party politics and to the expansion of the Yiddish press. As the numbers and popularity of competitors grew, the paper's producers searched for a style that might allow it to reach across ideological, geographic, and aesthetic divides that were increasingly differentiating Russian Yiddish readers one from another. It was a strategy that had succeeded once before. But by the close of the first decade of the twentieth century it would prove anachronistic.

Much to the chagrin of *Der fraynd*'s editorial board, Nokhem Shtif, a sometime-contributor to *Der fraynd*, proposed a similar hypothesis in a series of controversial articles that were published in the Russian-language daily *Razsvet* in 1908. *Der fraynd*, he argued, had

> gone from being respectable to being idealistic without an ideal, radical without a clear political stance, literary without a literary style. . . . Yiddish without pathos for Yiddish, and so on — all respectable, that is to say, static, certainly not haughty . . . something of a concocted Petersburg-intellectual journal without a stance and without appeal for the great majority of readers, [a paper] that existed for itself, for its editorial board.[88]

Shtif's insight is in many ways astute, though perhaps with one exception. Paradoxically, by being static or politically ambiguous, *Der fraynd* had not so much broken with its past as revived a tradition of caution that it had established in 1903 and overlooked in 1906. This was a tradition that, because it was defied by *Dos lebn,* had been forgotten.

Perhaps it was forgotten willfully. A stunning part of the history of *Dos lebn* is its utter lack of a sense of history. The journal is quite absent from studies of satire and caricature of the Russian Revolution of 1905–1907. Notably, the elision of Yiddish sources from the historiography is not a result of the relative quality of *Dos lebn* or other Yiddish satirical publications of the day. The cartoons from these papers certainly compare stylistically and in political incisiveness with cartoons that appeared in contemporary Russian-language journals. Perhaps the reason for the anonymity of Yiddish satirical sources is more political. As the history of Russian letters continues to be dominated by details about Russia's regional, ethnic, and linguistic hegemony, Yiddish radicalism is imagined to have a hermetic history, if it is allowed to claim any history at all. Perhaps, indeed, the imagined political cohesion of 1905–1907 (which seems to transfix many studies of the period) would be disrupted by recognition of its many strands.

The radical cartoons of *Dos lebn* are also barely mentioned in the memoirs and histories concerning the legacy of *Der fraynd*. Shoyl Ginzburg makes no mention of the journal in his memoir, *Amolike peterburg;* nor does Shabsay Rapoport, co-founder of the paper, in his extensive article written for the "10 Year Jubilee Anniversary Supplement" to *Der fraynd*.[89] This absence is mirrored in secondary literature focusing on the history of Russian Jewish journalism.[90] Further, information on Arnold Lakhovski is rare indeed: his name is left out of both memoirs and studies of the period. It is possible that these absences reflect a disdain for the medium of cartooning. It is possible, too, that *Dos lebn* received little attention because of the dwindling popularity of *Der fraynd* in the years after 1909. Moyshe Katz, who worked with *Der fraynd* after it relocated to Warsaw in 1909, recalled that after this point "*Der bezem* was sharp, funny, original, but just like *Der fraynd*, whose supplement it was, it was published irregularly, from time to time, with many mistakes, and didn't have a great success among readers."[91] What this suggests is that by 1909 (and even, as we have seen, by mid-1906), satire was less of a priority and less of a political necessity than it had once been. Its memory, indeed, may have become something of an embarrassment. One gathers that as Russian Jewish politics became increasingly partisan, those associated with *Der fraynd* preferred to overlook what could now be perceived as the paper's chameleon-like political nature in order to emphasize its Zionist legacy.

Images of pogrom violence have also been neglected, though for somewhat different reasons. The photographs of pogrom victims and violence that were featured in the pages of *Der fraynd baylage, Di blutige teg,* and *Der fraynd* have been fairly widely reproduced in many works of historical scholarship.[92] In every case, however, they have been employed as illustrations of fact rather than as texts that invite scrutiny. In the process, the complicated political nature of these photographs has been overlooked. This may be a sign that the aesthetic power of these images persists. Ironically, it is also a sign that *Der fraynd*'s ability to shape the news — and conceivably even to influence popular opinion — has proved remarkably enduring.

If the elision on *Dos lebn* and pogrom photography from scholarship and memoir writers of the early twentieth century is not inexplicable, it is nonetheless unfortunate. It serves as a reminder that the history of Jewish visual culture remains largely unwritten.[93] So, too, does it suggest the extent to which Russian Jewish party politics have been retroactively polemicized, not only in scholarly literature, but also in a popular consciousness that was to some extent initiated by memoirs and autobiographies penned by Russian Jewish intellectuals in the early decades of the twentieth century.

As we have seen, however, Russian Yiddish culture in print, and Russian Jewish politics more generally, were enormously elastic in the first decade of the twentieth century. During these years, Yiddish sources were juggling political alternatives at a moment in which Jewish political parties were not yet polarized. And they were drawing upon Russian-language sources while remaining aesthetically and politically independent from them. A certain subtlety governs the literary culture of this era, as it is often the implicit message of didactic texts that prove the most fascinating. Indeed, despite Moyshe Katz's suggestion that the Revolution of 1905–1907 enabled Jews to transcend fear, Yiddish newspapers of this period—much like Jewish politics more generally—were rarely as decisive as they appeared. Periodicals like *Der fraynd* could hide conservatism behind a radical mask, while satirical journals like *Der bezem* commentated soberly on the ever-evolving texture of Russian Jewish culture.

It was not only Jewish party politics that were malleable in the first decade of the century. Cartoons found their way into the Yiddish newspaper in an era in which political and ethnic distinctions could be bridged to serve a common goal, and when it was possible for Russian Jews to express optimism about the viability of democratic reform and the preservation (indeed, the protection) of multi-ethnicity. That this was a fleeting moment makes it all the more interesting. Photographs of Bialystok's dead reached readers at a time when possibilities seemed to dim—on the eve of the forcible annulment of public criticism and amidst growing skepticism about the viability of democratic reform. Together, these visual texts illustrate the complexity of the revolutionary moment and the imbrication of worlds Jewish and non-Jewish, Yiddish and Russian, Zionist and radical. They suggest that Russian Yiddish letters relied upon visual forms not only to narrate, but also to navigate and effect political change. The face of turn-of-the-century Russian Jewish culture was shifting and the Yiddish press was proving an instrument and a barometer of these refigurations.

4

THE SCIENCE OF HEALTHY LIVING

Readers of Ladino (like readers of Yiddish) received their news not only from daily newspapers, but also from supplemental journals and thematic weeklies. Weeklies and supplements conveyed their own variety of news. In their pages, readers encountered whole categories of information that were excluded from their daily newspapers: humor and satire, recipes and games, images and advice columns. Supplements and weeklies also addressed readers who were otherwise ignored by the daily press, including women, children, and families. These publications were experimental sources that expanded the scope of the popular press, the meaning of news, and the practice of reading.

This chapter turns to three supplemental periodicals that were published in association with *El tiempo.* The papers were called *El sol: revista sientifika y literaria* (Constantinople, 1877–78); *El amigo de la familia: revista periodika ilustrada* (Constantinople, 1881–86); and *El instruktor: revista sientifika y literaria* (Constantinople, 1888–89). All of these journals were created and edited by David Fresco, and all were nearly entirely composed of articles translated from contemporary (unattributed) English- and French-language periodicals. These articles were intended to educate readers about the latest trends in hygiene, child-rearing, nutrition, and the natural and human sciences. Together, they offered Jewish readers models of how to eat, drink, sleep, exercise, breath, and behave. They gave instructions about how the readers should look, what they should converse about, and in what manner they should clean and clothe themselves. In so doing, Ladino instructional journals created an itinerary for cultural transformation that fulfilled and expanded the central goal of the Alliance Israélite Universelle — that Ottoman Jewry ought to be educated (and thereby civilized) in the image of the Franco-Jewish bourgeoisie in order to compete in the emerging regional economy and be accepted as Ottoman citizens.

While instructional journals in Ladino presented readers with practical suggestions for how to embark on the "project" of Westernization, the publications also revealed how difficult a "process" this was.[1] For example, though the articles were inspired by Western sources, informant texts needed to be modified to render them appropriate for Ottoman Jewish readers. To this end, contributors to Westernizing Ladino journals embarked on cultural as well as literal acts of translations. Even if the writing was inspired by — or, indeed, lifted from — French- or English-language sources, Ladino instructional articles did not simply mimic their originals. Instead, these translated works took on different nuances and were published in such a different cultural context that they challenged and engaged various cultural models.[2] Readers of these sources, in turn, approached their reading matter actively, with interest, but also with humor and occasional disbelief.[3]

The following pages meditate on the turn-of-the-century experiences of Westernization and cultural change. Scholars of Jewish Studies have tended to fold these two phenomena into the more general historiographic categories of *assimilation* and *acculturation*. These are not terms I employ. By avoiding this language, I hope to emphasize that cultural change was never passive, transparent, or unidirectional. To some extent, this point can be generalized; in much of *fin-de-siècle* Europe, evolving Jewish cultural practices were meticulously triangulated around the poles of local custom, the emerging norms of national body politics, and traditional Jewish practice and ritual. In an Ottoman context, Jewish cultural change had an additional layer of complexity. To this more typical triangulation was added the powerful force of intra-Jewish cultural imperialism. Here (as in much of the Middle East and North Africa) Jews tended not to emulate or attempt to enter the culture of the surrounding majority but to turn for inspiration to a geographically foreign culture: the Western European Jewish bourgeoisie.[4] Accordingly, Ottoman Jewish cultural change was not triangulated but rectangulated. To be sure, this cultural geometry has parallels in other moments and contexts in European Jewish history.[5] In other cases, however, abstract influence was not encouraged by economic dependency and therefore could not be described as cultural semi-imperialism. The realization of this dynamic in the Ottoman (and wider Levantine) setting renders complex the application of historiographic vocabularies modeled on other contexts.

To suggest that the Ladino press bore the imprint of imperialism is not to suggest that it parroted Franco-Jewish texts or practices. On the contrary, the very process of mimicking the modes of the contemporary Franco-Jewish bourgeoisie enabled the Ladino press to produce new cultural forms that neither rejected the traditions of the past nor blindly followed local non-Jewish or extra-regional models. Instead, the new forms were original, creative, and self-consciously modern. By the same token, the widespread acceptance of Westernization by Ottoman Jews in Southeastern Europe — the religious elite included — ought not be assumed to have been accompanied by a dissociation from local milieus and networks.[6] Ottoman Jews did not become more Western or French, less Ottoman, or, indeed, passive recipients of semi-colonial cultural influences. Instead, the Ladino press helped synthesize a culture that resembled neither traditional Ottoman Jewish culture, nor contemporary French culture, nor the culture of the Ottoman Christian, Armenian, or Muslim bourgeoisie, though all served as influences. Ladino periodicals helped to shape a modern Ottoman Jewish culture that *borrowed* from regional, trans-national, extra-national, Jewish and non-Jewish models but also *transformed* them, creating, in the process, a culture — and a form of modernity — unique in texture and substance.

And yet Ottoman Jewish culture of the turn of the century was not infinitely hybrid, at least not in the sense implied by many contemporary theorists of identity.[7] At its core, Ottoman Jewish identity was not plural but self-consciously "Jewish," an essentialist category that held tremendous meaning, particularly insofar as it differentiated Ottoman Jews from their Christian and Muslim neighbors.[8] If Ottoman Jews viewed themselves as essentially (even quintessentially) Jewish, the Ladino press, too, came to be viewed by many as inherently Jewish regardless of content. David Fresco elaborated upon this point in the journal *El instruktor.* Because a particular journal was written for Jews, he explained, because it was written in a Jewish language and read by Jewish readers, its content — its very character — was necessarily Jewish.[9] To Fresco, informative articles about peacocks, the workings of electricity, or the circulation of air (all topics of scrutiny in the Ladino instructional press) maintained a Jewish character when and because they were published in Ladino and read by Jews. The following pages are in many ways an amplification of Fresco's argument. They consider how Ladino instructional literature — often because of and not despite its professedly non-Jewish content — reflected and affected turn-of-the-century Ottoman Jewish culture in transition, not least by encouraging readers to make themselves modern.

DISCIPLINING THE SENSES: WOMEN, CHILDREN, FAMILIES, AND THE LADINO INSTRUCTIONAL PRESS

The purpose of publishing Ladino journals of science, literature, and esoterica was clarified only in *El instruktor,* the last of three educative publications edited by David Fresco. In the first issue of the journal, Fresco outlined his motives. Ignorance, he declared, is the "mother of all crimes." Knowledge of science, on the other hand, alerts one to the existence of nature, the miracle of creation, and the supremacy of God. It leads one into a moral universe and helps bring about justice. Such abstract ambitions could also be turned to more practical uses. Fresco explained that if workers would read *El instruktor* to learn about the unknown, and if they turned to the journal with an ardor previously reserved for the Bible, the paper could become an "object of utility" for Ottoman Jews.[10]

The notions of the "useful" and the "useless" were returned to again and again in the pages of the Ladino instructional press. Educational reading, including the study of history, nature, and the French language were useful, these journals would argue, while idle hands and an ignorant woman were useless. These warnings, like the stated goals of *El instruktor,* echoed those that appeared in *El tiempo*'s first editorial, which emphasized the utility of Ladino news. The reigning assumption throughout was that turn-of-the-century Ottoman Jews desperately needed to acquire the skills that would allow them to succeed in a changing Ottoman world.

Ladino instructional journals encouraged readers to seek these skills in Western European models. In this way, the journals resembled their contemporary Turkish-language instructional sources, which also turned to French- and English-language models for inspiration.[11] Given that most turn-of-the-century Ladino journalists were more likely to be fluent in French than in Turkish, it is unlikely that Ladino sources borrowed from Turkish-language ones. Nonetheless, there is little question that the overlap in Turkish and Ladino letters reflects the shared historical mooring of the Ottoman press writ large. Turkish news in print, like Ladino news in print, was meant to be informative and useful, to help readers adjust to an evolving Ottoman economy and society. It often (though not always) reflected the enormous debt that the budding bourgeoisie owed to their British and French contemporaries.[12]

I have described this relationship as semi-imperial, an accurate term, but in a Jewish sense the concept does not fully convey the nuances in interactions between Ottoman Jews and the Franco-Jewish bourgeoisie. One reason that Ottoman Jews found contemporary French culture so compelling was that they saw in French Jewry a model of what they could and should become. In the view of Fresco and his Francophile colleagues, French Jews were emancipated, integrated into French culture, and economically successful. Their French was fluent and they considered themselves to be French rather than Jewish nationalists. But though French Jews felt comfortably French, they were also undeniably Jewish. In this sense, though French customs were not always the same as Sephardi or Ottoman Jewish practices, from the vantage of the creators of the Ladino instructional press, the majority of French customs were neither "foreign" nor "imported." The latest French trends, though often novel to Ottoman Jewish readers, were part of the corpus of modern Jewish knowledge.

Women, in particular, were regarded as the critical target for acquiring and transmitting this knowledge, and it was to women that a great number of the articles in the Ladino instructional press were directed. This fact reiterates a hypothesis advanced by other scholars of modern Sephardi culture: that is, that in the Southeastern European context, it was Jewish women rather than men who were responsible for promoting cultural change. This is quite a different model from that of Western and Central Europe, where Jewish women were often the guardians of tradition.[13] The targeting of female readers as proponents of change was a tactic that was defended in the first issue of *El instruktor.* There the first installment of a column entitled "La edukasion de la mujer" [The education of woman] appeared, the subject of which was a defense of Jewish women's right to a modern education. Education rids a woman of envy, vanity, superstition, and inarticulateness, the article argued, and it increases her knowledge of business and her sense of justice. It heightens her love of work, makes her prudent, sincere, courageous, and modest, while at the same time rendering her less false, hypocritical, intemperate, and egoistic. An educated woman gossips less and is more frank, sincere, courageous, and resigned.[14] Such lofty qualities were implicitly measured against others assumed to be prevalent among "uneducated" "Oriental Jews," and women in particular, including superstition, cunning, deceit, and wile.[15] The assumption of *El amigo de la familia* was that such instincts would fade once women adjusted their homes, bodies, and minds to suit the fashions of the West. The ordering of their space and person, it was suggested, would affect women's whole being — it would quell their passions, disabuse their faith in folk ways, and turn them, in short, into proper bourgeois subjects.

El amigo de la familia dedicated considerable time to offering female readers training in the habits of the modern woman. Much of this information was conveyed in a column entitled "Konsejos provechozos para la familia" [Helpful hints for the family]. The column advised readers how to tame unruly hair, a subject of much fascination in France.[16] It cautioned readers that when the weather was hot and humid, "the most beautiful women protect the color of their face when outdoors" in order to stay pale in complexion. Other articles counseled women to wear white to deflect the sun altogether.[17] Elsewhere, the paper reminded readers that "an honest woman washes only with water and wears her face in its natural color, conducts herself honestly and morally, for she is the queen of womanhood."[18] A treatise on the proper washing of the body encouraged women to wash their hands and face thoroughly at least once a day, and to use small quantities of soap or cognac to purify the skin.[19]

Such information served several purposes at once. On the one hand, it provided concrete advice that would allow women to emulate contemporary French meticulousness about the cleansing, scenting, and coifing of the female body.[20] On the other hand, such tips encouraged Ottoman Jewish readers to reject traditional practices and disassociate themselves from local customs. If protecting the light tone of one's skin could make one look French, such protection had the added "benefit" of distinguishing an Ottoman Jewish woman from her non-Jewish peers, many of whom were likely to have darker skin than she. And when *El amigo de la familia* encouraged women to wash "only with water," it implicitly criticized the common Levantine practice of washing with rose water. Similarly, advice on the removal of calluses (to smooth the hands, the paper suggested, soak them and abstain from heavy labor) encouraged both male and female readers to distinguish themselves from the less educated by adhering to an ethnic hierarchy of labor, with Jews dominating the "finer" professions.[21]

Even though disassociation from local practices was encouraged by Ladino instructional journals, success in pursuing this advice was by no means guaranteed. Changes in practice posed practical (if not philosophical) challenges to many readers. Western-imported toiletries were not easily available in Constantinople, and it was not until 1910 that the advertising pages of *El tiempo* included the posting of a toiletry merchant, B. Brown, who sold "all the latest goods for the toilette" in the neighborhood of Pera.[22] It was, however, in regard to the scent of roses that Jewish readers were most likely to be confounded by the Ladino press. Roses and rose water proved troublesome commodities for the contributors to *El amigo de la familia,* as these products were subjects of both scorn and praise. The heady smell of roses, one surmises, was perceived as evidence of the stagnation of the Levant and of the very stillness of its air. Elsewhere, however, readers were offered tips about the production and use of rose-scented goods. In one issue, readers could find a recipe for rose water; elsewhere, men were encouraged to use rose pomade to dye their greying temples.[23] In another issue, readers could find a recipe for an alcoholic drink made partly of rose water.[24]

The conflicting nature of such advice reflected a paradox that lay at the heart of contemporary French fashion. If in the Ottoman lands the smell of roses signified backwardness, in France it was coming to signify sophistication. Since the late eighteenth century, waters scented with rose, lavender, thyme, and rosemary — flowers and herbs common to the Mediterranean — were gaining favor in the French metropole.[25] To put this another way, while in one context the smell of roses could brand a woman as backward, in another it could distinguish her as cultivated. This was a distinction, one suspects, that was ultimately determined by ethnicity and class rather than by scent. It also produced a paradox that betrayed the complexity of the literary and cultural translation that Ladino instruction journals endeavored to achieve. Though a rose might smell the same in Paris and Constantinople, the cultural meaning of that smell was likely to differ. Similarly, articles about cuisine, couture, or cosmetics were likely to be read differently in different contexts or hands. In so many cases, the project of Westernization advocated by the Ladino press proved far more complex than its proponents would admit.

In the pages of *El amigo de la familia,* then, the scent of roses conjures up the complexity of the cultural encounter between French and Ottoman Jewish cultures. So too does it reflect the strain felt as cultural allegiances shifted and were reinvented. A sense of this strain is captured in the maudlin poem "The Rose," written by a Signora R. and published in *El amigo de la familia* in late 1881:

> In the early hours of morning,
> opening the window,
> I see a flower,
> a rose.
> I go to it and examine it,
> and with great desire,
> inhale its odor,
> admire its color.
> "Ah, my dear rose,
> you are so beautiful.
> Why is your fate,
> to die so soon?"
> And the rose said,
> "Ah, nothing is wrong, my daughter,
> Be happy,
> that I will die so soon."[26]

The rose, once irresistible, here stoically confronts its fate: to die so that newer blossoms might take its place. Here the rose serves as a metaphor for the attitude toward cultural change espoused by the Ladino press. In its adoption of the Westernizing project, presses like *El amigo de la familia* were inviting new cultural modes to replace indigenous and traditional ones.[27] That this process might inspire nostalgia in some — young women in particular — was not to be a deterrent.

In other instances, too, *El amigo de la familia* facilitated a conceptual and practical dependency on Western products and modes. Among the advice proffered by "Konsejos provechozos para la familia," for example, were hints on how to clean taffeta or remove stains from silk and other fabrics.[28] To contextualize such instructions, we must recall that for many years, the silk-producing industry — concentrated in the Ottoman city of Bursa — and the production, weaving, and dying of raw wool — based in Salonika and Safed — were dominated by Jews.[29] Though the Ottoman textile industry as a whole remained vibrant at the turn of the twentieth century, Ottoman Jewish readers were invited by Ladino sources to disassociate themselves from this economy, in part, one imagines, because Jews were less instrumental to its success.[30] Ironically, in attempting to offer Jews new economic relationships, advice like this unwittingly acknowledged the economic devolution of Ottoman Jews.

El amigo de la familia also offered advice about the running of families and homes. As it provided suggestions about dealing with children, supplying proper nutrition, using public and private spaces, and designing the layout of homes, *El amigo de la familia* continued to attempt to mold Ottoman Jewish families in the likeness of the French bourgeoisie. In the process, the journal protested the unsuitability of local (and local Jewish) practices.

El amigo de la familia supported women's education because of the many concrete benefits husbands and children would accrue. One contributor explained that while an ignorant woman was useless, an educated woman could help ensure the health, honor, and fortune of an entire family, whence the proverb "lucky is the man with an educated woman in the house."[31] Similar proverbs pepper the publication, as in phrases calling women "the flower of life," or "the natural friend of man."[32] Children, too, were assumed to benefit from a mother's knowledge. An article in *El instruktor* argued that 90 percent of the influence upon a child comes from his or her mother, a striking reversal of *halakhic* assumptions about children's education (the responsibility for which traditionally lay with fathers). Statements such as these echoed the views of the AIU.[33] In *El amigo de la familia,* practical suggestions were offered to ensure that a mother's influence would be proper. Warned one article: "First impressions are crucial!" This piece of advice was followed by a daunting litany: do not treat your child cruelly or unjustly or he will learn cruelty and injustice. Do not treat your children differently from one another, and do not impose different standards upon them. If you punish your child, do it gently, but not so gently that you coddle the child. Teach your children to speak well and to avoid base statements, so that people know they are from a good family. Teach them to be good to animals, for the child who is cruel to animals is crueler still to humans. Instill in your child kindness, a respect of God, a love of their neighbors, and a sense of charity. The same article cautioned parents (both mothers and fathers) to avoid immoral language and frivolous books.[34]

In "Konsejos provechozos para la familia," readers could discover how to prevent a child from sucking her thumb, a habit that was thought to cause teeth to grow improperly.[35] This series also taught mothers how to cure constipation and dehydration and how to prevent chilblains.[36] Worried mothers were further advised that the spread of contagious diseases would be limited if children were prevented from touching their eyes, face, and mouth.[37] Elsewhere, readers could learn how to staunch blood (by applying salt water to the wound) and to know what to do in the event of extreme blood-loss.[38] An article in *El instruktor* pointed out that if women could be taught simple rules of hygiene, they would keep a clean home and thereby prevent their children from contracting cholera.[39] To this end, a number of suggestions on the treatment of water were proffered, all undoubtedly borrowed from contemporary French journals, in which the proper use of water was frequently discussed in the mid to late nineteenth century.[40] Readers of *El amigo de la familia* were urged to heat their water to 78 degrees Celsius before consuming it (a process that "doesn't cost anything but can save a life").[41] They were told that mixing water with cognac, vinegar, coffee, or wine not only purified it but helped quench thirst — a useful tip against the threat of dehydration.[42] And they were instructed to identify healthy water by noting if it was clear and without scent or tint. For the particularly anxious, one could learn from *El tiempo*'s advertising pages that Krondorf mineral water was available for sale by Nissim Levy, a Sephardi merchant based in the Constantinople neighborhood of Galata.[43]

El amigo de la familia consistently warned parents that healthy children needed proper nutrition. Over the course of 1885, the column "Konsejos provechozos para la familia" was frequently devoted to the issues of hygiene and eating habits. Many contributing articles discussed the foods that were staples of a healthy diet (meat, eggs, milk, green vegetables, grains, and potatoes) and offered advice on choosing and preparing ingredients. Readers were told that meat was the most salutary food, and that beef and lamb were the most nutritious meats (one installment of "Konsejos provechozos para la familia" counseled that meat was particularly good for children and offered advice on its preparation: place the meat in a pot, pierce, salt, and bake).[44] Fish, it was argued, was less nutritious than red meat, and saltwater fish more nutritious than clearwater fish. Eggs were particularly good for the health of women, children, and convalescents, potatoes helpful for restoring energy to the infirm. Fresh butter was recommended over sour; green vegetables were nutritious, but only in small quantities. Consumption of fruit and compote was encouraged (with the warning that an excess of raw fruit leads to diarrhea). The drinking of milk was also a subject of tremendous concern, as it was in contemporary French journals of science.[45] While milk could come from a cow, goat, or sheep, *El amigo de la familia* counseled, the safest came from a goat. Chocolate imported from Mexico was considered of dubious nutritional value because its high level of milk fat was hard on the stomach.[46]

Such instructions must have been of mixed value to nineteenth-century Ottoman Jewish readers. Some of this advice was likely to be uncontroversial. For example, fish, eggs, and potatoes were all regular parts of a Southeastern European Jewish diet, as were fruits and compote.[47] Much of this

advice, however, relied on uncommon foods or directed that food be prepared in novel ways. One installment of the journal offered instructions
about cooking pasta, a food that by and large was not part of the traditional
Balkan Jewish diet. (Perhaps the author of the recipe was aware of this, for
the piece counsels that if readers do not have the proper ingredients for the
dish, numerous substitutions exist.)[48] And while beef, lamb, and poultry
were staples of Sephardi cooking, they were more often than not eaten in
small quantities, for example, in the filling of *pastelikos* or *borekas* (little pies).
This no doubt rendered curious the suggestion that beef be baked in one
large piece. Further, though Sephardi food was rich in vegetables (including eggplant, spinach, and artichokes), one suspects that of these, only
spinach might qualify as a "green vegetable," thus earning it the title "nutritious." Significant, too, were those products neglected by *El amigo de la
familia*'s list of recommended foods. Legumes (including fava and green
beans, lentils, and chickpeas), highly nutritious staples of Sephardi cooking, were not included in the list. Cheese — in particular goat and sheep
cheese — was a central part of the Balkan and Turkish diet, but neither
received the approval of this Ladino journal. Finally "Konsejos provechozos
para la familia" assiduously avoided mention of vinegars and spices. Cin-
namon, allspice, essence of orange, lemon, rose, vanilla, pepper, olives,
vinegar, and capers — all regular additions to Sephardi dishes — were never
mentioned in the many articles on cooking that appeared in *El amigo de la
familia*. Instead, such articles tended to recommend the use of butter (that
quintessential of French flavors) and salt for seasoning.

El amigo de la familia's frequent praise of butter and milk was particularly
rich with cultural meaning as it implicitly encouraged the secularization —
as well as the Westernization — of the Ottoman Jewish diet. Butter was a
commodity long treasured by the Ottoman administration, but was virtually
absent from the nineteenth-century Sephardi diet.[49] In contrast to many of
their non-Jewish neighbors, the Sephardim of Southeastern Europe avoided
butter because of the rules of *kashrut* (which forbids the mixing of milk and
meat) and relied, instead, on olive oil.[50] Meanwhile, it was quite unusual for
milk of any variety to be used in Sephardi cooking or to be given to children,
except during the holiday of Sevó (Shavuot), which was celebrated with the
preparation of milk-based dishes. In any case, the laws of *kashrut* were never
mentioned in *El amigo de la familia*'s recipes, not when they indirectly encouraged its transgression. This is a posture that would have been unthinkable in a contemporary Eastern European Yiddish periodical. In the absence of a Western Jewish imperial influence (among other factors), the
secularization of Ashkenazi cooking lagged several decades behind that of
Sephardi cooking.[51]

By sanctioning the use of milk fats, *El amigo de la familia* was encouraging
the gentrification as well as the secularization of the Sephardi diet. Milk and
butter were generally avoided by the Jewish population not only because of

the laws of *kashrut*, but because they were expensive commodities, particularly in cities where the necessity of refrigeration added to their cost.[52] For all of these reasons, it is not surprising that the attempted introduction of milk and milk fats into the Sephardi diet could be a potential source of intergenerational conflict. In the pages of the Salonikan Ladino press, the satirical character Benuta (the protagonist of a serialized humor column) was known to turn up her nose at her daughter-in-law's cooking of "inedible" Westernized dishes such as sardines with butter with the complaint: "the housewives of today are book-cooks!"[53] Perhaps it would have been more accurate for Benuta to condemn "journal-cooks," as it was the Ladino press that may have introduced Jewish readers like this fictional daughter-in-law to written recipes.

As *El amigo de la familia* offered female readers advice on how to cook and eat, so too did it advise them on the proper regulation of their time and space. Anxiety about gambling and the playing of cards and dominos surfaced often in the pages of *El amigo de la familia* and *El tiempo*.[54] More than once, the journal cautioned readers against playing cards, which it called "a dangerous passion" and a distraction from family time. If you cannot stop playing, one article recommended, don't let your children play, as it will cause young ladies to make a bad impression upon their suitors.[55] Attacks on card playing often pointed to the public nature of the game; the implication of the admonition against gambling by unwed daughters was not that gambling was inherently wicked, but that it could be perceived as wicked by a would-be suitor. And the use of public space for this hobby, we can conjecture, facilitated other dangerous practices — the speaking of Ladino, gossiping, the expression of passions, betting — all habits that the Ladino instructional press actively discouraged.

The playing of games in the privacy of one's home was encouraged as a healthy alternative. To this end, *El instruktor* featured puzzles and mathematical problems for readers to solve and *El amigo de la familia* provided readers with riddles and word games, a practice that was found in Turkish journals for women.[56] "When you know, you don't know me," reads one riddle published in *El amigo de la familia*, "but you know me even if you don't know me." The answer, published in the next issue: "history."[57] To further emphasize the value of private leisure, *El amigo de la familia* published a fictional exchange on the topic. A group of women meet in passing, and they gather to discuss the lottery. "My dear friend," one says to another, "what is this lottery you are following? I thought your dear husband has been dead for two years!" "Yes, over two and a half years, but what does that have to do with it?" the friend responds, adding, "I can play the lottery without ever having to leave my house!"[58] As long as they were protected by the security of their homes, this dialogue teaches, even women could enjoy gambling — a hobby once reserved for men. In presenting readers with new pastimes, Ladino instructional journals attempted to redefine — and draw rigid lines between — public and private spaces. Given that the reading of late-nineteenth-century newspapers was often more of a public than a private enterprise, a certain irony lay behind *El amigo de la familia*'s goal of reshaping readers' private lives. This irony reminds us that the intended impact of a newspaper was often subverted in the hands of readers.

Further advice about the proper use of public and private spaces appeared in "Hygiene, la syensya de gardar la salud" [Hygiene, the science of good health]. Here, readers were offered information on the proper dimensions and layout of homes. Ventilation was a subject of considerable reflection. Air circulation was considered critical to good health and poor ventilation was viewed as a potential cause of infant mortality. One article informed readers that the average room has eighty to ninety meters of air, enough to last eight to nine hours. As a result, the author warned, it is important to replenish a room with air on a daily basis, particularly if it houses a sick person (for dangerous gases could circulate and cause contagion or even spontaneous combustion, the article alerted readers).[59] To avoid such dangers, the article concluded, interior and exterior doors and windows had to be opened for several minutes a day. To maintain the purity of interior air, readers were advised to smoke only outdoors and were told to avoid displaying flowers and fruit with strong or unpleasant odors.[60] To guarantee that children had enough good air, meanwhile, readers were told to ensure that each resident of a home had fourteen square meters of space.[61] This space, warned another installment of the series, should be kept neat and well-ordered so that a "husband and wife" can "rest in comfort."[62] Other articles discussed the quality of air in various locations. The dangers of urban air were expounded in one issue, in another article ocean air was advocated over inland air, and elsewhere contact with the thin air of high altitudes was discouraged.[63] Jaffa was recommended as a particularly good destination for the sick, as in this town, the paper explained, northern ocean winds mixed with cool southern winds, producing a mild and pleasant climate.[64] Yet other articles encouraged readers to engage in regular exercise such as gymnastics or equestrian sports, both of which would increase the flow of oxygen to the brain.[65]

Anxieties about air purity and the threat of contagion from stagnant air were fueled by French journals such as *Revue d'hygiène* (Paris, 1879–1921), in which healthy air was a subject of much reflection. This publication and other contemporary journals elaborated upon the dangers of stagnant air and disease-infused interiors and offered suggestions about the size and shape of rooms, the placement of beds, and the dangers of cellars, vaults, and antechambers.[66] As Ann-Louise Shapiro has argued, the extensive debate over hygiene and the sanitation of public and private spaces in nineteenth-century Paris by social reformers allowed the bourgeoisie to define the terms of class and intra-class relationships.[67] Similarly, *El amigo de la familia* offered readers a model of how they could structure their physical lives according to European bourgeois standards. The difference, of course, was that while the social reformers of Paris were able to legislate reforms, the producers of *El amigo de la familia*—who had no legislative power — could do little more than offer advice. And much of this counsel was impossible to follow, even by members of the upper middle class. The notion that space should be sparsely inhabited, or inhabited only by nuclear families, for example, must have been anathema to Ottoman Jewish readers, for whom two-generational or one-family dwellings were the exception rather than the norm. Abraham Galanté has described how many of the Jews of Izmir lived in *cortijos,* communal structures with courtyards at their center, surrounded by walls in which one- or two-room homes were built. Each of these small homes housed several families and tended to be crowded and unhygienic.[68] To readers familiar with such conditions, articles on the dangers of over-populated urban space, the advice that healthy bodies needed eight hours of sleep a night, or warnings against sleeping on the floor or in the kitchen must have seemed little more than ethnographic details of a distant culture.[69] This disparity rendered somewhat ludicrous the hope that *El amigo de la familia* would truly become a "friend of the family." In fact, the family this journal gestured toward bore little resemblance to the Ottoman Jewish families the paper was likely to reach.

Though much of the counsel proffered by the Ladino instructional press must have been impossible to realize, the information these periodicals contained was still likely to be closely observed. Even if details of European bourgeois living were not mimicked, the contents could nonetheless be consumed by readers hungry for news. This hunger for information erased two critical distinctions that suffused the instructional Ladino literature: the distinction between the practical and the exotic, on the one hand, and the distinction between exemplary Western European norms and esoteric Oriental ones, on the other. As we will now see, the pages of the instructional Ladino press were steeped in exposés from the Orient, a category that seemed to include all regions of the world except Western and Central Europe. Reports such as these were meant to inform without necessarily personally influencing readers. And yet, ironically, to the eyes of readers of Ladino, descriptions of proper living spaces may have proved informative in much the same way as would exposés on Eskimos and ice-fishing. Both were ethnographic and both were news. These kinds of information were — to borrow from the terminology of the turn-of-the-century Ottoman Jewish milieu — equally useful and useless: enlightening, but difficult to emulate. Though offered as a sequence of juxtapositions, this variety of news inadvertently defined "modern science." To put this a slightly different way, the conceptual distinctions that the Ladino instructional press seemed to insist upon — the distinction between the West and the East and the analogous distinction between the exemplary and the exotic — proved impossible to enforce. Ladino instructional journals were illustrating how unpredictable and how very unruly was the process of Westernization.

COLONIALISM AND THE WESTERNIZING PROJECT

In *El amigo de la familia* and *El instruktor*, the highly detailed reports on the modes of contemporary France were almost exclusively textual. The journals provided few images of French people or their customs. The implication was that European appearances and habits were understood to be visually familiar to Ottoman Jewish readers; as visual icons, at least, Western European subjects were the norm rather than news. Bodies from the colonial world, by contrast, invited visual as well as textual taxonomy (see figure 4.1). These taxonomies were not invented by the Ladino press but were republished (without attribution) from contemporary French and English journals. The original captions in French and English were retained for many such images, while on others, the artist's English- or French-language signature is still apparent.[70] Yet other images appear inspired by George French Angas's atlas folio *The Kafirs illustrated in a series of drawings* of 1849, though whether Angas's lithographs reached Ladino publishers directly or indirectly cannot be ascertained.[71] Images of human types, as well as pictures of flora and fauna from Africa, Asia, and the Americas invited readers of Ladino to serve as literary colonialists. With the help of the Ladino instructional press, Ottoman Jews could benefit from imperial exploration by the act of reading. Depictions of Zulu tribes and Egyptian monuments, flowers of Ceylon, and tobacco of the

Figure 4.1. "Indigenous people." *El amigo de la familia*, unnumbered, 25 Tevet 5643 (1883).

Americas not only educated readers of Ladino but also presented them with the opportunity to recast themselves as colonial pioneers.[72]

Depictions of "curiosities" from other parts of the world inevitably encouraged readers of Ladino to identify with the Western European voyeur rather than with the colonial subject. Consider, as evidence of this impulse, a line sketch entitled "The voyage to Madagascar" that appeared in *El amigo de la familia* (figure 4.2). The depiction implicitly allies the reader with the imperial adventurer, a dapper white man seated on a platform that is held aloft by a cluster of Madagascans. The visitor rests casually on his

Figure 4.2. "The voyage to Madagascar." *El amigo de la familia,* unnumbered, 13 Iyar 5642 (1882).

perch, immaculately dressed, his eyes locked with the readers'. Visually and physically, he is the center of this image. The natives who surround him function as decoration. They are essentially support staff who offer the visitor his place of honor and mind his belongings (an umbrella, a satchel). For their efforts, the natives of Madagascar have been rewarded with a critical emblem of the Western colonial project: the sturdy explorer's hats. Like readers of the Ladino press, the natives of Madagascar have been made aware of the dangers of the Oriental sun.[73]

While the readers of *El amigo de la familia* were encouraged to assume the perspective of the imperial traveler, they were nonetheless reminded that they were (and that they looked) different from their Western peers. Consider the portraits of Baron Maurice de Hirsch and Baroness Clara de Hirsch that appeared in one of the early issues of the journal (figure 4.3). Baron de Hirsch was a French Jewish banker and philanthropist. In the last decades of the nineteenth century, he financed the creation of trade schools for Russian Jews, the construction of railways in European Turkey, and, with a gift of one million francs to the AIU in 1873, the education of Ottoman Jewry. The reproduction of their likenesses on the cover of *El amigo de la familia* was a means of lionizing these philanthropists, but also of signaling the peculiarity of the Franco-Jewish elite. The portrait of the Baron and Baroness reiterated that the couple's success was physical as well as economic. The Baron is shown clean-shaven, with an aristocratic mustache and a bare head, while the Baroness is depicted with her hair exposed: all signs of their acculturation into the European upper crust. The Baron

איל סיניזר באראן

מזרים די הירש

לה סיזיורה באראניסה

קלאדה די הירש.

Figure 4.3. "Baroness Clara de Hirsch (*on right*) and Baron Maurice de Hirsch (*on left*)." *El amigo de la familia,* unnumbered, 14 Tevet 5642 (1882).

and Baroness, readers could discern, were worthy of display not only for what they had done, but for how they looked.

In this regard, the role that the de Hirsches' portraits played was not entirely dissimilar to the role played by images of exotic natives and animals that appeared on other covers of *El amigo de la familia,* despite the obvious distinction that was meant to delineate the "cultured" European couple from the "wild" animals of the "uncivilized world." Let us turn, by way of example, to one such portrait: "Colonial subject" (figure 4.4).[74] Certain differences distinguish this portrait from that of the de Hirsches. While the de Hirsches are unquestionably the central focus of their portraits, the "Colonial subject" is depicted against a detailed backdrop including foliage, a house, and the edge of an elaborately decorated canoe. While we see only the de Hirsches' busts, the "Colonial subject" is depicted in full, allowing the reader to scrutinize his mostly bare musculature and informal posture,

כאלאנאת

Figure 4.4. "Colonial subject." *El amigo de la familia* #45, 11
Adar 5642 (1882).

his tattoos and hairstyle, and his "festive garb." Finally, the de Hirsches are
named, individuated, their accomplishments recognized, while the "Colonial subject" is an undifferentiated representative of native types. On this
basis, one could argue that while the portraits of the de Hirsches emphasize
their subjects' distinguished nature and standing, the portrait of the "Colo-

סו ס׳ יחוקים ג׳
גאסטיא"ק"ק איקס"נ"ט

Figure 4.5. "His Holiness,
Patriarch J. (Anthimus VI, né
Joannides)." *El amigo de la
familia,* unnumbered, 16
Kislev 5642 (1881).

nial subject" stresses its subject's animal nature and anonymity. In these ways, the images
of *El amigo de la familia* advance the principal
dichotomy of colonialism.[75] There is certainly
truth to this interpretation, but there is, perhaps, truth to a slightly different reading as
well. To many Ottoman Jewish readers, the de
Hirsches, like the "Colonial subject," must
have seemed like faces from a distant world, a
world to which the reader might (or might
not) wish to aspire, but nonetheless an exotic
world whose ritual garb, physiognomies, and
carriage invited scrutiny.

The exotic was, indeed, a complex concept
in the Ladino press. It was tied to the ideal as
well as the savage, to the local as well as the
foreign. For example, to alert readers to esoterica close to home, *El amigo de la familia* offered information about curiosities found in
Constantinople, most of them Christian holy
sights.[76] Such articles seem to align Ottoman
Jewish readers with the Western European
traveler. Articles on Constantinople published in *El amigo de la familia* read like guide
books designed for a first-time visitor (and
they were, no doubt, originally written for En-
glish- or French-language readers who might travel to this city). Such accounts may have encouraged readers to look at their city with new eyes, but
they also had the uncanny effect of rendering Constantinople a strange and
unwieldy place even though, presumably, it was also the city that most of
the journal's readers called home. Guides to the Ottoman capital implied
that readers were unfamiliar with their city. Ironically, they also encouraged literary rather than physical exploration. After all, though readers of
El amigo de la familia were directed by the journal to some of Constantinople's most notable Christian sites, they were simultaneously warned that the
city was made up of crowded, narrow, and dangerous streets. Finally, articles on the wonders of Constantinople implied that Western European–
informed sources were the most reputable sources on local affairs. Just as
"Konsejos provechozos para la familia" claimed the smell of roses as both
modern and Occidental, so too did *El amigo de la familia* promote the dynamism of Constantinople as a curiosity and a conquest of the West.

This dynamic was reasserted visually. The cover of one issue of *El amigo de
la familia* was devoted to "His Holiness the Greek Orthodox Patriarch J."

(Anthimus VI [1790–1878], né Joannides), whom the journal described as "the most celebrated of the Patriarchs," "informed, intelligent, energetic, [and] modest."[77] The accompanying portrait showed the Patriarch wearing a ceremonial head-covering and religious medallions, with a full beard and long hair (figure 4.5). From the accompanying article, readers learned that the Greek Ortho-dox Patriarch lived in Constantinople. Though the Patriarch was local, he was presented as something of a curiosity, in many ways as foreign as "The Em-press of the Zulu," whose portrait had appeared in

לה אישפיראמפירים די לוס זולוס

El amigo de la familia a few weeks earlier (figure 4.6). The portrait of the Empress is not, in fact, terribly dissimilar from that of the Patriarch. Both depict the head and torso of their subject. The Em-press, like the Patriarch, looks directly at the view-er. She, like he, is dressed in attire that might be perceived as exotic. She wears large hoop earrings, a thin bone through her nose, feathery ornamen-tation, and a loose cape: he the headgear, robes, and ornaments of his title. And if the portraits of

Figure 4.6. "The Empress of the Zulu." *El amigo de la familia,* unnumbered, 9 Kislev 5642 (1881).

the Zulu Empress and the Greek Orthodox Patriarch resembled each other visually, their placement within *El amigo de la familia* echoed each other textually, as both appeared on the cover of the journal (as, for that matter, did the portrait of the Baron and Baroness de Hirsch). This repetition in form integrated these three portraits into a corpus of scientific and literary knowledge. Discrete parts of this body of knowledge might have been in-tended to influence the way readers lived their daily lives: what they ate, how they presented themselves, how they spent their free time. As a whole, how-ever, the journal's repetitive form reminded readers that "supplemental news" was entertaining as well as instructional. Better put, in the pages of the Ladino supplement, the instructional and the entertaining merged into news. The thought that one could cook with butter or wear taffeta was no less fascinating and no more useful than were the detailed illustrations of ice-fishing Eskimos.[78]

These images begin to broaden our understanding of the complexity of the Westernizing project that informed the Ladino instructional press. The content of journals like *El amigo de la familia* encouraged readers of Ladino to delineate themselves from local cultures and to ally with the Western European bourgeois mode, both by assuming the vantage of the Western European colonialist and by distancing themselves from exotic figures like the Greek Orthodox Patriarch. They were meant to appreciate that first-

איל פאבון

Figure 4.7. "The peacock." *El amigo de la familia*, unnumbered, 12 Kislev 5643 (1882).

hand knowledge of Constantinople's narrow back streets was "useless," while second-hand knowledge of tourist sights of the city was "useful."

On some level, the success of this project can be judged by the fact that sources like *El amigo de la familia* introduced Ottoman Jewish readers to new forms of knowledge. That these sources existed, however, did not ensure the Westernizing project would be realized. For that, the medium of the newspaper was too malleable and the process of cultural translation too unpredictable. What the content of *El amigo de la familia* suggests, instead, is that most readers of Ladino could not but be aware that a gulf separated them from Franco-Jewish elite culture, and that this gulf was as wide as that which distinguished them from the native of Madagascar or the Greek Orthodox Patriarch of Constantinople. After all, though articles on these topics were presented in a certain didactic and ideological light, readers' reaction to them could not be controlled. Though a reader of *El amigo de la familia* could be encouraged to emulate Baroness de Hirsch, at the end of the day, it was olive oil and not butter that she might put on her bread. And if she washed with rose water, she was likely to smell not only like a French aristocrat, but also much like her grandmother.

In this regard, the Ladino instructional press was itself paralyzed by the illogical qualities of imperialism. Even as journals like *El amigo de la familia* urged readers to change their ways, they demonstrated that complete transformation — complete Westernization — was an unattainable goal. As the journal invited readers to marvel at the ways of the West, these modes themselves were transformed into subjects of the Ottoman Jewish imagination. Readers of Ladino could choose to emulate them, but they could also choose to be entertained by them, or, as the reminiscences of Leon Sciaky suggest with marvelous clarity, to view them with suspicion. Writes Sciaky:

> The century was drawing to a close. Stealthily the West was creeping in, trying to lure the East with her wonders. Almost inaudible yet was her

whisper. She dangled before our dazzled eyes the witchery of her science and the miracle of her inventions. We caught a glimpse of her brilliance, and timidly listened to the song of the siren. Like country folk at a banquet, we felt humble and awkward in our ways. But vaguely we sensed the coldness of her glitter and the price of her wooing. With uneasiness we gathered tighter the folds of our homespun mantles around our shoulders, enjoying their softness and warmth, and finding them good.[79]

As we shall now see, in much the same way that ethnographic images could inadvertently undermine the didactic nature of the instructional Ladino press, images of and articles about scientific marvels blurred the distinction between the exemplary and the exotic. Though designed to demonstrate the universal resonance of modern science, the Ladino instructional press nonetheless presented readers with what Sciaky might call witchery: conventions of the Westernizing project that seemed more spell than seminar, lessons that were at best unrealizable and at worst demeaning.

El amigo de la familia was particularly fond of plying readers with images of exotic flora and fauna: the hippopotamus, the peacock, the eagle, the whale, the bird of paradise (figures 4.7 and 4.8). Like the African natives that graced the journal's pages, these species were presented as the unearthing of proud colonial conquest. Often the pictures were printed without narration, and in some sense they required none as their picturing offered a lesson about

(12 פֿיגﬞורﬞה ﬞסﬞﬠﬞﬞ 3)   פﬞﬠﬞראﬞ די פﬞאראﬞזﬞﬞﬞ

Figure 4.8. "The bird of paradise." *El amigo de la familia,* unnumbered, 10 Nisan 5642 (1882).

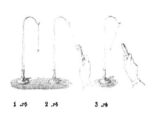

1 .୨୫   2 .୨୫   3 .୨୫

Figure 4.9. "Experiments with electricity." *El amigo de la familia* #132, 5 Tevet 5644 (1884).

the modern world. These images were meant to be "useful" to Ottoman Jewish readers simply because they expanded the body of knowledge considered germane for the culturally literate. In the worldview of the Westernizing Ladino journal, one could hardly be expected to emulate the peacock, but one was expected to know what a peacock looked like. The ability to recognize this animal was itself a modern skill, as critical as was relishing the taste of butter or relinquishing one's love of the smell of roses.

As this suggests, information proffered by the Ladino instructional press did not need to be put to any concrete use to be of value. "From a book," David Fresco wrote in *El instruktor,* "one learns of the mysteries of nature, of the miracle of creation and of moral beauty. Such knowledge is useful for those who never attended school or who did not learn from their studies." To resist learning, according to Fresco, was to fail to fulfill one's responsibility.[80] The act of knowing was itself a modern obligation — not only useful, but "just" and "moral."[81] Thus *El amigo de la familia* offered instruction about simple experiments with electricity that readers were expected to witness but not necessarily to enact (figure 4.9).

The importance of passive knowledge was illustrated by a drawing published in *El amigo de la familia* in 1881 featuring a telescope that was approximately twenty-five feet high. In front of the telescope stands a man who is all but overshadowed by the instrument. Arms behind his back, he stares up in awe. Barely discernible is a second figure, a man perched atop a ladder that leans against the telescope's side. This second figure appears to be adjusting the telescope's levers, perhaps readying it for the other's gaze. While the standing man stares at the telescope with wonder, this second man — his hands lost within the instrument's cogs — seems part of the telescope itself. Significantly, while the standing man is formally dressed, with a long beard and a dark hat, the second man is clean-shaven and more casually attired (figure 4.10). This image, like much of the scientific accounts offered by *El amigo de la familia,* posits readers of Ladino as witnesses to the achievements of the West, invited to marvel at the miracles of modern science at something of a distance. Like the standing man, they were attuned to the profundity rather than the workings of this instrument. Further, they, like he, could not but be aware of the differences that delineated them from the engineer at work before them. Differences in dress, facial hair, posture, expertise: these were details sure to remind readers of Ladino of the gulf that divided the passive learner from the scientific practitioner and, perhaps, the Ottoman setting from the Western European one.

Figure 4.10. "The telescope." *El amigo de la familia,* unnumbered, 23 Nisan 5642 (1882).

A telescope, of course, is designed to make distant things appear nearer and larger, to render discernible details otherwise not visible to the naked eye. The text that accompanied this image described with incredulity how a telescope can magnify even the mountains of the moon. Details such as this were made available to readers when *El amigo de la familia* reproduced microscopic images of the snowflake and telescopic pictures of the moon (figures 4.11 and 4.12). These images reminded readers that even seemingly similar objects could be subtly differentiated and that smooth surfaces could, in fact, be unevenly textured. This conclusion had implications for the way readers understood human as well as natural landscapes. In this way, images

צורת הרבה מינים שלג

Figure 4.11. "The many forms of
snowflakes." *El amigo de la familia,*
unnumbered, 27 Shevat 5642 (1882).

of microscopic curiosities returned readers to the complex
cultural terrain that *El amigo de la
familia*'s ethnographic exposés
had plumbed. These images
could thus serve as a reminder
that colonial subjects differed in
appearance from Frenchmen,
the Greek Patriarch from the
Zulu Empress, and the Baron
and Baroness de Hirsch from
the typical Ottoman Jew. The
journal's emphasis upon surface
and exteriors reiterated what images of these people had already
conveyed: that the way you
looked defined who you were
and, by extension, that the sub-
tlest modification to your person
could profoundly alter your
identity.

This point was substantiated
in anatomical studies of the
human body reproduced in
El amigo de la familia. Anatomical
pictures graphically illustrated that the insides of bodies were the same in
Madagascar, the Ottoman Empire, and France. An accompanying article
reinforced this point by describing the (universal) workings of the human
digestive tract (figure 4.13). Ironically, displays of human interiors could
have the effect of reminding readers of the importance of exteriors. Studies
of the workings of the human body implicitly reiterated that it was not how
bodies functioned that differentiated them but, instead, how these bodies
were fed, scented, dressed, and adorned that delineated them one from
another. In this sense, the journal's reproduction of the inside of humans
was in implicit dialogue with its depictions of human exteriors. Both demanded vivisection — one physical, the other political — and both offered a
lesson about the Ottoman Jews' need and ability to change themselves.

It is striking that the Ladino instructional press never turned its lens upon
Levantine Jewry. The same, after all, could not be said of the contemporary French-, German-, or English-language Jewish presses from which the
Ladino press was known to borrow.[82] Ironically, this blind spot did not mean
that Ottoman Jews were not subjects of journals like *El amigo de la familia*
or *El instruktor.* On the contrary, though these journals were outwardly
focused on the norms of the West and the curiosities of the East, they also

לה לונה

Figure 4.12. "The moon." *El amigo de la familia,* unnumbered, 23 Nisan 5642 (1882).

offered subtle but unmistakable lessons about Southeastern European Jewish culture and about the practices readers were meant to abandon. This implicit point of reference unambiguously marked the Ladino instructional press.

The Ladino instructional press was conditioned by a process of translation that was cultural as well as literary. As Fresco and his peers readied Western European sources for their readers, and as readers made sense of their contents, the meanings of informant texts changed. In myriad ways, these journals' coverage of fashion, hygiene, nutrition, ethnographic and scientific findings rubbed against the historical realities of late-nineteenth-century Ottoman Jewish life. The didactic messages they contained were often difficult to practice, even if they were not altogether unappealing. Further, instructive accounts often bled seamlessly into rather more exotic ones. In the process, the Ladino instructional press unintentionally pointed to the gulf that separated the Westernizing project from the actual process of cultural change. Rather than serve as itineraries for cultural transformation, this genre functioned as raconteur as well as pedagogue, a vehicle of entertainment as well as education.

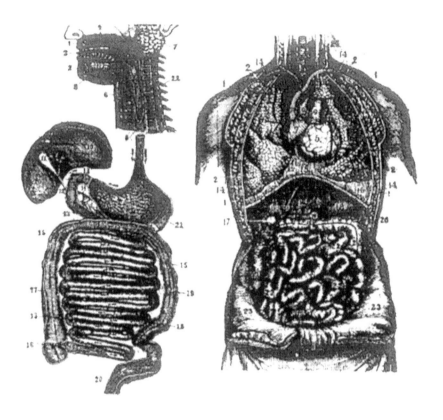

אִיל אוֹמבְּרִי

Figure 4.13. "The anatomy of man." *El amigo de la familia,*
unnumbered, 6 Hesvan 5643 (1882).

Ladino instructional literature offered readers a glimpse into foreign and
exotic worlds. To Fresco and his colleagues, the idiosyncrasies of these
worlds were the stuff of modern Jewish cultural literacy. But although journals such as *El amigo de la familia* attempted to align readers' gaze with that of
the European visitor to Madagascar, and though the journal attempted to
shape Ottoman Jews' sense of smell, taste, and propriety in the spirit of the

French bourgeoisie, in the end they could do little more than illuminate how culturally contingent were the senses. The stare of a visitor to Madagascar could be returned rather than shared and the scent of roses could evoke new meanings on Ottoman soil. In Leon Sciaky's words, the glitter of the West, "the witchery of her science and the miracle of her inventions" could be resisted, and "the price of her wooing" detected. To put this another way, no less than other corners of the Ladino press, instructional sources invited interaction and retort. This was the inevitable outcome of the process of reading, and a sign of the resiliency of Ottoman Jewish culture on the eve of the twentieth century.

PART THREE

ADVERTISING
ASPIRATION

5

IMAGES OF DAILY LIFE

In January 1904, the Warsavian merchant S. Yutman posted an advertisement in *Der fraynd*. "**There is no longer**," announced the ad in bold type, "any person in the world who isn't able to have, in his own house, the newly released 'Imperial Stereoscope,' which displays all kinds of images of daily life beautifully and naturally. The price of one stereoscope with 50 images is only 2 rubles and will be sent to you for free."[1] The ad, no larger than an inch square, featured in its upper corner an image of a woman serenely peering through the stereoscope, held upright by a dainty hand (figure 5.1).

The Imperial Stereoscope offered would-be owners the opportunity to peruse the world inexpensively and effortlessly from the safety of their homes. For the majority of readers of the Yiddish press—most of whom would never buy this product—this advertisement offered a similar prospect. Like the product it promoted, this text enabled a sedentary form of travel that demanded little expenditure of time, effort, or money. Printed in an era when leisure-oriented commodities were difficult to obtain and even to observe, this scrap of text offered readers a glimpse into an otherwise inaccessible reality while simultaneously acting as a source of news, entertainment, and commercial possibility.

עם איז נישטא

אימפעריאל סטערעאסקאפ

III. KOOTMAHЪ, Варшава, Долгая 27.   4—4

Figure 5.1. Advertisement for Imperial Stereoscope. *Der fraynd* #1, 1 January 1904.

Like other advertisements that appeared in the Yiddish popular press, this advertisement for the Imperial Stereoscope provides clues to the economic and cultural influence of Yiddish newspapers upon Russian Jewish readers in the first years of the twentieth century. Analyses of Yiddish advertisements allow us to extrapolate about the economic and cultural status of readers. Such statuses were challenged, and in some senses shaped, by the texts themselves. Advertisements in the Yiddish popular press capitalized upon a culture of social and economic aspiration, targeting Jewish readers who were literate but neither intellectuals nor professionals but rather members of a burgeoning consumer class; geographically scattered throughout the Russian Empire; both male and female; and religious and secular.

Advertising pages tell us about more than the readers who consumed them. They also illustrate how the Yiddish popular press was effecting economic interaction between Russian Jews. Taking *Der fraynd* as its case study, this chapter demonstrates that popular sources in Yiddish facilitated new relationships between Jewish merchants and readers of Yiddish, relationships that helped to cultivate a Russian Jewish economy with tentacles in the Russian economy. Yiddish newspapers did not promote a hermetic Russian Jewish economy. Arguably, such a discrete phenomenon could not exist. But

Der fraynd did facilitate an exchange of information about the production, distribution, and consumption of goods and services: what could be described as a Yiddish consumer culture.[2] The following pages turn to *Der fraynd*'s advertisements to explore this consumer culture. This exploration tells us more about Eastern European readers of Yiddish, uncovers a portrait of those merchants who advertised in the Yiddish press, and considers the economic impact of Yiddish popular sources.

ADVERTISING AND THE RUSSIAN JEWISH PRESS

By and large, the leading Hebrew-, Russian-, and Yiddish-language papers with a Jewish-target audience that had been created in the mid to late nineteenth century did not feature advertisements. Those that did published advertisements of a very different nature than would accompany the majority of early-twentieth-century Russian Jewish periodicals. The nineteenth-century Hebrew-language *Hamelits*, for example, mostly featured announcements promoting books, literary events, and journals. While these advertisements were no doubt published for a fee, one could argue that they reflected and encouraged literary rather than economic exchanges.[3] The literary *Hashiloah*, meanwhile, was published without advertisements, perhaps because it was funded by a contribution of 4,000 rubles by tea baron Kalman Vissotsky and was not in need (or was not imagined to be in need) of additional resources.[4] Most Yiddish periodicals of the late nineteenth and early twentieth centuries followed similar practices. Like *Hamelits*, the weekly *Der yud*, created in Kracow in 1899, contained no advertisements but did publish announcements about literary affairs.

These patterns reiterate a hypothesis proposed by other scholars of Jewish journalism in Russia: that late-nineteenth-century periodicals of this context were not designed for wide-reaching readerships and were funded — or, as was more often the case, were only barely supported — by patrons or loyal readers. The scarcity of advertisements in late-nineteenth-century Russian Jewish periodicals reminds us that these publications were aimed at a relatively narrow audience of *maskilim* and were not designed to have mass appeal.

In Western Europe and America, newspapers had been earning a substantial percentage of their income from advertisements for some decades. By contrast, advertising was a late development in Imperial Russia as the practice was forestalled by official interference.[5] As late as the early 1860s, editors of Russian journals were forbidden from printing advertisements paid for by individuals. Even after that year, advertisements were censored, though inconsistently and without clear standards.[6] Nonetheless, by the turn of the century general Russian-language periodicals — in contradistinction to Jewish-oriented ones — had quite sophisticated advertising mechanisms in place. By 1846, seven advertising agencies specialized in Russian-language publicity in St. Petersburg and thirteen existed in Moscow.[7] Further, by 1900 many Russian-language journals earned a significant portion of their revenue from advertising. In 1900, the Moscow-based *Russkoe slovo* (St. Petersburg, 1859–66), a periodical that targeted middle-class urban readers, paid a quarter of its expenses with money earned from advertisements. By 1903, this percentage exceeded one third. In the same year, *Russkie vedomosti*, a journal for professional readers, depended on advertisements for nearly half its income.[8]

Jews were among those who benefited from advances in the Russian advertising industry. Many Russian Jews could peruse advertisements in Russian-language sources whether or not they were fluent readers of Russian. Others subscribed to the Russian-language press as a matter of course. So too, were Jews among the merchants who advertised in Russian-language sources. Finally, like all residents of the empire, Russian Jews had access to a variety of goods sold in fairs, marketplaces, and by traveling merchants, and were thus exposed to the most quintessential of nineteenth-century advertising techniques: shouts, signs, and handbills.[9] By the turn of the twentieth century, however, the creation of Yiddish newspapers dramatically availed a new consuming public to advertisers and presented a novel concentration of advertisements to readers of Yiddish.

Although the first issues of *Der fraynd* boasted nearly a full page of advertisements, advertisements appeared only sporadically in 1903, the first year of the paper's production. Thereafter, however, the presence of advertisements in its pages became routine. By 1904, its typical four pages devoted one (the back page) to advertisements, which typically covered the entire or nearly all of the page (figure 5.2). An average issue of *Der fraynd* devoted 15 to 20 percent of its content to advertisements. When they spilled over onto the first page, advertisements could fill up to a quarter of the paper's content. The high proportion of spaces given over to advertising bespeaks its importance to the economic functioning of *Der fraynd*. What is more, advertisements were, from the vantage of readers, an important part of the day's news. For readers of the daily Yiddish press, advertising served as sources of entertainment and information, telling them "what there was to know about the world; [advertising] became what passed for knowledge; it became, to use the modern term, information."[10]

The variety of advertisements in *Der fraynd* was spectacular. Advertisements appeared in many sizes, with and without illustrations, for a day or for months or even years on end. The ads were a medium for the sale of a tremendous variety of merchandise: coffee, glasses, wigs, washing and sewing machines, ceremonial objects, cameras, musical instruments, bicycles, lighters, lights, boots, imported cigars, fabric, showers, Swiss cocoa, and implements for recorking bottles, grating vegetables, strengthening the upper body, and signing one's name. Advertisements were also posted by a wide

Figure 5.2. Page of advertisements from *Der fraynd* #1,
1 January 1904.

variety of sources, among them large factories and small shops, doctors, dentists, and lawyers offering their services, female readers looking for truant husbands, readers seeking jobs or advice, newspapers and authors in pursuit of readers. They also were written in many languages, including Russian, Hebrew, Polish, and German as well as Yiddish, and it was not uncommon for individual advertisements to utilize two or more languages.

In many of these respects (excepting their multi-lingual nature), *Der fraynd*'s advertising pages resembled those that were found in contemporary Russian-language sources. Still, *Der fraynd*'s advertisements were unique in that they were distributed to readers of Yiddish throughout the Russian interior and the Jewish Pale of Settlement. As a result, the genre of the Yiddish advertisement appealed to a particularly geographically diverse body of merchants. A single page of advertisements in *Der fraynd* could contain advertisements for stores in Warsaw, St. Petersburg, Odessa, Moscow, Berlin, and London.[11] In this way, *Der fraynd* differed from other periodicals designed for Jewish readers, as from most contemporary Russian-language dailies. The majority of advertisements in *Novoe vremia* (the most widely circulated Russian-language daily in 1900) were for St. Petersburg–based companies, the city in which the paper was based. And in marked contrast to *Der fraynd,* a substantial portion of the advertisements in *Novoe vremia* were classified advertisements announcing opportunities in the capital city—postings for available apartments, for example, or for jobs sought or offered. Such advertisements assumed that readers were aware they were reading about St. Petersburg as the city is more often than not unnamed, and street names and numbers alone direct readers to the goods they seek. Even the non-classified advertisements of *Novoe vremia* offered readers little more than a street address. Readers of such advertisements were simply assumed to understand that merchants advertising in the paper were located in the capital city. The same was true of the advertisements printed in *Peterburgskii listok.*[12]

The evolution of classified advertisements in *Der fraynd* points to the changing status of the paper itself. In the early years of the paper's run, classified advertisements were rare in *Der fraynd*. This was in part by design. Its editors believed that the absence of classified advertisements contributed to an aesthetic that was intended to distinguish the paper from "yellow" papers published in Russian and, increasingly, in Yiddish. *Der fraynd* was envisioned not only as a place to read the daily news, but also as a source for readers' cultural and literary sensibilities. At least so the editors had hoped. In fact, the reality was somewhat different. Even in the paper's first year of publication, classified advertisements sometimes appeared in *Der fraynd,* and they occurred with increasing frequency as the paper's popularity grew. Among them were advertisements for readers seeking or offering work and advertisements selling goods on an informal basis. Reads one: "A trapper has returned from Germany and will sell what he has caught."[13] Reads another: "An upstanding woman of middle age seeks a job in a virtuous house."[14] Terse obituaries were occasionally posted alongside such ads.[15] In general, classified advertisements were small and less skillfully rendered than other advertisements. By and large they were published on the paper's edges, perhaps because this space was cheaper to procure.

Classified advertisements such as these made the content of *Der fraynd*'s advertising papers close to that of Russian daily newspapers despite the professed ambitions of the paper's editors. Still, fundamental differences distinguished *Der fraynd*'s advertisements from their Russian-language contemporaries. There is, for example, the intriguing question of what is not represented in *Der fraynd*'s advertising pages. Advertisements for tobacco and alcohol, though plentiful in the Russian language press, are thin in *Der fraynd*. One can find occasional reproductions of the Shaposhnikov company's advertisements for *Krem* cigarettes in its pages, and not infrequent promotions for cigars. Other than these, advertisements for tobacco were few and far between.[16] While medicines for sexual potency and diet regimes were common in Russian-language journals, they, too, were rare in *Der fraynd*. Images of Mother Russia, a trope often drawn upon in Russian-language advertisements, were also virtually absent in the advertisements of *Der fraynd*. Finally, while Russian-language advertisements often reproduced official endorsements in the form of the state seal (featuring the double-headed imperial eagle), these accompanied Yiddish advertisements only occasionally.[17] Such absences suggest that readers of Yiddish were imagined to have different commercial and aesthetic needs than readers of Russian.

These differences notwithstanding, a portion of *Der fraynd*'s advertisements appeared in identical form in the most popular Russian-language papers based in St. Petersburg. A number were found in the conservative daily *Novoe vremia* and in the illustrated weekly *Niva* (St. Petersburg, 1870–1918). Given that approximately one fifth of the ads in *Der fraynd* were written in Russian, and that many more combine Russian and Yiddish, this is not entirely surprising. Russian-language advertisements that appeared in *Der fraynd* included those for Russian-language newspapers like *Rech, Nov,* or *Niva,* the *Novishaya biblioteka* publishers, for goods such as suits, shoes, cigars, and a variety of lights, and for the services of doctors and hypnotists. In 1903, *Novoe Vremia, Niva,* and *Der fraynd* all featured Russian-language advertisements for various kinds of cocoa — Nestlé, Lucerna, or Bensdorfs — and for the Warsaw-based merchant S. Feininshteyn, seller of pocket watches. With these exceptions and a few other advertisements, the ads that appeared in *Der fraynd* rarely appeared in *Novoe vremia* and only slightly more frequently in *Niva*. This was not only because the papers advertised different kinds of commodities. Instead, *Der fraynd* was gathering a clientele of advertisers whose merchandise was not, by and large, being promoted in contemporary Russian language papers.

Why would an advertiser choose to post an advertisement in *Der fraynd*? A careful perusal of the names of the merchants who advertised in *Der fraynd, Niva, Peterburgskii listok,* and *Novoe vremia* reveals that while the Russian-language papers (and especially *Niva*) included select advertisements for the goods or shops of Jewish merchants, the Yiddish-language press is dominated by such advertisements. Thus while readers of *Novoe vremia* might consider purchasing the corsets of M. M. Jacque (St. Petersburg) or G. Adolfin (Warsaw), readers of *Der fraynd* would read of the corset collection of Y. H. Ravnitsky (Warsaw). And while *Novoe vremia* advertised the gramophones of A. Burxard (St. Petersburg), *Der fraynd* posted ads for the gramophones of Zhulyen Faynboym (Warsaw).[18] It is true, the liberal Russian-language *Niva* printed many advertisements of merchants with Jewish names, among them the bag-merchant G. M. Levinsohn or watch-sellers A. S. Kaplan and Z. Fishman. But the number of advertisements for Jewish-owned businesses that appear in *Der fraynd* far outnumbered those found in *Niva*. The pages of *Der fraynd*, it would seem, served as a unique place of contact for Jewish merchants and readers of Yiddish.

Whether merchants who chose to post advertisements in *Der fraynd* had non-commercial motives as well as commercial ones is difficult to ascertain. It is possible that some were inclined to support the endeavor of a Yiddish daily for ideological reasons. It is also possible that they were convinced to do so by members of the paper's staff, all of whom were acutely aware of the need for patronage, particularly after 1905 when numerous Yiddish periodicals collapsed for lack of funds.[19] Most likely, these merchants sensed the enormous commercial possibilities latent in the Yiddish daily press and realized that shared language in print could serve as a catalyst to commercial exchange. To be sure, among those who did turn to *Der fraynd* to post advertisements, many continued to publish in Russian-language presses, while other Jewish merchants chose not to post advertisements in Yiddish language presses at all. *Der fraynd* did not, in other words, help to create a hermetic Russian Jewish economy. And yet the Yiddish press undoubtedly offered merchants an opportunity to communicate with Jewish consumers on an unprecedented scale.[20]

The Yiddish press did not, of course, encourage Jews' economic interaction single-handedly. A look at the contemporary St. Petersburg–based Hebrew daily-turned-weekly, *Hazman* (St. Petersburg, Vilna, 1903–14), suggests that for Jewish merchants, the quest for Yiddish-speaking consumers could not be separated from the quest for Jewish consumers writ large. Many (though not all) of *Hazman*'s advertisements appeared in *Der fraynd*, a strikingly higher proportion, indeed, than were shared by *Der fraynd* and *Niva*. The advertisements of *Hazman* that appeared in *Der fraynd* were nearly always identical, and more often than not they even appeared in *Hazman* in Yiddish. The same was true for the Hebrew weekly *Hamelits*, which published a number of Yiddish advertisements that could also be found in *Der fraynd*. Both *Hamelits* and *Hazman* featured far fewer advertisements than did *Der fraynd*, however, which perhaps indicates that while these newspapers created commercial opportunities for merchants and buyers, they were not considered to be as commercially influential as was the more widely circulated *Der fraynd*. As far as *Hamelits* was concerned, this was at least in part a result of small circulation, as the paper reached only 3,000 readers at the turn of the century. *Hazman*, too, was not able to achieve the circulation or funding necessary to sustain itself. By 1905, the paper reached nearly 10,000 readers, but financial troubles soon forced the paper to move to Vilna.[21] A year later, the editors of *Hazman* tried to create a Yiddish paper to rival *Der fraynd*, but the operation closed after a few months, leaving its owners with a debt of 10,000 rubles.[22]

IN PURSUIT OF THE *FOLKSMENTSH?*

One of the most striking features of *Der fraynd*'s advertising pages is that they were dominated by advertisements that were sensitive to the economic constraints of would-be buyers, a reasonable strategy given the poverty endemic to Russian Jewry. Editorial board member H. D. Horovits maintained that *Der fraynd* was intended to be read by the *folksmentsh*, a population of new readers who were neither particularly well off nor well educated (either religiously or secularly), and who were targeted as a non-professional population.[23] Many advertisements posted in *Der fraynd*, for example, were designed to appeal to readers in search of work. One advertisement, written in a combination of Yiddish, Hebrew, and Russian, attempted to persuade readers to send away for advice about how to earn an income: "For only a few rubles everyone can earn a living in his very own home, as I have described in a letter [for sale]."[24] Other advice-givers followed suit. Permutations of this advertisement (penned by numerous authors) occur throughout the paper. "Now is the time!" shrieked one, "to earn a steady income!"[25] Get-rich quick schemes, too, were common in *Der fraynd*. One with the header "helpless and without money" offered to sell a pamphlet that contained all the information readers needed to pull themselves out of poverty.[26] Such advertisements were joined by others that offered readers means of advancing their practical educations by studying writing, teaching, or medicine.

Other advertisements in *Der fraynd* announced the affordability of their products, stressing that they could be bought "for only a few rubles," or "as cheaply as possible." One advertisement for a pocket watch priced at 1 ruble and 80 kopeks boasted that it was as good quality as "a more expensive watch that sells for 15 rubles."[27] Indeed, with the exception of unusually

פיר העררען

322   אונר   10—7

פיר דאמען

BOR+Ⓦ+YL.

פאבריק־מארקע 3717

באראקסיל

אינע סליסעינקים (וועטערל) צום אויסרי־
שען דער חרים פאן דאס געוונם. עם פערי־
הים דאס גדזיבט פון אלץ שעדליכע לוספט־
צוזעללעע; קיהלם אן ערפרישם דאס גע־
זילם; מאכט די הוים דעליקאט אונד חיים.

◄ ☞ 1 פלאקאן 60 ק. ☜ ►

חרים פערטריב אין דער געשעפט

Ф. Заменгофъ,

Варшава, Желѣзная Брама, 8.

צו פערלאנגען אינעראל, ווענינסטענס

צו פלאקאן פיר 2 ר' פער נאכנאמע.

Figure 5.3. Advertisement for Boroxyl. *Der fraynd* #230, 21 October 1903.

luxurious goods such as washing machines (which one Warsaw-based merchant advertised for 30 rubles), nearly all goods advertised in the paper cost less than 5, and many less than 2 rubles. In this regard, *Der fraynd* was similar to its Russian-language peers, *Peterburgskii listok, Niva,* and *Novoe vremia,* papers whose advertising pages were dominated by pitches for inexpensive goods.

All the same, most readers were unlikely to be able to afford even the inexpensive goods available in *Der fraynd.* The majority of Russia's turn-of-the-century readers of Yiddish were poor and growing poorer. It was not unusual for Jewish artisans (who, depending on region, could comprise up to 90 percent of the Jewish workforce) to earn 3–8 rubles a week, and to receive paid employment only ten weeks a year.[28] But this did not make advertisements irrelevant to readers. Arguably, it added to their appeal. For readers of *Der fraynd,* advertisements could serve as an engaging reflection of contemporary trends. It could inform a reader that she might need a corset, that blotchy skin was avoidable (with regular use of Boroxyl cream, figure 5.3), that spectacles came in ever-changing shapes, that the best cigars were from Warsaw, that gas lighting was efficient, that it was important to tell time and to do so fashionably, that potatoes did not need to be sliced with a knife, that Avrom Reyzen had published a new book, and so on. To put this another way, advertisements offered readers images of what their lives might be like had they the money to change them. And, in conveying information that was new(s), the advertisements of *Der fraynd* helped to stimulate a culture of consumption among readers of Yiddish.

Among the items designed to change readers' daily lives were goods that would make the consumption of the daily news more efficient. Many of *Der fraynd*'s advertisements, for example, promoted pocket watches, reminding readers that they had an obligation to be as timely as the day's news. It was not unusual for a single issue of *Der fraynd* to contain advertisements for three to five sellers of watches (among them were S. Fayninshteyn, U. Guber, the "Simon" factory, M. Anker, L. P. Levit, Sh. Y. Kukher, and Y. Perlman).

Punctuality was not invented by the daily press, however. Arguably, the arrival of the train in Eastern Europe did far more to systematize people's daily and even hourly lives.[29] Still, while the daily press did not create a need for timeliness, it did help to cement its value, not least of all by drawing attention to the importance of time past, the stuff of news.

If the daily press capitalized on readers' increased sensitivity to time, it also mandated a need for reading in conducive environments. Thus *Der fraynd*, like its Russian-language peers, featured many advertisements for electric lights, commodities that had found their way into many of Russia's public places and wealthier homes by the turn of the century.[30] One such advertisement boasted that "the construction of this lamp is so good that one can adjust the light as one wishes, leaving no reason to strain the eyes. For this reason it is suited for every house, for use by every reader, and to stand by every desk and workspace."[31] Like eyeglasses, lamps facilitated the process of reading. Advertisers argued that their products would help readers ease their eyestrain. Typewriters and "home printing machines," meanwhile, emphasized that readers needed tools that would enable them to communicate regularly and efficiently, perhaps through penning their own advertisements or letters to the editor. If these advertisements overestimated the ambitions of readers of Yiddish, others promised to fulfill more modest goals. It was not uncommon for the paper to post advertisements for professional letter writers, readers, translators, language teachers, and dictionaries. Such advertisements indicate that not all consumers of *Der fraynd* could read the books the paper promoted or, for that matter, the press itself. Even if these advertisements targeted readers who listened to rather than read the days' news, advertisements for dictionaries, typewriters, glasses, lamps, and watches promised to fulfill needs conditioned, described, and produced by the daily press (figures 5.4 and 5.5).

Advertisers and contributors to *Der fraynd* were aware that a portion of their readership was not only literate but also members of an expanding polyglot reading public. Even as the paper's advertisers imagined some of their readers to be unschooled, these readers were nonetheless envisioned to be eager to read more sophisticated publications. Although *Der fraynd* targeted an audience composed of the *folksmentsh,* at the same time it had higher ambitions, too, neither a contradictory nor particularly uncommon fusion in early-twentieth-century Russian Jewish culture.[32] This is suggested by its many announcements heralding the publication of scholarly and literary material, among them monographs by Shimen Dubnov, Heinreich Graetz, Sholem Aleichem, Avrom Reyzen, and Sholem Ash. That readers of the Yiddish popular press could learn about scholarly publications distinguished the world of Yiddish letters from the world of French, English, and Russian journalism, which tended to maintain sharp distinctions between elite and popular sources.[33] Arguably in the turn-of-the-century East

אמיניסטער־לאמפ

דערלבע געהם איבער מים איחר קאנסמרוקציע אלע איבריגע שוין
בעקוממע לאמפען. זי איז אזוי איינצעריכם אז מען קען ליכם
רעגולירען דאם ציין חי איינער חיל און מען בעדארף ניט בי דער
ארביים אנשמרענגען די אויגען, און דריבער זאקי איז די נוימוועני־
דיג און אין יעדער הויז בים שרייב־מיש, צום לעזען אין פדרישערענג
מערקשמעלען א. ז. ח, דער פרייז שוין מים פעליסאקלאנג אין גאנצן
אייראפעאישע רוסלאנד 5 רובל. מים א נאכנאהמע אויף 12 קאפ.
864   מיערער. זיך צו חענדען לוים אדרעם: 2--6

Л. Айзенбергъ, Варшава, Дикая 38.

Figure 5.4. Advertisement for L. Eizenberg desk lamp. *Der fraynd* #270, 7 December 1903.

European Jewish context, the line between popular and intellectual print culture was far more blurred, in part because academic culture in Yiddish was yet in its infancy.

Thus though *Der fraynd* was self-consciously created in contrast with high-minded predecessors such as *Hashiloah* or *Hamelits,* it also cultivated a literary readership and set of contributors. Consider the contents of *Der fraynd*'s monthly literary supplement *Dos lebn* (not to be confused with the cartoon-bearing paper which appeared in 1906). Under the editorial hand of Khaym Aleksandrov (pseudonym of Khaym Miler), Mendele Moykher Sforim published the first section of *Dos vintshfingerl* in this supplement and Dovid Pinsky first aired his play *Di muter.*[34] Many other revered Yiddish writers contributed to *Dos lebn* and *Der fraynd,* among them S. An-sky, Sholem Ash, Bal-Makhshoves, Rokhl Faygnberg, Shimen Frug, Morris Rosenfeld, and Avrom Liessin. The advertisements in *Der fraynd* and *Dos lebn* naturally followed suit. One published in March of 1903 promoted a twelve-volume set entitled *Di yidishe familye* that presented songs, stories, biographies, and jokes by the best Jewish writers. Complete with "a magnificent binding" and the cost of shipping, the volumes could be bought for 2.75 rubles apiece.[35] *Der fraynd* was itself involved in the dispersal of books in both Yiddish and Russian. Numerous advertisements for books published by its publishers peppered the paper's advertising pages. The case of Morris Shaten illustrates that advertisements like these had concrete effects. Shaten and his friends sent away for books after reading of them in *Der fraynd*'s advertising pages, eventually building an informal library of more than forty volumes.[36]

164

Figure 5.5. Advertisement for a Yiddish writing machine. *Der fraynd* #166, 28 July 1903.

To understand the blurring of intellectual and popular sources in the world of Yiddish letters, one must remember that in the early years of the twentieth century Russian Jewish intellectuals were still not quite like — or were not allowed to be like — other intellectuals in Russia and beyond. They had by and large been forbidden to attend Russian universities until the 1850s, and those that did earn a degree from a university were not allowed to teach at one or to be hired into the civil service. Further, Hebrew- and Russian-language journals designed for Russian Jewish intellectuals were themselves new arrivals on the East European Jewish cultural scene. Finally, even the most popular of Yiddish writers were eager for forums in which to publish their writing and thus turned to the popular press with an intellectual hunger that these writers' non-Jewish peers arguably lacked. In sum, mass culture and elite culture palpably overlapped in the turn-of-the-century Russian Yiddish milieu. Ironically, as the Yiddish publishing industry grew, the contribution of prominent Jewish intellectuals to *Der fraynd* would come to be seen as a sign of the paper's shortcomings rather than the achievement it debatably was. By 1908, *Der fraynd* was criticized by Bal Makhshoves (a former contributor whose own work perceptibly traduced worlds popular and literary) for its intimacy with Jewish intellectuals and for its isolation from the vast majority of Yiddish readers.[37]

If *Der fraynd*'s advertisers crossed the line that divided the *folksmentsh* from the intellectual, they also evaded the line that delineated readers religious and secular. *Der fraynd* did not intentionally target religious readers, of course: recall Shoyl Ginzburg's insistence that the paper was neither written for nor read by the observant. The paper's advertisements, however, suggest that the reality was different from this editor's vision. Among *Der fraynd*'s advertisements were, for example, postings that announced the sale of items appropriate for celebrating Jewish holidays. In the weeks leading up to Passover, *Der fraynd* consistently published a flurry of advertisements promoting stringently prepared kosher-for-Passover food and drink. The most prominent purveyor of kosher wine (at least in the pages of *Der fraynd*) was Carmel, a company whose advertisements normally read: "Drink only Carmel wine." At Passover time, advertisers replaced this terse Yiddish text with an equally terse statement in Hebrew: "Drink Carmel wine for all the days of Passover."[38] Other Passover foods included tea sold in Moscow; sweets and meat sold in Warsaw; and kefir sold in Frankfurt.[39] Meanwhile, A. Aronovitch of Vilna offered readers a special implement for the preparation of *matzah*.[40]

Holidays stimulated emotions as well as the appetite, and advertisements were quick to cater to such needs. Thus one advertisement offered readers *di shenste ekht yidishe* (the most beautiful and most genuinely Jewish) New Year's cards. Another publicized the reproduction of a painting by artist M. Yafo that "shows in a life-like way the moving scene of Erev Yom Kippur, when grandfathers and grandmothers pray over their grandchildren before going to synagogue."[41] One could argue that M. Yafo's portrait was designed for consumers who were more nostalgic than pious. But while this may be true, this advertisement, like those designed for observant readers, nonetheless introduced the theme of religion to a space where it was otherwise ignored.

Advertisements for pious images and Passover foods suggest that despite the goals of Shoyl Ginzburg and other of the paper's producers, *Der fraynd*'s readers were not altogether secular, or perhaps that the editors' intention to produce a paper only for secular readers misjudged the extensive and often undetectable overlap between the religious and secular that was arguably a hallmark of modern Yiddish culture. To the extent that tension surrounded the wedding of advertisements designed for the religious and a newspaper designed (at least theoretically) for the secular, it is captured linguistically. Advertisements that targeted observant readers were often published at least in part in Hebrew, a gesture that seems to have kept these advertisements aloft from the medium in which they appeared. One advertisement for a kosher restaurant in St. Petersburg was complemented by a handwritten Hebrew note of approval and a *heksher* (seal of *kashrut*) by local Jewish authorities.[42] Such distinctions between the religious and the secular were, however, as irrelevant to advertisers as to readers, as one did not need to be observant to be able to read an advertisement in Hebrew, recognize a *heksher*, want to locate a kosher restaurant in Berlin, learn where to purchase religious texts or ritual objects in Warsaw, or be interested that a new book for cantors was being published.[43] The "secular" and the "religious" were categories that were blurred by merchants wise enough to understand that a secular Yiddish newspaper was bound to reach the hands of readers of a variety of convictions.

It was not only holidays and religious traditions that inspired merchants to capitalize on readers' Jewishness. Readers of the Yiddish press could learn of a variety of goods that would cater to everyday Jewish imaginations. One advertisement in *Der fraynd* encouraged consumers to purchase "original Jewish music for piano, violin, or singing."[44] Elsewhere, an advertisement promoted "Jewish historical pictures" that included twenty-seven illustrations of biblical figures and events.[45] The following posting promoted an item that was intended to appeal not only to religious but also to historically minded readers:

> The letter of Joseph the Righteous. What he sent his father Jacob through his brothers. It describes everything that happened to him from the time they threw him in the ditch until the time he was an advisor in Egypt. The letter is 104 pages long and written in the Roman alphabet. It is more than 2000 years old. Price with postage 40 kopecks. Send a postcard of request, Typografia B. Tursch, Warsaw, Nalevki 39.[46]

Other advertisements looked to the Jewish future instead of the Jewish past. The pages of *Der fraynd* (like the pages of *El tiempo*) were filled with advertisements for ships prepared to carry readers to new homes in England, Africa, Australia, America, or Canada. Advertisements for the shipping company Riga, for example, promised to deliver interested candidates to Quebec, New York, Boston, Baltimore, Philadelphia, and Johannesburg, cities with fast-growing Jewish immigrant populations. In 1908, the Jewish Emigration Information Bureau took to promoting a twice-monthly journal in the Yiddish press. Entitled "The Jewish Emigrant," this publication sold for 5 kopecks and promised to deliver the best advice and information on emigration. Finally, Russian Jewish readers were becoming peripatetic consumers of print as well as peripatetic travelers. Already in the paper's first years of publication, but increasingly by 1909, *Der fraynd* was becoming a site for competitors to promote other newspapers. *Der fraynd*'s advertising pages thus gradually became dominated by advertisements for periodicals designed for Jewish readers of Russian, Hebrew, Polish, and Yiddish. By 1907, *Der fraynd* itself took to publishing advertisements about itself, as it grew aware, perhaps, that advertisements had become as persuasive as the paper itself.

WOMEN'S EYES

A significant portion of *Der fraynd*'s advertisements were directed at female readers who, like their male counterparts, were envisioned as being interested in learning about (and possibly acquiring) the accoutrements of modern life. Advertisements that targeted female readers rightly assumed that women played an active role in commercial exchanges. By 1908, women constituted nearly 30 percent of the Russian Jewish industrial labor force.[47] The salaries of these women (like the salaries of their male peers) were undoubtedly used to support families more often than they were used to buy leisure items. But female readers, like their male equivalents, were nonetheless potential consumers. This is depicted vividly in the advertisement for the Imperial Stereoscope with which this chapter began. The accompanying image features a woman gazing through the stereoscope, eager to catch a glimpse of the "images of daily life" promised to her by an advertisement. A similar item called The World Panorama was promoted some weeks later by M. Shrayman of Warsaw. The World Panorama, like the Imperial Stereoscope promised consumers a glimpse of one hundred life-like images. It, too, presented an image of a woman staring curiously into her newly acquired apparatus.[48]

It would be an exaggeration to suggest that *Der fraynd*'s advertisers (like their British or Western European peers) imagined women to be their most eager consumers.[49] Many advertisements in *Der fraynd* did target women, but many more were addressed to both sexes or, by their exclusion of gender, implicitly toward men. Advertisements for the Imperial Stereoscope and the World Panorama notwithstanding, images of women were extraordinarily rare in *Der fraynd*'s advertisements, far rarer than they were in advertisements in the Russian language press or, for that matter, in the contemporaneous Ladino press.[50] Still, many of *Der fraynd*'s advertisements were designed to appeal to women's curiosity. Indeed, female readers seem to have had unique relationships to *Der fraynd*'s advertising pages, and women interacted with these far more than they did with the main body of the newspaper.

Among *Der fraynd*'s advertisements that targeted women were postings for baby carriages and cooking implements, items that would help simplify traditional women's work.[51] Other advertisements challenged traditional tools of labor, for example by picturing a woman operating a sewing machine, traditionally an occupational appliance utilized by men.[52] Women's education, too, was promoted in the pages of *Der fraynd*. Here female readers could find information about training in sewing or hairdressing (figure 5.6).[53] Still other advertisements promoted merchandise designed to attune women to the latest trends in fashion. Female readers of the paper could learn about Fru-Fru perfume, for example, or where to buy "elegant boots for all seasons."[54] Advertisements directed at female readers not only presumed that women read the Yiddish press, but that they read it (or at least its advertisements) carefully and thoroughly. One ad for a corset contained nearly a full column of text and boasted that the merchandise (elaborately named the "Patented English Platinum Anti-corset") ranged in cost

Figure 5.6. Advertisement for F. R. Muller, Teaching Institute for Hairdressers. *Der fraynd* #21, 26 January 1907.

from 4 to 8 rubles, could be easily washed, was light, made of stretchable elastic, and never broke (figure 5.7). (To purchase one, women were required to send measurements of: "the length around the body under the arms and over the chest . . . around the waist . . . and around the hips.")[55] Strikingly, aside from advertisements for this and other corsets, *Der fraynd* contained almost no advertisements for ready-to-wear clothes for either men or women, although advertisements for the services of tailors and the sale of fabric — professions in which Russian Jews were over-represented — were common to the paper. This stands in great contrast to *El tiempo*, in which advertisements for ready-to-wear clothes imported from Western Europe or based upon Western European models were highly visible (see chapter 6).

Other advertisements in *Der fraynd* sought to generate medical needs that were being invented at the turn of the century. Not all of these were directed solely at women. Advertisements for medicines that soothed the nerves or for hypnotists with curative powers targeted male as well as female readers,[56] while others announced new techniques for the care of pregnant women, for child-rearing, or for the prevention of cholera.[57] Other advertisements promoted medical remedies of particular concern to women and mothers. Postings by doctors specializing in women's and girls' health were also common to *Der fraynd* (as they were to *El tiempo*). Such advertisements were often quite small, published free of visual embellishment, and clung to the inner edges of *Der fraynd*'s advertising pages. In contrast to those advertisements for women's health care that appeared in *El tiempo*, those of *Der fraynd*

Figure 5.7. Advertisement for Patented English Platinum Anti-corset. *Der fraynd* #245, 8 November 1903.

were consistently vague and often failed to clarify precisely what maladies a particular doctor had in mind, promising, instead, to address all *froyen krankhaytn* (women's maladies).[58] It is possible that a certain modesty lay behind this vagueness. But the language also points to the relative simplicity of *Der fraynd*'s advertisements, particularly those that that were composed solely for the Yiddish press.

Not infrequently, the advertisement forum was utilized by female readers pursuing truant husbands. According to Jewish law, abandoned wives are not to remarry without approval of a rabbi, whose permission hinges on proof of a husband's death or his signed consent to grant her a divorce. In 1903, one such advertisement was posted with the full-caps heading "WHO KNOWS?" featuring the plea of a woman seeking her husband, "a tailor from Vasilevka" named Yankev Viderman, who abandoned her and her five-year-old child. "Is he alive or dead?" the text asks, pleading: "Jews, have mercy!"[59] A similar advertisement appeared with the bold-faced heading "Searching for my husband!" The text continued with the words, "It is already a year since my husband left for London," followed by:

> and since then my friend who lives there wrote me that he has left London with another woman. Here are his details: he is 36 years old, his hair already gray, with blond whiskers, a pock-marked face and long nose, he is of middling height, not very confident, his name Zalmen Hersh Skunk, a sock-maker, who lived in Braynsk. Have pity, Jews, on a young woman with three small children! If you know such a man, inform this address.[60]

Such advertisements testify to the way in which the mass-circulating daily Yiddish press renegotiated traditional media of communication and arbitration among Russian Jewry. While we have no reason to assume that the women who posted these advertisements did not simultaneously seek help from rabbinical courts, the fact that they would turn to the daily press to publicize their abandonment suggests that the abilities of rabbis were considered to be newly circumscribed or at least geographically limited in ways that the press was not. Further, a posting such as the one above speaks not only of new symbolic roles, but of new economic ones. These young women, left alone with their young children, were aware that their abandonment was as much an economic as a religious concern, best suited to a commercial, rather than (or as well as) to a communal or religious arbitrator. Abandoned Jewish women had turned to the daily press for assistance before: in the late 1860s, editor Eliezer Lipman Zilberman devoted the last page of the Hebrew periodical *Hamagid* (Lyck, Krakow, Vienna, 1856–1903) to advertisements searching for truant husbands; and by the 1890s, one or two such advertisements were published each day in the Hebrew newspaper *Hamelits*.[61] As with these Hebrew presses, those women who turned to *Der fraynd* literally wrote their way into the paper. And as women consulted and exploited the daily press for its prompt and wide-reaching connection to great numbers of Russian Jews, they renegotiated traditional sources of power.[62]

A short while after "Searching for my husband!" was published, *Der fraynd* seemed to prove that it could, indeed, help such female readers in their desperate quests. In February 1908, a small article appeared on the second page of *Der fraynd* with the title "Yisroel Prayse," and an accompanying photograph of a grim-looking man. "In order to warn Jewish daughters away from abandonment and swindling," the text reads, "we are printing a picture of the well-known Yisroel Prayse, who married thirty times in various towns, abandoning the women each time before he was arrested in Minsk."[63] Aware that women turned to the paper for defense against errant husbands, this article seemed to acknowledge the kind of influence *Der fraynd*—and the Yiddish press more generally—had acquired. Were readers tempted to shun the daily newspaper, this posting seemed to suggest, they would be jeopardizing their very security. This short article attests to the way in which *Der fraynd* "accrued power by stimulating needs that only [it] could satisfy," in this case, needs that involved living one's life knowledgeably and prudently.[64]

The story of Yisroel Prayse has another installment. About a week after *Der fraynd* published its warning about Prayse, it ran a cartoon in *Der bezem* satirizing the attention the scandal had received. The cartoon pictured two infants, one seated on a low stool, the other in a highchair. Each child grips in chubby fists a copy of an adult-sized newspaper with the heading *Hakhaver* [The Friend], while a doll lies on the ground in front of them, forsaken for this more interesting toy. The caption reads, "A scandal! A children's paper — and not a single reference to Yisroel Prayse and his eighty wives!" (figure 5.8).[65] Printed at a time when *Der fraynd* was beginning to lose control over its readers, this cartoon reflected the anxiety with which the paper reported on this cause célèbre, thereby appealing to readers' zeal for scandal while simultaneously poking fun at it. It indicates that the publication of an article about Yisroel Prayse was a way for the paper to respond to the needs that readers had aggressively introduced to the paper's advertising pages. Advertising space had rapidly come to serve as a medium of interaction between readers and producers of the Yiddish press. Though editors may have disdained readers' "childish" tastes, they had no choice but to consider and even cater to them. These tastes compelled the producers of the paper to become its readers, and readers, in turn, to become the paper's creators.

Der fraynd's advertising pages were unusual sites where Jewish readers and Jewish merchants could interact; they were places where a newspaper reader could shape the content of Yiddish news in print. Yiddish advertisements were also spaces in which readers were able to communicate with one another. As the Yiddish press matured and its popularity grew, exchanges between these groups intensified. Over time, *Der fraynd*'s advertising pages became denser, its advertisements diversified. These were changes that reflected the evolving role of the press itself. They demonstrated that merchants had come to appreciate the Yiddish press for its unique ability to reach Russian Jews of diverse classes, regions, gender, and religious sensibilities. The pages indicated that readers of Yiddish, too, were — in ways inadvertent and intentional — shaping the Yiddish press. In sum, the Yiddish press not only *reflected* that Jews were entering the Russian bourgeoisie, but it also actually *enabled* Russian Jewish economic ascension by facilitating commercial exchange.

If Yiddish advertisements functioned as agents of change, they may now serve as the historian's stereoscope, a lens through which one can peer into the world of early-twentieth-century Russian Jewish culture. Advertisements reveal this world to have been defined by porous boundaries. By targeting an enormous diversity of readers and by appealing to a wide range of (at

אַ סקאַנדאַל! אַ קינדערײַצײטונג – ...ון קײן װאָרט נט טענעט פּרײַס, טים ווינע סײַבערו!

Figure 5.8. "A scandal! A children's paper — and not a single reference to Yisroel Prayse and his 80 wives!" *Der fraynd baylage* #9, 2 March 1909.

least imagined) needs, advertisements crossed and, in some sense, under-mined the boundaries that are assumed to be central to modern Jewish culture: the boundaries that divide popular from elite; secular from re-ligious; political from apolitical; Jewish from non-Jewish; vernacular lan-guage from hegemonic, majority, or liturgical ones. In this important re-spect, the advertisements of *Der fraynd* may serve as a metonym for the turn-of-the-century Russian Yiddish press as a whole. Long understood as an agent of secularization and differentiation, this industry muddied rather than distilled the waters of Russian Jewish culture.

In all of these respects, the advertising pages of the Russian Yiddish press shared certain similarities with the advertising pages of the Ottoman Ladino press. Both depicted Jewish economies that were deeply immersed in local and regional economies; both depicted Jewish cultures in flux and with a texture all their own. Finally, both imagined Jewish readers to be eager to learn about, if not acquire, the trappings of bourgeois living. It is quite clear, however, that the trappings of embourgeoisement—and of change more generally—differed in the Eastern and Southeastern European settings. While advertisements in the Yiddish press enticed readers with descriptions of goods (watches, cigars, books, and lamps), advertisements in the Ladino press drew readers' attention to services (translators, insurance vendors, educators) that would facilitate their climb to the middle class. And while the Yiddish press encouraged Eastern European Jews to form economic alliances with one another, the Ladino press encouraged Jews of Southeastern Europe to cultivate economic relationships with merchants and peers in Western Europe. These important differences highlight asymmetries in the turn-of-the-century Russian and Ottoman (Jewish) cultural economies that the next chapter continues to explore.

6

ADVERTISING ANXIETY

In May 1910, a letter from a Signor Doctor De Misimi was reproduced in *El tiempo*. The letter described the doctor's recent success in curing a patient of a "debilitating ailment." When the patient first visited Dr. De Misimi (he reported), she had lost her appetite, could not sleep, and suffered from pains in her stomach. Her menstruation was irregular, she had constipation and poor digestion, and was of a nervous disposition. In response, Dr. De Misimi prescribed two tablets of *Pillules pink pour personnes pâles* (Pink pills for pale people) to be consumed with every meal. Shortly thereafter, the patient's appetite rebounded, her sleep returned to normal, and the pain in her stomach disappeared. "I consider Pink Pills a heroic medicine," Dr. De Misimi's letter triumphantly concluded, "a veritable panacea!"[1]

Dr. De Misimi's letter appeared not in *El tiempo*'s letters-to-the-editor column but in its advertising pages, as the first in a series of advertisements promoting the miraculous Pink Pills. If these advertisements were to be believed, Pink Pills were indeed a wonder of modern medicine. The drug, it seems, could cure stomach ailments, digestive problems, menstrual irregularities, anemia, incontinence, insomnia, nervous conditions, lethargy, impotence, and loss of appetite. Advertisements for this "veritable panacea" were joined by others. As early as the late 1890s, *El tiempo*'s pages were littered with advertisements for banks promoting financial security, fire insurance companies offering protection from the threat of lost capital, and translators assuring readers that they need not be cowed by the linguistic demands of the modern economy.

As this suggests, the majority of *El tiempo*'s advertisements promoted services that would alleviate readers' anxiety about the fragility of life under Ottoman rule. These texts attempted to capitalize on apprehensions about the ever present threats of fire, bankruptcy, bureaucratic inefficiency, poverty and political disenfranchisement, and, perhaps most important of all, on readers' nervousness about being left behind by a European economy increasingly dependent upon the West. An important minority of *El tiempo*'s advertisements abetted this function by selling goods that were foreign-made or that mimicked foreign trends. Advertisements for goods produced or services provided by Turkish, Greek, or Armenian businesses, meanwhile, were few and far between in the paper's pages.[2]

Together, these advertisements appear to confirm an important hypothesis of Ottoman and Ottoman Jewish historiography: that the late nineteenth and early twentieth centuries witnessed the rise of an Ottoman Jewish comprador class.[3] Certainly the pages of this newspaper reveal that select Jewish merchants in *fin-de-siècle* European Turkey and the Balkans were benefiting from economic relations with Western and Central Europe and, partly as a result, were entering the middle (and, in rarer cases, the upper) class.[4] As the advertisements in *El tiempo* make clear, however, the Ottoman Jewish importers who promoted their wares in the Ladino press were not — as foundational literature on the Ottoman comprador class has tended to imply — commercial or cultural ambassadors of distant lands. On the contrary, in light of the precarious state of the Southeastern European Jewish economy, building extra-regional economic ties allowed Jewish merchants a form of economic agency that was in some sense uniquely Ottoman. In this important sense, the advertisements of the Ladino press suggest that Ottoman Jewish merchants — even if they listed toward Western Europe — were deeply embedded in local economic and social webs.[5]

The following pages aim to suggest that while *El tiempo*'s advertising pages displayed the hopes of a burgeoning Ottoman Jewish bourgeoisie, they simultaneously exhibited the desperation of a population for whom embourgeoisement was still something of a distant goal. Although individual Jews were managing to pull themselves out of poverty, by and large Ottoman Jewry lacked a middle class as late as the eve of the Balkan Wars.[6] The Ladino press thus advertised aspiration despite the fact that its would-be readership was overwhelmingly poor and evinced little sign of class ascension. What is more, *El tiempo*'s advertisements made few of the concessions to resource constraints that were evident in contemporary Yiddish sources. In sum, if *El tiempo* had been designed for the common reader, its advertising pages appear entrenched in elite Jewish society (though significantly, this proved to be a sphere intensely anxious about its own stability). As a result of these dynamics, advertisements in the Ladino press mirrored the general paradox of vernacular Jewish publishing in the Ottoman context. Designed to transform Southeastern European Jewry, the Ladino press inadvertently revealed this society to be internally diverse and not always in harmony with the ambitions of Westernizing editors. Rubbed against the reality known to readers of Ladino, the press was all but ineffective as propaganda. Perhaps this very failure helped to ensure the paper's popularity.

Advertisements in the Ladino press serve as documents that illustrate the economic and social practices to which Jewish readers were encouraged to aspire; reveal both the aspirations and the anxieties associated with embourgeoisement in the Ottoman Jewish context; and indicate a great deal — sometimes through omission — about the constitution of the Ottoman Ladino reading public.

EYES FULL OF WONDER

In 1890, a new term entered *El tiempo*'s advertisements: the *magasin* (department store). This term was first used in an advertisement for the Parisian store "Grands Magasins du Printemps," but was quickly adopted by local clothiers in place of the more traditional *casa* (house, as in the House of Goldberg).[7] The term *casa,* with its suggestion of neighborly intimacy, was never abandoned by advertisers, but its use was limited significantly by the adoption of the term *magasin.* Unlike the *casa,* the *magasin* was meant to be admired at a distance. It was spacious and orderly, housed in a modern building that towered over its surroundings and the curious shoppers who gathered at its base. Rather than being invited to the *magasin,* readers of *El tiempo* were encouraged to peruse the store at a distance by sending away for a catalogue of the shop's contents.

Implicitly, advertisements for the Grands Magasins du Printemps contrasted the *magasin* with another commercial establishment, the Ottoman bazaar. While the *magasin* was neat and spacious, the bazaar was labyrinthine and crowded. While the *magasin* was to be observed at a distance, the bazaar was a tumultuous sight of multi-ethnic encounters.[8] This contrast was only implicit. Small shops such as one might find in a bazaar were not represented in the advertisements of *El tiempo.* Indeed, mention of how to procure food and household goods — staples of bazaar commerce — were virtually absent from the newspaper. In part, this is because the success (and, perhaps, the culture) of small shops did not depend upon their promotion in print. Instead, their clientele was determined by geography and their reputation secured by word of mouth.[9] It is also likely that the cost of an advertisement put this medium of promotion out of the reach of most small shop owners. In sum, there were functional reasons that the advertising pages of the Ladino press appealed to the kinds of establishments that were coming to represent bourgeois Constantinople, large department stores among them. At the same time, the content of *El tiempo*'s advertising pages reflected political realities, in particular the Westernizing orientation of *El tiempo*'s producers.

Elias Canetti has recalled that to residents of the Ottoman town of his youth, "the rest of the world was known as 'Europe,' and if someone sailed up the Danube to Vienna, people said he was going to Europe. Europe began where the Turkish Empire had once ended."[10] In reality, the relationship between lands Ottoman and European was rather more complex in the cultural geography of Ladino popular culture. Not only could bodies and goods travel along the Danube in two directions, but for Ottoman Jews, at least, the very idea of Europe was malleable. Consider, for example, the configuration of Ashkenazi merchants in the pages of the Ladino press. Advertisements for Ashkenazi-owned stores suggest that their owners promoted themselves (and their goods) as Western and European despite the fact that an Ashkenazi presence had existed in the Balkans — and in Constantinople in particular — for generations.[11] That Constantinople's Ashkenazi population included many wealthy merchants in its ranks is evidenced by *El tiempo*'s advertising pages, in which featured department stores were more often than not Ashkenazi owned.[12] Advertisements for these stores attempted to capitalize upon the cachet of the West, and upon their owners' presumed connections with Western modes and networks. A store such as the Grands Magasins Karlman and Blumberg, for example, went out of their way to announce that their stock was purchased in Paris and London and tailored in Berlin and Vienna.[13] The department store owned by the brothers Stein, meanwhile, promised to deliver readers the latest in French and English fashion, while the House of Spiegel offered goods "direct" from Paris.[14]

For Ashkenazi merchants, the cachet of Western goods was something of a double-edged sword. On the one hand, it provided them with what seemed to be a commercial advantage. On the other hand, promoting their Westernness actually marked Ashkenazi merchants as foreign. Indeed, by stressing the Western nature of Ashkenazi-sold goods, advertisements in the Ladino press pointed to (and, indeed, may have served to exacerbate) tensions that were beginning to surround Ashkenazi-Sephardi relations in the Ottoman capital.[15] This tension was manifested somewhat metaphorically in *El tiempo*'s advertisements, in which Ashkenazi names were transliterated into Ladino in an awkward and inconsistent manner. The owners of the Galata-based department store Stein, for example, had their name spelled in no less than three ways in their own advertisements. Sometimes even a single advertisement for the store contained multiple spellings. Errors such as these were no doubt innocent. But on an abstract level their meanings were rather more profound. They served to emphasize the dichotomies of

Ottoman/European and Eastern/Western, and to impose them on a context whose complexity they belied.

As advertisements for Ashkenazi-owned department stores suggested, clothing sold through *El tiempo* was not simply modeled on Western designs but was often imported ready-made. The advertisements in *El tiempo* thereby encouraged Ottoman Jewish shoppers to disassociate themselves from the still active (though by and large no longer Jewish) Ottoman textile industry, including the thriving ready-made garment industry of Constantinople.[16] If *El tiempo*'s advertisements emphasized goods imported from Western Europe, however, the paper nonetheless reflected and helped shape commercial activity at home. The vast majority of *El tiempo*'s advertisements promoted shops and offices located in Constantinople and, more specifically, in neighborhoods where Jews were increasingly concentrated, including Galata and Pera. Some advertisers did not include an address in their postings, under the assumption that name-recognition was enough to guide readers.[17] Other advertisements directed would-be shoppers to street addresses, describing where a particular site was located in relation to its surroundings. The specificity of such directions was no doubt mindful of the many unnamed streets of Ottoman cities.[18] But such advertisements also reflected an attempt to direct Jewish readers toward Constantinople's newly gentrified neighborhoods, especially Galata, which was earning a reputation as the city's most modern neighborhood.[19] In so doing, *El tiempo*'s advertisements implicitly discouraged Jewish shoppers from relying on more traditional — and more recognizably Ottoman — sites of commercial exchange. All the while, advertisements such as these tried to shape bourgeois shopping habits so that they would be modeled on the West.

What did it mean to model one's shopping habits on Western norms? As we have learned from the pages of *El amigo de la familiya*, one was, first and foremost, expected to adorn one's body according to the latest French mode. It has been suggested that the dress of turn-of-the-century Ottoman Jewish women, though diversified by city and region, tended to undergo three stages of sartorial modernization. First, women began to use imported fabrics cut in the Ottoman style with a number of concessions to European style (the introduction of cuffs on sleeves, set-in sleeves, darts, gloves, umbrellas, and other accessories). In the second stage, women wore European dress with a traditional headdress. In the final stage, they adopted European clothing completely, abandoning the head-cover altogether.[20] The advertisements of *El tiempo* trace women bridging the last two stages of sartorial transformation. For example, an advertisement published in the 1890s might have depicted a woman in an elaborately ruffled dress with a high neck and tight waist, a large bow at her bosom, and a hat atop her head (figure 6.1). Over the course of the first decade of the twentieth century, modestly attired women remained visible in the paper's advertisements. A promotion of 1912, for example, featured relatively less elaborate outfits,

Figure 6.1. Advertisement for Karlman and Blumberg
Department Store. *El tiempo* #1, 4 October 1894.

Figure 6.2. Advertisement for S. Stein Department Store.
El tiempo #38, 6 April 1908.

but continued to represent women with head coverings. In accordance with traditional laws of modesty, advertisements such as these did not challenge public codes of behavior overseen by *halakha*. Over time, however, advertisements in *El tiempo* featured ever more images of women cavorting about bareheaded. Indeed, hats were increasingly presented as one fashionable accouterment among many—joined by fans, lace kerchiefs, gloves, umbrellas, walking sticks, corsets, and handbags. Head-coverings, it would appear, had become an accessory rather than a necessity. Certain advertisements announced this didactically, featuring women with their hats in hand, or— more shocking still—using their hats to wave at male companions. In this way, though *El tiempo* did not explicitly eschew the laws of *halakha,* its advertising pages nonetheless trivialized them.

If *El tiempo*'s advertisements advised women readers on how they should dress in public, they also established standards for the use of public space. An advertisement rarely depicted women alone; they appeared, instead, in pairs or, more frequently, with their families, embarking on a family stroll (figure 6.2).[21] The familial stroll not only presumed the existence of fashionable clothing, but also the construction of new public spaces (parks and boulevards among them) that were being built in European and Ottoman cities at the turn of the century and that were, in Constantinople at least, newly accessible by tram.[22] Public spaces such as these turned the stroll into a public act. The stroll did not simply represent a time for families to share, but was an occasion for showing off clothing and admiring the acquisitions of others. Indeed, certain advertisements suggested that the park had trumped the home and the synagogue as a site for Jewish gatherings. In the weeks leading up to Passover, for example, advertisements urging readers to buy outfits for *el okasion de los fiestas de Pesach* (the occasion of the celebration of Passover) were accompanied by illustrations of families enjoying a meander in their holiday clothes.

As figure 6.2 makes clear, it was not only women who were understood to be on display in Constantinople's public spaces. Children, too, were meant to be dressed in the latest mode, and to sport it with a confident carriage. Leon Sciaky recalls an episode from his childhood in turn-of-the-century Salonika that tells us much about the importance of fashion in the shaping of a sense of self for bourgeois Ottoman Jewish children. When he was about eight years old, he joined his Nono (grandfather) at a cafe "in the shade of the large plane tree in the middle of a small white square":

> Nono would order coffee for himself and a *locoum* [sweetmeat] for me. At other little tables, or squatting on their heels against a tree, Turks silently enjoyed their *narghiles* or cigarettes, listening with half-closed eyes to the songs of a blind man accompanying himself on a lute. Children would sometimes run over from the near-by fountain to stand shyly before our table and look at the little boy in Western clothes, their eyes full of wonder. Nono would address them in Turkish. "Come here, *kozoum* [literally "little lambs"]; would you like a *locoum?*" They would look at each other and giggle. "What manners you have, children! Why don't you answer the *chorbadji* [gentleman]?" the man at the table next to ours would chide. But, laughing hilariously, they would run away, to peek at us mischievously from behind the carved marble back of the fountain.[23]

This remembered encounter is marked by distinctions of class and clothes. Sciaky is clearly upper class because he sits in a cafe, is entertained by his grandfather, and sports Western attire, including (as he describes elsewhere) a "Brittany hat pushed down on my forehead[,] . . . its elastic band tight under my chin . . . [and] an uncomfortably clean sailor suit and creaking new tan shoes."[24] The confining outfit renders Sciaky, that "little boy in Western clothes," still and silent (though he is quiet perhaps because he does not speak Turkish). In contrast, the Turkish boys are active, if shy: they laugh, giggle, run about, and stare, their "eyes full of wonder." Though young, Sciaky perceives that class has its accouterments. The Turks he encounters have their own carriage (they "squat against trees"), their own method of smoking (the *narghile*), and even their own way of enjoying music (with "half-closed eyes"). These are all part of the semiotics of apparel that differentiated the Ottoman classes from one another.

If Sciaky's memoir is representative, bourgeois children bore a great deal of the responsibility for upholding this semiotic system. As Sciaky describes, the older generations in his family wore clothes that were neither imported nor of the latest style. Recurring images of his Grandmother Plata, for example, show her crocheting a winter shawl. By contrast, children (and boys in particular) were meant to embody the aspirations of an entire family and to represent these aspirations in public. The advertisements of *El tiempo* thus show a marked interest in dressing Ottoman Jewish children in the latest Western garb. Children are, indeed, represented in this Ladino press more frequently than adults. (Advertisements for Meyer Clothiers, in particular, frequently pictured boys in the sailor suits, "creaking shoes," and Brittany hats that Sciaky recalled.) More often than not, these children are depicted in the street or in school. Girls, too, were depicted in *El tiempo*'s clothing advertisements, though less frequently. Like their male peers, girls are adorned with numerous accessories, including gloves, walking canes, and enormous hats. No less than boys, they are meant to be canny of the complex semiotics of dress. It is no wonder that advertisements often depict boys and girls looking at their fathers, seeking approval and reassurance that they are acting as well as dressing their part.

Men, too, were meant to be aware of numerous subtleties governing their dress. Perhaps because men were expected to play more public roles than women, there was a wider variety of men's fashion. Men's jackets, for example, came in various lengths: a waist-length jacket was suitable for work; jackets for leisurely activities might extend to the thigh; a winter jacket could be as long as one's shins; and a more formal jacket was knee-length (figure 6.3). It was always appropriate to wear a vest and tie, but bow ties and cravats could be added for whimsy. One could choose between a cane with a rounded handle or one that looked more like a riding crop. One could carry a bag over one's arm or diagonally across the chest, and could sport a monocle if one's vision (or sense of panache) demanded it.

Most of these accouterments reflected little more than aesthetic whimsy. Others were more laden with meaning. Consider the question of facial hair. Much as a woman's exposed hair marked her as secular, a man's trimmed facial hair was an unambiguous indication of his departure from religious observance. Thus when *El tiempo*'s fashion advertisements depicted men who were clean shaven or who had neatly trimmed moustaches (which they nearly always did), advertisers made the firm but implicit point that sartorial modernization was inseparable from secularization. Conversely, one could be labeled "fresh off the boat" based on the condition of one's facial hair. An advertisement for Cocolin cocoa branded its importer as foreign by depicting him with a groomed but nonetheless full beard and mustache (see figure 6.8, discussed below).

While men could sport their secularism on their chin, they could also wear it aloft their head. *El tiempo*'s advertisements featured a wide array of

Figure 6.3. Advertisement for Meyer Department Store. "The House of Meyer's clothes are better than best." *El tiempo* #3, 12 October 1905.

hats for readers to choose from: top hats, bowlers, straw hats, soft derbies. One could even choose to go about bareheaded, so long as one's hat was nearby, playing the role of fashionable accouterment.[25] Though *El tiempo* may have availed a wide assortment of hats to its readers, one item — the fez — was conspicuously denied them. The fez, originally of North African origin, was introduced to the Ottoman Empire in 1828 by Sultan Mahmud II. The sultan viewed the headgear as an alternative to the turban, which he considered symbolic opposition to his Westernizing agenda. At first, the fez was required only of the Sultan's military, but within a year the turban was banned and all Ottomans were required to wear the fez in its place. Over the course of the following century, the fez became a powerful symbol of the Ottoman Empire and of Islam, so much so that it was outlawed by Atatürk in 1925 amidst a flurry of modernizing sartorial reforms. By 1925, the fez had come to be seen as quintessential of both Ottoman society and of Islam, and the Panama hat was envisioned as more suitable attire for citizens of Turkey's new republic.[26] At the turn of the century, the fez was still widely worn by Jewish as well as Muslim men; indeed, for many Ottoman Jews, the fez was a symbol of Ottomanness *and* Jewishness.[27] Not only did it accord with the fashion choice of other Ottoman subjects, but it also satisfied the *halakhic* mandate that men cover their heads. Thus the fez became something of a symbol for Jewish (as well as Muslim) observance. In spite of the popular appeal of fezes among Ottoman Jews, however, very few were pictured in *El tiempo*. Two, as we will see in a moment, were integrated into advertisements for Pink Pills. Another was pictured in an advertisement for the fez manufacturer Hamidi Fezes, but appeared only a few times in the paper.[28] Other than this, fezes were absented from *El tiempo*'s advertising pages. According to the logic of the paper and its supporters, a fez was simply too "Eastern" and not "Western" enough. By erasing the fez as an option for male shoppers, *El tiempo*'s advertisements quietly endorsed a dramatic form of cultural change.

As *El tiempo*'s advertisements indicate, turn-of-the-century readers of Ladino encountered myriad sartorial options in the pages of their newspapers. As did the pages of the press, the department store specialized in consolidating these options under one roof. Clothing stores like Stein or Tiring made shoppers' tasks easier by selling fashion for men, women, and children under just one roof. Shopping (like strolling) was now a family enterprise and the department store became a site where the whole family could fulfill their commercial and aesthetic needs. By the second decade of the twentieth century, this advantage was capitalized upon by advertisers like the Tiring Department Store, which aimed to impress upon readers that it could satisfy any shopper. To this end, Tiring began to publish full-page advertisements in Constantinople's Ladino periodicals (figure 6.4).

The advertising strategy of Tiring is worth juxtaposing to the method employed in the Yiddish press. In *Der fraynd*, advertisement pages became denser over time. On the eve of the First World War, the paper was so cluttered with advertisements that they spilled over the last page, filling one or two additional pages and occasionally appearing on the paper's cover. In *El tiempo*, by contrast, the number of advertisements in the paper did not increase significantly over time. Instead, particular advertisers such as Tiring dominated more and more of the newspaper's advertising spaces. If the press is any indication, large-scale businesses owned by Ottoman Jews were finding a place within popular Ladino print culture at the expense of smaller-scale merchants.

Fashion, rarely the subject of advertisements in the turn-of-the-century Russian Yiddish press, was among the most visible motifs of contemporary

ב׳יראנו   ג ר א נ ד י ם   ב׳יראנו

1913   אוקאזייונים   1913

קליאינטים אי אמינום

פ׳ייפ׳ימאר׳ די נואיסטראם אוקאזיונים
פירקי זינקה נו ב׳יטיש סימי׳אנטים פרסייים.

קליאינטים אי אמינום

פרופ׳יטאר׳ די נואיסטראם אוקאזיונים
פירקי זינקה ג׳י ב׳יטיש סימי׳אנטים פרסייים

ביסטימיינטאם פור ראמאם

קוקטונים טמייול מוקטופה פ׳אנטאזי אה 120,80
קאל סוביר, מוי מודירנו 80,75,60
נלומאב גראנדי אקוליעזיונעו 10
קוקטאם טילה חלפאתה 28,23
זיסוניק 24,22,20

בויטיריאה

קאלוינאם טריק פ׳לי אה 5, 3 ¼
קוטון 15,10,7
קאלטון קוטון 12,8
קאלסאורקים רינאלוב, פאנטאזי 5, 3 ¼

ב׳יסטימיינטאם פור אומברים

קוקטונים פ׳אנטאזי, נ׳יגרו אינגלים 108,100,95
פאנדרוקי מוקטופה חלטה נילילאל 120,108,95
קוקטמום טילה אי פ׳אלאנילה קיטון 66,50 נר׳י
זאקשאלט חלפאתה פור נירו 40,33
זילם פ׳אנטאזי אה אין מוקטופה אי קילה 50,40,30
טילה בלאנקה אה קלור 18,16,12
פאנטאלון אין מוקטופה אלטה מילילאל 45,40,35
קוטון אה טילה, מוי מודירנו 30,20,15
קוקטונים רידינ׳וט, בינלזר, בוויזינג אי טולי
נ׳יגרו די ביקטיולם די נ׳אני אי די קשורט

גראנדים אי ב׳ירדאדיראם רידוק.
סיוניס אין לום ריאונים די
ג׳אפ׳אים, לינגיריאה, מאריקוגיריאה, ביז׳-
טריאה, הורלוי׳יריאה, איטם. איטם.

ב׳יסטימיינטאם פור קריאטוראם

קוקטונ מוקטופה פ׳אנטאזי אה 60,50,40 ג׳ל׳ו
טילה נאלא׳אני » 30,25,20
לירקי טריקו מוי פ׳ינו » 30,20
לינגיריה פור נ׳אב׳יים נאטירום

קאלסאר׳ים

בוטינים אמיריקאנים אין נ׳אנרו נינרו אה 70
» פור נ׳אמאב » 63
» פור חילום אי חינקים » 43
אי טולו נ׳ינירו די קאלנאדם אין טילה אי חו-
סרום פור אומנרים, דאמאם אי קריאטוראם.

טירינג
נאלאטה

Figure 6.4. Advertisement for Tiring Department Store.
El tiempo #112, 13 June 1913.

Ladino periodicals. This obsession with dress is a keen indicator of the importance of class aspiration to the workings of the Ladino press. Ottoman Jews were not wealthier than their Russian peers; on the contrary, available scholarship suggests that the development of a middle class was, if anything, more firmly rooted in the Russian Jewish context than in the Ottoman.[29] But if embourgeoisement had not permeated the Southeastern European Jewish street, a culture of aspiration nonetheless conditioned Ladino newspaper publishing. Editors and advertisers alike imagined readers of Ladino popular sources to share their faith in the inextricable projects of Westernization and embourgeoisement. Part and parcel to this assumption was the belief that how one dressed signaled and facilitated a social climb. This link between class and couture was undoubtedly perceived by Russian Jewish readers of the popular press as well. The difference, perhaps, is that readers of the Yiddish press were — or were perceived to be — more internally divided by class than were readers of the Ladino press. In the Ottoman context, sponsors of the Ladino press clearly attempted to target middle-class readers who were unified in their investment in the (French-inspired) mode. Thus the advertising pages of *El tiempo* were virtually devoid of inexpensive goods and flush with images of fashionably attired bodies. Advertisements in the Ladino press, it would appear, were more interested in influencing readers than catering to their needs. In this important sense, *El tiempo*'s advertising pages participated in the political project initiated in the main body of the paper.

PILLULES PINK POUR PERSONNES PÂLES

While advertisements for fashion provided readers with advice on adorning their exteriors, other advertisements urged them to confront internal ailments. To this end, advertisements for doctors, dentists, and quick-fix medical cures were among the most numerous to appear in *El tiempo*. These advertisements reflected the influence of European medical trends on Ottoman society, but were also barometers of anxieties that were perceived to be particularly prevalent among Jewish readers. Advertisements for miraculous nostrums like Pink Pills — whose healing properties we have already encountered — suggest that Ottoman Jews' material needs were perceived to have stimulated physical frailties. In the pages of *El tiempo*, sartorial, financial, and physical insecurities were not only intertwined, but developed alongside — and certainly fed off — one another.

Advertisements for medical quick fixes were among the earliest advertisements to appear in *El tiempo*'s pages. As early as 1891, the paper published the first in a series of advertisements for the Bisleri Cure, a "reconstituting stomach beverage" that could cure intestinal ailments. Promotions for Bisleri not only foreshadowed the publication of innumerable advertisements for medical cures, but also established a genre that would be imitated by other advertisers in the years to come: the confessional. Its advertisements were composed as letters written to Mr. Bisleri, creator of the Bisleri Cure. "I recently experimented with your elixir," began one, penned by a Professor Simula of the University of Naples, "and I can recommend that it is a preparation of the best quality for long-term ailments of the body."[30] Bisleri's promotional literature announced to readers that personal pains were worthy of public attention and that physical suffering was itself a form of news.

No advertiser embraced the genre of the confessional quite so thoroughly as did the promoters of Pink Pills. During the course of 1910, nearly every issue of *El tiempo* published a long advertisement for the product containing the testimonial of a patient or doctor. These columns were designed to appear inseparable from the day's news; indeed, when advertisements for Pink Pills drifted from *El tiempo*'s back page to the paper's middle, as they occasionally did, they would merge seamlessly with news pieces. In the many advertisements for the drug, one encounters the repeated story of people with stomach ailments who — before their introduction to Pink Pills — were obliged to adhere to a rigorous eating schedule in order to alleviate their suffering. If neglected "for only a moment," several testimonials swore, the victim would be tortured by the results ("sometimes for weeks").[31] Advertisements for Pink Pills linked ailments of the stomach to ailments of the mind. Anxiety, it was explained, promoted indigestion and vice versa. A low red blood cell count was the presumed cause of these problems, and anemia their outward expression. Because red blood cells absorb oxygen — one advertisement for Pink Pills explained — and because oxygen is needed for digestion, when the number of red blood cells is considerably reduced, a person becomes pale, anxious, weak, and unable to properly digest food.[32] Women were considered particularly vulnerable to such symptoms, and ads for Pink Pills pictured them in various postures of duress; plagued by a loss of strength, color, or weight; or by menstrual pain, irregular periods, hysteria, or nervous conditions.[33] Fortunately, these could be easily treated with Pink Pills, which were now available "in the best pharmacies and drugstores in Constantinople," or so its promoters claimed.[34]

Nervous conditions were, of course, being invented, discovered, and cured throughout *fin-de-siècle* Europe, and many of Pink Pills' advertisements reflected no more than contemporary trends. Indeed, it is likely that the many depictions of women that appeared in advertisements for the product were simply lifted from French journals, with Ladino text appended (this might explain why their images were occasionally printed upside down or sideways).[35] Nor did this product hold a monopoly on catering to infirm women. Other advertisers, too, sought to capitalize on women's fragile states. Dr. Hadrad was one of several doctors who advertised in the pages of *El tiempo;* his posting announced the doctor's recent arrival in

דיסגראסייה אלום פיב'רים די סאנגרי.

Figure 6.5. Advertisement for Pink Pills. "The
disgrace of poor blood." *El tiempo* #140,
29 August 1910.

Constantinople from Paris, where he had studied with celebrated professors
of neurology and gynecology. Now in the Ottoman capital, he was creating a
practice for treating women's infirmities, among them hysteria, palpita-
tions, nerves, frigidity, and anemia.[36] Ads for drugs such as *lejiporus* and
"gold dust," too, promised to cure the problems to which women were
uniquely prone.[37]

And yet something was different about Pink Pills. The product's appeal
seemed to lay partly in its miraculous medical properties and partly in its
ability to resolve infirmities of a rather more social nature. Advertisements
for the product stressed that Pink Pills could help consumers avert digestive
woes caused by novel social experiences, in particular by the act of eating
outside the home. One such promotional featured a woman seated at an
elegant table. Her back is to the viewer as she twists her body away from her
food, her hand raised as if to summon a waiter. "The disgrace of poor
blood," the accompanying text reports; "it can strike in any public place"
(figure 6.5).[38] In another advertisement, a man sits at the table's edge. His
hand is raised to his chin as he sits deep in thought, failing to consume the
food in front of him. The caption narrates his plight: "For sick stomachs, a

פור לום איסטומאנום מאלום

און בואין טראטאמיינטו.

Figure 6.6. Advertisement for Pink Pills. "For
sick stomachs, a good treatment." *El tiempo*
#140, 29 August 1910.

good treatment" (figure 6.6).[39] Advertisements like this suggested that to
find oneself unable to consume the food one is offered — and thus to be in a
position in which one cannot exhibit one's intimacy with tastes en vogue — is
a disgrace far worse than physical suffering. Because Pink Pills could avert
situations like this, they had curative powers that rendered the drug part of
the modern diet.

Ironically, no matter their familiarity with the latest cuisine, readers of the
Ladino press must have only rarely found themselves in the shoes of the
desperate restaurant goers that Pink Pills' advertisements depicted. If the
pages of *El tiempo* are any indication, turn-of-the-century Ottoman Jews had
little opportunity to frequent formal restaurants. Few such establishments
were advertised in the pages of *El tiempo*. Problems with digestion may have
been on the rise among readers of this Ladino press, particularly given the
fact that their newspaper introduced foods and recipes hitherto absent
from the Sephardi diet. But in truth, the indigestion to which Pink Pills'
advertisements referred was not so much corporeal as symbolic. Even if

Sephardi diets were slow to change, anxieties about digestion and appetite were being born of a hyper-consciousness about food consumption and health that was stoked by the press itself.

As this suggests, while ads for Pink Pills offered readers of Ladino cures for their physical problems, the notices reminded readers that the cure depended upon the intervention of Western knowledge. Digestive disorders, readers were told, could not be solved on one's own. "You are cautious with your time and money," one ad accused readers. "You are, in effect, the kind of person who tries to cure yourself. . . . If you have an infirmity, it is time for Pink Pills, the key to health and convalescence."[40] The implication was that if ailing readers could not be trusted to seek treatment on their own, they could be counted on to understand the value of other people's opinions and the concomitant importance of keeping up with fashion. Pink Pills was — advertisements implied — the day's drug of choice. One believer in Pink Pills described having heard about the drug "in Constantinople," another reported learning of it from a friend, and yet another ostensibly turned to Pink Pills after hearing "of this medicine about which the whole world seems to know."[41] This public exchange of knowledge was pictorially represented in an advertisement for Pink Pills that depicted a vial of the drug being discreetly offered by a feminine hand, as if to remind readers that one need not turn to doctors for healing. Female confidants (with the help of the daily press), could be just as useful.[42]

Men as well as women were perceived as potential consumers of Pink Pills. Significantly, the male subjects of Pink Pills' advertisements — in contradistinction to their female peers — were not only assigned a gender but also an ethnicity.[43] Among them were three Turks (Memed Iman Efendi, Ahmed Hamdi Bey, and Halil Asaf') and two Greeks (Dionesius Sigala and Constantine Yasufalus).[44] As if to reiterate these men's ethnicity, they are pictured wearing two of the rare fezes that graced El tiempo's pages. If fezes were anathema to the culture of El tiempo, why were they considered acceptable symbols for the success of Pink Pills? Arguably because they did not appear on Jewish heads. On the heads of ethnic Turks and Greeks, fezes were proof that Pink Pills could be Ottoman as well as French — an imported product with a local stamp of approval. Thus advertisers were able to draw upon the mystique of the fez without implying that modern Jews ought to wear it. Lest these images put off readers of the upper class, other advertisements for Pink Pills stressed the bourgeois status of Greek patrons by featuring them hatless (as were Dionesius Sigala and Constantine Yasufalus). One need not wear a fez, elite readers were reassured, to appreciate the appeal of Pink Pills.

Photography played a major role in the advertisements for Pink Pills. Indeed, the promoters of Pink Pills likely introduced the medium to El tiempo. Publishing photographs in this journal had been technically possible, but for reasons that have not been documented, the paper's producers chose (or were obliged) to limit the form. We can conjecture that the reason for this was expense. Perhaps the makers of Pink Pills perceived the added cachet of photographs to be worth the extra cost.

That budgetary constraints may have limited *El tiempo*'s abilities should remind us that despite the bourgeois feel of the paper's advertisements, the paper itself, like the vast majority of Ottoman Jews, was far from wealthy. Not only did its production depend upon advertisers and patrons for support, but it was also likely obliged to curtail its ambitions for financial reasons. *El tiempo* was not the only Jewish-owned business that was shaped in response to financial constraints. If the paper's advertisements are any indication, the vulnerability of Ottoman businesses was perceived to be a central concern of readers. To this end, the paper's advertising section consistently housed numerous advertisements for bankruptcy, fire, and health insurance. Though the pronounced visibility of insurers was a sign of the vulnerability of the Ottoman Jewish economy, it was also a sign that the promise of medical quick fixes was as much a distraction from as a solution to the challenges readers might face — more placebo than panacea.

ENSURING SECURITY

In his memoir of turn-of-the-century Jewish Salonika, Leon Sciaky recounts a story told by Yaco — formerly a professional arsonist — that points out the significance of insurance for residents of Ottoman cities. One day, Yaco was invited to the shop of a merchant who was on the brink of bankruptcy. " 'Yaco,' the merchant lamented, 'this building is old and needs many repairs, but it won't do to spend much money on it. Of course it's well insured.' 'I understand, *Chilibi* [sir],' " Yaco replied, " 'it would be a blessing from heaven if it caught fire.' 'God preserve us, Yaco! It would be a calamity. I wouldn't like to see it damaged.' 'Damaged?' I said. 'Damaged? When I do a job, I do it thoroughly.' " Put off by Yaco's fee, the merchant starts the fire himself, but the results are so feeble that the building is only partially destroyed ("a child could have done better!" Yaco snorts). In the end, the merchant is forced to bribe the police to convince them that the fire had been an accident, and in the process he spends more than Yaco had originally requested.[45]

Arson was no doubt the exception rather than the norm for Salonikan merchants short on cash. But the risk of fire was palpable in Ottoman cities, and it was one reason that insurance was increasingly seen as a necessity for urban landowners. Constantinople was particularly vulnerable to fire because of its reliance on timber and the narrowness of its streets, which prevented the quick passage of fire-fighting equipment. Between 1853 and 1906, 120 extensive fires took place in Constantinople; among these were the fire of Hocapasa in 1865, which destroyed a large portion of the city, and the fire of Pera in 1870, which destroyed more than three thousand buildings.[46] Other fires caused particular damage to Constantinople's Jewish neighborhoods: in 1890, a fire in Balat destroyed 70 houses and 35 shops owned by Jews; in 1891, a fire in Besiktas killed 216 Jews; in 1894, a fire claimed 320 Jewish lives and 72 Jewish homes; in 1896, a fire in Balat left 800 Jews homeless; in 1905, a fire in Haskoy left 1,500 Jews homeless, and so on.[47] The ever-present risks prompted providers of life and fire insurance to be among the most frequent contributors to *El tiempo*'s advertisement pages. Companies such as London and Lancashire Fire, La Fundaria, L'Union, and Imperial all offered fire insurance through offices in the Constantinople neighborhood of Galata.[48] Other promoters of fire insurance included Royal, Paternal, and Central Insurance Company Limited.[49]

Though the threat of fire was quite real, readers' need for insurance illuminated more than the vulnerability of Ottoman buildings. One must recall that even by the turn of the century, a majority of Jews in the Ottoman capital city had neither fixed employment nor a regular wage, a factor that rendered the risk of bankruptcy extraordinarily high.[50] Fear of bankruptcy is, indeed, a reappearing motif in memoirs by turn-of-the-century Ottoman Jews. Sciaky's tale of Yaco the fire starter, recall, begins with a bereft merchant desperate to eke a profit out of the remains of his profession, an empty, if mildly flammable, shop. Similar anxiety surfaces in the journal of Gabriel Arié, an AIU teacher and school director, whose writing reveals an almost obsessive fear of being without money. (Interestingly, Arié's anxieties seem to have been alleviated only after he resigned from the Alliance to work in the insurance business, where he met with great success.)[51]

As we have already learned, turn-of-the-century Ottoman Jews had good reason to fear bankruptcy, as many of the professions that Jews traditionally dominated were becoming obsolete and being taken over by other ethnic or extra-regional groups. To address this situation, many advertisements sought to lend security to readers by rooting them in a Western or Central European economy, where nearly all sellers of insurance that advertised in the pages of *El tiempo* were based.[52] That these companies were not local was offered as evidence of their reliability. The company Mourning assured readers that it operated "under the supervision and control of the Government of France."[53] Other companies relied on visual motifs to articulate both their steadfastness and their foreign origins. For example, many insurers adorned their advertisements with depictions of British crests of arms or the royal crown (among them Imperial Fire, London and Lancashire Fire, North British and Mercantile, and Northern Assurance). To further draw attention to a company's European nature, names of insurers were printed in English, French, or Italian rather than Ladino. It was not uncommon for a single page of *El tiempo* to contain advertisements for three or more insurers, each ad more polyglot than the one before (figure 6.7). Highlighting the European origins of insurance companies was not simply

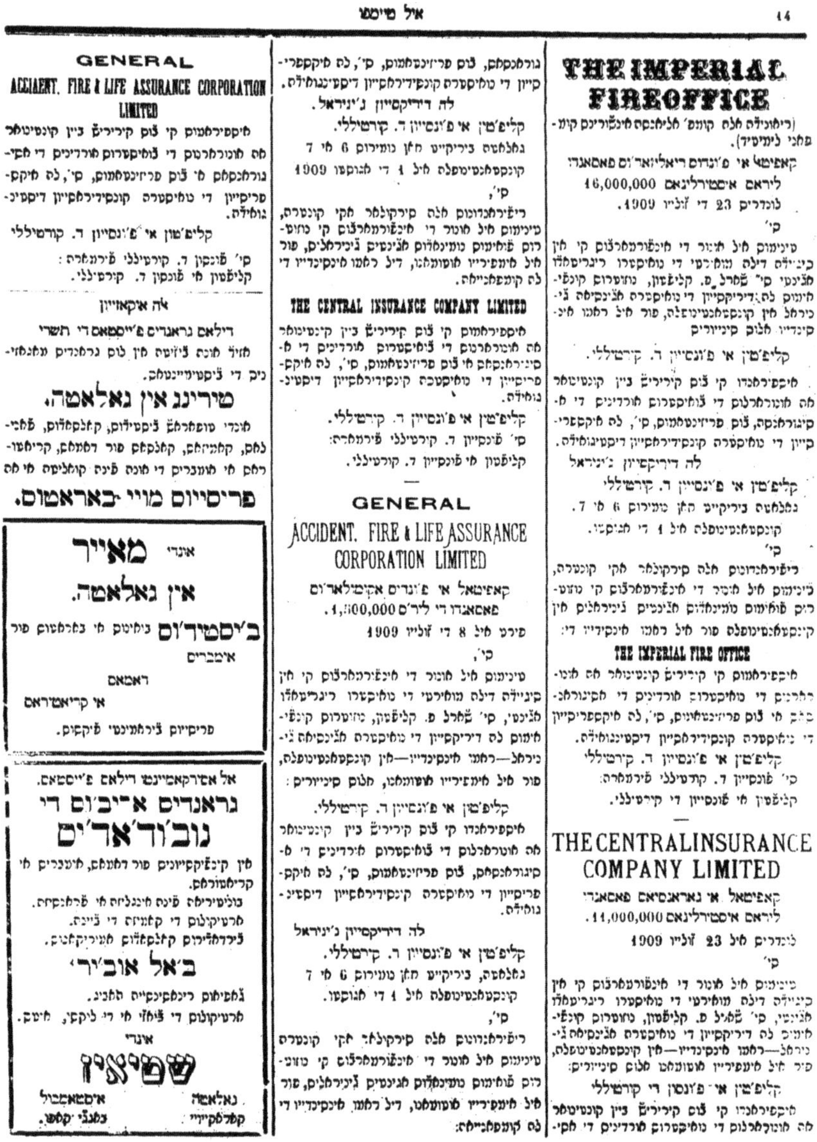

אל טיימפו 14

GENERAL

ACCIDENT, FIRE & LIFE ASSURANCE CORPORATION LIMITED

THE IMPERIAL FIREOFFICE

THE CENTRAL INSURANCE COMPANY LIMITED

GENERAL

ACCIDENT, FIRE & LIFE ASSURANCE CORPORATION LIMITED

THE IMPERIAL FIRE OFFICE

THE CENTRALINSURANCE COMPANY LIMITED

טירינג אין גאלאטה.

פריסיום מויי באראטוס.

מאייר

אין גאלאטה.

גראנדים אי־יב'וס די

נוב'וד'אד'יס

ב'אל אוב'יר'

שפייאר

Figure 6.7. Page of advertisements, including competing ads for Imperial Fire office, Central Fire Insurance, and General Accident, Fire and Life Insurance. *El tiempo* #2, 23 September 1909.

an aesthetic choice. It was a way for insurers to convince readers that they—like the empire as a whole—had little choice but to rely upon the European economy for stability, be it in the form of loans, the stabilization of currency, or security from potential disasters.

Advertisements for insurance would appear in the pages of *El tiempo* throughout the paper's run, but in the aftermath of the Young Turk Revolt, the symbolism upon which they relied changed. A striking example of this is manifest in advertisements for the "General Society of Ottoman Insurance," a company that began to advertise in *El tiempo* in the months after the 1908 revolt. In content and form, advertisements for the General Society differed from those of other insurance providers who promoted their services in *El tiempo*. To begin with, the General Society was not a foreign company, but a wing of the Ottoman Imperial Bank, founded, or so the advertisement announces, "by the virtuous order of his Majesty the Sultan." As if to reiterate this point, advertisements for the General Society featured neither European crests nor Roman letters but the Turkish crescent.[54] In fact, the Ottoman Imperial Bank had been created in 1861 with the help of the British and French; but it is precisely what this advertisement neglects that makes it so interesting. That advertisements for the General Society used both text and visuals to boast of the company's connection to the Sultan while eliding its Western European roots reflected a fundamental (if brief) shift in the way Ladino advertisers related to the Ottoman economy after the state's change of leadership. As did *El tiempo*'s editorials, the paper's advertising pages were both reflecting and attempting to influence Ottoman Jewish politics, in this case by articulating loyalty to the structure of empire.

While advertisements for fire, health, and bankruptcy insurance sought to protect readers of *El tiempo* from an insecure Ottoman economy, other advertisements attempted to lead them into safer economic waters. They often did so literally, as a significant portion of *El tiempo*'s advertising space was reserved for notices about maritime travel and overseas trade. Descriptions of the arrival time and cargo of ships in Constantinople's harbor were among the earliest kinds of financial information published in *El tiempo*, included in the first issues of the paper.[55] In subsequent years, other advertisements of relevance to maritime travel appeared in the paper as well. The Premier Imperial Company offered to guide ships through the Bosphorus and up the Danube, promising expertise in dealings with foreign countries and providing knowledge about the routes between Constantinople, Ruschuk, Budapest, Vienna, and Paris.[56] Elsewhere, readers could buy maritime insurance from the makers of Northern Assurance Life.[57]

By the second decade of the century, ships had become a symbol of all that was new in the Ottoman Empire, playing much the same metaphoric role as trains were playing in Russian society. In the pages of *El tiempo*, advertisers attempted to capitalize on the resonance of maritime travel. For example, advertisements for Cocolin cocoa pictured a man stepping off a

בְּיִם איסטאמוס טראאינדו

לה קוקולין

מאנטיקה בִ'יזְ'יטַאל נְאראנטיזאדְ'ה פּורה, פּור פְריאיר אי קוזיר

לס «קוקולין» חִיטַנליזְלַדה דיכְ'די דיס אכיוס חִין טודוס לוס פאחْחֵיכ די חִי-
חורופה קיכי חُמורה טרטמֵיר אין טורקיחה פאחמינין קוב לטחב קִאלַחֵים חֵתְכ-
טיניירכُחُ חׁי כוב לֵיזְْטַلֵים חִיקזنוליקוס.

8 פْחُבריקُهُ דיلُاؤ קוטיב 5 אين בِيزْ'וؤَه, 1 אין לֵיنﺲ (אחובٕטריúה) אׁו-
נﺓ חﭦ חיميريﭦ (חﺀيﭙﭛﺌ'ניﺋ), אﭝﭫﺓ אﭦ חﭫﺀﭙﭫ (קﭫחﭙﭛﭔﺓ), טﭫﭫﺀﭫﺔﭬﭫﺀﭫﭫﺓ דﭙﺓ
חﭨ גﭫﺔﭝ ﭫﺓ קﭫﭬﭫﭙ ﺀﺓ ﭫﺓﭔ ﺀﭫﭫﺓ ﭠﺀﭫﺓ ﭫﺓ קﭫﭝﭫ ﺓﭦ ﭫﺓﭝﭫﺌﺓﭙﭫﭝﺓ ﺀﭫﺓﭫﭝﭝﺓ
ﭫﺓ ﭝﭫﭦ ﭡﭫﺔﭫﭙ.

צﭫﭦ ﭔﭫﭝﭫ ﭝﭫﭔﭫﭥﭫ ﭔﭫﭫﭛﭫ ﭫﺓﭮ ﭫﭛﭫﭝﭙﭫﭝﺓﭮ   אﭫﭫ קﭫﭛﭫ ﭫﭫﭝﭫﺓﭝﭫ ﭫﭫ ﭫﭫﭝ קﭫﭫﭫ

נﭫﭮ ﭫﺓ ﭫﭫﭝﭫﭫﭮ לﺓ קﭫﭫﭫﭫﭫ   גﭫﭫﭫﭫﭮ 9.50

דﭫﭯﭫﭬﭫﭫﺔﭫ קﭫﺀﭫﭔﭫﭫﭫﭫﭫﭮ ﭫﺀﭫﭔﭫﭫﭫﭫﭫﭮ ﭫﭮ

בﭫ' פְﭫﭫﭫﭫ ﭫ. פְﭫﭫﭫﭫﭫ

גﭫﭫﭫﭫﭫﭔﭫﺓ , ﭫﭫﭫﭫﭫﭫﭫﭫﭫ ﭫﭫﭫ ﭫﭫ' 13-14 , ﭫﭫﭫﭫﭫﭫﭫﭫﭫﭫﭫﭫﭫﭫﭫﭫ

אﭫﭫﭫﭫﭫﭫ דﭫﭫﭫﭫﭫﭫﭫﭫﭫﭫﭫﭫﭫ ﭫﭫﭫ ﭫﺓ ﭫﭫﭫﭫﭫﭫﭫﭫ ﭫﭫ: די בּרואין ﭫﭫﭫﭫﭫﭫﭫﭫ, ﭫﭫﭫﭫﭫﭫﭫﭫﭫ

Figure 6.8. Advertisement for Cocolin. *El tiempo* #61,
27 February 1914.

boat in Constantinople, the city's minarets visible in the background. His clothing — a soft hat, thick beard, and three-piece suit — seems to mark him as foreign. In one hand he carries a leather satchel and the other holds aloft a tin of Cocolin cocoa (figure 6.8).[58] It is over water, this advertisement suggests, that the choicest goods reach the Ottoman capital city. It was also over water that one could leave. By 1912, readers interested in emigration could arrange trans-Atlantic crossings through the pages of *El tiempo*. The Cunard Line ("the biggest English company in the world"), for example offered to whisk readers away to Naples, Liverpool, Marseilles, New York, and Buenos Aires (figure 6.9).[59]

While ships could carry goods and people to and from the Ottoman capital, other services were needed to ensure that such transactions were properly executed. To this end, innumerable translators offered their services in the pages of *El tiempo*, promising to translate from Ladino to Turkish, English, French, Greek, Italian, German, Serbian, and Bulgarian, among other languages.[60] In 1910, an advertisement announced the sale of M. Fresco's *Practical Method*, a textbook designed to teach spoken French "in the shortest time."[61] Other advertisements allowed readers to purchase Ladino translations of recent French novels such as Eugène Sue's *Les Mystères de Paris* ("Men! Women! Old and young" the advertisement shrieks, "read this most interesting and instructive book!").[62] Elsewhere, *El tiempo*'s advertisements promised to help readers improve their written French. The Remington typewriter company became a regular advertiser in the newspaper after about 1902, boasting the sale of more than three hundred thousand typewriters. Significantly, that this typewriter had a Roman keyboard was implicit rather than stated outright. The underlying assumption was that few readers of *El tiempo* would have the need — or desire — for professional correspondence in Turkish or Ladino. Finally, while translators, foreign-language typewriters, and the latest novels helped smooth the linguistic complexity of international trade, hotel proprietors promised to ease the physical challenges of travel. Among the hotels listed in *El tiempo*'s advertisements were the Hotel Malka (Galata), Central Hotel (in the Constantinople neighborhood of Pera), Hotel International (located "on the Bosphorus"), Hotel Levi (Galata), and the Hotel France (Pera).[63]

If the promise of insurance against the risk of fire, bankruptcy, or unnatural death was not enough to comfort a reader of *El tiempo*, and if the service of maritime navigators, translators, or hotel proprietors could not better their economic footing, there was something else in the advertising pages of *El tiempo* to assuage the financial anxieties of readers: gambling. Although the paper's contributors were known to deride the practice of gambling, *El tiempo* frequently published elaborate lottery results, which often occupied an entire page of the newspaper (figure 6.10). Lotteries offered readers far more than did insurance insofar as they promised great riches and demanded little expenditure. In this sense, lotteries symbolized

CUNARD LINE

קוספולי, ליב׳רפול נייייורק ½1 4 דיאס

קוכפולי, טריאיסטה, נייייורק

„ נאפולי „

נאפולי אי בואינוס איירֿים
מארסֿילייה

ליניאה איבדוכאדארייה
דילה אכֿיריכה דיל נורד אי דיל סוד

קונארד לאאין אי אנכור לאאין.

לאס מאס גראנדים קומפאנייאס אינגליזאס דיל מונדו.

בֿאפֿורֿינטיה כֿימאֿהֿל פֿור הֿל מונדו אֿינֿכֿירו קֿיכֿה (תֿכֿֿלֿהֿנֿה). בֿהֿמֿיהֿה, הֿוכֿסֿטֿרֿלֿייֿה אֿיטֿס׳.

פֿרֿיֿסֿיֿיֿוֿס אֿלֿוֿהֿרֿה די כֿונֿכֿֿורֿינֿטֿיֿיֿה. לֿוֿב בֿאֿהֿכֿֿירֿיֿס די לֿה כֿוֿמֿפֿאֿנֿיֿיֿאֿהֿ בֿין טֿוֿלֿוֿס כֿוֿבֿֿמֿֿאֿלֿיֿס, גֿיֿלֿוֿס לֿרֿאֿֿגֿוֿהֿלֿוֿס, גֿרֿלֿ־
די פֿרֿוֿסֿפֿיֿס, אֿי דֿוֿכֿֿלֿוֿס אֿילֿוֿס.

דֿיֿיֿנֿסֿֿֿֿֿֿפֿרֿו דֿיֿל בֿֿלֿהֿכֿֿור כֿֿוֿפֿהֿרֿֿלֿאֿֿ מֿיֿלֿֿיֿכֿֿוֿבֿֿ, כֿֿירֿלֿֿֿֿֿֿֿֿֿוֿרֿֿֿיֿֿֿֿֿ, כֿֿֿֿיֿמֿֿֿיֿֿֿלֿֿֿֿֿֿֿֿאֿֿֿֿֿֿ אֿי נֿֿיֿֿֿֿֿֿֿֿֿֿֿֿאֿֿֿלֿֿֿֿֿֿֿו לֿֿֿֿֿֿֿֿֿֿֿֿֿֿֿ עֿֿלֿֿֿֿֿו לֿֿֿֿֿֿֿֿֿֿֿֿֿֿֿֿֿיֿֿֿֿֿ.

לֿה הֿֿוֿֿ.

פֿוֿר טֿֿֿ 20–10 אֿֿֿֿֿֿֿֿֿֿֿֿֿֿֿֿֿֿֿ לֿה דֿֿֿֿֿֿֿֿֿֿֿֿֿ די גֿֿֿֿֿֿֿֿֿֿֿֿֿֿֿֿֿֿֿֿ.

לֿה כֿֿֿ.

קאד׳ה סימאנה

פֿארֿטֿֿֿֿֿֿֿֿֿֿֿֿֿיֿה די כֿונֿֿסֿֿֿֿטֿֿֿֿֿֿֿֿֿֿֿֿֿֿֿֿֿ . טֿֿֿֿֿֿֿֿֿֿֿֿֿ, מֿֿֿֿֿֿֿֿֿֿֿֿֿֿֿֿֿֿֿֿֿ אֿי נֿֿֿֿֿֿֿ
גֿֿֿֿֿֿֿֿֿֿ אֿי בֿֿֿֿֿֿֿֿֿֿֿ.

Figure 6.9. Advertisement for Cunard Line. *El tiempo* #111,
24 June 1912.

economic desperation and yearning, sentiments that characterized the vast
majority of *El tiempo*'s advertisements.

In the Ottoman Jewish world, lotteries did not simply provide individuals
with the opportunity to better their circumstances. Organizations, too,
could profit from the game: the lottery results in figure 6.10, for example,
were sponsored by the Jewish Hospital of Izmir. Thus it was not only individual readers of the Ladino press that sought opportunity in the pages of the

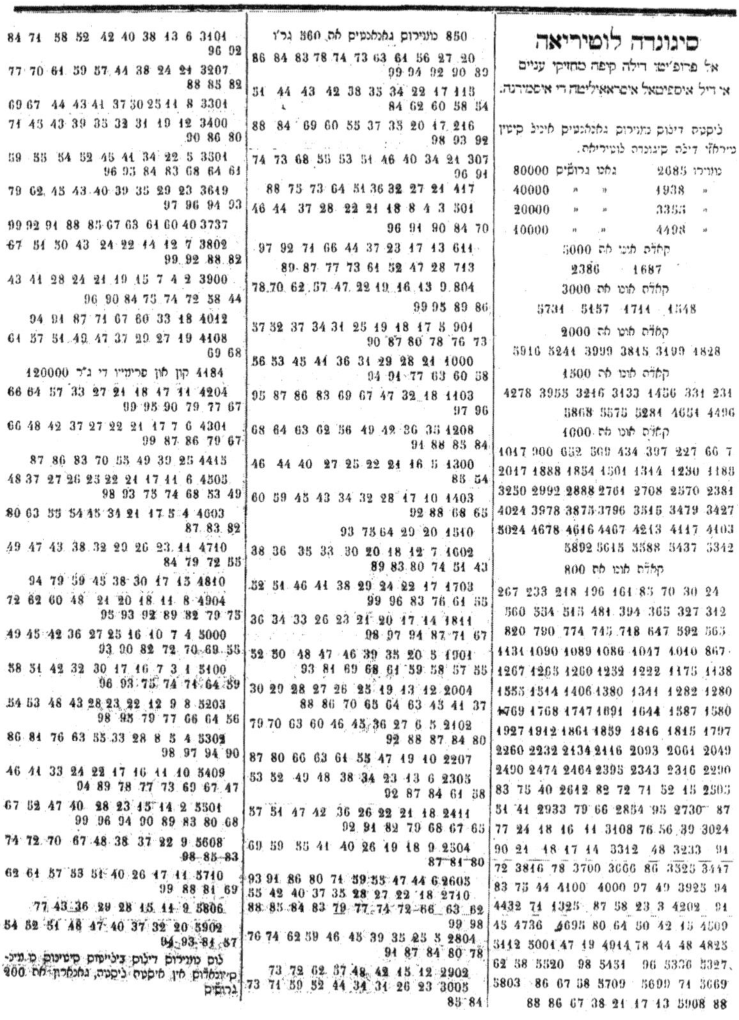

Figure 6.10. Lottery Results. *El tiempo* #7, 6 October 1904.

Ladino press. Communal institutions, too, perceived the press as a catalyst to economic change. For this reason, organizations took to publicizing their budgets in the pages of *El tiempo* (a practice, it is worth noting, that was anathema in the contemporary Yiddish press). Thus in *El tiempo*'s pages, readers could peruse the budget of the Jewish community of Galata and of Constantinople as a whole: budgets of the organizations Ahavat hesed, Hesed v'emet, and Tseror hahayim; budgets of the Hospital Or hahayim; and of the offices of the Chief Rabbi and the Ottoman military (to name but a few examples among many). And these budgets did not appear infrequently. The updated budget of Bursa of Galata, for example, was reprinted every month.

Esther Benbassa has demonstrated that these budgets can tell us a great deal about the economic need of Ottoman Jewry at the turn of the century. In her study of the evolutions in communal budgets published in the Ladino press over a span of some six decades (from 1846 to 1910), Benbassa concludes that the number of Ottoman Jews being taxed by communal authorities increased while the amount paid by individuals decreased. Given that the amount one paid in taxes was calculated on the basis of one's income, Benbassa has argued that not only did Jews in the Ottoman interior *not* undergo a radical economic change in the decades straddling the turn of the century, but, in fact, during this period the number of Jewish artisans actually stagnated, preventing the creation of a Jewish working class and weakening traditionally strong communal institutions.[64]

It is worth comparing these findings to those of the imperial Russian Jewish context. In turn-of-the-century Russia, Jews were disproportionately represented as artisans and, partly as a result, exhibited a certain resiliency as Russia industrialized.[65] If industrialization wrought the expansion of Jewish economic and cultural opportunity in the Russian context, in Ottoman-controlled Southeastern Europe the reverse seems to have occurred. Here, Jews witnessed a compression of professional opportunities on the eve of the twentieth century, at which point they were without a strong — or even a nascent — middle or working class. As will be explored in more detail in the epilogue, these dynamics had a profound impact on Jewish vernacular culture in the Russian and Ottoman settings. In Russia, the class composition of Jews stimulated their embrace of the labor movement, which in turn fueled a cultural revolution in Yiddish; in the Ottoman setting, by way of contrast, a relative absence of working-class politics left Ottoman Jews disinclined to utilize Ladino as a language of cultural or political expression.

While the micro-economic manifestations of this comparison await study, the textual and symbolic expressions of these trends may be tracked in the Jewish popular press. Studying *El tiempo* and *Der fraynd* suggests that while the advertisements of the Yiddish press provided a forum for myriad economic encounters, in the Ottoman setting, the Jewish popular press was imagined as a vehicle of class aspiration more than a forum for multi-faceted economic exchange. In this important sense, the advertising pages of *El tiempo*—in contrast to those of *Der fraynd*—did not cater to the class constitution of its would-be readership.

This comparison of the worlds of modern Yiddish and Ladino letters suggests that Jewish economic aspiration assumed different form in different contexts. In both the Eastern and Southeastern European settings, popular newspapers in the Jewish vernacular promoted embourgeoisement to readers who could peruse, if not necessarily afford, the trappings of a bourgeois life. But while Yiddish newspapers facilitated the acquisition of goods that would mark and promote this process (typewriters, record players, cigars, watches, corsets), readers of the Ladino press were warned that such goods might adorn but could not ensure economic ascension. Rather than focusing their exclusive attention on plastic goods, the advertisements of *El tiempo* urged readers to protect themselves against threats that might jeopardize their financial stability: physical ailments, financial insolvency, linguistic obstacles, and sartorial shortcomings. The bulwarks against these dangers included medical elixirs; fire, health, and bankruptcy insurance; translators; and myriad trappings of modern fashion. If such guarantors of embourgeoisement were by and large imported from Western Europe, in the pages of *El tiempo* they became the symbols of an Ottoman and Sephardi sensibility. Advertisements in Ladino promoted goods and services that were designed to appeal to Jewish readers who faced economic constraints at home but who retained the power to interpret rather than parrot offered norms. By inviting the act of interpretation, the press enabled Jews to imagine a modernity all their own.

EPILOGUE: IMPRINTS OF EMPIRE

To write about the history of Russian and Ottoman Jewries — and about the history of Yiddish and Ladino popular cultures — is to write about destroyed worlds. In the wake of the Holocaust, Eastern and Southeastern European Jewish culture and society are no more than distant echoes. In the course of the Second World War, the majority of Jews of Eastern and Southeastern Europe were extinguished, and with them were destroyed the cultural heartlands of Yiddish and Ladino. Those who managed to elude the death camps — among them the Jews of Turkey, Bulgaria, and the Soviet Union — found their way of life profoundly and irrevocably transformed. European Jewish culture remained dynamic in the wake of the Second World War, but those centers that had reigned in the nineteenth or early twentieth century — cities like Salonika and Warsaw — effectively disappeared from the Jewish map.[1]

While the vast majority of European Jewries did not survive the twentieth century, the Russian and Ottoman Empires did not outlast the interwar period. By the mid-1920s, these empires had fragmented into myriad nation-states and republics. Many of these new polities adopted constitutions that guaranteed citizens voting rights, the protection of religious freedom, and the maintenance of communal languages and institutions. Partly as a result, secular and religious Jewish culture bloomed in the interwar period and particularly in the 1920s, materializing in as many languages and forms as were known to Eastern and Southeastern Europe. A certain segment of Jews found their standard of living improved by these new social landscapes, including many who chose to take on the mores of the cultural or hegemonic majority.[2] On average, however, the Jews of Eastern and Southeastern Europe remained poor during the interwar period. Many faced intense pauperization, particularly in the aftermath of the Great Depression of 1929. (It did not help matters that the Jews in these regions had not entered the interwar period in a position of economic strength. Some of the most protracted fighting of the Balkan and First World Wars had taken place in areas densely settled by Jews and resulted in tremendous poverty, homelessness, and dislocation.)[3]

Further, for Jews as for other ethnic minorities, the creation of nation-states and republics in Eastern and Southeastern Europe brought constraints as well as opportunities. With their emergence came border and civil wars, population transfers, pogroms, and political and ethnic purges. Beginning in the 1920s and particularly in the decades that followed, legislation that attempted to enforce linguistic, religious, and cultural homogenization was adopted through much of the Balkans and Eastern Europe, as well as in Turkey and the Soviet Union.[4] Some of this legislation was explicitly antisemitic. But whether it targeted Jews or others, such policy signaled the precarious status of ethnic and religious minorities in nation-states, republics, and unions that seemed intent on forcibly manufacturing homogeneity.

If Jews in Eastern and Southeastern Europe faced hardships in the interwar period, it was partly because the "acceptance" initiated by emancipatory decrees was juridical rather than social in nature. The philosophical transition from "imperial subject" to "citizen," it turned out, could not be guaranteed by the stroke of a pen.[5] The fate and cultures of Jews in Eastern and Southeastern Europe, however, were shaped not only by an abstract relationship between Jews and the modern nation-state, but also by legacies inherited from the imperial era. It is the task of this epilogue to explore some of the legacies of empire that influenced Jewish culture in Eastern and Southeastern Europe after the structure of empire had disappeared. The following pages seek traces of such legacies in the worlds of Yiddish and Ladino letters in the interwar period. How, they ask, did the industries of the Yiddish and Ladino press — and their reading publics — continue to evolve? Were the statuses of these languages altered in the era of the nation-state? Finally, what can these developments retroactively tell us about the relative state of Jewish culture under the rule of the Russian and Ottoman Empires? By addressing these questions, this epilogue weaves together insights of the previous chapters and carries this book's themes forward in time.

THE YIDDISH AND LADINO PRESS IN THE INTERWAR PERIOD

Let us begin by turning to the case studies that this book has relied upon: the newspapers *El tiempo* and *Der fraynd*. These newspapers both ceased publication roughly around the interwar period, though for quite different reasons. *Der fraynd*'s last issue was published before the interwar period began, in October of 1913. Its closure was due largely to financial pressures. The paper, never profitable, had become too expensive to produce. Financial constraints were reflective of an even greater weakness. *Der fraynd* was failing to attract readers and was beset by competition. In its desperate attempts to satisfy a diverse readership, *Der fraynd* had lost its readers altogether. Ironically, the paper's move to Warsaw in 1909 — envisioned as an attempt at resuscitation — only served to highlight its deficiencies. *Der fraynd* was too sensational for its traditional readers and not sensational enough for others. It was neither assimilationist, religious, or nationalist in a city where Jews (and Jewish presses) were increasingly divided among these three camps.[6] By 1913, Yiddish readers in Warsaw could acquire their daily news from a dizzying array of sources. *Der fraynd* parodied this predicament in a cartoon entitled "Insanity and Death for Two Kopecks," in which a reader was depicted collapsing under the weight of the numerous Yiddish periodicals delivered to him in the course of the day.[7]

Some months before it closed, *Der fraynd* published an "anniversary volume" to which many of the paper's original editorial staff contributed.[8] Though this special issue did not allude to the paper's imminent closure, it appeared as much eulogy as homage. Tellingly, contributors' writing dwelt almost entirely on the paper's early years, when *Der fraynd*'s successes were incontestable. In the first years of the twentieth century, it reminded readers, the paper had introduced Russian Jewish readers of Yiddish to the genre of the Yiddish daily. It had attracted luminary contributors, and had acquired a circulation that far exceeded that which had been reached by any Russian Jewish periodical to date. When the paper did close, it happened quite suddenly, without forewarning or farewell. That *Der fraynd* could cease to exist so abruptly was a sign of how reduced was its status by 1913. But it was also a reminder that amidst the new sea of Yiddish periodicals, the survival of any single newspaper had become almost inconsequential. Perhaps there was no more fitting way for the paper to fold: *Der fraynd*'s innocuous end illustrated that the paper's legacy was not to be found in its influence, strength, or even quality, but instead in the success of the Yiddish publishing industry it had ushered in. In the short span of a decade — from *Der fraynd*'s creation in 1903 to its closure in 1913 — the Yiddish daily had been invented and reinvented, transformed into one of the most influential and wide-reaching forms of Russian Jewish secular print culture.

El tiempo's closure, by contrast, was neither subtle nor humble, but was an ending perfectly suited to the newspaper's history, which had always been marked by bravado. The paper's cessation was the focus of the entire last issue, published in the early winter of 1930. This issue was not so much a tribute to *El tiempo* as a farewell by David Fresco. After fifty-five years in journalism, Fresco wrote, "due to my health, and for familial and financial reasons, I can no longer assume the responsibility for publishing *El tiempo.*" Fresco went on to offer fond remembrances, expressing thanks to individuals to whom he was indebted and to the AIU. He continued with a final condemnation of Zionism and a brief complaint. ("Think for a moment what it means for one man to take responsibility for a paper," wrote Fresco; to work day after day, with no break, year after year, and on top of this to face "moral and financial" difficulties. "I have not had an easy time," Fresco concluded, "but my good humor and serenity of spirit saw me through.")[9] Fresco's farewell paid obeisance to his extraordinary career, but was also a reminder that Ladino newspapers — at least in the early years — remained balanced on the boundary of elite and popular cultures, part private fiefdom, part popular product.

The closing issues of *Der fraynd* and *El tiempo* also gestured toward the new role assigned to Jews within the multi-ethnic landscape of Eastern and Southeastern Europe. In the last issue of *El tiempo*, David Fresco described his aspirations for the future of Turkish Jewry. "I desire," he wrote, "that Turkey will remain a place of liberty and equality and justice for all the children of this country, where Jews can live unmolested," where Muslim compatriots could view Turkish Jews "with sympathy." These were dreams, but they also were concessions. When Fresco penned this editorial in 1930, it was not enough to hope for the sympathy of one's Muslim compatriots, one had to prepare for communal self-defense as well.[10] In the Ottoman concept, this was an unthinkable notion in the era of empire. Prior to the dismantling of the *millet* system and the emergence of regional nationalism, by and large antisemitism was all but absent from the Ottoman lands. Fresco's farewell, in other words, served as implicit recognition of how very much had changed, and arguably not for the better, since *El tiempo* began publication half a century before.

Der fraynd's disappearance, too, signaled that Jews' place within Russia's multi-ethnic landscape was more unstable than ever. The fact that the paper's closure went unacknowledged was in large part because this event — like so much else — was overshadowed by the sensational Beilis trial. Mendel Beilis, a Jew living in Kiev, had been accused of killing a thirteen-year-old boy in a ritual murder. After two years in prison, Beilis was tried and found not guilty. The trial captivated the Jewish presses of Europe. *Der fraynd*, too, presented a daily accounting of the proceedings, introducing each issue with the runner "Beilis Trial: Day 1" (and so on). This coverage bore the mark of sensationalism, but readers' interest was politically motivated as well. Though not organized at the highest level of the imperial regime, the

Beilis trial was proving how entrenched was official Russian antisemitism or, at best, how willing the regime was to acquiesce to the right wing.[11]

By the time that *Der fraynd* and *El tiempo* ceased publication, they had secured similar symbolic roles in the worlds of Yiddish and Ladino letters. Both were recognized — by friends and foes alike — as pioneers of the Jewish popular press. Both were credited with proving that a daily publication in a Jewish autochthonous language could be successful, professional, and influential, even if it could not remain a daily for long. These newspapers were recognized for their shortcomings as well as their achievements: shortcomings that stemmed from their inability to adapt to the rapid changes that transformed Jewish publishing in the Russian and Ottoman Empires in the early twentieth century. Both were newspapers that had managed to maneuver around (and to capitalize upon) imperial censors. Both had benefited from a political landscape that was far less contentious than that which would succeed it. Finally, these newspapers were created by editors who shared the expansive visions of reaching across the geographic, political, and aesthetic boundaries that internally divided Russian and Ottoman Jews. By the interwar period, this vision seemed hopelessly anachronistic. But that *Der fraynd* and *El tiempo* survived to become obsolete was itself a sign of the phenomenal success of the Yiddish and Ladino daily newspaper industries. These were, in effect, industries that these newspapers inaugurated.

Indeed, by the close of the interwar period, Yiddish and Ladino publishing was entirely transformed. More than three hundred Ladino periodicals were now published in Turkey and the Balkans, while the number of Yiddish periodicals in print ran into the thousands.[12] These periodicals of the interwar era were substantially different from their predecessors. They tended to be written for readers in a single city (even if their readership was geographically wide-reaching). They prioritized coverage of local and regional news. Editorials were shortened and were less didactic. Coverage of sensational news was the norm rather than the exception. Yiddish and Ladino newspapers of the interwar era were internally more diverse than their predecessors, in part because they exploited relatively new genres and media of the popular press (among them theater reviews, gossip columns, biographical essays, photographs, cartoons, and classified advertisements). Meanwhile, individual newspapers sought to fill social niches that the earliest Yiddish and Ladino newspapers had eschewed, or that had not yet crystallized in full. There were now newspapers for the religious reader, newspapers for the socialist or Zionist reader, newspapers for the Polonized or the Hellenized, newspapers for the wealthy, and newspapers for the poor. Yiddish and Ladino newspaper cultures had become increasingly fractured in order to appeal to readers whose number and diversity had grown exponentially.

The diversification of Yiddish and Ladino sources was at least in part a product of changes in newspaper production methods. Street sales were introduced around the time of the First World War, dramatically increasing the visibility of individual newspapers and newspaper cultures as a whole. Meanwhile, nearly every city with a sizable Jewish population could now boast at least one Jewish newspaper, which meant that Jewish readers could attain their news faster and more easily than before. Photographs from the era suggest these newspapers commanded a more public role than ever: they were posted on kiosks, sold in cafés, read on streetcars.[13] The dropping cost of newspapers also helped to widen their influence; the introduction of Yiddish penny dailies in Eastern Europe, for example, rendered them affordable to all but the poorest reader.[14] In sum, that the Yiddish and Ladino press had fragmented along geographic, political, aesthetic, and class lines was a sign of its cultural vivacity and popular influence.

YIDDISH AND LADINO CULTURES AFTER EMPIRE

It was not, of course, only the Yiddish and Ladino press that had evolved by the interwar period. Readers of these languages, too, had changed considerably. At the outset of the interbellum period, the majority of Jews in Eastern and Southeastern Europe still pointed to Jewish vernacular languages as their mother tongues — despite growing rates of fluency in the language of the state. In the Soviet setting, Yiddish had an unnatural impetus to survive. As a result of the state's determination that there be a national Jewish language, 72 percent of Jews in the Soviet Union claimed Yiddish as their mother tongue by the early 1920s.[15] Six years later, nearly 80 percent of Polish Jewry did the same (and this most likely underestimated the number of speakers of Yiddish who claimed Polish as their mother tongue). Meanwhile, 85 percent of Turkish Jews identified Ladino as their mother tongue in 1926. The number of contemporary Bulgarian Jews who did the same was higher still.[16] Familiarity with Yiddish and Ladino did not translate into symmetrical dependencies upon Yiddish and Ladino sources. By the interwar period, it appears that in certain areas of Eastern Europe, readers of Yiddish were growing younger, while in Southeastern Europe, readers of Ladino were growing older.[17] Memoirs gestured toward these dynamics and surveys confirmed them, but new forms of literature narrated them somewhat more graphically. In interwar Eastern Europe and in North and South America, a rich genre of children's literature and school primers in Yiddish was being created for young readers. In the Ladino-speaking world, however, a paucity of comparable sources existed.[18] Similarly, the penning of Yiddish autobiographies was increasingly captivating the interest of young adult writers in Poland and beyond, while the Sephardi diaspora witnessed no such blossoming of Ladino literary creativity.[19] Availability exacerbated these inequities still further. In the Yiddish cultural area of Eastern Europe, many Jewish communities maintained libraries and stocked them with Yiddish sources. One study conducted in interwar Poland documents that Yiddish books represented over 60 percent of the books in 138 Jewish libraries surveyed.[20] Contemporary readers of Ladino in the former territories of the Ottoman Empire, meanwhile, confronted a paucity of Jewish libraries. Those that existed tended to stock few sources in Ladino.[21]

Cultural proclivities inherited from the imperial period had a great deal to do with these trends, but demographics and economics, too, were relevant. Patterns of emigration contributed to the relative youth of the Yiddish reading public and to the greying of readers of Ladino. To a certain extent, the Ashkenazi and Sephardi populations of Eastern and Southeastern Europe (respectively) conformed to similar migratory patterns. Both regions witnessed a great deal of migration, both intra- and extra-regionally. And in both contexts, it was young men and women who were most likely to emigrate abroad. But why Jews left their homes, and when they chose to do so, differed from context to context. The greatest wave of Eastern European Jewish emigration occurred in the last two or three decades of the nineteenth century and in the first decade of the twentieth. During these years, more than a million Jews left the region, most of them young men and women in search of economic and social opportunities.[22] By the interwar period, however, when Jewish emigration from Eastern Europe was slowing, Jewish emigration from Southeastern Europe was on the rise. Indeed, it was in the first decade of the twentieth century that this region saw the greatest upsurge of Jewish emigration. In other words, while Russian Jewry experienced a drain of its youthful population under the rule of empire, Southeastern Jewry experienced a drain of its youthful population in the empire's fading days.[23] In sum, at precisely the same moment that the Ladino cultural area of Southeastern Europe was greying, the Yiddish cultural area of Eastern Europe was retaining — and replenishing — its youth.

These trends might not have affected the status of Yiddish and Ladino in the particular ways that they did had it not been for the relative size of the Jewish population in Eastern and Southeastern Europe. In the interwar period the number of Jews in the successor states of the Russian Empire exceeded six million, while in 1914 the number living within the boundaries of the Ottoman Empire was approximately two hundred thousand.[24] The larger Jewish population was more resilient in part because of its size. According to this theory, while large-scale emigration from the Russian Empire would inevitably have had an effect on Jewish culture in the region, large-scale emigration from the Ottoman Empire and its successor states would have been felt much more acutely. Similarly, though Jews in Eastern and Southeastern Europe both experienced declining rates of fertility in the interwar period, these shifts would have had a more profound impact in the Southeast than in the East.[25] These hypotheses await testing; certainly they are beyond the scope of this epilogue. One other test of these hypotheses, however, has already been demonstrated. As we have seen, the large

Russian Jewish population had always served as a buoy to Yiddish culture. This population contained ample consumers of Yiddish in print, and, perhaps more importantly, provided the social and economic infrastructure that allowed Yiddish to have uses as a language of social ascension and, at least to some extent, as an international tongue. Because of its relatively smaller size, the Southeastern Jewish population, and thus the Ladino language, was less self-sufficient. Perhaps, all other things being equal — the relative strength of regional economies, the pace of emigration, the appeal of non-Jewish languages — the Sephardim of the (former) Ottoman Empire, because they were fewer in number, were simply more vulnerable to a reversal of fortune.

To be sure, though Yiddish and Ladino cultures were both vibrant in the interwar period, these languages were not destined for identical fates, at least in the short term. There is evidence that in the wake of the First World War, the cultural value of the Yiddish word continued to grow while the cultural value of the Ladino word was threatened, if not in decline. This was in part the result of educational practices. In Poland and in the Soviet Socialist Republics of Ukraine and Belorussia, the number of primary schools in which Yiddish was the main language of instruction (or in which literacy in Yiddish was taught) rose dramatically in the 1920s.[26] (In the Soviet setting, Yiddish schools were erected as sovietizing instruments and in some regions their attendance depended upon coercion. By 1930, these schools were essentially Jewish in language alone.)[27] If in the Soviet Union the production of Yiddish culture could rest on draconian motives, in Poland and Lithuania the Yiddish school movement was supported by — and in turn fueled by — a secular Yiddishist (Diaspora Nationalist) movement.[28] Perhaps the greatest achievement of this circle was the creation of the Yiddish Scientific Institute (YIVO) in Vilna in 1925. The YIVO Institute maintained an ambitious scholarly agenda, of which the study and preservation of Yiddish was one dimension. The YIVO Institute also contributed to the standardization of Yiddish that — in contradistinction to Soviet Yiddish, which was required by all Soviet publications — continues to be recognized as authoritative by most scholars.[29] Finally, the development of a prolific Yiddish cultural milieu in North and South America in the last decades of the nineteenth century and first decades of the twentieth — a Yiddish-speaking diaspora, if you will — heightened the allure and sustainability of Yiddish culture further still. Indeed, some Jewish writers and activists from Eastern Europe adopted Yiddish only after encountering Yiddishist culture in the United States.[30]

No such scholarly or popular activism emerged in the Ladino cultural world. By the interwar period, the number of Jewish children in the shrunken Ottoman Empire and its successor states who were educated in schools in which Ladino was likely to be taught was on the decline and, in any case, these schools were less and less likely to utilize Ladino as a primary language of instruction.[31] The virtual lack of a Sephardism movement, meanwhile, meant that no energy was put behind the attempt to promote Ladino among youth. This was not only true of the former Ottoman lands. By the turn of the century, a Levantine Jewish diaspora had emerged, and a lively Ladino culture had developed in New York as elsewhere in the Americas. But this émigré community was small, and perhaps the pressure to join the American (and the Ashkenazi Jewish) mainstream was acute enough to render impossible the reversal of Ladino's devolving status.[32] Meanwhile, no language academy or central organization that would oversee the standardization or promotion of Ladino was ever created.[33] Thus when Turkish was romanized in the 1920s, nearly all writers of Ladino followed suit, abandoning Rashi script in favor of the Roman alphabet. In the absence of a linguistic authority to oversee this process, speakers and writers of Ladino were now inclined more than ever toward linguistic borrowing.[34] Thus, while by some measures Ladino popular culture thrived in the interwar period, the future of Ladino culture was by no means secure.

Continued challenges to the stability of Ladino culture — and to the status of Ladino more generally — were but symptoms of a more complete metamorphosis that transformed Southeastern Jewish culture in the wake of empire. Though the era of the nation-state brought certain hardships to the Jews of Southeastern Europe, perhaps the single most significant reality was that the era of empire had ended. This book has argued that Ottoman Jews had long benefited from an association with the imperial regime and, largely for this reason, those who remained under the rule of empire tended to eschew nationalism and irredentism.[35] Indeed, I have argued that popular Ladino sources exhibited a persistent loyalty to empire — and a disinclination toward nationalism — even after the potency of empire seemed to be fading. Relative to Jews elsewhere in Europe, the Jews of the successor states of the Ottoman Empire could be said to have suffered a reversal of fortune in the era of the nation-state not only *relative* to their experience under the rule of empire, but precisely *because* they had experienced tranquility under the Ottoman old regime.[36]

Perhaps there is no better graphic representation of this theory than the Sephardi love for the Ottoman fez. Banned in the Turkish Republic as a symbol of the old regime, the fez appears in a startling number of photographs of Southeastern Jewish émigrés. This was an item that may have sparked memories of otherwise distant families and homes, but it was also an icon with political potency. Because it was a symbol that the Turkish Republic sought to eradicate, the Jews of the region wore the fez as an act of willful nostalgia.[37] Jews were not the only ones whose memories of their imperial alliances lingered. Other former subjects of the Ottoman Empire, now majority populations of new nation-states, were inclined to punish Jews for their historic alliances with the imperial regime. In many of the new nation-states of Southeastern Europe, Jews were judged as an alien, if not a colonizing, force. As a result, antisemitism, which was hitherto lacking in the region, gradually gained a popular following.[38] For Jews, modernity itself could be said to have assumed negative characteristics in this context. This, at any rate, was the conclusion of the fictional character of a leading Ladino satirical series, who in 1940 mused to his wife, "Doesn't 'modernism' mean . . . 'anti-Semitism'?"[39]

In sum, the erosion of the status of Ladino and the Ladino reading public — an erosion that began under empire and accelerated under the rule of nation-states — reflected the enduring legacy of empire in a post-imperial context. For Jews in Southeastern Europe, the end of empire had inspired a symbolic, if not a real, reversal of fortune. The Jews of the Russian Empire and its successor states harbored diametrical memories of empire. For Russian Jews, the old regime tended to be associated with adversity. With imperial rule came limitations upon professional, geographic, and educational mobility, economic hardship and social disenfranchisement, and a tolerance — if not the promotion — of antisemitic actions. It is true, imperial law was kinder at some moments than others, and kinder to some individuals than others. One thinks, for example, of official attempts to seek allies among a new generation of rabbinical leaders in the late nineteenth century, or of the official strategy of employing Jewish officials in Congress Poland.[40] But instances like these were neither common nor compelling enough to translate into a long-lasting affinity for the Russian autocracy, particularly after the structure of empire had disappeared. This is one reason why Jewish support for a multi-ethnic Russia in the era of the Revolution of 1905–1907 is so noteworthy. But it also explains why so many Russian Jews participated in forms of political expression that promoted the disintegration of empire and the cultivation of anti- and post-imperial politics, among them emigration, Communism, Socialism, Zionism, and other forms of nationalism.

If the fez evokes the way in which Jews remembered the Ottoman Empire, perhaps the best symbol of how Jews remembered Imperial Russia is the pogrom. There is considerable evidence that the Russian authorities did not, as a practice, stimulate or sanction pogroms (indeed, the government was often unable to halt them), just as there is evidence that pogroms did not catalyze Jewish emigration abroad.[41] Nonetheless, popular Jewish recollections of life in Russia generated in or after the 1940s often remember anti-Jewish violence in Russia as acts of official antisemitism and as stimulants to Jewish exit. These misperceptions were born of and in turn fueled Russian Jewish antipathy toward the structure of empire and, perhaps, evinced unusually acute sentimentality for the Jewish world it contained.[42] If a Jewish distrust for empire lingered when imperial Russia was strong, it did not wane after the old regime was dismantled. Although the Jews of Eastern Europe did not uniformly experience a positive reversal of fortune in the era of the nation-state, there is little to suggest that the hardships they did experience translated into a nostalgia for empire (even if, in the American setting, it bore a wistfulness for the lost world of the Jewish *shtetl*).

In conclusion, the shifting status and social function of Yiddish and Ladino in the years just before and during the interwar period can be understood as a barometer of the state of Jewish culture under the rule of the new nation-states of Eastern and Southeastern Europe. These processes also testify to the enduring influence of practices and memories inherited from the imperial period. In the successor states of the Russian and Ottoman Empires — and far beyond them — the legacy of empire outlived the structure of empire itself, influencing relations between Jews and non-Jews and between Jews and the nation-states in which they lived, and continuing to shape Jewish cultures and lives.

TOWARD THE WRITING OF COMPARATIVE JEWISH HISTORY

This study has introduced a comparative approach to the field of Jewish history. Such a focus affords certain unusual advantages. First, this exercise demonstrates that modern European Jewish culture was far from singular in nature. Instead, the trends we associate with European Jewish modernity unfolded in different ways and at different paces in heterogeneous contexts. While Jewish nationalism (both in the form of Zionism and of Diaspora nationalism) was gaining popularity in the Russian lands in the nineteenth century, these movements secured virtually no foothold in the Ottoman Empire. Conversely, while many Jews in the Ottoman lands expressed a deep distrust for irredentism and nationalism and an enduring loyalty to the structure of empire, in Russia's western territories many Jews supported cultural and political movements that would facilitate the dismantling of empire. And if many Sephardim in Southeastern Europe emulated Western European cultural mores at the turn of the twentieth century, resisting the adoption of hegemonic or regional languages and cultural norms until the nation-states of the interwar period required it, many Jews in Eastern Europe were comfortable operating in a Russian milieu (even as they contributed to the development of Yiddish and Hebrew culture) by the close of the nineteenth century.

The value of comparative scholarship in this context is to find evidence to support a theoretical preconception long held by scholars of Jewish History. Scholars of Jewish Studies have long appreciated variances in Jewish culture across Europe. We presume that the texture of Jewish life depended upon local laws, conditions, and economies, upon relationships between Jews and the state and between Jews and the minority and majority cultures they lived alongside. Accordingly, we would expect Russian and Ottoman Jewries to have existed in discrete worlds. All this the field has presumed. And yet, in the absence of comparative scholarship, these suppositions have remained theoretical and the products of inference. Part of what is compelling about comparing Russian and Ottoman Jewish cultures, then, is that their differences have not been observed before. Until now, we have lacked tangible evidence of the heterogeneous nature of Eastern and Southeastern European Jewish cultures.

Though this study has offered evidence of Jewish heterogeneity, it has also deepened our understanding of the things that Russian and Ottoman Jewries — and the polities in which they lived — had in common. These cultures and contexts witnessed similar trends at the turn of the twentieth century: the uneven erosion of empire, transformations in the juridical and social status of the imperial subject, the emergence of print cultures in ethnic vernaculars and of nationalist and anti-nationalist movements, and, finally, the disintegration of multi-ethnicity as a functional reality. The Jewries of Eastern and Southeastern Europe discussed and described these changes in a new genre of turn-of-the-century Europe — the popular press. In the Russian and Ottoman settings, Jews were drawn to popular sources in Yiddish and in Ladino (respectively), because such readers tended to be highly literate in Jewish languages and because they lived in cities and towns, where it was easy to distribute and acquire news in print. They flocked to these sources because they perceived them to be vectors of social and economic ascension, and because of the importance of newspapers in the worlds of Russian and Ottoman letters writ large. In both contexts, Jews delighted in newspapers as sources of information, education, and entertainment. They read them, listened to them being read aloud, and passed them lovingly from hand to hand.

Further, despite the enormous differences in turn-of-the-century Russian and Ottoman Jewish life, readers of the Yiddish and Ladino popular press were engaged in strikingly comparable negotiations. They used Jewish languages to articulate a wide array of political postures, among them nationalist and anti-nationalist sentiments. They struggled to create new cultural forms that preserved important aspects of their cultures but were not necessarily nationalistic, and that integrated useful aspects of other cultures — though not necessarily the culture of the majority that surrounded them — without abandoning one model for another. Finally, in both contexts, readers expressed awareness that they — and the newspapers they read — were circulating in a new era, an era that the Yiddish and Ladino press described as modern.

Depending upon whether it was invoked in the pages of a Yiddish or Ladino newspaper, "modern" could mean any number of things. Indeed, even within the pages of a single newspaper, this term had shifting meanings. But this did not render the term meaningless. For readers of Yiddish and Ladino, modernity was a moment in which the future looked different than it had before. It was a moment in which one was compelled to rethink what it meant to live as a Jew. It was a time of new possibilities and new constraints, a time that raised new questions and stimulated new kinds of discussions and desires. In the pages of the Yiddish and Ladino press, modernity was, above all, a restless state. It was a state in which one feared falling behind: behind one's non-Jewish peers, behind one's co-religionists to the West, behind the times, behind, even, the successes of one's own past. And it was a state in which one struggled to progress: to learn new languages, to educate one's children differently than before, to dress and eat in new ways, to inhabit new gendered norms. The strategies broached by readers and writers of Yiddish and Ladino differed dramatically. But they nonetheless returned to a single complex question: Should one, and how could one, make oneself modern?

The most exciting possibility afforded by the comparative study of Jewish history is of fathoming the coincidence of heterogeneity and consistency that has marked modern Jewish culture. This exercise allows us to unravel certain inherited dichotomies that have defined the field of Jewish history, and Russian, Ottoman, European, and Middle Eastern history along with it. By illuminating new linkages between Sephardim and Ashkenazim, and between Europe, Russia, and the Middle East, this process challenges the notion that there existed "Eastern," "Western," "European," or "Levantine" ways of being. Conversely, by exploring historical forces that delineated Europe's Jewries from one another, this project queries the notion that there existed a single, unified Jewish people or culture. These concepts have had a profound influence on the way Jewish history has been written, and yet a comparison of Russian and Ottoman Jewish history indicates that — despite their long service in Jewish historiography — they are typologies that may no longer be useful.

In place of these concomitant and yet contradictory visions, this project charts a new map of European Jewish culture. It envisions Jewish cultures linked and fissured by local politics and economics, by cuisine and couture, by humor and hubris, by aspiration, adaptation, and imagination, and, finally, by the arabesques of Jewish language in print. It envisions overlapping terrains of Jewish readers: readers both voracious and lazy, readers who shared coveted texts and readers who used them to cover holes in their walls, readers who saw secular print culture as the messiah, and readers who eschewed it as a shibboleth; readers who were, above all else, transformed by the emergence of Yiddish and Ladino newspaper cultures in the Russian and Ottoman Empires, and who themselves helped to usher in a moment they labeled modern.

NOTES

1. Habsburg Jewry represents an enormously compelling point of comparison for both Russian and Ottoman Jewries, though for rather different reasons. Like the Ottoman state, the Habsburg state could be said to have inadvertently sponsored pluralism, as in this context Jews were allowed to ascend the social hierarchy virtually unchecked (at least until the end of the nineteenth century). Further, in the Austro-Hungarian context — as in the Ottoman — Jews proved among the most reliable allies of the monarchy and in turn developed into the greatest supporter of the structure (and eventually, the maintenance) of the multi-ethnic empire. However, Habsburg Jewry did not so much resemble as inspire Jews in Russia. So unfettered was the cultural environment of Habsburg society — at least relatively speaking — that it served as a sort of proxy for Jews who dwelt in Russia. For example, when the Russian state's check on minority cultural expression was at its most intense, Yiddish cultural forms that were designed and destined for Russian Jews were not infrequently developed on Austro-Hungarian soil. (One thinks of the Yiddish periodicals published in Habsburg cities and read by Russian Jews, or of the 1908 Conference for the Yiddish Language, which was convened in the Austro-Hungarian city of Czernowitz — though the vast majority of its delegates were Russian Jews — precisely because such an event would never have been permitted in Russia.) What is more, because of the way in which Habsburg society treated its minority populations (and as a result of its relatively democratic political structure), the Austro-Hungarian Empire became a model for certain Russian Jewish advocates of imperial reform. Those Russian Jews who were involved in opposition politics, meanwhile, looked to the Austro-Marxists and liberal parties for inspiration. The exclusion of the Habsburg case from the current study is not meant to deride its relevance; on the contrary, I hope the comparative focus of this book invites auxiliary comparisons.

Among the influential works on Habsburg Jewry are Istvan Deák, *Beyond Nationalism: A Social and Political History of the Habsburg Officer Corps 1848–1918* (New York: Oxford University Press, 1990); Lois Dubin, *The Port Jews of Habsburg Trieste: Absolutist Politics and Enlightenment Culture* (Stanford, Calif.: Stanford University Press, 2000); William McCagg, *A History of Habsburg Jews, 1670–1918* (Bloomington: Indiana University Press, 1989); Marsha Rozenblit, *Reconstructing a National Identity: The Jews of Habsburg Austria during World War I* (Oxford: Oxford University Press, 2001);

Robert S. Wistrich, *The Jews of Vienna in the Age of Franz Joseph* (Oxford: Oxford University Press, 1989). For an extraordinary comparison of the transition between empire and nation-state in the Russian, Ottoman, and Habsburg settings, see Karen Barkey and Mark Von Hagen, *After Empire: Multiethnic Societies and Nation-Building: The Soviet Union and the Russian, Ottoman, and Habsburg Empires* (Boulder, Colo.: Westview Press, 1997).

2. For more on the education of Jewish girls in the modern Ottoman setting, see Esther Benbassa, "L'éducation féminine en Orient: l'école de filles de l'Alliance Israélite Universelle à Galata, Istanbul (1879–1912)," *Histoire, économie, et société* 4 (1991) and Benbassa's revised English version published in *Studies in Contemporary Jewry;* Aron Rodrigue, *French Jews, Turkish Jews: The Alliance Israélite Universelle and the Politics of Jewish Schooling in Turkey, 1860–1925* (Bloomington: Indiana University Press, 1990). On the Russian context, see Shaul Stampfer, "Gender Differentiation and Education of the Jewish Woman in Nineteenth-Century Eastern Europe," *Polin* 7 (1994). For a comparison of gendered practices among Eastern and Western European Jewries, Paula A. Hyman, *Gender and Assimilation in Modern Jewish History: The Roles and Representation of Women* (Seattle: University of Washington Press, 1995).

3. I borrow the term "selective integration" from Benjamin Nathans, *Beyond the Pale: The Jewish Encounter with Late Imperial Russia* (Berkeley: University of California Press, 2002); see especially pp. 23–82. For a literary study of the Russified Jewish elite, see Gabriella Safran, *Rewriting the Jew: Assimilation Narratives in the Russian Empire* (Stanford, Calif.: Stanford University Press, 2000).

4. Discussion of Jews' rates of literacy in Yiddish and Ladino (in the imperial and post-imperial contexts) may be found in a number of sources and will be discussed in detail in chapters 1 and 2. On Sephardi Jewry, see Kalev Astruc, "Data Concerning the Demographic Situation of the Bulgarian Jews, 1887–1949," *Annual* 16 (1981); Harriet Pass Freidenreich, *The Jews of Yugoslavia: A Quest for Community* (Philadelphia: Jewish Publication Society, 1979); Eyal Ginio, " 'Learning the Beautiful Language of Homer': Judeo-Spanish Speaking Jews and the Greek Language and Culture between the Wars," *Jewish History* 6, no. 3 (2002); Saul Mézan, *Les juifs espagnols en Bulgarie* (Sofia: "Hamishpat" Publishers, 1925); Bracha Rivlin, ed., *Pinkas hakehilot — Greece* (Jerusalem: Yad Vashem, 1998); Walter F. Weiker, *Ottomans, Turks, and the Jewish Polity* (New York and London: University Press of America, 1992). The percentage of Russian Jews fluent in Yiddish is derived from the Russian census of 1897, an admittedly imperfect source (the reasons for this will be explored in chapter 1). Results of the census may be found in "Gramotnost' evreev v Rossii," in *Evreiskaia entsiklopediia,* ed. Albert Harkavy (St. Petersburg: Obshchestva dlia nauchnykh evreiskikh izdanii, 1908–13). This information is also summarized in English by I. M. Rubinow, *Economic Conditions of the Jews in Russia,* vol. 15 (New York: U.S. Bureau of Labor Bulletin, 1907 [reprinted New York, 1976]). At roughly the same time as the Russian census was collected, the Jewish Colonization Association undertook its own study of Russian Jewry. These findings are reported in *Sbornik materialov ob ekonomicheskom polozhenii evreev v Rossii* (St. Petersburg: Jewish Colonization Association, 1904). Russian and Ottoman Jews' rates of fluency and literacy in Yiddish and Ladino (respectively) and in regional and hegemonic languages will be discussed in detail in chapters 1 and 2.

5. Among the sources that offer (incomplete) lists of Yiddish and Ladino periodicals of the Russian and Ottoman Empire are the following: Joshua Fishman, *Yiddish: Turning to Life* (New York: John Benjamin's Publishing Co., 1991); Abraham Galanté, *La presse judéo-espagnole mondiale* (Istanbul: Société anonyme de papeterie et d'imprimerie [Fratelli Haim], 1935); Moshe David Gaon, *Haitonut beladino: bibliografia* (Jerusalem: Ben Zvi, 1965); A. Kirzhnits, *Di yidishe prese in der gevezener rusisher imperye (1823–1916)* (Moscow: Tsentraler felker-farlag fun fssr, 1930); Avigdor Levy,

The Sephardim in the Ottoman Empire (Princeton, N.J.: Darwin Press, 1992); Gad Nassi, "Synoptic List of Ottoman-Turkish-Jewish and Other Sephardic Journals," in *Jewish Journalism and Printing Houses in the Ottoman Empire and Modern Turkey,* ed. Gad Nassi (Istanbul: Isis Press, 2001); Leonard Prager, *Yiddish Literary and Linguistic Periodicals and Miscellanies* (New York: Norward Editions, 1982); Y. Shayn, "Materialn tsu a bibliografye fun yidisher periodike in poyln, 1918–1939," in *Shtudyes vegn yidn in poyln, 1919–1939,* ed. Joshua Fishman (New York: YIVO Institute, 1963); Avraham Yaari, *Reshimat sifrei ladino hanimtsaim bevethasefarim haleumi vehauniversitai biyerushalayim* (Jerusalem: Hevrah lehotsaat sefarim al yad hauniversitah haivrit, 1934).

6. English-language scholarship on Ottoman and Russian presses is scarcely twenty years old. See Ami Ayalon, *The Press in the Arab Middle East: A History* (Oxford: Oxford University Press, 1995); Jeffrey Brooks, *Thank You, Comrade Stalin! Soviet Public Culture from Revolution to Cold War* (Princeton, N.J.: Princeton University Press, 2000) and *When Russia Learned to Read: Literacy and Popular Literature, 1861–1917* (Princeton, N.J.: Princeton University Press, 1985); Elizabeth Brown Frierson, "Unimagined Communities: State, Press, and Gender in the Hamidian Era" (Ph.D. dissertation, Princeton University, 1996); Elizabeth Kendall, "Between Politics and Literature: Journals in Alexandria and Istanbul at the End of the Nineteenth Century," in *Modernity & Culture from the Mediterranean to the Indian Ocean,* ed. C. A. Bayly and Leila Fawaz (New York: Columbia University Press, 2002); Louise McReynolds, *The News under Russia's Old Regime: The Development of a Mass-Circulating Press* (Princeton, N.J.: Princeton University Press, 1991); Charles A. Ruud, "The Printing Press as an Agent of Political Change in Early-Twentieth Century Russia," *The Russian Review* 40, no. 4 (1981); Sally West, "Constructing Consumer Culture: Advertising in Imperial Russia to 1914" (Ph.D. dissertation, University of Illinois at Urbana-Champaign, 1987). The following chapters also rely on secondary sources in Russian and Turkish; these will be cited as necessary.

7. Exploration of Yiddish and Ladino periodicals of the nineteenth century may be found in Dovid Druk, *Tsu der geshikhte fun der yidisher prese in rusland un poylen* (Varshe: farlag zikhroynes, 1920); Abraham Elmaleh, "Hasifrut vehaitonut haespanoliot," *Hashiloah* 26, no. 1 (1912); Galanté, *La presse judéo-espagnole mondiale;* Eli Lederhendler, *The Road to Modern Jewish Politics: Political Tradition and Political Reconstruction in the Jewish Community of Tsarist Russia* (Oxford: Oxford University Press, 1989); Avner Levi, "Alexander Ben Ghiat and His Contribution to Journalism and Belles-Lettres in Ladino" (in Hebrew), in *The Heritage of Sephardi and Oriental Jews,* ed. Issachar Ben-Ami (Jerusalem: Magnes Press, 1982); Michael Molho, *Literatura séfardita de Oriente* (Madrid and Barcelona: CSIC and Instituto Arias Montano, 1960); Alexander Orbach, *New Voices of Russian Jewry* (Leiden: E. J. Brill, 1980); Yakov Shatzky, "Geshikhte fun der yidisher prese," in *Algemeyne entsiklopedye* (New York: Dubnov fund un TSIKO, 1942); S. L. Tsinberg, *Istoriia evreiskoi pechati v rossii v sviazi s obshchestvennymi techeniiami* (Petrograd: Tip. I. Fleitmana, 1915); Shmuel Leyb Tsitron, *Di geshikhte fun der yidisher prese fun yorn 1863–1889, fareyn fun yidishe literatn un zhurnalistn in vilne* (Vilna: Aygner farlag, 1923); Steven J. Zipperstein, *Elusive Prophet: Ahad Ha'am and the Origins of Zionism* (Berkeley: University of California Press, 1993).

8. In the worlds of Yiddish and Ladino letters, a "daily" was never published more than six times a week, as even the most avowedly secular of editors resisted publishing on the Sabbath. In any case, both *Der fraynd* and *El tiempo* had difficulty ⸱ing to this printing regime. For more information about the regularity of these ⸱ls, see chapters 1 and 2.

⸱n between Ladino journalists and the religious leadership of Constan-⸱lonika are discussed in chapter 2 and described in the following ⸱nco, *Essai sur l'histoire des Israélites de l'empire Ottoman depuis les origines jusqu'à nos jours* (Hildesheim, New York: Georg Olms Verlag, 1897 [reissued 1973]), 187–89; Robyn Lowenthal, "Elia Carmona's Autobiography: Judeo-Spanish Popular Press and Novel Publishing Milieu in Constantinople, Ottoman Empire, circa 1860–1932" (Ph.D. dissertation, University of Nebraska, 1984), 179, 214, 233; Abraham Galanté, *Histoire des juifs de Turquie*, 9 vols. (Istanbul: Isis, 1985), vol. 2, 137, 261–63. Discussion of the relationship between the secular Yiddish press and religious readers and leaders can be found in chapter 1. It is also discussed in the following sources: Shoyl Ginzburg, *Amolike peterburg*, 3 vols., vol. 1: *Historishe verk* (New York: Shoyl ginzburg shriftn-komitet, 1944); Ya'akov Lifshits, *Zikhron ya'akov*, 3 vols., vol. 2 (Frankfurt and Kovno: N. H. Lifshits, 1924–30); Ehud Luz, *Parallels Meet: Religion and Nationalism in the Early Zionist Movement (1882–1904)* (Philadelphia: Jewish Publication Society, 1988).

10. David Fresco, "Alos lektores," *El instruktor*, no. 1, Iyar 5648 (1888).

11. In the turn-of-the-century Sephardi context in particular, the religious elite proved amenable to discussing and accommodating change. But even in Russia, where the religious elite was arguably more successful in waging a campaign against secularization, the imprint of the observant was inevitably felt in the pages of the professedly secular *Der faynd*. I describe the artificial attempt to create a secular Yiddish literary milieu in "Divining the Secular in the Yiddish Popular Press," in *Sacred Stories: Religion and Culture in Russia*, ed. Mark Steinberg and Heather Coleman (forthcoming). See also Imanuel Etkes, ed., *Hadat vehahayim: tenu'at hahaskala hayehudit bemizrah eropa* (Jerusalem: Merkaz zalman shazar le-toldot yisra'el, 1993); Jacob Katz, "Orthodoxy in Historical Perspective," *Studies in Contemporary Jewry* 2 (1986). On the Ottoman and wider Sephardi milieu, see Matthias Lehmann, "Judeo-Spanish Musar Literature and the Transformation of Ottoman-Sephardic Society (Eighteenth through Nineteenth Centuries)" (Ph.D. dissertation, Freie Universität, 2001); Norman Stillman, *Sephardi Religious Responses to Modernity* (London: Harwood, 1996); and the articles by Zvi Zohar cited in the bibliography to this work.

12. "La questyon de la lingua," *El tiempo*, no. 63 (17 June 1901); "La literatura hebraika," *El tiempo*, no. 30 (30 December 1904); Veridades, "La konkurensya de la mujer con el hombre," *El tiempo*, no. 90 (3 September 1906); "Medicine i hygiene," *El tiempo*, no. 82 (6 July 1908).

13. *Der faynd*, no. 1 (5 [18] January 1903).

14. On which, see Max Weinreich, *History of the Yiddish Language*, trans. by Shlomo Noble with the assistance of Joshua A. Fishman (Chicago: University of Chicago Press, 1980); Paloma Diaz Mas, *Los sefardies: historia, lengua, y cultura* (Barcelona: Riopiedras ediciones, 1993); Tracy K. Harris, *Death of a Language: The History of Judeo-Spanish* (Newark, N.J.: Associated University Press, 1994); Raymond Robert Renard, *Sépharad, le monde et la langue judéoespagnole des séphardim* (Mons: Annales universitaires de Mons, 1966); Vidal Sephia, *Le judéo-espagnol* (Paris: Entente, 1986).

15. The growing discrepancy between these two populations was largely a result of the tremendous expansion in the Russian Jewish population over the course of the nineteenth century, an expansion whose causes remain open to debate. From 1820 to 1880 this population grew 150 percent, in comparison to an 87 percent increase among the general population: over the subsequent thirty years it grew 40 percent larger still. Jacob Lestchinsky, *Dos yidishe folk in tsifern* (Berlin: Klal-farlag, 1922) and "Di antviklung fun yidishn folk far di letste 100 yor," *Shriftn far ekonomik un statistik* 1 (1928). See also Rubinow, *Economic Conditions of the Jews in Russia, Sbornik materialov*. My assessment of the Ottoman Jewish population is based upon Ottoman statistics that excluded Jews of foreign nationality. Jewish sources identify almost double this number. Kemal H. Karpat, *Ottoman Population, 1830–1914: Demographic and Social Characteristics* (Madison: University of Wisconsin Press, 1985), 169.

16. During the same period, the Jewish population in smaller cities of the Otto-

man Empire (particularly in the regions of the Aegean and Thrace) increased as well. Walter F. Weiker, *Ottomans, Turks, and the Jewish Polity* (New York and London: University Press of America, 1992), 132–48.

17. Lestchinsky, *Dos yidishe folk in tsifern* and "Di antviklung fun yidishn folk."

18. Just over 300,000 Jews lived outside the Pale at the turn of the twentieth century, of whom approximately 200,000 lived in European Russia and approximately 100,000 lived in the empire's eastern territories. On the formation of the Pale, see John Klier, *Russia Gathers Her Jews: The Origins of the "Jewish Question" in Russia, 1772–1825* (DeKalb: Northern Illinois University Press, 1986); Richard Pipes, "Catherine II and the Jews: The Origins of the Pale of Settlement," *Soviet Jewish Affairs*, no. 5 (1975).

19. According to traditionalist and textualist views of Islam, the *shari'a* divided Ottoman society into two: the elite (a group accessible only to Muslims that was exempt from the payment of taxes and that consisted of the bureaucracy, the military and janissary corps [slave army], and the clergy) and the *reaya* (the flock), who were subject to heavy tributary taxes. Metin Heper, *The State Tradition in Turkey* (Atlantic Highlands, N.J.: Eothen Press, 1985); Serif Mardin, "Power, Civil Society and Culture in the Ottoman Empire," *Comparative Studies in Society and History*, no. 11 (1969).

20. On the importance of the state's respect for "difference," see Aron Rodrigue and Nancy Reynolds, " 'Difference' and Tolerance in the Ottoman Empire," *Stanford Humanities Review* 5 (Fall 1995). More on the evolution and status of the *dhimmi* in the modern Ottoman setting may be found in: Benjamin Braude and Bernard Lewis, eds., *Christians and Jews in the Ottoman Empire: The Functioning of a Plural Society* (New York: Holmes & Meier, 1982); Amnon Cohen and Elisheva Pikali, *Jews in the Moslem Religious Court: Society, Economy, and Communal Organization in the XVIth Century* (Jerusalem: Ben-Zvi Institute, 1993); Bernard Lewis, *The Jews of Islam* (Princeton, N.J.: Princeton University Press, 1984); Bruce Masters, *Christians and Jews in the Ottoman Arab World: The Roots of Sectarianism* (Cambridge: Cambridge University Press, 2001). A uniquely comparative study of Jewish life under Islamic and Christian rule has been written by Mark R. Cohen, *Under Crescent and Cross* (Princeton, N.J.: Princeton University Press, 1994). A discussion of the historiographic debates that have surrounded the status of Jews under the rule of Islam is offered by Mark Cohen in his introduction to the aforementioned and in his "The Neo-Lachrymose Conception of Jewish-Arab History," *Tikkun* 6 (May–June 1991). See also Sarah Abrevaya Stein, "Sephardi and Middle Eastern Jewries since 1492," in *The Oxford Handbook of Jewish Studies*, ed. Martin Goodman (Oxford: Oxford University Press, 2002).

21. Among the many works that contain theoretical discussion of Russia's policy toward its multi-ethnic population are Hosking, *Russia: People and Empire;* Marc Raeff, "In the Imperial Manner," in *Catherine the Great: A Profile*, ed. Marc Raeff (New York: Hill & Wang, 1972); Von Hagen, "Russia as Empire"; Theodore Weeks, *Nation and State in Late Imperial Russia: Nationalism and Russification on the Western Frontier, 1863–1914* (DeKalb: Northern Illinois University Press, 1996). See also the contributions by Pearson and Waldon in *Civil Rights in Imperial Russia*, ed. Linda Edmondson (Oxford: Clarendon Press, 1989), and those by Raeff and Starr in *Soviet Nationality Problems*, ed. Edward Allworth (New York: 1972).

22. For example, see Robert E. Blobaum, *Rewolucja: Russian Poland, 1904–1907* (Ithaca, N.Y.: Cornell University Press, 1995); Andrzej Sulima Kaminsky, *Republic vs. Autocracy: Poland-Lithuania and Russia 1686–1697* (Cambridge, Mass.: Harvard University Press, 1993); Raeff, "Russian Imperial Policy"; Edward Thaden, *Russification in the Baltic Provinces and Finland, 1855–1914* (Princeton, N.J.: Princeton University Press, 1982); Weeks, *Nation and State*. See also the contributions to Brower and Lazzerini, eds., *Russia's Orient*.

23. For a splendid discussion of the terms of integration employed by the Russian state, see Nathans, *Beyond the Pale,* 72−79; and Michael Stanislawski, "Russian Jewry, the Russian State, and the Dynamics of Russian Jewish Emancipation," in *Paths of Emancipation: Jews, States, and Citizenship,* ed. Ira Katznelson (Princeton, N.J.: Princeton University Press, 1995), 267. For a more general account of the social structure of Russian society, see Gregory Freeze, "The *Soslovie* (Estate) Paradigm and Russian Social History," *American Historical Review* 91, no. 1 (1986).

24. John Doyle Klier, *Imperial Russia's Jewish Question, 1855–1881* (Cambridge: Cambridge University Press, 1995), Pearson, "Privileges, Rights, and Russification."

25. Lederhendler, *Modern Jewish Politics;* Azriel Shohat, *Mosad harabanut mitaam berusya: parasha bamaavak hatarbut ben haredim leven maskilim* (Haifa: University of Haifa, 1975); Michael Stanislawski, *Tsar Nicholas I and the Jews: The Transformation of Jewish Society in Russia, 1825–1855* (Philadelphia: Jewish Publication Society of America, 1983).

26. On Jews' role in the Polish uprising of 1863, see Stephen D. Corrsin, *Warsaw before the First World War: Poles and Jews in the Third City of the Russian Empire 1880–1914* (Boulder, Colo.: East European Monographs, 1989); Jonathan Frankel, *Prophecy and Politics: Socialism, Nationalism, and the Russian Jews, 1862–1917* (Cambridge: Cambridge University Press, 1981); John Doyle Klier, "Russification and the Polish Revolt of 1863: Bad for the Jews?" *Polin* I (1989); Michael Jerry Ochs, "St. Petersburg and the Jews of Russian Poland, 1862–1905" (Ph.D. dissertation, Harvard University, 1986); Yakov Shatzky, "Yidn in dem poylishn ufshtand fun 1863," *YIVO historishe shriftn,* no. I (1929).

27. On the experience of Jews in Russian universities, see Nathans, *Beyond the Pale,* 201–310. See also Klier, *Imperial Russia's Jewish Question;* Gr. Vol'tke, "Prosveshchenie," in *Evreiskaia entsiklopediia,* ed. Lev Izrailevich Katsnelson et al. (St. Petersburg: Brokhaus-Efron, 1906–13); and Steven J. Zipperstein, *The Jews of Odessa: A Cultural History, 1794–1881* (Stanford, Calif.: Stanford University Press, 1985).

28. "Gramotnost' evreev v Rossii"; Stampfer, "Gender Differentiation."

29. Arcadius Kahan, *Essays in Jewish Social and Economic History,* ed. Roger Weiss (Chicago: University of Chicago Press, 1986); see esp. 82–101, Simon Kuznets, "Immigration of Russian Jews to the United States: Nature and Background and Structure," *Perspectives in American History* 9 (1975); Lestchinsky, *Dos yidishe folk in tsifern.*

30. The study of nineteenth- and twentieth-century Russian Jews' class composition has been marked by dramatic ideological rifts: these are described in detail by Stanislawski, *Tsar Nicholas I and the Jews,* 170–82. See also Arcadius Kahan, "Impact of Industrialization on the Jews in Tsarist Russia," in *Essays in Jewish Social and Economic History,* ed. Roger Weiss (Chicago: University of Chicago Press, 1986).

31. Benjamin Braude, "The Rise and Fall of Salonika Woollens, 1500–1650: Technology Transfer and Western Competition," *Mediterranean Historical Review* 6, no. 2 (1991); Snezhka Panova, "The Development of the Textile Industry in the Balkan Countries and the Role of the Jewish Population in the XVIth–XVIIth Centuries," *Annual: Social, Cultural and Educational Organization of the Jews in the People's Republic of Bulgaria,* no. 11 (1976); Minna Rozen, "Contest and Rivalry in Mediterranean Maritime Commerce in the First Half of the Eighteenth Century: The Jews of Salonika and the European Presence," *Revue des études juives,* no. 147 (1988); Azriel Shohat, "The King's Cloth in Salonika," *Sefunot,* no. 12 (1971–78). A fascinating reconsideration of the Ottoman Empire's place within early modern Europe is offered by Daniel Goffman, *The Ottoman Empire and Early Modern Europe* (Cambridge: Cambridge University Press, 2002).

32. Daniel Goffman, *Izmir and the Levantine World* (Seattle: University of Washington Press, 1990), and "Izmir: From Village to Colonial Port City," in *The Ottoman*

City between East and West, ed. Daniel Goffman, Edhem Eldem, and Bruce Masters (Cambridge: Cambridge University Press, 1999).

33. Virginia Aksan, "Locating the Ottomans among Early Modern Empires," *Journal of Early Modern History* 3, no. 2 (1999).

34. On the Ottoman Empire's relationship to the shifting regional economy, see Suraiya Faroqhi et al., *An Economic and Social History of the Ottoman Empire,* 2 vols., vol. 2 (Cambridge: Cambridge University Press, 1994); Huri Islamoglu-Inan, ed., *The Ottoman Empire and the World Economy* (Cambridge and Paris: Cambridge University Press and Editions de la Maison des Sciences de l'Homme, 1987); Reşat Kasaba, *The Ottoman Empire and the World Economy in the Nineteenth Century* (New York: State University of New York Press, 1988); Çaglar Keyder, *State and Class in Turkey: A Study in Capitalist Development* (London and New York: Verso, 1987); Roger Owen, *The Middle East in the World Economy* (London and New York: Methuen, 1981); Sevket Pamuk, *The Ottoman Empire and European Capitalism, 1820−1913: Trade, Investment, and Production* (Cambridge: Cambridge University Press, 1987).

35. See, for example, Beshara Doumani, *Rediscovering Palestine* (Berkeley: University of California Press, 1995); Reşat Kasaba, "Economic Foundations of a Civil Society: Greeks in the Trade of Western Anatolia, 1840−1876," in *Ottoman Greeks in the Age of Nationalism: Politics, Economy, and Society in the Nineteenth Century,* ed. Dimitri Gondicas and Charles Issawi (Princeton, N.J.: Princeton University Press, 1999); Donald Quataert, *Ottoman Manufacturing in the Age of the Industrial Revolution* (Cambridge: Cambridge University Press, 1993); Ehud Toledano, "The Emergence of Ottoman-Local Elites (1700−1900): A Framework for Research," in *Middle East Politics and Ideas: A History from Within,* ed. Ilan Pappe and Mose Ma'oz (London: I. B. Tauris, 1997); and the contributions to Edhem Eldem, Daniel Goffman, and Bruce Masters, eds., *The Ottoman City between East and West: Aleppo, Izmir, and Istanbul* (Cambridge: Cambridge University Press, 1999).

36. For a detailed study of Ottoman Jewry's experience of this period, see Aron Rodrigue and Esther Benbassa, *Jews of the Balkans: The Judeo-Spanish Community, Fifteenth to Twentieth Century* (Oxford: Blackwell, 1995). On the shifting economic roles of Ottoman *millets,* see the contributions to Benjamin Braude and Bernard Lewis, eds., *Christians and Jews in the Ottoman Empire: The Functioning of a Plural Society* (New York: Holmes & Meier, 1982).

37. Benbassa, "L' éducation feminine en Orient"; Paul Dumont, "Jewish Communities in Turkey during the Last Decades of the Nineteenth Century in Light of the Archives of the Alliance Israélite Universelle," in *Christians and Jews in the Ottoman Empire: The Functioning of a Plural Society,* ed. Benjamin Braude and Bernard Lewis (New York: Holmes & Meier, 1982); Rodrigue, *French Jews, Turkish Jews.*

38. On the economic state of late imperial Russia, see Linda Edmondson and Peter Waldron, eds., *Economy and Society in Russia and the Soviet Union, 1860−1930: Essays for Olga Crisp* (New York: St. Martin's Press; Basingstoke: Macmillan, 1992); Peter Gatrell, *The Tsarist Economy, 1850−1917* (London: Batsford, 1986); Arcadius Kahan and Roger Weiss, *Russian Economic History: The Nineteenth Century* (Chicago: University of Chicago Press, 1989); Esther Kingston-Mann and Timothy Mixter, eds., *Peasant Economy, Culture, and the Politics of European Russia* (Princeton, N.J.: Princeton University Press, 1991).

39. There is good reason to question the government's sincerity in implementing the Tanzimat reforms, or its ability to carry them out. In certain regions of the empire — the Arab Middle East, in particular — it was nearly two decades before the Tanzimat reforms were implemented and their effects were, in any case, unpredictable. In Palestine, for example, these reforms gave local merchants access to official political posts and institutions (such as the Advisory Councils), which in turn allowed them to manipulate and resist the central government's economic policies. Dou-

mani, *Rediscovering Palestine.* See also Masters, *Christians and Jews;* Hasan Kayali, *Arabs and Young Turks: Ottomanism, Arabism and Islamism in the Ottoman Empire, 1908–1918* (Berkeley: University of California Press, 1997); Ussama Makdisi, *The Culture of Sectarianism: Community, History, and Violence in Nineteenth-Century Lebanon* (Berkeley: University of California Press, 2000). On the formulation of the Tanzimat Reforms more generally, see Feroz Ahmad, *The Making of Modern Turkey* (London and New York: Routledge, 1993).

40. For example, though the traditional Ottoman political system was considerably eroded by the 1890s, no unitary juridical system had been established to take its place, leaving Jews (and many other non-Muslims) excluded from the benefits of Ottoman civil reform. Kemal Karpat, "*Millets* and Nationality: The Roots of the Incongruity of Nation and State in the Post-Ottoman Era," in *Christians and Jews in the Ottoman Empire: The Functioning of a Plural Society,* ed. Bernard Lewis (New York: Holmes & Meier, 1982); Aron Rodrigue, "From *Millet* to Minority: Turkish Jewry," in *Paths of Emancipation: Jews, States, and Citizenship,* ed. Pierre Birnbaum and Ira Katznelson (Princeton, N.J.: Princeton University Press, 1995), 260; and "Eastern Sephardi Jewry and New Nation-States in the Balkans in the Nineteenth and Twentieth Centuries," in *Sephardi and Middle Eastern Jewries: History and Culture in the Modern Era,* ed. Harvey E. Goldberg (Bloomington: Indiana University Press, 1996).

41. Eliyahu Feldman, *Yehude rusya biyeme hamapekha harishona vehapogromim* (Jerusalem: Magnes Press, Hebrew University, 1999).

42. On the importance of the pogroms of 1881 for the reorientation of Russian Jewish intellectuals, see Frankel, *Prophecy and Politics;* Jehuda Reinharz and Anita Shapira, eds., *Essential Papers on Zionism* (New York: New York University Press, 1995); Michael Stanislawski, *For Whom Do I Toil? Judah Leib Gordon and the Crisis of Russian Jewry* (New York: Oxford University Press, 1988); David Vital, *Zionism: The Formative Years* (Oxford: Oxford University Press, 1982) and *Zionism: The Crucial Phase* (Oxford: Clarendon Press, 1987); Zipperstein, *Jews of Odessa.* Recent scholarship has questioned the watershed nature of 1881 and 1882: for a discussion of the issues at stake, see Stanislawski, *For Whom Do I Toil?* 146–47; Haberer, Erich. "Cosmopolitanism, Antisemitism, and Populism: A Reappraisal of the Russian and Jewish Socialist Response to the Pogroms of 1881–1882," in *Pogroms: Anti-Jewish Violence in Modern Russian History,* ed. John D. Klier and Shlomo Lambroza, 62–97 (Cambridge: Cambridge University Press, 1992).

43. Benjamin Harshav, *Language in Time of Revolution* (Berkeley: University of California Press, 1993) and *The Meaning of Yiddish* (Berkeley: University of California Press, 1990); Dan Miron, *Bodedim bemoadam* (Tel Aviv: Am oved, 1987); Dan Miron, *A Traveler Disguised: A Study in the Rise of Modern Yiddish Fiction in the Nineteenth Century* (New York: Schocken Books, 1973); Yehuda Slutzky, *Haitonut hayehudit-rusit bemea haesrim (1900–1918)* (Tel Aviv: Ha'agudah leheker toldot hayahadut, hamakhon leheher hatefutsot, 1978).

44. Recent scholarship has suggested that many of the empire's ethnic groups remained loyal to the multi-ethnic structure of empire far longer than historians have traditionally assumed. See, for example Engin Deniz Akarli, *The Long Peace: Ottoman Lebanon, 1861–1920* (Berkeley: University of California Press, 1993); Kayali, *Arabs and Young Turks.* Ottoman Jews' loyalty to Ottomanism reflected their positive sentiments to empire more generally. As will be explored in the epilogue, Jews in this context benefited from their cooperation with the imperial regime and, just as importantly, tended to view the alternative to empire — that is, the break-up of empire into successor states — with considerable trepidation. On the popularity of Ottomanism among Jews in Ottoman-controlled Palestine, see Michelle Campos, "A 'Shared Homeland' and Its Boundaries: Late Ottoman Palestine between Imperial Commitment and Communal Identification, 1908–1914" (Ph.D. dissertation, Stan-

ford University, 2003). See also the essays by Rodrigue and Benbassa in *Sephardi and Middle Eastern Jewries: History and Culture in the Modern Era*, ed. Harvey E. Goldberg (Bloomington: Indiana University Press, 1996).

45. There exists a rich literature on the events of 1905–1907. Among the sources that have informed this study are Abraham Ascher, *The Revolution of 1905*, 2 vols. (Stanford, Calif.: Stanford University Press, 1988); Walter Sablinsky, *The Road to Bloody Sunday: Father Gapon and the St. Petersburg Massacre of 1905* (Princeton, N.J.: Princeton University Press, 1976); Gerald Surh, *1905 in St. Petersburg: Labor, Society, and Revolution* (Stanford, Calif.: Stanford University Press, 1989); and Andrew M. Verner, *The Crisis of Russian Autocracy: Nicholas II and the 1905 Revolution* (Princeton, N.J.: Princeton University Press, 1990).

46. On Russian Jews' involvement in opposition and socialist politics, see Blobaum, *Rewolucja;* Frankel, *Prophecy and Politics;* Cristoph Gassenschmidt, *Jewish Liberal Politics in Tsarist Russia, 1900–1914: The Modernization of Russian Jewry* (Oxford: Macmillan, 1995); Jacob S. Hertz, ed., *Doyres bundistn*, 3 vols. (New York: Unzer tsayt farlag, 1958–68); Henry J. Tobias, *The Jewish Bund in Russia from Its Origins to 1905* (Stanford, Calif.: Stanford University Press, 1972). On pogroms, see Feldman, *Yehude rusya biyeme hamapekha harishona;* Shlomo Lambroza, "The Pogrom Movement in Russia, 1903–1905" (Ph.D. dissertation, Rutgers University, 1981) and "The Pogroms of 1903–1906," in *Pogroms: Anti-Jewish Violence in Modern Russian History,* ed. John D. Klier and Shlomo Lambroza (Cambridge: Cambridge University Press, 1992).

47. Hans Rogger, "The Formation of the Russian Right: 1900–1906," in *Jewish Policies and Right-Wing Politics in Imperial Russia* (Berkeley: University of California Press, 1986).

48. A uniquely comparative study of this process may be found in the contributions to Barkey and Von Hagen, *After Empire.*

49. Among the most influential works on this subject are Benedict Anderson, *Imagined Communities* (New York: Verso Press, 1983); Eric J. Hobsbawm, *Nations and Nationalism since 1870* (Cambridge: Cambridge University Press, 1992); Miroslav Hroch, *Social Preconditions of National Revival in Europe: A Comparative Analysis of the Social Composition of Patriotic Groups among the Smaller European Nations* (New York: Cambridge University Press, 1985); Anthony Smith, *The Ethnic Origins of Nations* (Oxford: Blackwell Press, 1986).

50. I refer, here, to the paucity of Ladino primary sources from the turn of the century relative to Yiddish ones. There exists, for example, a wealth of autobiographies and memoirs written by Russian Jews in the first decades of the twentieth century (in Hebrew, Yiddish, and Russian). In the Sephardi milieu, by contrast, this genre was all but non-existent. Similarly, historians of Russian Jewry may rely on the rich collection of literature produced by Russian Jews and Russian Jewish émigrés, while the historian of Ottoman Jewry has few such sources at her disposal. I analyze the cause and results of these disparities in the epilogue to this book.

51. For example, scholars of Ottoman Jewry, like scholars of Ottoman culture as a whole, remain preoccupied with weighing and reconsidering the influence of "the West" upon indigenous economic, political, and cultural forms, and, by extension, with dismantling the narrative of Ottoman "decline." Recent scholarship on the Russian context, on the other hand, has been rather more oriented toward "intracolonial" relationships and toward the question of whether it is fruitful to speak of Russia as an empire or imperial power. In reference to the Ottoman context, see previously cited works by Kayali, Doumani, Aksan, and U. Makdisi. See also George Makdisi, "Corrupting the Sublime Sultanate," *Comparative Studies in Society and History* 42 (2000). In reference to the Russian context, consider, for example, Michael Doyle, *Empires* (Ithaca, N.Y.: Cornell University Press, 1986); Geoffrey Hosking, *Rus-*

sia, People and Empire (Cambridge, Mass.: Harvard University Press, 1997); Andreas Kappeler, *The Russian Empire: A Multiethnic History* (New York: Pearson Education, 2001); Dominic Lieven, *Empire: The Russian Empire and Its Rivals* (New Haven, Conn.: Yale University Press, 2000); Mark Von Hagen, "Writing the History of Russia as Empire: The Perspective of Federalism," in *Kazan, Moscow, St. Petersburg: Multiple Faces of the Russian Empire,* ed. Catherine Evtuhov (Moscow: O. G. I., 1997). See also the contributions to Barkey and Von Hagen, *After Empire;* Daniel R. Brower and Edward Lazzerini, eds., *Russia's Orient: Imperial Borderlands and Peoples, 1700–1917* (Bloomington: Indiana University Press, 1997); and Thomas Sanders, ed. *Historiography of Imperial Russia: The Profession and Writing of History in a Multinational State* (Armonk, N.Y.: M. E. Sharpe, 1999).

1. CREATING A YIDDISH NEWSPAPER CULTURE

1. Information about Morris Shaten has been culled from an interview conducted by his son, Dr. Haim Shaten, in 1965. It is held in the archives of the Jewish Institute for Scientific Research (YIVO), as a part of its collection of oral histories of American Jewish labor activists. Shaten, "Interview with Morris Shaten." In 1908, the Jewish population of Kutno numbered 8,978, 63.1 percent of the population writ large. David Sztokfisz, *Sefer kutnah veha-sevivah* (Tel Aviv: Irgun yotse kutnah, 1968).

2. Shaten, "Interview with Morris Shaten," 4.

3. Shaten's phraseology contains a pun that eludes this English translation. *Gevisen frayndshaft* might be understood both as "a certain friendship" and "a certain *fraynd*-ship." Ibid., 5. To put this another way, readers of *Der fraynd* were loyal to one another as well as to the paper itself.

4. For more on the existence of formal and informal libraries catering to Jewish readers in Minsk, Vilna, Libau, and Verzshbolov, see Ezra Mendelsohn, *Class Struggle in the Pale: The Formative Years of the Jewish Workers' Movement in Tsarist Russia* (Oxford: Oxford University Press, 1970), 120–22.

5. Shaten, "Interview with Morris Shaten," 5–6.

6. This figure will be enumerated in chapter 1.

7. Michael C. Steinlauf, "The Polish-Jewish Daily Press," *Polin* 2 (1987).

8. Zipperstein, *The Jews of Odessa.*

9. The history of Jewish Odessa and the related history of the earliest Russian Jewish periodicals—*Razsvet* (Odessa, 1860–61), *Hamelits* (St. Petersburg, 1860–1904), *Sion* (Odessa, 1861–62), *Kol mevaser* (Odessa, 1862–70), and *Den* (Odessa, 1869–71)—may be found in Orbach, *New Voices;* Tsitron, *Di geshikhte;* Zipperstein, *Jews of Odessa.* For a discussion of the posture of early *maskilim* toward Yiddish, see Frankel, *Prophecy and Politics;* Emanuel Goldsmith, *Modern Yiddish Culture: The Story of the Modern Yiddish Language Movement* (New York: Shapolsky Publishers, 1987); Miron, *A Traveler Disguised;* Naomi Seidman, *A Marriage Made in Heaven: The Sexual Politics of Hebrew and Yiddish* (Berkeley: University of California Press, 1997).

10. Arguably, Zederbaum's success with the ministry was a result of his skills as a *shtadlan* (intercessor on behalf of the Jewish community before Gentile officialdom). Like Shoyl Ginzburg and Shabsay Rapoport, future co-editors of *Der fraynd,* Zederbaum was able to impress upon officials of Russia's Ministry of Interior his loyalty and conservative political predilections. Orbach, *New Voices;* Zalman Reyzen, *Leksikon fun die yiddisher literature, prese, un filologye* (Vilna: Tsentral, 1926). For more on the tradition of *shtadlanut,* see Lederhendler, *Modern Jewish Politics.*

11. For twenty-five years (from 1836 to 1861), the state permitted only two Jewish

printers to operate in the empire: both were based in Zhitomir and were controlled by Hasidim. This arrangement made it very difficult for *maskilim* to publish secular material. Shoyl Ginzburg, "Tsu der geshikhte fun yidishn drukvezn," in *Historishe verk, fun yidishen leben un shafen in tsarishen rusland* (New York: Shoyl ginzburg shriftn-komitet, 1937).

12. Y. S. Hertz, "Di umlegale prese un literatur fun bund," in *Pinkes far der forshung fun der yidisher literatur un prese*, ed. Khaym Bas (New York: Alveltlekher yidisher kultur-kongres, 1972), and *Doyres bundistn*.

13. Shabsay Rapoport, co-editor of *Der fraynd*, himself submitted three unsuccessful requests to publish a Yiddish newspaper. Shabsay Rapoport, "Der onheyb fun 'fraynd,'" *Yubileum-baylage fraynd, tsenter yorgang*, no. 12 (1913). See also Druk, *Tsu der geshikhte;* D. A. Eliashevich, *Pravitel'stvennaia politika i evreiskaia pechat' v rossii, 1797–1917: ocherki istorii tsenzury* (St. Petersburg and Jerusalem: Mosty kul'tury, Gesharim, 1999); Ginzburg, *Amolike peterburg;* David E. Fishman, "The Politics of Yiddish in Tsarist Russia," in *From Ancient Israel to Modern Judaism: Intellect in Quest of Understanding—Essays in Honor of Marvin Fox*, vol. 4: *The Modern Age: Theology, Literature, History*, ed. Jacob Neusner, Ernest Frerichs, and Nahum Sarna (Atlanta: Scholars Press, 1989); Viktoriia Khiterer, *Dokumenty sobrannye evreiskoi istoriko-arkheograficheskoi komissiei* (Kiev and Jerusalem: Instytut Iudaiki and Gesharim, 1999); Tsitron, *Di geshikhte.*

14. Brower and Lazzerini, *Russia's Orient;* Corrsin, *Warsaw* and "Language Use in Cultural and Political Change in Pre-1914 Warsaw: Poles, Jews, and Russification," *Slavonic and East European Review* 68, no. 1 (1990); Thaden, *Russification.*

15. Recent explorations of Russian archives have considerably deepened our understanding of Russian censorship of Yiddish sources. Eliashevich, *Pravitel'stvennaia politika i evreiskaia pechat;* Khiterer, *Dokumenty.*

16. Druk, *Tsu der geshikhte*, 10; H. D. Horovits, "Unzer ershte teglikhe tsaytung (tsu der tsen-yoriger geshikhte fun'm fraynd)," in *Der pinkes, yorbukh fun der geshikhte fun der yidisher literatur un shprakh, far folklor, kritik un bibliographye*, ed. Shmuel Niger (Vilna: B. A. Kletzkin, 1912), 240.

17. Miron, *A Traveler Disguised;* Ruth Wisse, "Not the 'Pintele Yid' but the Full-Fledged Jew," *Prooftexts* 15, January (1995).

18. The weekly *Yisrolik* (Lemberg, 1875–76), for example, was successfully mailed to Russian Jewish readers from outside the empire until the authorities intervened. A similar tactic was attempted with *Kol laam* (Koenigsburg, 1876–79). Even radical newspapers that were distributed within single cities, like the *Bialystoker arbayter* (London, 1899–1902), were often published abroad: the latter paper printed no less than a thousand papers at a time. Tsitron, *Di geshikhte*, 89–116; A. Kirzhnits, *Di yidishe prese in der gevezener rusisher imperye (1823–1916)* (Moscow: Tsentraler felker-farlag fun fssr, 1930).

19. Yakov Shatzky, *Geshikhte fun yidn in varshe, 1863–1896*, 3 vols., vol. 3 (New York: YIVO Publishers, 1953), 308.

20. This relatively large readership was the accomplishment of editor Nahum Sokolow, who more than doubled *Hatsefira's* circulation from 1886 to 1896, and who eventually turned the weekly into a daily. Ibid., 308.

21. Steven Zipperstein has shown that the publishing house Ahiasaf estimated that *Hashiloah* could not remain afloat with fewer than a thousand subscribers. This challenge prompted then-editor Ahad Ha'am to campaign vigorously on the paper's behalf: nonetheless, in 1897 its circulation fell to five hundred. Zipperstein, *Elusive Prophet*, 166–68.

22. Ginzburg, *Amolike peterburg*, 216; Druk, *Tsu der geshikhte*, 20. For more on the content and orientation of *Hamelits*, see Stanislawski, *For Whom Do I Toil?*

23. Miron, *A Traveler Disguised*, 3.

24. Wisse, "Not the 'Pintele Yid,' " 35.

25. "Gramotnost' evreev v Rossii," Rubinow, *Economic Conditions; Sbornik materialov.* In judging literacy levels, the census defined Jews by language, not nationality. Thus nearly 200,000 Jews who identified their mother tongue as Russian (including some who desired to disassociate themselves from Yiddish for political reasons) were not counted as literate Jews. "Gramotnost' evreev v Rossii"; Rubinow, *Economic Conditions.*

26. Shaul Stampfer, "What Did 'Knowing Hebrew' Mean in Eastern Europe?" in *Hebrew in Ashkenaz,* ed. Lewis Gilnert (New York: Oxford University Press, 1993).

27. An article published in *Der fraynd* asserted that while 56 percent of all Russian women could claim literacy, 80 percent of Jewish women could claim literacy in at least one language, adding, "this is why Jewish women are not ashamed of Yiddish." "Di yidn in peterburg," *Der fraynd,* no. 92 (10 [27] May 1903). In fact, the figure of 80 percent measured St. Petersburg's Jewish women's rate of literacy in Russian and not in Yiddish, at least according to the Russian census of 1897. By this count, 59 percent of Jewish women in St. Petersburg declared themselves fluent in Yiddish. As Benjamin Nathans has documented, relative to other factions of the city's population, St. Petersburg's Jews were unusual in that they were experiencing a *rise* in Russian-language fluency at the turn of the century. Nathans, *Beyond the Pale,* 110–13, especially table 6. *Der fraynd's* statistics are cited from the "folk census of 1900," which might refer to the study conducted by the Jewish Colonization Association, on which see *Sbornik materialov.* For more on the general theme of Jewish women's literacy, Stampfer, "Gender Differentiation."

28. Goldenberg, "Ha'yesh korim evrim?" Interestingly enough, this point was often criticized in the pages of *Der fraynd.* While articles in the paper often pointed to the intimacy women felt for Yiddish, contributors seemed unwilling to imagine women as constituting a significant portion of their readers. One "letter from a woman," which we will have further opportunity to explore, extolled the relationship between women and the Yiddish language while simultaneously degrading women's interest in reading the Yiddish press. "Jewish women read few books and newspapers in Yiddish," the article begins; "[t]he average woman doesn't have enough time, while upper-class women have no interest in reading in Yiddish. Very few of us women, mind you, will open a Yiddish book or newspaper and when we do, we understand very little of what is written there." Dine Tseytlin, "Fun a fremder velt (a briv fun a froy)," *Der fraynd,* no. 6 (12 [25] January 1903).

29. For an explanation of why the census underestimated Jews' rates of literacy in Russian and Yiddish, see note 25, above.

30. Kahan, *Jewish Social and Economic History,* 4, especially footnote 3. As Kahan points out, most of these Jews were concentrated in Warsaw, Łódź, Odessa, and Kiev.

31. Slutzky, *Haitonut hayehudit-rusit.*

32. For a detailed study of the Jewish community of St. Petersburg, see Nathans, *Beyond the Pale,* especially pp. 83–201. For a statistical study of Jewish populations in cities inside and outside the Pale, see Lestchinsky, *Dos yidishe folk in tsifern,* and "Di antviklung fun yidishn folk." For more on the Russian press and publishing industries, see Brooks, *When Russia Learned to Read;* Beth Holmgren, *Rewriting Capitalism: Literature and the Market in Late Tsarist Russia and the Kingdom of Poland* (Pittsburgh: University of Pittsburgh Press, 1998); McReynolds, *Russia's Old Regime,* especially tables 6–8; Joan Neuberger, *Hooliganism: Crime, Culture, and Power in St. Petersburg, 1900–1914* (Berkeley: University of California Press, 1993); Ruud, "The Printing Press"; Sally West, "Constructing Consumer Culture: Advertising in Imperial Russia to 1914" (Ph.D. dissertation, University of Illinois at Urbana-Champaign, 1987).

33. Goldenberg, "Ha'yesh korim evrim?" In certain general libraries that catered to Jewish readers, the stock of Russian-language literature seems to have been fairly

rich (certainly richer than that of periodicals). However, other libraries that catered to Jewish workers were stocked almost exclusively with Yiddish-language sources. On this, see Mendelsohn, *Class Struggle in the Pale*, 120–22, 154.

34. *Halevanon* (1863–86) was among the first Orthodox newspapers circulated in Eastern Europe, though it was based alternately in Jerusalem, Paris, Mainz, and London. Its founder, Ya'akov Lifshits, sensed an opportunity to use the medium of the newspaper to combat the influence of the *Haskalah* and of Zionism. According to its (no doubt overly optimistic) founder, the newspaper was read by almost every rabbi in Poland, Lithuania, and the Ukraine. Lifshits, *Zikhron ya'akov*, 99. A brief discussion of the history of *Halevanon* may be found in: Luz, *Parallels Meet*, 15–16.

35. S. An-sky, "Mendl Turk," in *The Dybbuk and Other Writings*, ed. David Roskies (New York: Random House, 1986), 94.

36. Memoiristic literature of the period suggests that Mendl Turk was not alone in the way he gathered news or in the effect it had upon him. Yiddish common parlance has a term for the kind of political discussion favored by Mendl and his peers: the activity itself is referred to as *lezhanke politik* (stove-side politics) and the (sometimes limited) knowledge it presupposes *khokmey lezhanke* (stove-side smarts). The citation from An-sky's story is found on p. 100 of Roskies' edition.

37. Horovits, "Unzer ershte teglikhe tsaytung," 246.

38. Avrom Reyzen attributes the lowest circulation to *Der fraynd*: 50,000. Ginzburg estimates it to have been 90,000; Druk 100,000. Druk, *Tsu der geshikhte*, 20; Ginzburg, *Amolike peterburg*; Reyzen, *Leksikon fun der yidisher literatur*, 569.

39. Druk, *Tsu der geshikhte*, 38.

40. The number of dailies sold on St. Petersburg's streets is quantified by McReynolds, *Russia's Old Regime*, tables 4 and 5.

41. *Der fraynd*'s wide geographic base rendered the paper similar to *Niva*, a literary journal that circulated throughout Russia, and distinguished it from Russian-language dailies such as *Peterburgskii listok*, whose circulation was by and large dependent upon a single city. This was a point of pride for the paper's editors, for it brought them (at least theoretically) closer to their goal of producing a paper for "all" the Jews of the Russian Empire. In 1908, *Der fraynd* took to publishing its list of distributing "agents" in its advertising pages. See, for example, *Der fraynd*, no. 18 (22 January [4 February] 1908). For reference to sellers abroad (including L. Friedman of Oxford and P. Gontser of Berlin), see *Der fraynd*, no. 195 (27 August [9 September] 1908).

42. In the early years of Yiddish publishing, it was assumed that dailies would not appear on the Sabbath. For the first three years of its run, *Der fraynd*'s editors succeeded in publishing the paper six times a week, but from 1908 until its final year, it appeared only five times weekly. The number of issues of *Der fraynd* by year are as follows: 1903, 296; 1904, 299; 1907, 289; 1907, 289; 1908, 245 (though the paper was not published between the first of October and the first of December, when it relocated from St. Petersburg to Warsaw); 1909, 248; 1910, 280; 1911, 286; 1912, 301. By imperial decree, *Der fraynd* was not published from December 12, 1905, until July 31, 1906; during these months it was published instead under the name *Dos lebn*. From the beginning of August 1906 until the year's end, *Der fraynd* published 122 issues. Kirzhnits, *Di yidishe prese*.

43. Ibid.

44. The RTA received official approval from the government in 1866. Charles A. Ruud, *Fighting Words: Imperial Censorship and the Russian Press, 1804–1906* (Buffalo: University of Toronto Press, 1982), 202–203. McReynolds, *Russia's Old Regime*, 47–48.

45. Druk, *Tsu der geshikhte*.

46. McReynolds, *Russia's Old Regime*, tables 16–23.

47. Mendelsohn, *Class Struggle in the Pale*, 1–27.

48. The 1903 minutes of a painters' union (*fereyn*) meeting testifies to just such a practice: "We have now enlarged our library [and] have subscribed to the daily Yiddish paper, *Der fraynd*, which is always to be found in our painters' quarters; our *ferayn* [*sic*] is also considering the acquisition of new books, because the number of readers increases every day." Ibid., 147.

49. Ginzburg, *Amolike peterburg*, 218, 217.

50. Joseph Buloff, *In the Old Marketplace* (Cambridge, Mass.: Harvard University Press, 1991), 13. For more on the practice of public reading, see Natalie Zemon Davis, "Printing and the People," in *Society and Culture in Early Modern France* (Stanford, Calif.: Stanford University Press, 1975).

51. Louise McReynolds, for example, has suggested that five to ten readers can be estimated to have had "access" to Russian-language papers of the early twentieth century: Shaul Stampfer has proposed that late-nineteenth-century Hebrew periodicals like *Hamelits* may have reached fifteen readers per copy. McReynolds, *Russia's Old Regime*, 72; Stampfer, "Knowing Hebrew," 106.

52. Weinreich, *History of the Yiddish Language*, 695.

53. Horovits, "Unzer ershte teglikhe tsaytung," 248.

54. Ginzburg, *Amolike peterburg*.

55. Druk, *Tsu der geshikhte*.

56. In the years before 1905, many newspapers were based in St. Petersburg, due to official resistance to publishing in the empire's borderlands. Thus the most popular Polish journal published in the empire in the pre-1905 period was also based in the capital city. Weeks, *Nation and State*, 81.

57. Ginzburg, *Amolike peterburg*, 192.

58. On the social and cultural texture of Jewish life in St. Petersburg, see Nathans, *Beyond the Pale*, 83–200; Stanislawski, *For Whom Do I Toil?* 106–28. On the history of Vilna, Odessa, and Warsaw as Jewish centers, see Israel Cohen, *Vilna* (Philadelphia: Jewish Publication Society, 1992); Corrsin, *Warsaw*; Orbach, *New Voices*; Chone Shmeruk, "Aspects of the History of Warsaw as a Yiddish Literary Center," in *The Jews in Warsaw: A History*, ed. Wladyslay T. Bartoszewski and Antony Polonsky (Oxford: Basil Blackwell, 1991); Zipperstein, *The Jews of Odessa*.

59. Ginzburg, *Amolike peterburg*, 192.

60. Ibid., 200.

61. Ibid., 201–202.

62. As Mark Steinberg has demonstrated, it was not unusual for printing presses to be run by "immigrants" from lands annexed by the Russian Empire. Indeed, in 1881, 12 percent of the printing firms in St. Petersburg were run by Jews from the Pale. Mark D. Steinberg, *Moral Communities: The Culture of Class Relations in the Russian Printing Industry, 1867–1907* (Berkeley: University of California Press, 1992), 13.

63. Ginzburg, *Amolike peterburg*, 191, 192, 199.

64. Niger, *Fun noentn over*, 188. The letter is dated St. Petersburg, 1909. A year earlier, Niger and Vayter had begun to co-publish the monthly *Literarishe monatshriftn* in Vilna.

65. Wisse, "Not the 'Pintele Yid.' "

66. Rapoport, "Der onheybe fun 'fraynd.' "

67. As Chone Shmeruk has noted, "the growth of the Yiddish press established the economic base for a modern Yiddish intelligentsia and for the Yiddish writer." Shmeruk, "A Yiddish Literary Center," 240.

68. Horovits, "Unzer ershte teglikhe tsaytung," 251. For more on Brokhes, see Wisse, "Not the 'Pintele Yid,' " 50. For more on the careers of leading Russian Jewish women writers, see Carol B. Bailin, *To Reveal Our Hearts: Jewish Women Writers in Tsarist Russia* (Cincinnati: Hebrew Union College Press, 2000).

69. Ruth Wisse has identified a similar dynamic effecting the editorial staff of the Yiddish weekly *Der yud.* Because the paper remained indifferent to the question of language, she argues, the editorial staff remained atypically diverse. Wisse, "Not the 'Pintele Yid.' "

70. *Der fraynd*, no. 1 (January 5 [18] 1903).

71. This column, signed with the pseudonym Emes (Truth), bears the same title as a column penned by Y. L. Peretz in the weekly *Der yud.* References to the series in an article by Bal Makhshoves, however, attribute it to S. An-sky. Wisse, "Not the 'Pintele Yid.' " Bal Makhshoves (Isador Eliashev), "Notitsn fun a kritik," *Kunst un lebn*, no. 1 (June 1908). See note 119 for more in this regard.

72. "Shtet un shtetlakh," *Der fraynd*, no. 21 (29 January [11 February] 1903).

73. "Shtet un shtetlakh," *Der fraynd*, no. 60 (17 [30] March 1903).

74. "Di rusishe shprakh in yeshives," *Der fraynd*, no. 36 (3 [17] March 1903).

75. Ginzburg, *Amolike peterburg*, 231.

76. See discussion of "Mendl Turk," above. See also Lifshits, *Zikhron yaakov*, 99. A brief discussion of the history of *Halevanon* may be found in Luz, *Parallels Meet*, 15–16.

77. Shaten, "Interview with Morris Shaten."

78. The article "Di rusishe shprakh in yeshives," for example, responded to a letter published in the preceding issue of *Der fraynd.* This letter, penned by a (self-proclaimed) religious reader, criticized the assumption that yeshiva students ought to be fluent in Russian. "Di rusishe shprakhe in yeshivas," *Der fraynd*, no. 36 (3 [17] March 1903).

79. The practice of hiring Hasidic censors was not an uncommon one for the state: the Hasidim, who were (at least theoretically) hostile to secular Jewish culture, were thought to be checks upon the spread of radicalism. This did not mean that the authorities did not view Hasidic censors with suspicion, but rather that they proved necessary allies in the government's offensive against secular Jewish culture. Druk, "Tsu der geshikhte"; Ginzburg, "Tsu der geshikhte"; Tsitron, "Di geshikhte."

80. Ginzburg's lengthy description of Landau can be found in his memoirs. Ginzburg, *Amolike peterburg*, 224–27.

81. As has already been described, because the industry of Yiddish publishing in Russia had since the early nineteenth century been dominated by the religious, few secular Jews were able to learn how to operate Yiddish printing presses. Ginzburg, *Amolike peterburg*, 196, and "Tsu der geshikhte."

82. This point is echoed by Benjamin Nathans, who has suggested that in late-nineteenth-century St. Petersburg, "religious categories were becoming less rather than more sharply definable." In this regard, *Der fraynd* was eminently suited to the urban terrain it called home. Nathans, *Beyond the Pale*, 146–49.

83. It is noteworthy that *Der fraynd*'s coverage of cultural affairs in the United States had a profound impact on young émigrés. In his unpublished autobiography, Elbert Aidline Trommer has recalled how strongly *Der fraynd*'s coverage of American Jewish writers affected him in the years before he left Russia for New York. Elbert Aidline (Khaym eliezer ben mordkhe-dov) Trommer, "Far vos ikh bin avek fun der alter heym un vos ikh hob dergreykht in amerike" (YIVO Institute, American Autobiography, Folder 182), 35.

84. Zipperstein, *Elusive Prophet*, 118–19.

85. "Di yidn in peterburg," *Der fraynd*, no. 92 (10 [27] May 1903).

86. "Shtet un shtetlakh," *Der fraynd*, no. 21 (29 January [11 February] 1903).

87. *Der fraynd*, no. 1 (January 5 [18] 1903).

88. See, for example, Dr. Yosef Luria's "Zelbst-bashtimung, zhargon als folks-shprakhe," *Dos lebn* 37 (22 December 1905 [11 January 1906]).

89. Shimen Dubnov, *Fun "zhargon" tsu yidish un andere artiklen: literarishe zikhroynes* (Vilna: B. Kletskin, 1929). See also Miron, *A Traveler Disguised.*

90. Druk, *Tsu der geshikhte,* 26.

91. Ginzburg, *Amolike peterburg,* 198.

92. *Der fraynd,* no. 178–80 (3 [11], 4 [17], 5 [19] August 1904). Zhitlowsky's poem reads:

> You don't say "windses" [*vender*]
> when you hear the wind [*vind*]
> and neither "edgeses" [*render*] nor "landses" [*lender*]
> come from the words edge [*rand*] or land [*land*].
> In proper speech, ribbons [*bender*]
> are made from ribbon [*band*]
> so we will not take Frug by the "handses" [*hender*]
> we take him, instead, with loving hands [*hend*]
> we will not dress him up in ribbons [*bender*]
> but bind his writings in a volume [*band*].

93. Dr. Yosef Luria, "Zelbst-beshtimung 4, zhargon als folks-shprakhe," *Dos lebn,* no. 7 (22 December 1905 [4 January 1906]).

94. Ibid.

95. Dr. Yosef Luria, "Zelbst-beshtimung 5, yidish un natsionale kultur," *Dos lebn,* no. 8 (23 December 1905 [5 January 1906]).

96. Dr. Yosef Luria, "Zelbst-beshtimung 4, zhargon als folks-shprakhe," *Dos lebn,* no. 7 (22 December 1905 [4 January 1906]).

97. *Der fraynd,* no. 178–80 (3 [11], 4 [17], 5 [19] August 1904).

98. See, for example, "Di folks literatur," *Der fraynd,* no. 43–45 (24 February [9 March]–7 [20] March 1903); "Di mode in der shprakhe," *Der fraynd,* no. 24 (8 [21] July 1903); Dr. Yosef Luria, "Zelbst bashtimung," *Der fraynd,* no. 220 (11 [20] October 1905).

99. "A bisl kongres loshn," *Der fraynd,* nos. 177, 178 (10 [23] August, 11 [24] August 1903).

100. Though the various Eastern European Yiddish dialects were mutually intelligible, there tended to be a great variance in spelling, word-choice, and pronunciation, which prompted many proponents of Yiddish to call for standardization of the language. Movement toward the creation of a standard Yiddish began in the interwar period, when scholars of Vilna's YIVO Institute (Jewish Institute of Scientific Research) proposed a standard Yiddish based upon the dialect employed by Vilna's intellectual elite. For more on the history of Yiddish, see Weinreich, *History of the Yiddish Language. Der fraynd*'s call for a standardization of the language was articulated in: "Vegn der yidisher ortographia," *Der fraynd,* no. 124 (4 [17] June 1908). For reflections on the paper's use of Yiddish orthography, see Horovits, "Unzer ershte teglikhe tsaytung," 251.

101. *Der fraynd* offered daily coverage of the conference and a great deal of commentary in its wake. This coverage began on August 25, 1908, and continued throughout the following month.

102. One interesting result of the conference was that, in the debates that followed, the personality of participating journalists became almost as important as the news itself. The most vociferous defender of the conference was the fiery delegate Ester Frumkin, who argued that it was in Czernowitz that Yiddishism (as a term and a movement) had been coined. On the basis of her arguments and personality, Ester (as she was known) gained a highly public reputation — though not, by and large, a flattering one — in the wake of the conference. So too did Moshe Kleynman, editor of the Warsaw-based *Der togblat,* Hillel Tseytlin, contributor to the Warsaw-based *Haynt,* and Avrom Reyzen, then a reporter for the New York *Der forverts.* Ester elabo-

rated her view of the language question in: "Di ershte yidishe shprakh konferents," *Di naye tsayt* 34 (New York, 1908).

103. Dine Tseytlin, "Fun a fremder velt (a briv fun a froy)," *Der fraynd*, no. 6 (12 [25] January 1903).

104. Horovits, "Unzer ershte teglikhe tsaytung," 251.

105. Seidman, *A Marriage Made in Heaven.*

106. A. L. Levinski, "A bisl kongres-loshn (fun an altn delegat)," *Der fraynd*, no. 177 (10 [23] August 1903), no. 178 (11 [24] August 1903).

107. Horovits, "Unzer ershte teglikhe tsaytung," 249. The selection is from *Der fraynd*, no. 82 (15 April 1903). The paper's treatment of this and other pogroms of the 1903–1905 era will be discussed in more detail in chapter 3. For more on the Zionist movement's reaction to the pogroms, see Eliyahu Feldman, *Yehude rusya biyeme hamapekha harishona vehapogromim* (Jerusalem: Magnes Press, Hebrew University, 1999); Frankel, *Prophecy and Politics;* Yitzhak Maor, *Hatenuah hatsiyonit berusyah* (Jerusalem: Hasifriya hatsionit, 1986); Michael Stanislawski, *Zionism and the Fin de Siècle: Cosmopolitanism and Nationalism from Nordau to Jabotinsky* (Berkeley: University of California Press, 2001).

108. Maor, *Hatenuah hatsiyonit berusyah;* Reinharz and Shapira, *Essential Papers on Zionism;* Stanislawski, *Zionism and the Fin de Siècle;* Vital, *The Formative Years* and *The Crucial Phase;* Zipperstein, *Elusive Prophet.*

109. The issue in question is *Der fraynd*, 12 (25) October 1903. After the publication of the St. Petersburg–based daily *Der tog* in 1904, *Der fraynd*'s supplement was renamed *Der bezem.* That year, the supplement appeared only once, during Purim, and again was published within the body of *Der fraynd.* Beginning in 1906, *Der bezem* appeared as an independent satirical supplement: it is to this journal that we turn our attention in chapter 3. Thanks to Edward Portnoy for drawing this issue of *Der tog* to my attention.

110. *Der fraynd baylage*, no. 148 (29 July 1904).

111. Michael Berkowitz, "Art in Zionist Popular Culture and Jewish National Self-Consciousness, 1897–1914," in *Studies in Contemporary Jewry: An Annual*, ed. Ezra Mendelsohn and Richard I. Cohen (Oxford: Oxford University Press, 1990), and *The Jewish Self-Image in the West* (New York: New York University Press, 2000); Stanislawski, *Zionism and the Fin de Siècle.*

112. Zipperstein, *Elusive Prophet.* See especially pp. 105–70.

113. McReynolds, *Russia's Old Regime*, table 13.

114. Until 1906, *Dos lebn* had been the name of *Der fraynd*'s monthly literary supplement, ed. Chaim Aleksandrov (pseudonym of Chaim Miler). On December 15, 1905, however, the publication of *Der fraynd* was suspended for one year after the paper was found guilty of violating Article 129 of the criminal code. At this point, the daily was renamed *Dos lebn* in order to continue publication. *Der fraynd*'s encounter with the imperial censors is described in *Dos lebn*, no. 1 (15 December 1905).

115. Brooks, *When Russia Learned to Read*, 28–29; Druk, *Tsu der geshikhte*, 31; McReynolds, *Russia's Old Regime*, 192–223. For an anecdotal account of Russian Jewish readers' interest in wartime news, see An-sky, "Mendl Turk." See also Buloff, *In the Old Marketplace.*

116. Druk, *Tsu der geshikhte*, 45. For more on Yiddish publishing in Warsaw in these years, see Ber Kutsher, *Geven amol varshe: zikhroynes* (Paris: n.p., 1955).

117. *Der veg* aimed to be a paper of Warsaw, and gained the support of Warsaw-based writers like Y. L. Peretz. The paper also instituted a theater column (a first in Yiddish publishing), which was a great sensation. Druk, *Tsu der geshikhte*, 45; Keith Ian Weiser, "The Politics of Yiddish: Noyekh Prilutski and the Folkspartey in Poland, 1900–1926" (Ph.D. dissertation, Columbia University, 2001).

118. See the essays by Mendel Mayzes, Yitzhak Greenboym, Nahman Mayzel, and Moshe Sena in in *Di yidishe prese vos iz geven*, ed. Dovid Flinker, Mordechai Tsanin, and Sholem Rosenfeld (Tel Aviv: Veltfarband fun di yidishe zhurnalistn, 1975).

119. Kutsher, *Geven amol varshe*. As Peter Fritzshe has reminded us, "newspapers tell stories, and they also wrap fish and make paper hats." Peter Fritzsche, *Reading Berlin 1900* (Cambridge, Mass.: Harvard University Press, 1996).

120. Shmeruk, "A Yiddish Literary Center." See also Weiser, "The Politics of Yiddish."

121. In 1908, A. Litvak (former editor of *Der varshaver arbayter*) became editor of *Der fraynd*, a position he would retain until 1912.

122. Greenboym, "Zikhroynes vegn 'haynt.' "

123. Ginzburg, *Amolike peterburg*.

124. Shmeruk, "A Yiddish Literary Center." Ruth Wisse, *I. L. Peretz and the Making of Modern Jewish Culture* (Seattle: University of Washington Press, 1991).

125. "*Traytel-faytel-kadetishe* politics" refers with obvious sarcasm to *Der fraynd*'s sympathies with the liberal Kadet (or Constitutional Democratic) party. For Bal Makhshoves, *Der fraynd*'s loyalty to the Kadets reflected the paper's bourgeois orientation and its lack of interest in more radical politics: a tendency that will be explored in more detail in chapter 3.

126. Makhshoves, "Notizn fun a kritik," *Kunst un lebn*, no. 1 (June 1908): 49–54. The citation is from pages 50–51.

127. This refers to a column on economics penned by H. D. Horovitz and signed with the pseudonym *a soykher* (business man).

128. Makhshoves, *Notitsn fun a kritik*, 51. This reference to S. Ash's *shtetl* likely refers to his penning of a book by this name. Bal Makhshoves's reference to folksy articles by *a soykher* (a businessman) refers to a series on economics by editorial board member H. D. Horovitz, who employed this pseudonym.

129. Druk, *Tsu der geshikhte*, 92–93.

130. Vayter's comment is made to literary critic Shmuel Niger in a letter dated 1909. It is cited in Niger, *Fun noentn over*, 188.

131. "Tsu unzer lezer," *Der fraynd*, no. 241 (25 October [10 November] 1908).

132. Mayzel, *Geven a mol a lebn*.

133. Marcus Moseley has described the importance of the act of reading and writing — and the reading and writing of new and experimental genres, in particular — for Poland's interwar Jewish youth: Marcus Moseley, "Life, Literature: Autobiographies of Jewish Youth in Interwar Poland," *Jewish Social Studies* 7, no. 3 (2001). See also Jeffrey Shandler, *Awakening Lives: Autobiographies of Jewish Youth in Poland before the Holocaust* (New Haven: Yale University Press, 2002).

134. Druk, *Tsu der geshikhte*, 92, 96.

135. Carla Hesse, *Publishing and Cutural Politics in Revolutionary Paris, 1789–1810* (Berkeley: University of California Press, 1991), 176.

136. See, among others, Gunther Barth, "Metropolitan Press," in *City People: The Rise of Modern City Culture in Nineteenth-Century America* (New York: Oxford University Press, 1980); Fritzsche, *Reading Berlin 1900;* David Henkin, *City Reading: Written Words and Public Spaces in Antebellum New York* (New York: Columbia University Press, 1998); Henri Lefebvre, *Everyday Life in the Modern World* (New York: Harper and Row, 1971); Thomas Richards, *The Commodity Culture of Victorian England: Advertising and Spectacle, 1851–1914* (Stanford, Calif.: Stanford University Press, 1990); Richard Terdiman, *Discourse/Counter-Discourse: The Theory and Practice of Symbolic Resistance in Nineteenth-Century France* (Ithaca, N.Y.: Cornell University Press, 1985).

137. I borrow this phrase from Benedict Anderson, who has argued that it is with the emergence of print-languages that a national community can be imagined.

Anderson, *Imagined Communities*. See also Ernest Gellner, *Nationalism* (New York: New York University Press, 1997); Smith, *The Ethnic Origins of Nations*.

2. CREATING A LADINO NEWSPAPER CULTURE

1. This provocative reference to *El tiempo*'s sacred status was offered by David Fresco in the pages of *El instructor*, one of the newspaper's informal supplements. David Fresco, "Alos lektores," *El instruktor*, no. 1, Iyar 5648 (1888). *El instruktor* and other Ladino supplements will be explored in more detail in chapter 4.

2. Galanté, *La presse judeo-espagnole mondiale;* Moshe David Gaon, *Haitonut beladino: bibliografia* (Jerusalem: Ben Zvi, 1965); Levy, *The Sephardim;* Avner Levy, "The Jewish Press in Turkey," in *Jewish Journalism and Printing Houses in the Ottoman Empire and Modern Turkey*, ed. Gad Nassi (Istanbul: Isis Press, 2001); Nassi, *Jewish Journalism.*

3. The quotation is selected from an annual report issued by Alliance teacher M[oïse] Fresco in 1908. Translated and cited by Aron Rodrigue, *Images of Sephardi and Eastern Jewries in Transition: The Teachers of the Alliance Israélite Universelle, 1860–1939* (Seattle: University of Washington Press, 1993), 131.

4. For a survey of the Jewish debate over language, see David M. Bunis, "Modernization and the Language Question among Judezmo-Speaking Sephardim of the Ottoman Empire." In *Sephardi and Middle Eastern Jewries: History and Culture in the Modern Era*, ed. Harvey E. Goldberg (Bloomington: Indiana University Press, 1996), 226–39.

5. As we have seen, this tension also surrounded the publication of secular Yiddish in print, especially in the early days of Yiddish newspaper publishing. Arguably in the Ottoman setting, disdain for Ladino was at once more widespread and more persistent than was the disdain for Yiddish voiced in Russian Jewish circles. And though critics of Ladino employed similar vocabulary as critics of Yiddish, in the Ottoman context, the social and economic forces that girded their critique were arguably more dire.

6. Numerous sources, both primary and secondary, refer to *El tiempo*'s influence. See, for example, Galanté, *La presse judéo-espagnole mondiale;* Franco, *Essai sur l'histoire des Israélites;* Benbassa and Rodrigue, *The Jews of the Balkans;* Gaon, *Haitonut beladino;* Iacob Hassan, "El estudio del periodismo sefard," *Sefarad* 26 (1988); Lowenthal, *Elia Carmona's Autobiography;* Avner Levi, "The Ladino 'El tiempo' of Istanbul during 1882–83," *Qesher*, no. 13 (May 1993); Levy, "The Jewish Press in Turkey."

7. *El tiempo* was created by Merkado Fresco, David Fresco, Sami Alkabez, and Isaac Carmona, and was at first patronized by Hayim Carmona, scion of a prominent family of Constantinople. After Carmona's death in 1883, patronage of the paper was assumed by Hayim's son Isaac, who had served as *El tiempo*'s editor since 1872. Until 1878, the paper was edited by Sami Alkabez and Merkado Fresco. Thereafter, the position was assumed by David Fresco, whose tenure lasted until the paper folded in 1930. Levi, "The Ladino 'El tiempo' of Istanbul"; Gaon, *Haitonut beladino*, 55.

8. Franco, *Essai sur l'histoire des Israélites*, 281.

9. Rodrigue, *French Jews, Turkish Jews*, 85–90.

10. One visitor to Constantinople noted in 1886 that there were only 66 Jewish children in the city who were being schooled in Turkish. Cited in Dumont, "Jewish Communities in Turkey," 215. After the state passed a decree making the teaching of Turkish mandatory in all non-Muslim schools, it began furnishing schools with the requisite teachers. As a result, AIU schools began to increase the number of hours students were required to spend studying the language. Rodrigue, *French Jews, Turkish Jews*, 86–88.

11. Franco, *Essai sur l'histoire des Israélites*, 249.

12. Abraham Galanté has, for example, described an official meeting between Sultan Abdülhamid II and Constantinople's Chief Rabbi Moshe Levy that took place in 1900. Because the Chief Rabbi lacked fluency in Turkish, the rabbi's grandson was obliged to serve as translator. Avram Galanté, *Histoire des juifs de Turquie*, 9 vols. (Istanbul: Isis, 1985), vol. IX, 183. For more on the evolving role of the Chief Rabbi, see Esther Benbassa, *Haim Nahum: A Sephardic Chief Rabbi in Politics, 1892–1923* (Tuscaloosa: University of Alabama Press, 1995) and *Une diaspora sépharade;* Ilan Karmi, *The Jewish Community of Istanbul in the Nineteenth Century: Social, Legal and Administrative Transformations* (Istanbul: Isis, 1996), 34–46.

13. Sam Levy has offered a poignant description of his father, who, though a liberal autodidact, retained a keen appreciation of the Bible. In Levy's words, his father understood the Bible to have contained a "germ of all of the greatest scientific discoveries." Sam Levy, "Mes memoires: Salonique à la fin du XIXᵉ siècle," in *Tesoro de los Judios Sefardies: estudios sobre la historia de los judios sefardies y su cultura* (Paris: Archives of the Alliance Israélite Universelle, 1961), 75.

14. The AIU schools, for example, mandated that boys study Hebrew a minimum of five and a maximum of ten hours a week, and girls two hours a week. This proved difficult to implement, as AIU teachers often lacked sufficient training in the language (or the will to teach it), while students exhibited less interest in learning Hebrew than French. Rodrigue, *French Jews, Turkish Jews*, 80–81. See also Benbassa, "L'éducation feminine en Orient." For more on the relative laxity of the Sephardi religious authorities, see Stillman, *Sephardi Religious Responses*, Matthias Lehmann, "The Intended Reader of Ladino Rabbinic Literature and Judeo-Spanish Reading Culture," *Jewish History* 6, no. 3 (2002), and "Judeo-Spanish Musar Literature."

15. By the nineteenth century many of the Hebrew books published in Constantinople were printed by Armenian printers. Yaron Ben-Naeh, "Hebrew Printing Houses in the Ottoman Empire," in *Jewish Journalism and Printing Houses in the Ottoman Empire and Modern Turkey*, ed. Gad Nassi (Istanbul: Isis Press, 2001), 84–85. Avraham Yaari, *Hadefus haivri bekushta* (Jerusalem: Hotsaat sefarim al shem Y. L. Magnes, hauniversitah haivrit, 1967). See also Benbassa and Rodrigue, *Jews of the Balkans*, 112.

16. Hebrew language journals in Palestine—and in Jerusalem in particular—proved more popular and long-lived than those in Southeastern Europe. Michelle Campos, "Between 'Haviva Otomania' and 'Eretz Israel': Ottomanism among Palestine's Sephardi and Maghrebi Jews, 1908–13," in *Coexistence and Conflict in Ottoman Society*, ed. R. Kasaba and S. Stein (forthcoming). For more on attempts to create Hebrew periodicals in the European regions of the empire, see Dov HaCohen, "Hadafus haivri beizmir," *Kiryat hasefer* 64, no. 4 (1992); Avner Levy, "Jewish Journals in Izmir," *Pea'mim* 12 (1982); Levy, "The Jewish Press in Turkey"; Aryeh Shmuelevitz, "Two Hebrew-Language Weeklies in Turkey: An Appeal to Revive Concept of a National Culture," in *Türkiye'de yabanci dilde basin* (Istanbul: Istanbul Universitesi Yayinlari, 1985).

17. No reliable statistics document the rise of Ottoman Jewish literacy rates in French. Writing in 1897, Moïse Franco suggested that somewhere between 80,000 and 100,000 Ottoman Jews, or nearly half (by his estimation) of all Jews in the empire, "think and speak" in French. Franco, *Essai sur l'histoire des Israélites*. For a detailed study of French language acquisition among Ottoman Jewry facilitated by the AIU, see Rodrigue, *French Jews, Turkish Jews* and Benbassa, *Une diaspora sépharade*. On the AIU in the Middle East and North Africa, see Michael M. Laskier, *The Alliance Israélite Universelle and the Jewish Communities of Morocco: 1862–1962* (Albany: State University of New York Press, 1983); Amnon Netzer, *The Jews of Persia and the Alliance in the Late Nineteenth Century: Some Aspects* (Jerusalem: Hebrew University of Jeru-

salem and Ben-Zvi Institute, 1974); Yaron Tsur, "Haskalah in a Sectional Colonial Society Mahdia (Tunisia) 1884," in *Sephardi and Middle Eastern Jewries: History and Culture in the Modern Era,* ed. Harvey E. Goldberg (Bloomington: Indiana University Press, 1996); Georges Weill, "The Alliance Israélite Universelle and the Emancipation of the Jewish Communities of the Mediterranean," *The Jewish Journal of Sociology* 24, no. 2 (1982); Zvi Yehuda, "Iraqi Jewry and Cultural Change in the Educational Activity of the Alliance Israelite Universelle," in *Sephardi and Middle Eastern Jewries: History and Culture in the Modern Era,* ed. Harvey E. Goldberg (Bloomington: Indiana University Press, 1996).

18. David Altabe, "The Romanso, 1900–1932: A Bibliographical Survey," *The Sephardic Scholar* 3 (1977–78): 104.

19. Upon visiting the Ottoman capital in 1897, one English tourist remarked that the works of Shakespeare, Milton, Dante, Molière, Voltaire, and Racine, though all prohibited by imperial censor, were available along the Grande Rue de Pera at a cost that little exceeded what one would pay in Paris or London. Richard Davey, *The Sultan and His People* (London: Chapman and Hall, 1897), 296. Lucy Garnett's memoirs of her travels through Constantinople also contain reflections on the state of censorship and reading. Lucy Garnett, *Home Life in Turkey* (New York: Macmillan, 1909).

20. Avner Levy notes that the few attempts to produce a French Jewish periodical either failed or remained marginal to the Ottoman Jewish reading public. For an incomplete list of Ottoman Jewish periodicals published in multiple languages, see Levy, "The Jewish Press in Turkey"; Nassi, "Synoptic List."

21. In 1877, Sa'adi Bezalel HaLevy produced the Ladino weekly *La epoka* and eight years later with Vitalis Cohen (alias Sheridan), the French-language Jewish biweekly *Journal de Salonique.* For more on this newspaper and the publishing culture of Salonika, see David M. Bunis, *Voices from Jewish Salonika: Selections from the Judezmo Satirical Series tio Ezrá i su mujer benuta and tio bohor i su mujer jamila* (Jerusalem: Misgav yerushalayim, 1999); Paul Dumont, "Le français d'abord," in *Salonique, 1850–1918: La 'ville des juifs' et le réveil des Balkans,* ed. Gilles Veinstein (Paris: Editions Autrement-Series Memoires, 1992); Eyal Ginio, " 'Learning the Beautiful Language of Homer': Judeo-Spanish Speaking Jews and the Greek Language and Culture between the Wars," *Jewish History* 6, no. 3 (2002); Levy, *Mes Memoires;* Michael Molho, "Haitonut espanyolit besaloniki," in *Saloniki, ir veam beyisrael* (Jerusalem: hamakhon leheker yahadut saloniki, 1967); Joseph Nehama, *Histoire des Israélites de Salonique,* vol. 7 (Salonique: Molho, 1978).

22. In his adulation of the *Journal de Salonique,* Levy was not alone. Young readers of the *Journal de Salonique* were avid consumers of its reports of local scandals and celebrations, its coverage of local and international affairs, and its provocative queries, to which they responded eagerly and profusely (one of Levy's earliest contributions asked readers "do you prefer blondes or brunettes, and why," a question that was met by a surge of replies so prolific they clogged the local mail for days). The *Journal de Salonique,* it would appear, was confidante, pedagogue, and status symbol rolled into one: a text that could make as much as mark Salonika's young Jewish bourgeoisie. Levy, *Mes mémoires,* 74, 79.

23. Dumont, "Le français d'abord," 218.

24. Rodrigue, *Sephardi and Eastern Jewries,* 130–31.

25. In 1895, 80.35 percent of Serbian Jews spoke Ladino: in 1931, this number had fallen to 29.86 percent. Conversely, only 2.79 percent of Serbian Jews claimed fluency in Serbo-Croat in 1895, while in 1931 this number had risen to 48.99 percent. In 1926, meanwhile, 89.43 percent of Bulgarian Jews labeled themselves Ladino speakers; in 1934, in the wake of state-sponsored Bulgarization policies, this number had fallen to 57.86 percent. Conversely, between 1926 and 1934, the per-

centage of Bulgarian Jews who claimed Bulgarian as their mother tongue rose from 7.62 percent to 39.8 percent. Finally, in 1928, 62,000 of Greece's 73,000 Jews (most of them from Macedonia and Thrace) identified Ladino as their native language. Reasons for declining rates of literacy in Ladino will be discussed in the epilogue. Freidenreich, *The Jews of Yugoslavia,* 32–33; Ginio, "Language of Homer"; Mézan, *Les Juifs espagnols en Bulgarie,* 68; Astruc, "Data Concerning the Demographic Situation," 90; Rivlin, ed., *Pinkas hakehilot;* Weiker, *The Jewish Polity.*

26. See the description of Talmud Torah study by Franco, *Essai sur l'histoire des Israélites,* 262–63. A more extensive examination of the Talmud Torah schools of Salonika may be found in *Saloniki, ir veam beyisrael,* 57–98. On the publication and content of the *Me'am Loez,* see Yaari, *Reshimat sifrei ladino.* Michael Molho, *Le meam loez: enclopédie popularire du sépharadisme levantin* (Thessalonica: n.p., 1945). For more on rabbinic sanctions of the practice of reading aloud, see Lehmann, "Judeo-Spanish Musar Literature" and "The Intended Reader of Ladino Rabbinic Literature."

27. Lehmann, "Judeo-Spanish Musar Literature."

28. Matthias Lehmann has discussed how authors of Ladino vernacular rabbinic literature composed their works in order to make them accessible to women readers. Further, authors of this literature encouraged women and girls to study their writing, as did Yehuda Papo in the introduction to the nineteenth-century *Pele Yoets:* "How laudable it is if women, friends and relatives meet one Sabbath in the home of one friend, and the other Sabbath in another friend's home, and each group appoints a woman who can read and they spend the hour with [learning], and they will want to make sure their daughters learn to read." Lehmann, "The Intended Reader," 298, and "Judeo-Spanish Musar Literature." See also Stillman, *Sephardi Religious Responses;* Molho, *Literatura séfardita,* 91–129; Lowenthal, *Elia Carmona's Autobiography,* 61–62; Franco, *Essai sur l'histoire des Israélites,* 262–63; Rachel Simon, "Between the Family and the Outside World: Jewish Girls in the Modern Middle East and North Africa," *Jewish Social Studies* 7, no. 1 (2000).

29. The first effort to introduce Jewish libraries with secular works in their collections seems to have been undertaken by the Alliance Israélite Universelle in 1882. Because of the AIU's efforts, by the late 1880s small reading rooms and literary societies had been founded in numerous communities. These successes notwithstanding, a questionnaire circulated in 1904 by the Spanish senator Angel Pulido Fernández revealed that in locals as diverse as Alexandria, Cairo, and Izmir, not only Jewish libraries but reading matter in Spanish and Ladino were a rarity. For more on Senator Pulido's intentions, see footnote 78 of this chapter. Lowenthal, *Elia Carmona's Autobiography,* 66–67, 221.

30. Until now, literature translated into Ladino has been dismissed as derivative and inauthentic. But as recent research by Olga Borovaia suggests, this genre in fact constitutes a fascinating testimony to the way in which Sephardi culture was translating, adopting, and transforming contemporary literary traditions. Olga V. Borovaia, "The Role of Translation in Shaping the Ladino Novel at the Time of Westernization in the Ottoman Empire," *Jewish History* 16, no. 3 (2002), and "Translation and Westernization: *Gulliver's Travels* in Ladino," *Jewish Social Studies* 7, no. 2 (2001). For a discussion of the Ladino literary corpus writ large, see Aviva Ben-Ur, "Ladino in Print: Towards a Comprehensive Bibliography," *Jewish History* 16, no. 3 (2002).

31. Hassan, "El estudio del periodismo Sefardi," 230.

32. To this trend, *La epoka* was the rare exception. *La epoka* was not only published in folksy Ladino, but also contained articles that defended Ladino as a modern language that should be employed by Sephardim. Bunis, *Voices from Jewish Salonika.*

33. "El jurnalizmo judio en turkia" *El tiempo,* no. 42 (7 March 1892).

34. Lehmann, "The Intended Reader," and "Judeo-Spanish Musar Literature."

For a discussion of the divisions between the modernizing and traditionalist camps in the Ottoman capital, see Karmi, *The Jewish Community of Istanbul.*

35. The Chief Rabbinate emerged in the seventeenth to eighteenth centuries and supplanted local congregational rabbis. In certain towns, two or more rabbis shared the position; in others, pressure groups ensured that a particular rabbi would assume the post. The legal office of Chief Rabbi, modeled on that of the Greek and Armenian Patriarchs, was officially introduced in 1835 by the imperial administration. Thereafter, the Chief Rabbi was to be elected by the community and his appointment ratified by the sultan. It was not until Chief Rabbi Haim Nahum assumed the position in 1908 that a single Chief Rabbi attempted to rule over all of Ottoman Jewry. Benbassa, *Une diaspora sépharade* and *Haim Nahum.* For a study of the Chief Rabbi of Constantinople, see Karmi, *The Jewish Community in Istanbul.* The budget and editorial that sparked the crisis between *El tiempo* and the religious authorities can be found in *El tiempo,* no. 17 (January 1873).

36. Franco, *Essai sur l'histoire des Israélites,* 187–89. The episode is also described in the Ladino-language autobiography of Elia Carmona, who served as a typographer at *El tiempo,* and discussed by Robyn Lowenthal in her unpublished doctoral dissertation: Lowenthal, *Elia Carmona's Autobiography,* 179, 214, 233. See also Galanté, *Histoire des juifs de Turquie,* vol. 2, 137, 261–63.

37. Lowenthal, *Elia Carmona's Autobiography,* 233, Mark Mazower, "Salonica between East and West, 1860–1912," *Diagolos Hellenic Studies Review,* no. 1 (1989): 118.

38. See the contributions by Barsoumian, Clogg, Issawi, and Dumont in Braude and Lewis, *Christians and Jews in the Ottoman Empire.* See also Karmi, *The Jewish Community in Istanbul;* Kasaba, "Economic Foundations"; Turgay, "Trade and Merchants"; Kasaba, *The Ottoman Empire;* Rodrigue, "From *Millet* to Minority"; Rodrigue and Benbassa, *Jews of the Balkans;* Stanford Shaw, *The Jews of the Ottoman Empire and the Turkish Republic* (New York: New York University Press, 1991); Weiker, *The Jewish Polity.*

39. In 1885, Greeks and Armenians represented 22.5 percent and 20.6 percent of the active population of Constantinople and 25.4 percent and 27 percent of the population working in trade craft and industry, while Jews represented 5.6 percent of the active population and 5.2 percent of the population working in trade, craft, and industry. Shaw, "Population of Istanbul."

40. Carter V. Findley, "The Acid Test of Ottomanism: The Acceptance of Non-Muslims in the Late Ottoman Bureaucracy," in *Christians and Jews in the Ottoman Empire: The Functioning of a Plural Society,* ed. Benjamin Braude and Bernard Lewis (New York: Holmes & Meier, 1982).

41. It is unfortunate that most studies of the Ottoman press have tended to focus exclusively upon Turkish-language sources. Similarly, the non-Turkish language presses of the empire tend to be discussed in isolation. As a result, our knowledge of the circulation of non-Turkish-language popular sources is limited, while our understanding of their *relative* popularity is almost non-existent. This is in great part a result of linguistic constraints, but it also reflects the extent to which our understanding of Ottoman society continues to be bifurcated along ethnic and linguistic lines. Whether or not this accurately reflects the nature of this society is a question rarely asked and difficult to answer. For more on the rise of the Turkish-language press, see M. Orhan Bayrak, *Türkiye'de gazeteler ve dergiler sözlügü, 1831–1993* (Istanbul: KÜLL Yayinlari, 1994); Nesim Benbanaste, *Örneklerle Türk Musevi basininin tarihçesi* (Istanbul: N. Benbanaste, 1988); Brummett, *Image and Imperialism; Bildiriler, Türk Kütüphaneciler Dernegi* (Ankara: Türk Kütüphaneciler Dernegi, 1979); Hasan Duman, *Istanbul kütüphaneleri arap harfli süreli yayinlari toplu katalogu, 1828–1928,* Bibliographical Series/Research Centre for Islamic History, Art, and Culture, 3

(Besiktas and Istanbul: Islâm Tarih, Sanat, ve Kültür Arastirma Merkezi, Islâm Konferansi Teskilâti, 1986); Selim Nüzet Gerçek, *Türk matbaaciligi* (Istanbul: Istanbul
Devlet Basimevi, 1939); Server Iskit, *Türkiyede matbuat idareleri ve politikalari* (Istanbul: Tan Basimevi, 1943); *Türkiyede matbuat rejimleri* (Istanbul: Ülkü matbaasi, 1939)
and, *Türkiyede nesriyat hareketleri tarihine bir bakis* (Istanbul: Devlet Basimevi, 1939);
Alpay Kabacali, *Baslangiçtan günümüze Türkiye'de basin sansürü* (Istanbul: Gazeteciler
Cemiyeti Yayinlari, 1990); Fuat Süreyya Oral, *Türk basin tarihi*, 2 vols., vol. 1 (Ankara: Yeni Adim Matbaasi, 1967); Zafer Toprak, "Fikir dergiciliginin yuzyili," in
Türkiye'de dergiler, ansiklopediler (1849–1984) (Istanbul: Gelisim Yayinlari, 1984);
A. D. Zheltiakov, *Matbaaciligin 250. Kurulus yildönümüne srmagan — Türkiye'nin dosyo-
politik ve kültürel hayatinda basin* (Ankara and Leningrad: Basin Yayin Genel Müdürlügü, 1979).

42. In the first decade of the twentieth century, the leading Armenian dailies of
Constantinople (*Manzoumei-Efkiar* and *Sourhantag*) reached three thousand readers
combined. On the basis of the Ottoman census, Justin McCarthy estimates the adult
Armenian population of the Ottoman capital at 83,000. Justin McCarthy, *Muslims
and Minorities: The Population of Ottoman Anatolia and the End of the Empire* (New York:
New York University Press, 1983), 121–24. The number of Armenian periodicals in
the city is recorded by Gia Aivazian, "The Role of the Armenian Press in Istanbul,
1908–1915 in the Shaping of the Armenian National Identity" (paper presented at
the Middle East Studies Association, San Francisco, 1997). The circulation of the
leading eight Armenian periodicals (including five dailies) is referred to in Paul
Fesch, "La presse et la censure," in *Constantinople aux derniers jours d'Abdul-Hamid*
(Paris: Librairie des Sciences Politiques et Sociales, 1907).

43. The Greek population of Constantinople has been measured differently by
different sources. The official Turkish census of 1910 suggested there were 70,906
Greeks in the city, while in 1912 the Greek Patriarch counted 74,457. These population statistics are cited by McCarthy, *Muslims and Minorities*, 91. The circulation of
Greek papers in the city is drawn from Fesch, "La presse et la censure." For more on
the Greek press, see John Dimakis, "The Greek Press," in *Greece in Transition: Essays in
the History of Modern Greece, 1821–1974*, ed. John T. A. Koumoulides (London: Zeno,
1977).

44. For studies of the shifting economic roles of the Greek, Armenian, and Turkish *millets* at this time, see the contributions by Issawi, Barsoumian, Clogg, Dumont,
and Turgay in Braude and Lewis, *Christians and Jews in the Ottoman Empire*. See also
Kasaba, "Economic Foundations."

45. Findley, "The Acid Test of Ottomanism," 356, 360.

46. The former reference to *El tiempo*'s circulation may be found in a travel
memoir by Paul Fesch, whose *Constantinople aux derniers jours d'Abdul-Hamid* was
published in the 1930s. According to Fesch, in 1908, *El tiempo* had a circulation of
900, while the Constantinople-based *El telegrafo* (1878–1930) had a circulation of
500. A vastly different circulation is identified by historian Avner Levy, who has
estimated that the circulation of *El tiempo* reached 10,000 subscribers at its peak.
Unfortunately, neither Fesch nor Levy offers evidence in support of their claims.
Fesch, "La Presse et la Censure," 68; Levy, "The Jewish Press in Turkey."

47. Speaking very roughly indeed, *Der fraynd* could be said to reach one subscriber
for every five thousand Russian Jewish subjects. *El tiempo*, on the other hand, could be
said to reach one out of every twenty-five Ottoman Jewish subjects. These figures
assume an Ottoman Jewish population of 250,000 and a Russian Jewish population
of five million, both of which are based on official figures. By comparing these
figures, and the circulations of *El tiempo* and *Der fraynd*, I do not mean to suggest that
either paper was distributed evenly throughout the empire in which it was produced,
nor, indeed, that it would be accessible (or of interest) to all Jewish subjects.

48. Elias Canetti, *The Tongue Set Free: Remembrance of a European Childhood*, trans. Joachim Neugroschel (New York: Seabury Press, 1979).

49. Arguably such interlocution was the norm rather than the exception. Ladino newspapers of the late nineteenth and early twentieth centuries tended to be in conversation with one another and their editors, friends or foe, often knew one another well, collaborated on projects, or, indeed, were related. Consider, for example, the close relationship between Abraham Galanté (editor of the Cairo-based *La vara*) and David Fresco, or the relationship between Fresco and Elia Carmona, editor of the humorist *El gugeton* (the longest-lived Ladino journal after *El tiempo*). In both instances, these writers and editors exhibited a profound influence on one another. Albert E. Kalderon, *Abraham Galanté: A Biography* (New York: Sepher-Hermon Press, 1983); Lowenthal, *Elia Carmona's Autobiography*. Mention of *El tiempo*'s influence on the Ladino press of Jerusalem has been made by Michelle Campos in her unpublished Ph.D. dissertation, in which she notes that the Jerusalem-based Ladino newspaper *Haherut* ran numerous articles responding to *El tiempo*'s coverage of Zionism. See *Haherut*, nos. 49 and 50 (19 and 21 January 1910); Campos, "A Shared Homeland." On the culture of Ladino publishing in Izmir, see Henri Nahum, *Juifs de Smyrne, XIXᵉ–XIXᵉ siècle* (Paris: Aubier, 1997).

50. This hypothesis is based, first, on Levy's attribution of a circulation of 10,000 and, second, on two demographic studies of Constantinople's Jewish population. The number of Jews living in Constantinople is cited by: Riva Kastoryano, ed., *Ottoman and Turkish Jewry: Community and Leadership,* Indiana University Turkish Studies Series, vol. 12 (Bloomington: Indiana University Turkish Studies, 1992), 255; Shaw, *The Jews of the Ottoman Empire,* 11. The percentage of Jewish adults in the city is derived from Justin McCarthy's age pyramids, based upon the Ottoman census of 1912. McCarthy, *Muslims and Minorities,* Appendix 4, 193–226.

51. Levy's concern was not misplaced: *La epoka* does seem to have reached only a small minority of Salonika's Ladino reading public. Various and conflicting accounts of the circulation of this newspaper exist, and no doubt the journal's circulation changed over time. At one point, Sam Levy cites the figure 50; at another, he speaks of a conflict with the paper's printer, who was printing twice as many of the 700–800 newspapers whose sale he reported. In the pages of *La epoka* itself, a circulation of 200 was cited in 1877. Levy, *Mes mémoires,* vol. VII, lxi–lxii. "Komo se sostene un jurnal?" *La epoka,* no. 109 (28 November 1877). For more on the Ladino press of Salonika, see Bunis, *Voices from Jewish Salonika;* Dumont, "Le français d'abord"; Ginio, "Language of Homer"; Levy, *Mes mémoires;* Molho, "Haitonut espanyolit besaloniki"; Nehama, *Histoire des Israélites de Salonique.*

52. Franco, *Essai sur l'histoire des Israélites,* 281.

53. Levy, *Mes mémoires,* 78.

54. Lowenthal, *Elia Carmona's Autobiography,* 169.

55. As has already been mentioned, in its earliest years, *El tiempo* was patronized by the Carmona family. After the Alliancist Chief Rabbi Haim Nahum assumed the position in 1909, this organization, too, contributed to the paper's budget. *El tiempo,* no. 109 (14 June 1909).

56. Rodrigue, *French Jews, Turkish Jews,* Benbassa, *Une diaspora sépharade.*

57. David Fresco, "Alas lekturas," *El instruktor,* no. 1, 1 Ayer 5648. According to this article, Fresco founded *El instruktor* to fill a void that he once envisioned *El telegrafo* as addressing.

58. See, for example: "A mueva kompanyero del 'telegrafo,'" *El tiempo,* no. 86 (10 August 1899); "Los amabilidados del direktor del 'telegrafo' por el direktor del 'tiempo,'" *El tiempo,* no. 91 (28 August 1899). In 1909, this accusation would be applied to *El tiempo* by Nahum Sokolow, editor of the Berlin-based Zionist newspaper *Die Welt.* Sokolow accused Fresco of employing the pseudonym Gad Franko as a way

of multiplying his attacks on Zionism, a charge that Fresco called an outrage and an insult. Gad Franko (1881–1954) did in fact exist: he was an important constitutional lawyer, an avid anti-Zionist, and a founder of the journal *El commercial*. Sokolow's false accusation provides some fodder to the claim that Zionism's leading theoreticians were estranged from the Ottoman Jewish political landscape. David Fresco, "El tsionizmo," *El tiempo*, no. 17 (3 November 1909). Reference to Gad Franko can be found in Shaw, *Jews of the Ottoman Empire*, 182.

59. See, for example, "Los mashgiahes de galata i '*El telegrafo*,' " *El tiempo*, no. 90 (24 August 1899).

60. In 1892, *El tiempo* published one such panegyric, an unsigned article (often a signal that the piece was penned by David Fresco) on the history of journalism in Turkey. After detailing a bit of this history, the article suggested that one man, "a great Jew," who is too modest to allow himself to be mentioned, was singlehandedly responsible for reviving Jewish culture in Constantinople (a footnote specified that this individual was responsible for the publication of *El tiempo*, in case there was any doubt just who was being referred to). A poem was included that sang the praises of the "heroic writer, David" who "devoted his life to his nation." It began with the following stanza:

> On the banks of the Bosphorous
> Every day a man breathes,
> A good soul, a noble heart,
> with a pure and celebrated name.

The poem goes on to offer a passionate description of this David, who has armed himself with a lance to combat ignorance in the Diaspora, an ignorance so deeply rooted that David must fight it strenuously and continuously. "El junalizmo judio in turkia," *El tiempo*, no. 43 (10 March 1892).

61. "La lucha de las lenguas," *El tiempo*, no. 398 (24 September 1891).

62. "Orijin i dezvelopamiento de la lengua franseza," *El tiempo*, nos. 37 and 38 (1 and 22 February 1892).

63. Bunis, *Voices from Jewish Salonika*.

64. Nissim Yehuda Pardo "El judeoespanyol," *El tiempo*, no. 72 (22 June 1893).

65. Examples taken from "El esprito del judaismo," *El tiempo*, no. 40 (8 February 1894); "El alegria en el judaismo," *El tiempo*, no. 3 (8 October 1897). Abraham Galanté has also commented on this practice. Galanté, *La presse judéo-espagnole mondiale*, 6.

66. Rodrigue, "From *Millet* to Minority," 253.

67. Borovaia, "Translation and Westernization" and "The Role of Translation."

68. Rodrigue, *Sephardi and Eastern Jewries* and *French Jews, Turkish Jews*.

69. Rodrigue, *French Jews, Turkish Jews*, 86–88, 165.

70. "Otomanizmo i otomanizasyon," *El tiempo*, no. 116 (6 July 1910).

71. Rodrigue and Benbassa, *The Jews of the Balkans*, 116–43.

72. "Las israelitas i la turkia," *El tiempo*, no. 46 (9 March 1899).

73. "La lengua turka i los judios de turkia," *El tiempo*, no. 31 (17 January 1901).

74. "Otomanizmo i otomanizasyon," *El tiempo*, no. 116 (6 July 1910). On the development of Turkism, see Haldun Gulalp, "Modernization Policies and Islamist Politics in Turkey," in *Rethinking Modernity and National Identity in Turkey*, ed. Sibel Bozdogan and Reşat Kasaba (Seattle: University of Washington Press, 1997); Reşat Kasaba, "Kemalist Certainties and Modern Ambiguities," in *Rethinking Modernity and National Identity in Turkey*, ed. Sibel Bozdogan and Reşat Kasaba (Seattle: University of Washington Press, 1997); Jacob M. Landau, ed., *Ataturk and the Modernization of Turkey* (Boulder, Colo.: Westview Press, 1984).

75. Isaac Ferrara, "De la literatura otomana," *El tiempo*, no. 52 (20 March 1902).

76. Isaac Ferrara, "De la literatura otomana," *El tiempo,* no. 36 (27 February 1902).

77. Isaac Ferrara, "De la literatura otomana," *El tiempo,* no. 52 (20 March 1902).

78. The idea that Sephardi Jews should cultivate their ties with Spain had been raised in a letter to *El tiempo* penned by Dr. Angel Pulido Fernandez of Spain. Dr. Pulido's *Españoles sin Patria y la Raza Sefardi* would attempt to raise Spaniards' interest in the culture of the Sephardim with the hope of establishing good relations between Spain and the Spanish Jews of the Levant. Isaac Ferrara, "La lengua judeo-espanyol i sr. polido," *El tiempo,* no. 89 (11 August 1902).

79. Isaac Ferrara, "Los verbos turkos en el judeoespanyol," *El tiempo,* no. 95 (1 September 1902).

80. Isaac Ferrara, "Su ekselensia ahmed midhat efendi i los israelitas de turkia," *El tiempo,* no. 2 (16 September 1902).

81. Isaac Ferrara, "De la literatura otomana," *El tiempo,* no. 48 (20 March 1902).

82. G. L. Lewis, "Ataturk's Language Reform as an Aspect of Modernization in the Republic of Turkey," in *Ataturk and the Modernization of Turkey,* ed. Jacob Landau (Boulder, Colo., and Leiden: Westview Press and E. J. Brill, 1984).

83. "El judeoespanyol," *El tiempo,* no. 72 (22 June 1893).

84. "El judeoespanyol," *El tiempo,* no. 24 (14 December 1893).

85. "El judeoespanyol," *El tiempo,* no. 26 (26 December 1893).

86. "La komunidad del gran rabinato por la propagasyon de la lengua turka," *El tiempo,* no. 35 (10 March 1900).

87. "La lengua turka i los judios de turkia," *El tiempo,* no. 31 (17 January 1901).

88. Galanté, *La presse judéo-espagnole mondiale,* 4–6.

89. "El judeoespanyol," *El tiempo,* no. 69 (9 July 1901).

90. "El tsionizmo asembrando la diskordia entre los judios de bulgaria," *El tiempo,* no. 102 (1 June 1910).

91. David Fresco, "La kestyon de la lengua," *El tiempo,* no. 62 (13 June 1901).

92. David Fresco, "La kestyon de la lengua," *El tiempo,* no. 63 (17 June 1901).

93. Paul Dumont, "La structure sociale de la communauté juive de Salonique à la fin du dix-neuvième siècle," *Revue historique* 263 (April–June 1980); Ginio, "Language of Homer"; Rena Molho, "Le renouveau," in *Salonique, 1850–1918: La 'ville des juifs' et le réveil des Balkans,* ed. Gilles Veinstein (Paris: Editions Autrement-Series Memoires, 1992), 65; Michael Molho, "Haitonut espanyolit besaloniki." Two very fine collections of essays on Salonika also exist: Veinstein, ed., *Salonique, 1850–1918,* and *Saloniki, ir veam beyisrael.* Recent pioneering work by Eyal Ginio also offers a uniquely multi-ethnic glimpse of the city, "Aspects of Muslim Culture in the Ottoman Balkans during the 18th Century: A View from Salonika" (Ph.D. dissertation, Hebrew University, 1999). See also Mazower, "Salonica between East and West," and Nehama, *Histoire des Israélites de Salonique.* For a map of Salonika's religious quarters, see *Salonique 1850–1918,* 283.

94. Sa'adi Bezalel HaLevy, "El judeoespanyol," *La epoka,* no. 1294 (21 June 1901).

95. Bunis, *Voices from Jewish Salonika,* 26–27.

96. Sa'adi Bezalel HaLevy, "El judeoespanyol," *La epoka,* no. 1295 (28 June 1901).

97. Ibid.

98. "Novedades politikas, el movimento de la lengua turka," *La epoka,* no. 953 (24 August 1894).

99. Satri, "La lengua turka en eskolas non muzulmanas," *La epoka,* no. 954 (14 September 1894).

100. See Haim Behmuares, "En adrinopla, konferensya sovre la lengua turka," *La epoka,* no. 1319 (December 1901 [undated]); Leon Moshe Saporta, "La lengua turka," *La epoka,* no. 1336 (18 April 1902).

101. Sa'adi Bezalel HaLevy, "El judeoespanyol," *La epoka,* no. 1294 (21 June 1901).

102. Benbassa, *Une diaspora sépharade*, 173.

103. Roderic Davison, *Reform in the Ottoman Empire 1856–1876* (Princeton, N.J.: Princeton University Press, 1963), 358–409. On the events of 1908, see Sukru M. Hanioglu, *The Young Turks in Opposition* (New York: Oxford University Press, 1995); Aykut Kansu, *The Revolution of 1908 in Turkey* (Leiden and New York: Brill, 1997).

104. "El imperio otomano salvado por la justisya," *El tiempo*, no. 88 (27 July 1908).

105. Kalderon, *Abraham Galanté: A Biography*, 37.

106. David Fresco, "La publikasyon d'*El tiempo*," *El tiempo*, no. 88 (27 July 1908).

107. Brummett, *Image and Imperialism*, 31–32.

108. Feroz Ahmad, "Unionist Relations with the Greek, Armenian, and Jewish Communities of the Ottoman Empire, 1908–1914," in *Christians and Jews in the Ottoman Empire, the Functioning of a Plural Society*, ed. Benjamin Braude and Bernard Lewis (New York: Holmes & Meier, 1982); Rodrigue, "From *Millet* to Minority," 255.

109. Benbassa, *Une diaspora sépharade* and *Haim Nahum*.

110. Esther Benbassa, "Presse d'Istanbul et de Salonique au service du sionisme (1908–1914)," *Revue historique* 560 (1986). For a more general treatment of the lifting of censorship in the post-revolutionary era, see Brummett, *Image and Imperialism*.

111. Benbassa, *Une diaspora sépharade*.

112. *L'Aurore* and *Le Jeune Turc*, for example, were to gain circulations of 1,500 and 15,000, respectively, in the post-1908 period. For presses in other languages, this was a period of greater, rather than fewer restrictions: Armenian presses suffered greatly under the new leadership, and almost all were forcibly closed after 1914. Aivazian, "The Armenian Press."

113. Benbassa, "Presse d'Istanbul et de Salonique" and *Une diaspora sépharade*, 97.

114. "Las israelitas i la lengua turka," *El tiempo*, no. 20 (20 November 1908); David Fresco "El tsionizmo," *El tiempo*, no. 13 (25 October 1909).

115. Response to a letter to the editor by David Fresco, *El tiempo*, no. 34 (15 December 1909); "El eksplotasyon tsionista, el muev kongreso," *El tiempo*, no. 132 (12 August 1910).

116. David Fresco, "El tsionizmo," *El tiempo*, no. 14 (27 October 1909).

117. Ibid., and no. 16 (1 November 1909).

118. Jed Franko, "El tsionizmo," *El tiempo*, no. 8 (13 September 1909).

119. David Fresco, "La monstrozo impostura, a sr. sokolow," *El tiempo*, no. 20 (12 November 1909).

120. David Fresco, "El tsionizmo," *El tiempo*, no. 17 (3 November 1909).

121. La nasion, "Tsionizmo, judaizmo, otomanizmo," *El tiempo*, no. 26 (14 December 1911).

122. "Kursos gratuitas de lengua turka en los kuartieras israelitas de konstantinopla," *El tiempo*, no. 19 (25 November 1910); David Fresco, "La kestyon de la lengua evraika," *El tiempo*, no. 25 (12 December 1910).

123. Weiker, *The Jewish Polity*, 303.

124. Karmi, *The Jewish Community in Istanbul*, 116–24. Rodrigue, *French Jews, Turkish Jews*, 86.

125. Hasan Kayali and Engin Akarli have argued that in the wake of the 1908 revolt, the empire witnessed a rise in cultural (as opposed to political or territorial) nationalisms and that these were forms of nationalist expression that accommodated Ottomanism. These scholars both conclude that the empire's ethnic groups by and large remained loyal to the multi-ethnic structure of empire until the close of the First World War. Akarli, *The Long Peace;* Kayali, *Arabs and Young Turks*.

126. "El lenguaje de oro del apostolo del tsionizmo," *El tiempo*, no. 118 (23 August 1911).

127. Roderic Davison, "The Armenian Crisis, 1912–1914," *American Historical Review* 53, no. 3 (1948): 481–505; Fikret Adanir, "Armenian Deportations and

Massacres in 1915," in *Ethnopolitical Warfare: Causes, Consequences, and Possible Solutions*, ed. D. Chirot and M. Seligman (Washington, D.C.: Psychological Association, 2001); and Hilmar Keiser, "The Armenian Genocide, Governing Myths Revisited," in *Conflict and Coexistence in Ottoman Society*, ed. R. Kasaba and S. Stein (forthcoming).

128. "Por la defensa del imperio otomano," *El tiempo*, no. 120 (19 July 1909).

129. "Por la defensa de muestra kerida patria," *El tiempo*, no. 54 (2 February 1910). That Jews "voted with their feet" in 1909 by emigrating may tarnish Çaglar Keyder's suggestion that the period between the fall of 1909 and elections in March 1912 hinted at the potential success of a multi-ethnic political sensibility. Çaglar Keyder, "The Ottoman Empire," in *After Empire: Multiethnic Societies and Nation-Building*, ed. Karen Barkley and Mark Von Hagen (Boulder, Colo.: Westview Press, 1997), 38.

130. Bosnia and Herzegovina (including the Jewish center of Sarajevo) had been annexed by Austria-Hungary in 1878, and Bulgaria declared independence the same year. In the course of the next three years, Crete and Greece would announce their union; Italy would attack the Ottoman Tripolitania; and a series of wars would be declared between Turkey and its Balkan neighbors. The kingdom of Greece, independent since 1830, seized the Sephardi center of Salonika in 1912. Macedonia was divided among Bulgaria, Greece, and Serbia. The much-reduced empire would face an additional decade of fighting before the emergence of the Turkish Republic in 1923, by which point the kingdoms of the Serbs, Croats, and Slovenes had also been established.

131. N. M. Gelber, "An Attempt to Internationalize Salonika, 1912–1913," *Jewish Social Studies* 17, no. 2 (1955); Rodrigue and Benbassa, *The Jews of the Balkans*, 96.

132. On the process of Turkicization, see Rifat N. Bali, *Bir türklestirme serüveni (1923–1945)* (Istanbul: Iletisim, 1999); Avner Levi, *Turkiye Cümhuriyeti'nde Yahudiler, hukuki ve siyasi durumlari* (Istanbul: Iletisim, 1992); Weiker, *The Jewish Polity*. On the process of Hellenization, see Ginio, "Language of Homer"; Rena Molho, "Popular Antisemitism and State Policy in Salonika during the City's Annexation to Greece," *Jewish Social Studies* 50, no. 3–4 (1988–93); Rivlin, *Pinkas hakehilot — Greece*.

133. For a comparative study of these policies, see Rogers Brubaker, "Aftermaths of Empire and the Unmixing of Peoples," in *After Empire: Multiethnic Societies and Nation-Building: The Soviet Union and Russian, Ottoman, and Habsburg Empires*, ed. Mark Von Hagen and Karen Barkey (Boulder, Colo.: Westview Press, 1997). On the Armenian genocide, see Adanir, "Armenian Deportations and Massacres"; Davison, "The Armenian Crisis"; and Keiser, "The Armenian Genocide."

134. Rodrigue and Benbassa, *Jews of the Balkans*, 184–88; Weiker, *The Jewish Polity*, 263–69.

135. See, for example, "A traverso el mundo," *El tiempo*, no. 64 (14 February 1913).

3. Iconographies of Agitation

1. The following studies of the cartoons of the 1905 era have informed this study: Margaret Bridget Betz, "The Caricatures and Cartoons of the 1905 Revolution: Images of the Opposition" (Ph.D. dissertation, City University of New York, 1984); Vladimir Botsiavnovskii and E. F. Gollerbakh, eds., *Russkaia satira pervoi revoliutsii 1905–1906* (Leningrad: Gosudarstvennoe izdatel'stvo, 1925); E. P. [Evgeniia Petrovna] Demchenko, *Politicheskaia grafika kieva, perioda revoliutsii, 1905–1907* (Kiev: Haukova dumka, 1976) and *Politicheskaia grafika v pechati ukrainy, 1905–1907* (Kiev: Naukova dumka, 1984); S. Isakov, *1905 god v satire i karikature* (Leningrad: Priboi, 1928); David King and Cathy Porter, *Images of Revolution: Graphic Art from 1905 Russia*

(New York: Pantheon Books, 1983); E. L. [Evgenii Lvovich] Nemirovskii, ed., *Russkaia satiricheskaia periodika, 1905–1907* (Moscow: Gosudarstvennaia biblioteka SSSR im. V.I. Lenina, 1980); V. V. [Vladimir Vasil'evich] Shleev, ed., *Revoliutsiia 1905–1907 goda i izobrazitel'noe iskusstvo,* 3 vols. (Moscow: Izobrazitel'noe iskusstvo, 1977).

On the rather more corporeal manifestations of the Revolution of 1905–1907, see Ascher, *The Revolution of 1905;* Victoria Bonnell, *Roots of Rebellion: Workers' Politics and Organizations in St. Petersburg and Moscow, 1900–1914* (Berkeley: University of California Press, 1983); John Bushnell, *Mutiny amid Repression: Russian Soldiers in the Revolution of 1905–1906* (Bloomington: Indiana University Press, 1985); Laura Engelstein, *Moscow, 1905: Working-Class Organization and Political Conflict* (Stanford, Calif.: Stanford University Press, 1982); William C. Fuller, "Civil-Military Conflict in the Russian Revolution, 1905–1907," in *Civil-Military Conflict in Imperial Russia, 1881–1914* (Princeton, N.J.: Princeton University Press, 1985); Stephen P. Frank, *Crime, Cultural Conflict, and Justice in Rural Russia* (Berkeley: University of California Press, 1999); Henry Reichman, *Railwaymen and Revolution: Russia, 1905* (Berkeley: University of California Press, 1987); Sablinsky, *The Road to Bloody Sunday;* Surh, *1905 in St. Petersburg;* Verner, *The Crisis of Russian Autocracy;* Robert Weinberg, *The Revolution of 1905 in Odessa: Blood on the Steps* (Bloomington: Indiana University Press, 1993).

2. The most complete list of Yiddish satirical journals of the 1905 era may be found in Botsiavnovskii and Gollerbakh, *Russkaia satira pervoi revoliutsii.*

3. Moyshe Katz, *A dor, vos hot farloyrn di moyre, bleter zikhroynes fun arum 1905* (New York: Moyshe kats yubiley-komitet, 1956), 18. A second compelling memoir of this period by a Russian Jewish activist is that by A. Yuditsky, *Der veg tsu oktober, revbavegung in rusland (1895–1917)* (Kiev: Kultur lige, 1925).

4. Botsiavnovskii and Gollerbakh, *Russkaia satira pervoi revoliutsii.*

5. Feldman, *Yehude rusya biyeme hamapekha harishona.* Shlomo Lambroza, "The Pogrom Movement in Russia, 1903–1905" and "The Pogroms of 1903–1906."

6. The most thorough exploration of the Bund's rise to power may be found in Frankel, *Prophecy and Politics.* See also Gassenschmidt, *Jewish Liberal Politics;* Tobias, *The Jewish Bund.*

7. In 1903, in the wake of the Kishinev pogrom, Theodor Herzl proposed that the Zionist movement accept the British government's tentative offer of Uganda as a destination for the mass settlement of Jews. The proposal caused a schism in the movement between those territorialists who would settle for nothing less than the settlement of the Jews in Palestine and those who sought an immediate solution to the Russian Jewish "problem." The failure of Herzl's proposal caused widespread disillusionment with the movement, which was failing to realize its territorial ambitions. See, for example, Jacques Kornberg, *Theodor Herzl: From Assimilation to Zionism* (Bloomington: Indiana University Press, 1993); Maor, *Hatenuah hatsiyonit berusyah;* Stanislawski, *Zionism and the Fin de Siècle,* especially chapter 1; Vital, *The Formative Years.*

8. Steven Zipperstein has described how, in the era of the Revolution of 1905–1907, Zionist theoretician Ahad Ha'am watched with concern as Russian Jews subordinated their call for Jewish national rights to the struggle for democratic reform in Russia. However, Ahad Ha'am, too, was unable to resist becoming preoccupied with the struggle for parliamentary reform. Zipperstein, *Elusive Prophet.* For general treatment of the evolution of Russian Jewish politics in this era, see Frankel, *Prophecy and Politics.* Gassenschmidt, *Jewish Liberal Politics.*

9. "Thankfully, today Turkey severed its relationship with the leadership in Macedonia," celebrated an article of February 1903, "despite a great danger that Turkey would never give up her greatest state." "Macedonia," *Der fraynd,* no. 31 (10 [23] February 1903).

10. One might say that *Der fraynd* experienced minor but not insignificant tangles with the censor. In an article describing Tsar Nicholas, for example, a reference to the emperor's *eygene hent* (own hands) was "mistakenly" replaced with a reference to his *ayzene hent* (iron hands). The author, Yankev Dineson, was threatened with arrest, but was able to prove the reference a mistake and suffered no consequences. Whether the mistake was accidental or the result of a mischievous typesetter or editor we have no way of knowing. Regardless, it was gleefully noted and remembered by readers who, for months after this episode, signed their letters to the paper's staff with the phrase, "don't forget the 'g'!" Ginzburg, *Amolike peterburg,* 199, 224–25, 227, 229–30. As this episode suggests, while *Der fraynd* was cautious in its first two years of publication, it was not uncritical of Russian state politics, but rather relied on highly metaphoric forms of critique. This strategy was far from an anomalous practice among Russian writers. On the contrary, since Alexander I had imposed strict censorship laws in 1825, journalists had perfected strategies of literary subtlety: Vasili Kurochkin's famous satirical journal of the 1850s, for example, featured a daily column, "Chronicle of Progress," which was always blank. (Alexander's restrictions, in fact, sought to counteract a precedent set by Tsarina Catherine II, who secretly edited a satirical journal, thereby introducing the genre to many Russians.) Yiddish authors, too, relied upon such techniques of concealment. Y. L. Petez's *Yontev bletlakh,* for example, were published as "holiday pamphlets," and each issue had the appearance of being devoted to a different Jewish holiday. A. N. [Aleksandr Nikolaevich] Afanas'ev, *Russkie satiricheskie zhurnaly 1769–1774* (Kazan: Molodyia sily, 1920); King and Porter, *Images of Revolution;* Wisse, *I. L. Peretz,* 41.

11. *Der bezem* predated *Dos lebn,* but appeared as an independent supplement only in 1906. Prior to this year, *Der fraynd* had published two satirical issues within the main body of the newspaper. On both occasions, the supplement was titled *Der tog.* Edward Portnoy has suggested that the first Yiddish cartoon appeared in 1904 in the Warsaw-based *Peysekh-blat,* a collection of poems related to Passover. As Portnoy notes, this cartoon is interesting because it was the first, but it did not immediately initiate a trend. Significantly, it was also not created for this journal, but was appropriated from another (the New York *Der yidisher pok*). Edward Portnoy, "Exploiting Tradition: Religious Iconography in Cartoons of the Polish Yiddish Press," *Polin* 16 (forthcoming November 2003).

12. Lakhovski rarely signed his contributions to *Dos lebn,* making it difficult to determine with certainty which cartoons he penned. However, the stylistic conformity of *Dos lebn*'s cartoons do persuasively suggest that nearly all were created by the artist. Those cartoons that Lakhovski did sign bear the Russian initials "A.L." Neither the publication of anonymous cartoons, nor the signing of one's name in Russian was exceptional in the still-young world of Yiddish cartooning. The fact that Lakhovski chose to sign his name in Russian reflects his comfort in the language — the language in which he was being trained as an artist. But it also points to the ease with which he moved between the symbiotic worlds of Yiddish and Russian letters, and between the intersecting worlds of Jewish and Russian politics. References to Lakhovski's publications in *Udav* and *Serii volk* can be found in Nemirovskii, *Russkaia satiricheskaia periodika,* 98, 106.

13. John E. Bowlt, "Jewish Artists and the Russian Silver Age," in *Russian Jewish Artists in a Century of Change,* ed. Susan Tumarkin Goodman (New York: Prestel, 1995), 45; John Milner, *A Dictionary of Russian and Soviet Artists, 1420–1970* (Woodbridge, Suffolk: Antique Collectors Club, 1933), 244; Shleev, *Revoliutsiia 1905–1907 goda,* 110. Lakhovski also exhibited with the Kuindzhi Society, the *Assotsiatsiia khudozhnikov revoliutsii,* and The Sixteen. After the Russian Revolution of 1917, he produced Agitprop decorations. He later emigrated and exhibited internationally. Information about *Mir iskusstva* may be found in Bowlt, *The Silver Age.* See also

Alesander Kamenskii and Vsevolod Petrov, *The World of Art Movement in Early Twentieth Century Russia* (Leningrad: Aurora Art Publishers, 1991); Janet Kennedy, *The "Mir Iskusstva" Group and Russian Art, 1898–1912* (New York: Garland Publishers, 1977); Sergei Parshin, *Mir iskusstva* (Moscow: Izobrazitel noe iskusstvo, 1993); Aleksandr Strelkov, *Mir iskusstva* (Moscow: Aleksandr Strelkov, 1923).

14. *Dos lebn,* no. 88 (12 April [4 May] 1906).

15. *Dos lebn,* no. 93 (27 April [10 May] 1906).

16. *Dos lebn,* no. 144 (30 June [13 July] 1906); *Dos lebn,* no. 59 (13 [26] March 1906).

17. A reproduction of Brodsky's poster can be found in V. V. [Vladimir Vasil'evich] Shleev, "Peterburg," in *Revoliutsiia 1905–1907 goda.*

18. *Dos lebn,* no. 89 (23 April [6 May] 1906).

19. Botsiavnovskii and Gollerbakh, *Russkaia satira pervoi revoliutsii.*

20. Ruud, "The Printing Press," 24; McReynolds, *Russia's Old Regime.*

21. By way of contrast, most satirical journals of the 1905 period were designed for a narrow and often internal readership, and one that was recognized as fleeting. The authors of *Russkaia satira,* a volume published in Leningrad in 1925, suggested that each copy of Russian satirical journals reached between five and ten readers, and that each journal could claim a circulation of around 15,000. These seem inflated figures — perhaps a product of the ideological euphoria marking the era in which this work was produced. Botsiavnovskii and Gollerbakh, *Russkaia satira pervoi revoliutsii,* 37.

22. At least one exception to this rule may be noted: a cartoon entitled "The arrival of the *dergraykher* [Congress of the Union for Equal Rights]" (figure 3.11) was published in color. *Der bezem,* no. 42 (1 [14] March 1906).

23. See, for example, the cartoons reproduced in King and Porter, *Images of Revolution.*

24. Lakhovski's devilish characters also appeared in the Yiddish *Der sheygets,* a satirical newspaper more radical than *Dos lebn* or *Der bezem.* The radical nature of *Der sheygets* was illustrated by its masthead, in which weapons spell out the journal's name.

25. *Piatsii* (undated, 1906). This cartoon is reproduced in *Russkaia satira,* where it is incorrectly attributed to B. Anisfeld. Botsiavnovskii and Gollerbakh, *Russkaia satira pervoi revoliutsii.*

26. *Piatsii* (undated, 1906).

27. *Leshii,* no. 3 (1906).

28. Cited by Ascher, *The Revolution of 1905,* vol. 1, 17. For more on surveillance in the tsarist period and beyond, see Peter Holquist, " 'Information Is the Alpha and Omega of Our Work': Bolshevik Surveillance in Its Pan-European Context," *Journal of Modern History* 69, no. 3 (1997).

29. *Dos lebn,* no. 64 (20 March [2 April] 1906).

30. *Dos lebn,* no. 81 (13 [26] April 1906).

31. *Dos lebn,* no. 69 (26 March [7 April] 1906).

32. *Dos lebn,* no. 63 (18 [21] March 1906).

33. This and related visual diagnostics have been informed by the following collections of photographs of late imperial Russian society: David Elliott, *Photography in Russia 1840–1940* (London: Thames and Hudson, 1992); Kyril FitzLyon and Tatiana Browning, *Before the Revolution: A View of Russia under the Last Tsar* (London: Allen Lane, 1977); Marvin Lyons, *Nicholas II, the Last Tsar* (New York: Routledge & Kegan Paul, 1974); Chloe Obolensky, *The Russian Empire: A Portrait in Photographs* (New York: Random House, 1979).

34. *Dos lebn,* no. 112 (25 May [7 June] 1906).

35. *Dos lebn,* no. 14 (26 June [9 July] 1906).

36. *Ovod*, no. 1 (undated, 1906), 5.

37. *Svoboda* (undated, 1906).

38. *Sekira* (6 January 1906).

39. *Dos lebn*, no. 132 (17 [30] June 1906).

40. For example, Laura Engelstein, *The Keys to Happiness: Sex and the Search for Modernity in Fin-De-Siècle Russia* (Ithaca, N.Y.: Cornell University Press, 1992); Neuberger, *Hooliganism*. One thinks also of the feverish coverage of student suicides (by young women as well as young men) during the revolutionary era, a trend that Susan Morrissey has associated with the rejection of the corruption and mundane nature of daily life in early-twentieth-century Russia. Susan K. Morrissey, *Heralds of Revolution, Russian Students and the Mythologies of Radicalism* (Oxford: Oxford University Press, 1998), 178–205.

41. Paula Hyman has explored ways in which this gender dynamic was experienced socially and economically, while Naomi Seidman has considered its more metaphoric incarnations. Hyman, *Gender and Assimilation;* Seidman, *A Marriage Made in Heaven*. See also Stampfer, "Gender Differentiation."

42. Hans Rogger, *Jewish Policies and Right-Wing Politics in Imperial Russia* (Berkeley: University of California Press, 1986), 188–212. Engelstein, *The Keys to Happiness*.

43. *Signal*, 18 January 1906.

44. *Dos lebn*, no. 102 (9 [22] May 1906).

45. *Dos lebn*, no. 103 (10 [23] May 1906).

46. *Dos lebn*, no. 70 (26 March [8 April] 1906). The padlocks in this cartoon may refer to the failure of the Vyborg Manifesto, a proclamation issued by the Kadet and Trudovk Duma factions (who had temporarily relocated to Vyborg, Finland) in the wake of the dissolution of the Duma. The manifesto included a general critique of governmental policy and a call for action on the part of Russian population. The Manifesto met with scant enthusiasm, and had little tangible effect. I have been unable to discern just who is being silenced in Lakhovski's rendition.

47. *Der fraynd*, no. 78 (10 [23] April 1906).

48. See, for example, *Dos lebn*, no. 135 (20 June [4 July] 1906).

49. These images are similar to others; in the Russian-language, St. Petersburg–based satirical journal *Leshii*, for example, unnamed officials are shown metamorphosing into bulldogs, roosters, frogs, and pigs. See, for example, *Leshii* (undated, 1906). Other example are reproduced in E. P. [Eleonora Petrovna] Gomberg-Verzhbinskaia, *Russkoe iskusstvo i revoliutsiia 1905 g.; grafika, zhivopis'* (Leningrad: Izdatel'stvo Leningradskogo Universiteta, 1960), 33.

50. *Der sheygets* (undated, 1906).

51. Additionally, some of the cartoons of *Der bezem* relied on "Jewish" motifs to satirize imperial politics, such as a cartoon that depicted representatives of the Duma drowning in the ocean while a large group of "Israelites," a Moses-figure at their fore, looked on from shore. *Der bezem*, no. 72 (10 April [28 March] 1906).

52. Israel Zangwill, a British Jew, formed and led the Jewish Territorial Organization. Manya Vilbushevitsh advocated the large-scale collective settlement of Jews in Palestine, and their subsequent use of mechanical farming. She was also briefly involved in the terrorist section of the SR party. In 1904, she migrated to Palestine. Thereafter, she traveled in the United States and Europe, purchasing arms in the West and shipping them to self-defense organizations in Russia. "Telefon," *Der bezem*, no. 72 (28 March [10 April] 1906): 6.

53. In Russian, the Union was known as *Soiuz dlia dostizheniia polnopraviia evreiskago naroda v rossii*. For more on the party's development and impact, see Gassenschmidt, *Jewish Liberal Politics*.

54. *Der bezem*, no. 42 (March 1 [14] 1906).

55. I elaborate upon this argument in "Divining the Secular." Edward Portnoy

makes a similar argument about the importance of religious motifs in Yiddish satirical cartoons published in Poland in the interwar period. Portnoy, "Exploiting Tradition."

56. One could argue that *Der bezem* is an anti-Zionist hero as well. Images of Orthodox men had become increasingly central to Zionist art of the early twentieth century, where they tended to "possess an air of wisdom and rich character." See Berkowitz, "Art in Zionist Popular Culture," 20. By displaying its Orthodox reader as a gawky buffoon, *Der bezem* capitalized upon the mystique of the Orthodox reader while simultaneously subverting the reigning Zionist narrative.

57. Historians have differed in their calculation of the number of pogroms in this period: for a survey of these historiographic differences, see Lambroza, "The Pogroms of 1903–1906," 226–28. See also Feldman, *Yehude rusya biyeme hamapekha harishona;* Lambroza, *The Pogrom Movement in Russia;* Robert Weinberg, "The Pogrom of 1905 in Odessa: A Case Study," in Klier and Lambroza, *Pogroms.* Contemporary accounts of pogrom violence include S. An-sky, "Pogromnye vpechatleniia," in *Sobranie sochinenii* (St. Petersburg: T-vo prosviashchenie, 1911); "From Kishineff to Bialystok: A Tale of Pogroms from 1903–1906," in *American Jewish Year Book* (Philadelphia: American Jewish Committee, 1906–1907); Avrohm Shmuel Hershberg, *Pinkes Bialystok,* vol. 2 (New York: Bialystok Jewish Historical Association, 1950).

58. *Der fraynd baylage,* nos. 171 and 183 (undated, 1903). Interestingly enough, these images have been widely reproduced in scholarly studies of the era, which is in itself suggestive of the lasting influence of *Der fraynd*'s coverage of contemporary events.

59. The newspaper was not alone in anticipating the appeal of an album devoted to commemorating and documenting the 1905–1906 pogroms. Just three years after the publication of *Di blutige teg,* the World Zionist Organization published a German-language pogrom commemoration entitled *Die Judenpogrome in Russland* (Berlin, 1909), edited by Leo[n] Motzkin.

60. Four pages of the album were devoted to images from Odessa, three to Warsaw, and one each to Kiev, Vilna, and Kishinev.

61. In Western European, and, for that matter, much Russian revolutionary art, it is a woman who tends to carry the bough and/or wreath. The gender of Lakhovski's seated figure is unclear, but what is evident is that she or he has rejected the strident stance one might expect of Lady Liberty. In subduing her pose, Lakhovski emphasizes that he is borrowing motifs but doctoring them to suit the needs of the Yiddish press: in this case, the careful balancing of Zionist and radical tropes. For more detailed discussions of images of the French Revolution, see Maurice Agulhon, *Marianne into Battle: Republican Imagery and Symbolism in France, 1870–1880* (Cambridge: Cambridge University Press, 1981); Lynn Hunt, *Politics, Culture, and Class in the French Revolution* (Berkeley: University of California Press, 1984); Jean Starobinski, *1789: The Emblems of Reason* (Cambridge, Mass.: MIT Press, 1988).

62. The association between Lilien and Zionism was consolidated after works by the artist were displayed during the course of the Fifth Zionist Congress of 1901 and, thereafter, widely dispersed in postcard form. For more on the presence of Lilien's images at the Zionist Congress, see Berkowitz, "Art in Zionist Popular Culture"; Richard Cohen, *Jewish Icons: Art and Society in Modern Europe* (Berkeley: University of California Press, 1998), 209–10; Stanislawksi, *Zionism and the Fin de Siècle,* especially chapter 5.

63. Consider, for example, Lilien's illustrations for Morris Rosenfeld's *Lider des Ghetto* of 1902, his portrait of Herzl used for a Jewish National Fund stamp, or his postcard for the Fifth Zionist Congress. All feature figures crouched in a corner, peering at Jerusalem's walls. Reproductions of these images may be found in Berko-

witz, *The Jewish Self-Image,* 21, 58; Cohen, *Jewish Icons,* 210; Stanislawski, *Zionism and the Fin de Siècle,* figures 1–15, 100–101.

64. Sharing the title page of *Di blutige teg* with Lakhovski's cartoon is a poem by Shimen Frug entitled "Tombstones" that further illustrates this political metamorphosis. The poem pushes readers beyond grief, encouraging them to abandon mourning for the cause of freedom. The first stanza reads:

> Victims holy and beautiful
> For our freedom, happiness, and joy
> The angry enemy drove in the slaughterer's knife
> And returned it to its sheath.
> The blood has not yet been washed away
> From their murderous hands
> The old locks are still in place
> The old woes still stand.
> There is no time to mourn
> Wind has absorbed our hate
> The heart is full with lament and sorrow
> The storm blows, the storm calls. . . .

This chapter will return to the genre of the pogrom poem. See also Bal Makhshoves [Isador Eliashev], "Pogrom Literature," in *Geklibene shriftn* (Vilna: S. Sreberk, 1910); Alan Mintz, *Hurban: Responses to Catastrophe in Hebrew Literature* (New York: Columbia University Press, 1984), 109–56; David Roskies, *Against the Apocalypse: Responses to Catastrophe in Modern Jewish Culture* (Cambridge, Mass.: Harvard University Press, 1984), 79–108.

65. According to John Bowlt, it is possible that Lakhovski's departure from Palestine was not a personal choice, but was "owing to intolerable interference of the administrative committee in Berlin, which preferred its own candidate for the job." See Bowlt, "Jewish Artists," 45–48. There is also evidence that Lakhovski found the conditions in Jerusalem intolerable. In any case, in assuming a position at the Bezalel Academy—and in subsequently returning to Europe—Lakhovski was again following in Lilien's footsteps and in the footsteps of other turn-of-the-century European Jewish artists. After returning to Russia, Lakhovski displayed his work as part of the first exhibition of the Jewish Society for the Encouragement of the Arts (JSEA) in the spring of 1916. The JSEA sought to develop and encourage Russian Jewish artists, in part by sponsoring exhibitions, opening galleries, and encouraging formal affiliations between artists. For more on the Bezalel Academy, see Berkowitz, "Art in Zionist Popular Culture," 33–34; Cohen, *Jewish Icons,* 214–18. Nurit Shilo-Cohen, ed., *Betsalel 1906–1929* (Jerusalem: Israel Museum, 1983); Bowlt, "Jewish Artists," 45–48.

66. Michael Stanislawski has made a similar argument in regard to the artist E. M. Lilien. Lilien, he has proposed, managed to "glide from Galician poverty to socialism, cosmopolitanism, decadence, and then to Jewish nationalism." In so doing, Stanislawski argues, Lilien was not unusual but typical of many leading Zionists of the day. Stanislawski, *Zionism and the Fin de Siècle,* 101.

67. For a firsthand account of the pogroms, see Hershberg, *Pinkes bialystok,* An-sky, "Pogromnye vpechatleniia." For more on the pogroms of 1905 and 1906, see Feldman, *Yehude rusya biyeme hamapekha harishona;* Lambrozo, "The pogroms of 1903–1906" and *The Pogrom Movement in Russia.*

68. For a detailed mapping of the violence of 1903–1906, see "From Kishineff to Bialystok."

69. This in itself reflected a recent evolution in Jewish political philosophy: the

pogroms of 1881, by way of contrast, had been widely viewed as an agent of—rather than an obstacle to—revolution, a conclusion that led many Russian Jews away from universalist causes. S. An-sky, *Der fraynd*'s future correspondent in pogrom-torn Bialystok, described this dynamic thusly: "the revolutionaries who twenty years earlier were considered enemies of the people [by "the Russian Jewish people"] . . . emerged now as its most reliable champions." Cited in Frankel, *Prophecy and Politics*, 143. The article from which this quotation is culled was originally published in the Russian-language newspaper *Voskhod* in February of 1906. My analysis here echoes Frankel's: Frankel, *Prophecy and Politics*, 134–43. For more on the debates among Jewish intellectuals in the wake of the 1881 pogroms, see Erich Haberer, "Cosmopolitanism, Antisemitism, and Populism."

70. *Der fraynd*, too, launched such accusations in the wake of the violence in Bialystok. S. An-sky's correspondences from Bialystok were particularly influential in the formation of this stance. Read one article: "[n]o one is as guilty of the pogrom as the administration. . . . or, better put, no one is as guilty as the whole bureaucracy and its arbitrary rule." *Der fraynd*, no. 120 (2 [15] July 1906). This complaint was echoed in the paper's editorials: "[t]he bureaucracy will conduct new pogroms, the Duma will conduct new inquiries, send new commissars, and we Jews will be helped not at all." *Der fraynd*, no. 134 (10 [23] July 1906). Whether the central government was in fact guilty of instigating (or simply tolerating) the violence has been a subject of some debate. See, for example, "From Kishineff to Bialystok"; Lambrozo, "The Pogroms of 1903–1906"; Feldman, *Yehude rusya biyeme hamapekha harishona*, 191–268; Frankel, *Prophey and Politics*, 150–54. For a comparative study, see Weinberg, "The Pogrom of 1905" and *The Revolution of 1905*. For more on the extension of the powers of the state and the right, see Rogger, *Jewish Policies;* Frank, *Crime, Cultural Conflict, and Justice;* Fuller, "Civil-Military Conflict."

71. This dynamic is described by Jonathan Frankel in *Prophecy and Politics*, 153–69.

72. This stance was upheld even after the Bialystok pogrom ended. In the months after the pogrom, both cartoons and photography were absented from the main section of the paper. In time, both genres were resurrected, with photography in December of 1908 and cartoons a year or so later. By 1909, however, both genres seemed depleted of political content: partly for this reason, neither genre was employed as a documentary device.

73. I borrow this phrase from Richard Cohen, *Jewish Icons;* see especially pp. 220–55.

74. Lilien's famous drawing depicted a Jewish victim swathed in a prayer shawl and tied to a stake. It appeared first in Maksim Gorky's *Zbornik* in 1903 and was later republished in a German-language volume on the Kishinev pogroms (Berthold Feiwel's *Die Judenmassacres in Kischinew von Told*). As Richard Cohen has demonstrated, artists Samuel Hirszenberg, Leopold Pilichowski, Mauriey Minkowski, and Leonid Pasternak all produced oil paintings depicting pogrom violence or victims in the years after 1905. Thereafter, these images were displayed fairly widely in Europe and Palestine. For more on Lilien's image, see Cohen, *Jewish Icons*, 321. Lilien's image is also analyzed and reproduced in Roskies, *Against the Apocalypse*, 85.

75. Among the varied newspapers that reproduced images from Bialystok were the Warsaw-based, Yiddish-language, and Zionist-leaning *Der veg* and the radical Polish-language *Tygodnik illustrowany.* Thanks to Scott Ury for leading me to these sources.

76. Elena Barkhatova, "Pictorialism: Photography as Art," in *Photography in Russia 1840–1940*, ed. David Elliott (London: Thames and Hudson, 1992).

77. Sylvie Anne Goldberg, *Crossing the Jabbok: Illness and Death in Ashkenazi Judaism in Sixteenth-through-Nineteenth-Century Prague* (Berkeley: University of California Press,

1996). *Der fraynd* was not the only source to exaggerate or invent the Jewishness or martyralogical quality of Bialystok's victims. One of the lasting images of the Kishinev pogroms of 1903 was of a synagogue attendant whose murder was said to take place in front of the Holy Ark. It was later determined that the man was killed outside the synagogue rather than in its inner sanctum, but this fact did not prevent him from being transformed into a symbol of suffering and martyrdom. Roskies, *Against the Apocalypse*, 84.

This uneasy coexistence of images and traditional practices is reminiscent of dynamics that Malek Alloula describes in *Colonial Harem*, a study of erotic photographs of Algerian women taken by Europeans and transformed into postcards. The women pictured in these texts, argues Alloula, embody relationships—between women and men, women and women, women and their jewelry, women and their breasts—that were "unthinkable possibilit[ies] in Algerian society," and that illuminated far more about the interests and fantasies of their European photographers than the subjects themselves. This comparison is not meant to elide the very different relationship between photographer and subject in violence-ridden Bialystok and imperially controlled Algeria. It is, instead, to remind us that the photographs of Bialystok's recorded deaths were not so much spontaneous as posed. See Malek Alloula, *The Colonial Harem* (Minneapolis: University of Minnesota Press, 1986), 38. Other studies of the political contours of photography that have influenced this reading include Seth Koven, "Dr. Barnardo's 'Artistic Fictions': Photography, Sexuality, and the Ragged Child in Victorian London," *Radical History Review* 69 (Fall 1997); Christopher Pinney, *Camera Indica: The Social Life of Indian Photographers* (Chicago: University of Chicago Press, 1997); James R. Ryan, *Picturing Empire: Photography and the Visualization of the British Empire* (Chicago: University of Chicago Press, 1997); Allan Sekula, "The Body and the Archive," *October* 39 (Winter 1986); Julia Thomas, "Photography, National Identity, and the 'Cataract of Times': Wartime Images and the Case of Japan," *The American Historical Review* 103, no. 5 (1998).

78. *Der fraynd*, no. 124 (7 [20] July).

79. An-sky also penned reflections on the Bialystok pogroms in Russian and contributed them to the journal *Voskhod*. These essays are included in the 1911 Russian-language collection of his works, An-sky, "Pogromnye vpechatleniia."

80. *Der fraynd*, no. 120 (2 [15] July 1906).

81. Bialik's poem has received considerable attention from scholars. See, for example, Mintz, *Hurban;* Roskies, *Against the Apocalypse;* Stanislawski, *Zionism and the Fin de Siècle*, 184–87. An English translation of Bialik's poem may be found in David Roskies, ed., *The Literature of Destruction: Jewish Responses to Catastrophe* (Philadelphia: Jewish Publication Society, 1989).

82. Roskies, *Against the Apocalypse*, 91.

83. *Der fraynd* borrowed something else from the budding poet of Jewish nationalism: the assumption that photographs, politics, and the written word were intricately intertwined. Bialik, it should be noted, had not traveled to Kishinev with the intention of producing poetry. His goal, instead, was to collect eyewitness accounts and to photograph the damage. This mission was sponsored by a group of nationally minded Jewish intellectuals from Odessa, among them historian Shimen Dubnov, theoretician Ahad Ha'am, and Hebrew poet Mordecai Rabinowitch (Ben-Ami). Reference to the formation of this ad-hoc group, and to Bialik's trip to Kishinev, is made in Roskies, *Against the Apocalypse*, 84–86; Zipperstein, *Elusive Prophet*, 201–208. Discussion of the creation of a Zionist myth of martyrdom in visual form may be found in Stanislawski, *Zionism and the Fin de Siècle* and Berkowitz, *The Jewish Self-Image*.

84. In this sense, this chapter joins a varied literature on the relationship between photography and the national (or imperial) imagination. To cite but a few sources

among many: Anderson, *Imagined Communities;* Ryan, *Picturing Empire;* Thomas, "Photography"; Nicholas Thomas, *Entangled Objects: Exchange, Material Culture, and Colonialism in the Pacific* (Cambridge, Mass.: Harvard University Press, 1991).

85. Two exceptions are worth noting. One of the first cartoons published by *Der fraynd* is a busy tale in thirteen frames with tiny handwritten captions, which surveys, as its title announces, the "culture of 1907." Among the events chronicled are the destruction of the Second Duma by pigs in official uniforms, the consumption of new literary talent by the demons of Article 129, and graphic images of police brutality and bureaucratic excess. A second cartoon depicts the constitution being buried as part of "a poor man's funeral," complete with a tattered shroud and hand-drawn carriage. *Der bezem,* no. 18 (22 March 1908); *Der bezem,* no. 52 (2 March 1908).

86. *Der bezem,* no. 59 (11 March 1908).

87. *Der bezem,* no. 205 (3 September 1908).

88. Nahum Shtif, "Autobiographia fun nahum shtif," *Yivo bleter, hoydesh-shrift fun yidishn visenshaft institute* 5, no. 3–5 (1933): 203.

89. Rapoport, "Der onheyb fun 'fraynd,' " 2–5.

90. In his study of the history of the Yiddish press, for example, Dovid Druk comments only that *Dos lebn* "demanded rights through revolution." Similarly, in his exploration of the nineteenth-century Russian Jewish press, Yehuda Slutzky fails even to mention the periodical. Druk, *Tsu der geshikhte,* 30; Slutzky, *Haitonut hayehudit-rusit.*

91. Katz, *A dor.*

92. See, for example, Frankel, *Prophecy and Politics;* Klier and Lambrozo, *Pogroms.*

93. This point has also been made by the editors of and various contributors to a special issue of *Studies of Contemporary Jewry* devoted to visual culture. Ezra Mendelsohn and Richard I. Cohen, eds., *Art and Its Uses: The Visual Image and Modern Jewish Society, Studies in Contemporary Jewry* (Oxford: Oxford University Press, 1990). See also Matthew Baigell and Milly Heyd, eds., *Complex Identities: Jewish Consciousness and Modern Art* (New Brunswick, N.J.: Rutgers University Press, 2001); Cohen, *Jewish Icons.*

4. THE SCIENCE OF HEALTHY LIVING

1. I borrow the distinction between *project* and *process* from Paula Hyman, who has written of the difference between the "project" and the "process" of assimilation. However, I avoid the term *assimilation* in the pages that follow, preferring, instead, to speak of a more meandering process of cultural change. I do find Hyman's delineation of "project" and "process" useful as it emphasizes the difference between elite ambitions and popular experiences. Hyman, *Gender and Assimilation.*

2. Borovaia, "Translation and Westernization" and "The Role of Translation."

3. Documenting the actual impact of these journals upon readers proves difficult because of the scarcity of autobiographies and memoirs by Jews of the region. As a result, the following pages rely on a combination of speculative and textual evidence that allows us to ponder the reaction of readers. On the rarity of the autobiographical form, see Esther Benbassa and Aron Rodrigue, *A Sephardi Life in Southeastern Europe: The Autobiography and Journal of Gabriel Arié, 1863–1939* (Seattle: University of Washington Press, 1998). On the difficulty of documenting the reaction of the reader of Ladino, see Lehmann, "The Intended Reader."

4. Arguably, this trend remained true at least until the wake of the Balkan and First World Wars. At that point, the Westernizing impulse was replaced by nationalistic or patriotic sentiments, not only as the Zionist movement grew, but as Jews devoted themselves to the national cultures emerging in their new states. Eyal Ginio

has traced the emergence of a Hellenizing impulse among Greek Jews in the wake of the Balkan Wars. Ginio, "Language of Homer." More scholarship has addressed the Turkification of Turkey's Jews, including Bali, *Bir Türklestirme serüveni;* Levi, *Turkiye Cümhuriyeti'nde Yahudiler;* Shaw, *Jews of the Ottoman Empire;* Weiker, *The Jewish Polity.* For a comparative study of Jews in the Arab provinces of the empire, see Joel Beinin, *The Dispersion of Egyptian Jewry: Culture, Politics, and the Formation of a Modern Diaspora* (Berkeley: University of California Press, 1997), and Gudrun Krämer, *The Jews in Modern Egypt, 1914–1952* (Seattle: University of Washington Press, 1989). It is striking that there is so little scholarship on Sephardi and Middle Eastern Jews' involvement in or reactions to the processes of state-building: a reflection, perhaps, of the overriding assumption that Jews were not only alienated from, but victims of Arab, Turkish, and Balkan nationalism.

5. The early Eastern European *maskilim,* for example, were highly indebted to German cultural models as well as to traditional Jewish, regional, and Russian hegemonic modes.

6. Jews' disassociation from local cultural landscapes is more often than not implicitly rather than explicitly advanced. In general scholarship on turn-of-the-century Ottoman history, this hypothesis sometimes surfaces through the labeling of Jews as *compradors,* a term that assumes Jews — and, for that matter, other non-Muslim bourgeoisie — were somehow coincidentally stationed on Ottoman soil. In scholarship in the field of Jewish Studies, by contrast, Jews' alienation from local practices and contexts is often assumed (Mark Cohen has termed this impulse "neolachrymose"). Mark R. Cohen, "Islam and the Jews: Myth, Counter-Myth, History," *Jerusalem Quarterly,* no. 38 (1986); "The Neo-Lachrymose Conception"; and *Under Crescent and Cross.* I elaborate upon these historiographic themes elsewhere; see Stein, "Sephardi and Middle Eastern Jewries." On the receptivity of the Sephardi religious leadership to Westernization, see Stillman, *Sephardi Religious Responses.*

7. I refer here, in particular, to Homi Bhabha's notion of hybrid identity as a site of colonial resistance. To quote Bhabha, "Hybridity is the sign of the productivity of colonial power, its shifting forces and fixities; it is the name for the strategic reversal of the process of domination through disavowal. . . . [Hybridity] unsettles the mimetic or narcissistic demands of colonial power but reimplicates its identifications in strategic subversion that turn the gaze of the discriminated back upon the eye of power." Homi Bhabha, "Signs Taken for Wonders: Questions of Ambivalence and Authority under a Tree Outside Delhi, May 1817," in *The Location of Culture* (New York: Routledge, 1994), 113.

Though Bhabha's theories of hybridity have helped shape my understanding of Ottoman Jewish cultural identity, I depart from him in several significant regards. First, I stop short of equating Ottoman Jews' ability to marvel at French culture with a political process of "resistance." This term, I would suggest, fails to describe the many nuances in the relationship between Ottoman Jewry and French Jewry and between France and the Ottoman Empire. In particular, Bhabha's theory elides the eagerness with which many Ottoman Jews embraced the influence of Franco-Jewry and the various cultural and material reasons that lay behind this choice. For Bhabha, the absorption of Western influence by colonial (or semi-colonial, in this case) subjects is always born of inauthenticity or cultural or material corruption. For Jews of the turn-of-the-century Ottoman Empire, however, Westernization represented not the demise of modern Ladino culture, but its reformulation. Such a reformulation was necessary in part because the changing political landscape of the Ottoman Empire was turning Jews into a minority (and nonindigenous) culture. In this sense, by the turn of the century, Ottoman Jews were becoming doubly imperial subjects, quite unlike Bhabha's much-simplified imperial subject. See also Homi Bhabha, "Of Mimicry and Man: The Ambivalence of Colonial Discourse," *October* 28 (1984).

8. Bruce Masters has made a similar point about Jewish culture in the Arab regions of the empire. Masters, *Christians and Jews*.

9. David Fresco, "Alos lektores," *El instruktor,* no. 1, Iyar, 5648 (1888).

10. Ibid.

11. For a more extensive treatment of the Turkish instructional press, see Frierson, "Unimagined Communities," 154–55.

12. For more on the genesis and content of the Ottoman Turkish-language press, see Bayrak, *Türkiye'de gazeteler ve dergiler sözlügü;* Benbanaste, *Örneklerle Türk Musevi basininin tarihçesi;* Brummett, *Image and Imperialism;* Dernegi, *Basim ve Yayinciligimizin 250;* Duman, *Istanbul kütüphaneleri arap harfli;* Frierson, "Unimagined Communities"; Gerçek, *Türk matbaaciligi;* Iskit, *Turkiye'de matbuat hareketleri ve politikalari, Türkiyede matbuat idareleri ve politikalari,* and *Türkiyede nesriyat hareketleri tarihine;* Kabacali, *Baslangiçtan günümüze Türkiye'de basin sansürü;* Oral, *Türk basin tarihi;* Toprak,"Fikir dergiciliginin yuzyili"; Zheltiakov, *Matbaaciligin 250. Kurulus Yildönümüne Armagan.*

13. Benbassa, "L'education féminine en Orient"; Rodrigue, *French Jews, Turkish Jews.* For more on the relationship between gender and modernity in Western, Central, and Eastern Europe, see Hyman, *Gender and Assimilation;* Marion Kaplan, *The Making of the Jewish Middle Class: Women, Family, and Identity in Imperial Germany* (Oxford: Oxford University Press, 1991). For a comparative approach, see also the contributing essays to Judith Baskin, *Jewish Women in Historical Perspective* (Detroit: Wayne State Press, 1991).

14. Unsigned. "La edukasyon de la mujer," *El instruktor,* no. 1, Iyar 5648 (1888).

15. Diffusing "native" qualities was a central goal of the AIU as a whole. Consider the following selection from the AIU's "Instructions for teachers": "One of the principal tasks of the teachers will be to combat the bad habits which are more or less prevalent among Eastern populations: selfishness, pride, exaggerated egotism, lack of original thinking, blind respect for wealth and power, and violent, petty passions." "Instructions pour les professeurs," Archives of the AIU, France XI.E.1. Cited in Rodrigue, *Sephardi and Eastern Jewries,* 72. For a more detailed discussion of the gendered dimensions of the AIU's activities, see Benbassa, "L'education féminine en Orient"; Rodrigue, *Sephardi and Eastern Jewries,* 80–93. See also "El abito de la lektura," *El amigo de la familia,* no. 1, 1 Iyar 5648 (1888).

16. "Konsejos provechozos para la familia," *El amigo de la familia,* unnumbered, 14 Tevet, 5642 (1882). On the historical development of French hair care, see Alain Corbin, *The Foul and the Fragrant: Odor and the French Social Imagination* (Cambridge, Mass.: Harvard University Press, 1986), 179.

17. "Konsejos provechozos para la familia," *El amigo de la familia,* unnumbered, 6 Shevat, 5642; "Hygiene, la syensya de gardar la salud," *El amigo de la familia,* unnumbered, 18 Av, 5645 (1885).

18. "Diversos," *El amigo de la familia,* unnumbered, 23 Kislev, 5642 (1882).

19. "Hygiene, la syensya de gardar la salud," *El amigo de la familia,* unnumbered, 18 Kislev, 5646 (1886).

20. Corbin, *The Foul and the Fragrant;* Julia Csergo, *Liberté, égalité, propreté: la morale de l'hygiène au XIXe Siècle* (Paris: Albin Michel, 1988); Jean-Pierre Goubert, *The Conquest of Water,* trans. Andrew Wilson (Oxford: Polity Press, 1986); Georges Vigarello, *Concepts of Cleanliness: Changing Attitudes in France since the Middle Ages* (Cambridge: Cambridge University Press, 1988).

21. "Hygiene, la syensya de gardar la salud," *El amigo de la familia,* unnumbered, 4 Kislev, 5646 (1886).

22. *El tiempo,* no. 102 (1 June 1910).

23. "Konsejos provechozos para la familia," *El amigo de la familia,* unnumbered, 20 Shevat, 5642 (1888); 30 Adar, 5642 (1888).

24. "Konsejos provechozos para la familia," *El amigo de la familia,* unnumbered, 15 Iyar, 5642 (1888).

25. Corbin, *The Foul and the Fragrant,* 74.

26. "Poezia de sienyora R.," *El amigo de la familia,* unnumbered, 16 Kislev, 5642 (1888).

27. That France would emerge as a source of roses and rose-scented products may have had commercial as well as cosmetic manifestations. In his memoir of Jewish life in Salonika, Leon Sciaky recalls that in the late nineteenth century, Ottoman Jews with an interest in botany (such as his father) were beginning to import their prize roses from Paris. Leon Sciaky, *Farewell to Salonica: Portrait of an Era* (New York: Current Books, 1946), 11.

28. "Konsejos provechozos para la familia," *El amigo de la familia,* unnumbered, 16 Kislev, 5642 (1888); no. 66 (undated) Av 5642 (1888).

29. The timing of the decline of Jewish textile production is a subject of some debate. For more on this theme, see Benjamin Braude, "The Cloth Industry of Salonika in the Mediterranean Economy," *Pe'amim* 15 (1983); "International Competition and Domestic Cloth in the Ottoman Empire, 1500–1650: A Study in Underdevelopment," *Review* 2 (1979) and "Salonika Woollens"; Daniel Goffman, *Izmir and the Levantine World* (Seattle: University of Washington Press, 1990); Panova, "Textile Industry"; Rozen, "Contest and Rivalry"; Shohat, "The King's Cloth in Salonika."

30. Donald Quataert has demonstrated that though the Ottoman textile industry had declined in international relative terms, it nonetheless remained dynamic, producing by 1914 higher volumes of textiles than it had during the nineteenth century. Quataert, *Ottoman Manufacturing.*

31. "La edukasyon de la mujer," *El instruktor,* no. 1, Iyar 5648 (1888).

32. "La mujer," *El amigo de la familia,* unnumbered, 23 Kislev, 5642 (1882).

33. "La edukasyon de la mujer," *El instruktor,* no. 1, Iyar 5648 (1888).

34. "Komportamiento del padre i madre kon sus kreaturas," *El amigo de la familia,* no. 61, 12 Tamuz, 5642 (1881).

35. "Konsejos provechozos para la familia," *El amigo de la familia,* no. 61, 12 Tamuz, 5642 (1881).

36. "Konsejos provechozos para la familia," *El amigo de la familia,* no. 61, 12 Tamuz, 5642 (1881); no. 1, 16 Kislev, 5642 (1881).

37. "Hygiene, la syensya de gardar la salud," *El amigo de la familia,* unnumbered, 22 Shevat, 5646.

38. "Konsejos provechozos para la familia," *El amigo de la familia,* unnumbered, 23 Kislev, 5642.

39. "La edukasyon de la mujer," *El instruktor,* no. 1, Iyar 5648 (1888).

40. Goubert, *The Conquest of Water,* 117–28.

41. "Konsejos provechozos para la familia," *El amigo de la familia,* unnumbered, 25 Adar, 5642.

42. "Hygiene, la syensya de gardar la salud," *El amigo de la familia,* unnumbered, 28 Sivan, 5645; unnumbered, 18 Av 5645 (1885).

43. *El amigo de la familia,* unnumbered, 14 Sivan, 5645 (1885). Advertisements for Krondorf appeared in *El tiempo* for almost the duration of the paper's run.

44. "Consejos provecozos para la familia," *El amigo de la familia,* unnumbered, 26 Tevet 5642 (1882).

45. Ann LaBerge, "Nurses and Nursing: Alfred Donné and the Medicalization of Child Care in Nineteenth-Century France," *Journal of the History of Medicine and Allied Sciences* 46, no. 1 (1991).

46. "Hygiene, la syensya de gardar la salud," *El amigo de la familia,* unnumbered, 16 Adar, 5645 (1885).

47. In referring here to the "Southeastern European Jewish diet," or, as I do in the

following paragraph, to a Sephardi diet, I am referring rather generally to the cooking habits of the Sephardi Jews of European Turkey and the Balkans. This is meant to distinguish these Jews from Sephardim of the Magrehb — Morocco, Tunisia, Algeria, and Libya — and from Mizrahim — the Jews of Syria, Iraq, Iran, Lebanon, and Yemen — all of whom had their own forms of Jewish cuisine.

48. "Konsejos provechozos para la familia," *El amigo de la familia,* unnumbered, 25 Adar, 5642 (1888).

49. Sami Zubaida reminds us that clarified butter was regulated and guarded by the Ottoman administration, and was a particularly prized commodity in Istanbul. Sami Zubaida, "National, Communal and Global Dimensions in Middle East Food Cultures," in *Culinary Cultures of the Middle East,* ed. Sami Zubaida and Richard Tapper (London: I. B. Tauris, 1994), 42.

50. According to the pre-eminent scholar of Jewish cuisine, Claudia Roden, the laws of *kashrut* meant that in some regions, "one could smell a Jewish home from the cooking fat." Roden, "Jewish Food in the Middle East," in Zuabida and Tapper, *Culinary Cultures,* 155.

51. Ibid., 154.

52. In her memoir of Jewish life in early-twentieth-century Rhodes, Rebecca Amato Levy details the foodways of Rhodesli Jews. "You will note," she writes in conclusion, "that milk has never been mentioned. The reason is that milk was reserved for the sickly, or sometimes for use in cooking, since it was very expensive." Rebecca Amato Levy, *I Remember Rhodes . . .* (New York: Sepher-Hermon Press for Sephardic House at Congregation Shearith Israel, 1987), 8.

53. As cited in Bunis, *Voices from Jewish Salonika.*

54. Card and domino playing was also a source of vexation for the teachers of the AIU. See Rodrigue, *Sephardi and Eastern Jewries,* 75–76.

55. "Komportiamiento del padre i madre kon sus kreaturas," *El amigo de la familia,* no. 61, 12 Tamuz, 5642 (1881).

56. Frierson, "Unimagined Communities," 126. For an example of the type of puzzle that was published in the Ladino press, see "Kalkolo de pastiempo [math to pass the time]." *El instructor,* no. 20, 16 Eylul, 5648 (1888).

57. "Enigma," *El amigo de la familia,* unnumbered, 6 Shevat, 5642 (1882); 20 Shevat, 5642 (1882).

58. "Diversos," *El Amigo de la Familliya,* unnumbered, 14 Tevet, 5642 (1882).

59. "Hygiene, la syensya de gardar la salud," *El amigo de la familia,* unnumbered, 6 Tishrei 5645 (1884).

60. "Hygiene, la syensya de gardar la salud," *El amigo de la familia,* unnumbered, 16 Eylul, 5645 (1885).

61. "Hygiene, la syensya de gardar la salud," *El amigo de la familia,* unnumbered, 23 Eylul, 5645 (1885).

62. "Hygiene, la syensya de gardar la salud," *El amigo de la familia,* unnumbered, 9 Eylul, 5645 (1885).

63. "Hygiene, la syensya de gardar la salud," *El amigo de la familia,* unnumbered, 6 Adar, 5646 (1886); unnumbered, 26 Tammuz, 5645 (1885); unnumbered, 26 Tammuz, 5645 (1885).

64. "Hygiene, la syensya de gardar la salud," *El amigo de la familia,* unnumbered, 18 Av, 5645 (1885).

65. "Hygiene, la syensya de gardar la salud," *El amigo de la familia,* unnumbered, 2 Tevet, 5646 (1885); 9 Tevet, 5646 (1885).

66. Corbin, *The Foul and the Fragrant.*

67. Ann-Louise Shapiro, *Housing the Poor of Paris, 1850–1902* (Madison: University of Wisconsin Press, 1985).

68. Galanté, *Histoire des juifs de Turquie,* 116–17. See also David Bunis's description

of the physical layout of Salonikan Jewish homes. Bunis, *Voices from Jewish Salonika*, 199–200.

69. "Hygiene, la syensya de gardar la salud," *El amigo de la familia*, unnumbered, 2 Tevet, 5646 (1886).

70. Sketches of Jerusalem and Jaffa, for example, retain the signature "H. Fenn" and the name of the travel society that sponsored his journey.

71. George French Angas, *The Kafirs Illustrated in a Series of Drawings Taken among the Amazulu, Amaponda, and Amakosa Tribes: Also, Portraits of the Hottentot, Malay, Fingo, and Other Races Inhabiting Southern Africa: Together with Sketches of Landscape Scenery in the Zulu Country, Natal, and the Cape Colony* (London: J. Hogarth, 1849).

72. I am inspired, here, by Mary Louise Pratt's broad understanding of colonial tourism. Mary Louise Pratt, *Imperial Eyes: Travel Writing and Transculturation* (London: Routledge, 1992). See also Stephan Greenblatt, *Marvelous Possessions: The Wonder of the New World* (Chicago: University of Chicago Press, 1991). Studies of the Zulu can be found in *El amigo de la familia*, unnumbered, 7 Tevet, 5642 (1882) and unnumbered, 23 Kislev, 5642 (1881). A feature on odalisques; no. 72, 21 Tevet, 5642 (1882). Botanical oddities from Ceylon; unnumbered, 25 Adar, 5642 (1882). American tobacco; unnumbered, 3 Nisan, 5642 (1882).

73. *El amigo de la familia*, unnumbered, 15 Iyar, 5642 (1882).

74. The image of "Zulu in festive garb" may be found in *El amigo de la familia*, no. 45, 11 Adar, 5642 (1882). The resemblance between this image and George French Angas's "Young Zulus in Dancing Costume" is striking. Angas, *The Kafirs Illustrated*.

75. There is a rich and expanding body of scholarship on the connection between visual imagery and the colonial project. To list a few among many useful works: Alloula, *The Colonial Harem;* Timothy Burke, *Lifebuoy Men, Lux Women: Commodification, Consumption, and Cleanliness in Modern Zimbabwe* (Durham and London: Duke University Press, 1996); Anne McClintock, *Imperial Leather: Race, Gender and Sexuality in the Colonial Contest* (London: Routledge, 1995); Timothy Mitchell, *Colonizing Egypt* (Berkeley: University of California Press, 1988); Pinney, *Camera Indica;* Pratt, *Imperial Eyes;* Ryan, *Picturing Empire*.

76. "Alguno de los lugares kuriozos en konstantinopla," *El amigo de la familia*, unnumbered, 3 Nisan, 5642 (1882).

77. "His holiness, J. [Anthimus VI, né Joannides]," *El amigo de la familia*, unnumbered, 16 Kislev, 5642 (1881).

78. See, for example, *El amigo de la familia*, unnumbered, 9 Kislev, 5642 (1881).

79. Sciaky, *Farewell to Salonica*, 17.

80. "El abito de la lektura," *El instructor*, no. 1, 1 Iyar, 5648 (1888).

81. "Los estudyos rekomendables," *El instructor*, no. 3, 15 Iyar, 5648 (1888).

82. Consider, for example, the extensive coverage of the Damascus Affair that had riveted Western and Central European Jewish readers some decades before, or German Jewish doctors' emerging interest in race theories. On the former, see Jonathan Frankel, *The Damascus Affair: "Ritual Murder," Politics, and the Jews in 1840* (Cambridge: Cambridge University Press, 1997); on the latter, John Efron, *Defenders of the Race: Jewish Doctors and Race Science in fin-de-siècle Europe* (New Haven, Conn.: Yale University Press, 1994).

5. IMAGES OF DAILY LIFE

1. *Der fraynd*, no. 1 (1 [13] March 1904).

2. I borrow this term from Thomas Richards, who has described "commodity culture" as being rooted in a discourse about the "production, distribution, and consumption of commodities." Richards, *Commodity Culture*, 268, especially footnote 26.

3. This phrase is employed by Michael Schudson, historian of American news-papers. Michael Schudson, *Discovering the News: A Social History of American Newspapers* (New York: Basic Books, 1967), 19. *Hamelits* did also publish advertisements that would reappear in *Der fraynd* (most of which appeared in *Hamelits* in Yiddish).

4. Zipperstein, *Elusive Prophet*, 116.

5. Studies of advertising in the Western European and American context that have informed this study include Simon Bronner, "Reading Consumer Culture," in *Consuming Visions: Accumulation and Display of Goods in America 1880–1920*, ed. Simon Bronner (New York: Norton, 1989); Henkin, *City Reading;* William Leach, *Land of Desire: Merchants, Power, and the Rise of a New American Culture* (New York: Vintage Books, 1994); Jackson Lears, *Fables of Abundance: A Cultural History of Advertising in America* (New York: Basic Books, 1994); Lori Anne Loeb, *Consuming Angels: Advertising and Victorian Women* (Oxford: Oxford University Press, 1994); McClintock, "Soft-Soaping Empire: Commodity Racism and Imperial Advertising," in *Imperial Leather;* Terdiman, *Discourse/Counter-Discourse;* Raymond Williams, "Advertising: The Magical System," in *Problems in Materialism and Culture* (London: Verso, 1980).

6. Tsarist control of advertising is discussed in McReynolds, *Russia's Old Regime*, 25, and West, "Constructing Consumer Culture."

7. West, "Constructing Consumer Culture," 46–47.

8. Ibid., 39–41.

9. A limited study of the role of the market in the economic affairs of Russian Jews can be found in Nachum Gross, ed., *Economic History of the Jews* (New York: Schocken Books, 1975), 248–51. A detailed study of the Nizhnii Novgorod Fair has been conducted by Anne Lincoln Fitzpatrick, *The Great Russian Fair: Nizhnii Novgorod, 1840–90* (New York: St. Martin's Press, 1990). Sally West provides a brief history of pre-modern advertising in her study of Russian shop signs: West, "Constructing Consumer Culture," 17–30. On Russian entrepreneurial culture more generally, see Alfred J. Rieber, *Merchants and Entrepreneurs in Imperial Russia* (Chapel Hill: University of North Carolina Press, 1982).

10. Richards, *Commodity Culture*, 257.

11. *Der fraynd*, no. 245 (21 February [5 March] 1908).

12. This observation is based upon copies of *Peterburgskii listok* held by the Hoover Institute at Stanford University.

13. *Der fraynd*, no. 27 (1 [14] February 1908).

14. *Der fraynd*, no. 242 (28 December [10 January] 1908).

15. See, for example, *Der fraynd*, no. 118 (27 [9] January 1907).

16. *Der fraynd*, no. 242 (28 December [10 January] 1908). Tobacco seller F. C. Ginzberg also advertised in *Der fraynd*. For reference to Shaposhnikov's advertisement's appearance in *Russkoe slovo* and for a discussion of the role of advertisements for tobacco in the contemporaneous Russian language press, see West, "Constructing Consumer Culture," 294–95.

17. This list of images and goods common to Russian language advertisements has been culled from West, "Constructing Consumer Culture." The official state seal could only accompany officially recognized goods or signs, an honor that may have been bestowed upon Jewish merchants less frequently than their non-Jewish peers. Still, this in itself is an incomplete explanation. The official seal was often illegally reproduced in Russian-language advertisements, and could have been similarly used by advertisers who relied on the Yiddish press.

18. This is, of course, as much a commentary on the predilections of *Novoe vremia*, a conservative paper known to publish state advertisements, as it is a comparison for the advertising patterns of *Der fraynd*. McReynolds, *Russia's Old Regime*, 25.

19. Druk, *Tsu der geshikhte*.

20. This thesis is supported by the findings of economic historian Arcadius Kahan, who has argued that while pre-industrial Russia produced "horizontal" economic

relationships between Jews and non-Jews, as Russia became industrialized, "vertical integration" among Jews (that is, their economic self-reliance) "was crucial for [their] economic survival." Kahan, *Jewish Social and Economic History*. Kahan, it should be noted, re-engages a conversation about Jews' role in the Russian economy that was the source of extensive debate by Bundist and Zionist intellectuals in the early years of the twentieth century, and that continued to divide Soviet and American scholars of Russian Jewry well into the twentieth century. Kahan's position affirms the Bundist and materialist argument that the Jewish working class was part of Russia's wage-earning proletariat class. The Zionist perspective, by way of comparison, argued that although Russian Jews could be found in marginal sectors of industry, they did not represent a true proletariat largely because they were denied social and political equality and a territory of their own. For more on the Bundist perspective, see Hertz, *Doyres bundistn*. For a scholarly case study that applies Bundist theory to Russian Jewish economic history, see H. Landau, *Der onteyl fun yidn in der rusish-ukraynisher tsuker-industrye, shriftn far ekonomik un statistik* (Vilna: Yivo Institute for Jewish Research, 1929). For more on the Zionist struggle with class, see Vital, *The Formative Years*. For a summary of these historical and historiographic debates, see Jonathan Frankel's introduction to Kahan's work, Frankel, *Prophecy and Politics*, 329–63, and Stanislawski, *For Whom Do I Toil?* 155–82.

21. Much of this information is gathered from the memoir of Ben Tsien Kats, one of *Hazman*'s editors. Ben Tsien Kats, *Zihronot: hamishim shana behistorya shel yehude rusya* (Tel Aviv: Hotsaot sefarim n. tevarski, 1963). The other editors of *Hazman* included L. Salkovitsh, M. Rivkin, and S. F. Margolin. More information about *Hazman* may be found in Horovits, "Unzer ershte teglikhe tsaytung," 256.

22. Druk, *Tsu der geshikhte*, 50.

23. Horovits, "Unzer ershte teglikhe tsaytung," 247.

24. *Der fraynd*, no. 146 (2 [16] July 1903). The same advertisement was published in the Hebrew daily *Hazman* throughout 1903.

25. *Der fraynd*, no. 127 (8 [21] June 1908).

26. *Der fraynd*, no. 54 (23 [11] March 1903).

27. *Der fraynd*, no. 205 (8 [21] September 1908).

28. Mendelsohn, *Class Struggle in the Pale*, 1–27.

29. In 1903, Sholem Rabinovich (the much-loved writer of folk fiction, known by his pseudonym Sholem Aleichem) was inspired to write a series of humorous stories about Jews and railroad travel. The stories were told through the voice of a narrator who was a "good friend and practical man, a commercial traveler." They have been translated and gathered in a single volume by Hillel Halkin, ed., *Tevye the Dairyman and the Railroad Stories* (New York: Schocken Books, 1987), 284. See also Leah Garrett, "Trains and Train Travel in Modern Yiddish Literature," *Jewish Social Studies* 7, no. 2 (2001).

30. This is not to underestimate the continued importance of gas lighting in the turn-of-the-century East European context. Stephen Corrsin has noted that in Warsaw, gas lighting was used primarily by the poor: in 1919, one-half of the city's property lacked electricity. Corrsin, *Warsaw*, 15. For more on advertisements for electricity in the Russian language press, see West, "Constructing Consumer Culture," 153–57.

31. *Der fraynd*, no. 270 (7 [20] December 1903).

32. In this regard, the Yiddish newspaper industry resembled the rapidly expanding Russian and Polish publishing industries of the same era. As Beth Holmgren has demonstrated, these industries, even as they worked to broaden their market appeal, were loath to relinquish the notion of "serious" authors, readers, or literature. Holmgren, *Rewriting Capitalism*.

33. Richard Terdiman, for example, has suggested that the first popular presses in France were written "against" the discourse of the intelligentsia. Thus in nineteenth-

century France, the first mass-circulating papers were distinguished from their pre-decessors in that they were written neither for nor by the intelligentsia. Louise McReynolds has developed a similar thesis about the Russian context. The most popular presses in Russian, she has argued, challenged the journalistic tradition that had been established by Russian intellectuals. Terdiman, *Discourse/Counter-Discourse;* McReynolds, *Russia's Old Regime.*

34. Prager, *Literary and Linguistic Periodicals.*

35. See *Der fraynd,* no. 23 (11 [23] March 1903).

36. Shaten, "Interview with Morris Shaten."

37. Bal Makhshoves, "Notitsn fun a kritik."

38. See, for example, *Der fraynd,* no. 59 (11 [24] March 1904).

39. The latter two advertisements can be found in *Der fraynd,* no. 45 (1 [14] March 1905); the advertisements for meat may be found in *Der fraynd,* no. 59 (11 [24] March 1904); and the advertisement for tea in *Der fraynd,* no. 42 (11 [23] March 1903).

40. *Der fraynd,* no. 27 (1 [14] February 1908).

41. The latter two advertisements may be found in *Der fraynd,* no. 173 (9 [22] August 1905). M. Yafo's painting was promoted in the pages of *Der fraynd* around the time of Yom Kippur for years to come.

42. *Der fraynd,* no. 228 (10 [23] December 1908).

43. Advertisements for the Hotel Orient's kosher restaurant appeared in *Der fraynd* for years on end. Ritual objects could be bought from Y. Shekman (among other sellers). See *Der fraynd,* no. 195 (27 August [9 September] 1908). The guide for cantors was promoted in *Der fraynd,* no. 173 (1 [14] August 1908).

44. *Der fryand,* no. 227 (9 [22] December 1908).

45. *Der fraynd,* no. 235 (25 October [10 November] 1903).

46. *Der fraynd,* no. 54 (23 [11] March 1903).

47. Kahan, *Jewish Social and Economic History,* 5.

48. *Der fraynd,* no. 108 (12 [25] May 1904).

49. See, for example, Loeb, *Consuming Angels;* Judith Walkowitz, *City of Dreadful Delight* (Chicago: University of Chicago Press, 1992).

50. Sally West argues that relative to early-twentieth-century Britain, Russian advertisers, too, addressed men as much if not more than women. And yet her study of gender roles in Russian advertising suggests that relative to the Yiddish press, at least, the Russian language press targeted and depicted consuming women with regularity. West, "Constructing Consumer Culture." See especially chapter 6, "Sex Appeal: Gender Roles and Sexuality in Advertising."

51. See, for example, *Der fraynd,* no. 151 (9 [22] July 1903); *Der fraynd,* no. 270 (7 [20] December 1903).

52. See, for example, *Der fraynd,* no. 151 (9 [22] July 1903). Similar advertisements appeared in the Russian-language press: West, "Constructing Consumer Culture," 197.

53. See, for example, *Der fraynd,* no. 173 (1 [14] August 1908); *Der fraynd,* no. 21 (26 January [8 February] 1907).

54. See, for example, *Der fraynd,* no. 13 (3 [16] January 1904); *Der fraynd,* no. 129 (16 [29] June 1905).

55. *Der fraynd,* no. 245 (8 [21] November 1903). The same ad appeared in Russian in *Niva* throughout the preceding year. See, for example, *Niva,* no. 32 (10 August 1902). As Sally West has demonstrated, advertisements for corsets and implements to help women improve upon their figure were common in the Russian language press of the day. See West, "Creating Consumer Culture," 244–300.

56. Karl Hartmann of St. Petersburg, for example, promoted pills that would combat nervous conditions: *Der fraynd,* no. 67 (20 March [2 April] 1908). Interestingly enough, advertisements for hypnotists were among the few advertisements

published entirely in Russian, perhaps because Jewish hypnotists were an uncommon breed. *Der fraynd,* no. 50 (2 [15] March 1907).

57. Advertisements for "Boroxyl," a medicine "for women and girls," and for Y. H. Ravnitsky's *The Jewish Treasure,* an instructional pamphlet on child-rearing, can be found in *Der fraynd,* no. 230 (21 October [4 November] 1903).

58. Among the many advertisements for doctors claiming a specialty in women's health are those for the offices of Drs. Jakob Goldenberg and J. Mucha of Warsaw: *Der fraynd,* no. 71 (31 October [13 November] 1906); *Der fraynd,* no. 1 (3 [16] January 1904).

59. *Der fraynd,* no. 245 (8 [21] November 1903).

60. *Der fraynd,* no. 25 (31 January [13 February] 1907).

61. Mark Baker, "The Voice of the Deserted Jewish Women, 1867–1870," *Jewish Social Studies* 2, no. 1 (1995); Freeze, *Jewish Marriage,* 233. Arguably, the need for such postings was exacerbated by the fact that Jewish widows were considerably more prevalent than Jewish widowers in late-nineteenth- and early-twentieth-century Russia. As ChaeRan Freeze has demonstrated, this configuration was made worse by patterns of emigration. Kahan, *Jewish Social and Economic History,* 5; Freeze, *Jewish Marriage,* 131–200.

62. This state of affairs can be compared to that in England, where the daily press was used to politicize the disadvantaged status of the widow. Lisa Tickner, *The Spectacle of Women: Imagery of the Suffrage Campaign 1907–1914* (Chicago: University of Chicago Press, 1987). See especially the cartoon reprinted on p. 157.

63. *Der fraynd,* no. 44 (21 February [5 March] 1908).

64. The phrase is borrowed from McReynolds. McReynolds, *Russia's Old Regime.*

65. *Der fraynd baylage,* no. 9 (2 March 1908).

6. Advertising Anxiety

1. "Observations of a Doctor," *El tiempo,* no. 90 (4 May 1910).

2. The exceptions are strikingly few and appeared once or twice before disappearing altogether. They include the sale of fezes, furs, olive soap, and cigarette paper. The Papadopolus Brothers advertised for their clothing shop a number of times in 1894: *El tiempo,* no. 1 (8 October 1894). Aram Kyomgeon's advertisement for *samaras* (fur wraps) can be found in *El tiempo,* no. 30 (8 December 1911). The Tchaoussi Brothers promoted cigarette paper: *El tiempo,* no. 95 (28 August 1902). Olive soap could be bought from the Greek Company Rizo Prahi: *El tiempo,* no. 63 (23 May 1899). Hamidi Fezes were advertised in *El tiempo,* no. 58 (10 April 1902). Ironically, of the three Turkish cigarette-paper brands advertised in *El tiempo,* one was sold to benefit the Jewish Hospital Or HaHayim, and another was named "Emile Zola." See, for example, *El tiempo,* no. 48 (17 March 1899). Emile Zola cigarettes can be found in *El tiempo,* no. 88 (24 August 1898).

3. This view of Ottoman Jews' role in the evolving regional economy is expressed by Charles Issawi, *The Economic History of Turkey, 1800–1914* (Chicago: University of Chicago Press, 1980); Pamuk, *The Ottoman Empire.* Reşat Kasaba presents a similar critique of the literature on the Ottoman Jewish compradors in his *The Ottoman Empire.*

4. Jewish movement into the middle class, it should be specified, was largely catalyzed by the acquisition of skills taught in AIU schools. To wit, Benbassa, "L'education feminine en Orient"; Esther Benbassa and Aron Rodrigue, "L'artisanat juif en Turquie à la fin du XIXe siécle: l'Alliance Israélite universelle et des oeuvres s'apprentissage," *Turcica* 17 (1985); Rodrigue, *French Jews, Turkish Jews,* 111–20. Because the Jewish middle class expanded more rapidly in Salonika than elsewhere in the empire, there is considerably more literature on this context. See, for example Dumont, "La structure sociale." For a close study of an exceptional Jewish financier who became

influential in the Ottoman and wider European sphere, see Aron Rodrigue, "Abraham De Camondo of Istanbul: The Transformation of Jewish Philanthropy," in *From East and West: Jews in a Changing Europe, 1750–1870,* ed. Frances Malino and David Sorkin (Oxford: Basil Blackwell, 1990).

5. This point has been echoed by Reşat Kasaba, who has demonstrated on a rather more material level that the local (primarily non-Muslim) intermediaries who made market exchange the "pivotal axis of integration in the dissolving empire," in fact *relied* on local relations rather than existing (as a previous generation of scholars suggested they did) "as mere offshoots of foreign interests and capital." Kasaba, *The Ottoman Empire,* 114.

6. Benbassa, *Une diaspora sépharade,* 59–70. Aron Rodrigue has documented the prevailing inability of families to pay even the symbolic fees charged by the Alliance schools. High rates of attrition from these schools, he argues, were prompted by widespread poverty. Rodrigue, *French Jews, Turkish Jews,* 111–20. For a general discussion of Jewish poverty in turn-of-the-century Southeastern Europe, see Benbassa and Rodrigue, *The Jews of the Balkans,* 80–83.

7. The Grands Magasin du Printemps, created in 1865, was one of Paris's first department stores (following on the heels of the Bon Marché, which opened in 1852, and the Louvre, which opened in 1855). By the late 1860s, the Bon Marché could boast a turnover of seven million francs. Mitchell, *Colonizing Egypt,* 10. An example of the Grands Magasins du Printemps' advertisement can be found in *El tiempo,* no. 87 (25 May 1892).

8. Aron Rodrigue discusses the bazaar as a site of multi-ethnic identity in Rodrigue, " 'Difference' and Tolerance."

9. For a nostalgic picture of the role of a general store owned by Jews in an Ottoman city, see Elias Canetti's memoir of his youth in Ruschuk. Canetti, *The Tongue Set Free,* 7–10. For a description of an open market in the Ottoman provinces, see Sciaky, *Farewell to Salonica,* 66–67.

10. Canetti, *The Tongue Set Free,* 4–5.

11. It is also true that the majority of Ashkenazim in turn-of-the-century Constantinople were recent immigrants, while a significant percentage of the remainder held foreign passports. An article published in *El tiempo* in 1912 suggested that 5,500 of the city's roughly 10,000 Ashkenazim were foreigners. It is important to note that many Ottoman Sephardim, too, held foreign passports, a fact that complicated but did not defuse growing tensions between Ashkenazim and Sephardim in the Ottoman capital. *El tiempo,* no. 62 (23 February 1912).

12. Among the most frequently advertised department stores were those of D. H. Pollack; the brothers Goldberg; Karlman and Blumberg; the brothers H. and S. Stein; A. L. Spiegel; Tiring; and Meyer. The Tiring Department Store, located in the neighborhood of Galata from 1843 to 1925, was owned by an Austrian Jewish family. The department store owned by the Stein family was also located in Galata, in the Place du Tunnel. Reference to the Tiring family can be found in Lowenthal, *Elia Carmona's Autobiography,* 36, 119.

13. See, for example, *El tiempo,* no. 46 (13 March 1893).

14. See, for example, *El tiempo,* no. 102 (1 June 1910); *El tiempo,* no. 13 (11 November 1910).

15. Prior to the Young Turk Revolt, this divide was by and large cultural, but in the wake of 1908 it became infused with politics. Constantinople's Ashkenazim tended to support Zionism, while the AIU retained the support of the majority of the city's Sephardim. By 1912, the Sephardi-Ashkenazi divide had become so rife that the president of the Ashkenzi community, Henri Reisner, and the community's head rabbi, David Marcus, advocated that Constantinople's Ashkenazim be fused under one communal authority, placing them outside of the influence of the (Sephardi and

Alliancist) Chief Rabbi, Haim Nahum. Ever a supporter of the AIU and Rabbi Nahum, *El tiempo* vociferously opposed the measure. Benbassa, *Une diaspora sépharade*, 158–70, see especially p. 164, note 41.

16. On the continued stability of the Ottoman textile economy, see Quataert, *Ottoman Manufacturing*. His discussion of the ready-made garment industry of Istanbul can be found on p. 56.

17. The advertising practices tell us something, too, about the demography of *El tiempo*'s readership, for they assume readers' familiarity with the city. Indeed, the paper's heavy concentration of advertisements for Constantinople-based shops seems a convincing indication that the paper was distributed mainly in the capital city. Were it to have reached many readers in other cities with large Jewish populations, one would expect the advertisements to have reflected local commercial options as well, or to have offered directions more accessible to shoppers outside of Constantinople's limits.

18. Writes Leon Sciaky of contemporary Salonika: "Few of the streets of Salonica had names, nor were the houses numbered. Vaguely bounded sections of the city had acquired unofficial appellations, either from events which had occurred in the neighborhood or from the owners of outstanding buildings." Sciaky, *Farewell to Salonica*, 108.

19. The attempt to turn Galata into Constantinople's most "European" city dates to the 1860s, when the walls surrounding the city were torn down to create space for the construction of new and wider arteries linking the neighborhood to Pera and Istanbul. Zeynep Çelik, *The Remaking of Istanbul: Portrait of an Ottoman City in the Nineteenth Century* (Seattle: University of Washington Press, 1986), 70–81.

20. Esther Juhasz, ed., *Sephardi Jews in the Ottoman Empire: Aspects of Material Culture* (Jerusalem: Israel Museum, 1990), 130. Linda Welters has argued that Greek dress of the turn of the century was marked not only by ethnicity but by region. The same is certainly true of traditional dress of the Ottoman Sephardim, as of patterns of sartorial acculturation. Linda Welters, "Ethnicity in Greek Dress," in *Dress and Ethnicity: Change across Space and Time*, ed. Joanne B. Eicher (Oxford and Washington, D.C.: Berg, 1995).

21. See, for example, the advertisements in *El tiempo*, no. 75 (25 March 1912); *El tiempo*, no. 117 (8 July 1912).

22. Çelik, *The Remaking of Istanbul*.

23. Sciaky, *Farewell to Salonica*, 59.

24. Ibid., 67.

25. Advertisements for Stein clothiers, for example, frequently pictured bareheaded men. *El tiempo*, no. 104 (5 September 1908).

26. For more on the history of the fez, see Nancy Lindisfarne-Tapper and Bruce Ingham, eds., *Languages of Dress in the Middle East* (Surrey: Curzon, 1997), John Norton, "Faith and Fashion in Turkey," in *Languages of Dress*, and Jeremy Seal, *A Fez of the Heart: Travels around Turkey in Search of a Hat* (San Diego, New York, and London: Harcourt Brace and Co., 1996).

27. Juhasz, *Sephardi Jews*, 126–39.

28. *El tiempo*, no. 58 (10 April 1902).

29. While no single body of scholarship has attempted to compare the class composition of turn-of-the-century Russian and Ottoman Jewries, studies of these two contexts point to such an asymmetry in their economic development. We will return to this theme at the close of this chapter.

30. *El tiempo*, no. 16 (7 December 1891).

31. See, for example, *El tiempo*, no. 98 (23 May 1910); *El tiempo*, no. 140 (29 August 1910).

32. *El tiempo*, no. 93 (11 May 1910).

33. See, for example, *El tiempo*, no. 145 (12 September 1910); *El tiempo*, no. 151 (28 September 1910); *El tiempo*, no. 13 (11 November 1910).

34. Each ad for Pink Pills appended a number of addresses identifying where readers might buy the drug.

35. See, for example, *El tiempo*, no. 151 (28 September 1910).

36. *El tiempo*, no. 44 (10 January 1910). For similar advertisements, see *El tiempo*, no. 86 (10 August 1899); *El tiempo*, no. 142 (5 September 1910).

37. *El tiempo*, no. 136 (22 August 1910); *El tiempo*, no. 6 (16 October 1908). In *El tiempo*'s advertisements, the treatment of children's health, also, emerged as a field of its own. *El tiempo*'s advertisements include postings by the pediatricians Alfandri and Milafolo. *El tiempo*, no. 142 (5 September 1910); *El tiempo*, no. 86 (10 August 1899).

38. *El tiempo*, no. 142 (5 September 1910).

39. *El tiempo*, no. 140 (29 August 1910).

40. *El tiempo*, no. 151 (28 September 1910).

41. *El tiempo*, no. 140 (29 August 1910); *El tiempo*, no. 95 (16 May 1910); *El tiempo*, no. 236 (22 August 1910).

42. Advertisement for Pink Pills, *El tiempo*, no. 13 (11 November 1910). A similar advertisement depicted a woman comforting a companion, whose hand was raised to her chin in despair. See, for example, *El tiempo*, no. 145 (12 September 1910).

43. Of the many testimonials for Pink Pills that spoke of women's ailments, only one claimed to be written by (rather than about) a woman. In her letter, Mademoiselle Esther Bras described how her anemia resulted in poor circulation in her hands and feet, an inability to sleep or digest food, and a general state of languor, all of which were instantly remedied by Pink Pills. Mlle. Bras's ethnic identity is not definitively established in her testimonial or accompanying photograph, though her first name suggests she was Jewish. *El tiempo*, no. 22 (20 November 1911).

44. *El tiempo*, no. 95 (16 May 1910); *El tiempo*, no. 133 (15 August 1910).

45. Sciaky, *Farewell to Salonica*, 41–42.

46. Çelik, *The Remaking of Istanbul*, 49–81.

47. Galanté, *Histoire des juifs de Turquie*, 142–49.

48. See, for example, *El tiempo*, no. 46 (13 March 1893); *El tiempo*, no. 87 (25 May 1892); *El tiempo*, no. 63 (23 May 1899).

49. See, for example, *El tiempo*, no. 4 (27 October 1891); *El tiempo*, no. 90 (20 August 1905); *El tiempo*, no. 23 (20 November 1909).

50. Benbassa, *Une diaspora sépharade*, 59–70.

51. Rodrigue and Benbassa, *A Sephardi Life*, 37.

52. A significant minority of insurance providers were based in the United States, among them Mutual Life and Mutual Reserve, and the Life Fund of New York. *El tiempo*, no. 43 (6 April 1900).

53. *El tiempo*, no. 43 (6 April 1900).

54. Advertisement for General Society of Ottoman Insurance, *El tiempo*, no. 104 (5 September 1908).

55. *El tiempo*, no. 31 (10 November 1872).

56. *El tiempo*, no. 78 (18 March 1876).

57. See, for example, *El tiempo*, no. 43 (6 April 1901).

58. *El tiempo*, no. 61 (27 February 1914).

59. *El tiempo*, no. 111 (24 June 1912).

60. See, for example, *El tiempo*, no. 31 (10 November 1872); *El tiempo*, no. 151 (28 September 1910).

61. *El tiempo*, no. 136 (22 August 1910).

62. *El tiempo*, no. 79 (16 July 1893).

63. *El tiempo*, no. 88 (25 August 1898); *El tiempo*, no. 21 (12 December 1898); *El tiempo*, no. 63 (23 May 1899); *El tiempo*, no. 8 (2 November 1905).

64. Benbassa, *Une diaspora sépharade*, 59–70. On the absence of a Jewish working class, see also Benbassa, "L'éducation feminine en Orient"; Benbassa and Rodrigue, "L'artisanat juif en Turquie"; Rodrigue, *French Jews, Turkish Jews*, 111–20; Benbassa and Rodrigue, *The Jews of the Balkans*, 80–83.

65. Of course, Russian Jewry was overwhelmingly poor and unemployed on the eve of the twentieth century, but in this setting, traditional Jewish skills afforded artisans — even unemployed ones — a range of options that their Ottoman contemporaries did not posses. Russian Jews could participate in the strike and labor movements, join the industrial workforce, or choose to throw in their lot with the enormous swell of Jewish émigrés, the vast majority of whom were skilled workers who had left Russia in search of economic opportunity. On Russian Jews' poverty and attraction to working class politics, see Kahan, *Essays in Jewish Social and Economic History*, 1–69; Mendelsohn, *Class Struggle in the Pale;* Tobias, *The Jewish Bund in Russia.* On the relationship between emigration and class aspiration, see Simon Kuznets, "Immigration of Russian Jews to the United States: Nature and Background and Structure." *Perspectives in American History* 9 (1975) and Kahan, *Essays in Jewish Social and Economic History*, 101–48.

EPILOGUE

1. Immigration was one force that kept Western and Central European Jewry dynamic in the wake of the Second World War. The arrival of Jews from North Africa and the Middle East, for example, rendered new neighborhoods and cities centers of European Jewish life. This process inevitably changed the texture of European Jewish culture. Jöelle Bahloul, among others, has developed a compelling argument about cultural dynamism in post-war Europe that presents a useful antidote to scholarship that imagines European Jewish history to end with the Holocaust. See Jöelle Bahloul, "The Sephardi Family and the Challenge of Assimilation: Family Ritual and Ethnic Reproduction," in Goldberg, *Sephardi and Middle Eastern Jewries*. A rather different and far more lachrymose view may be found in Bernard Wasserstein, *Vanishing Diaspora: The Jews in Europe since 1945* (Cambridge, Mass.: Harvard University Press, 1996).

2. This was true, at least for a time, in the Soviet setting, where Jews occupied visible and privileged positions in the Soviet state (occupying, for example, elite stations in the Communist Party, the Red Army and the Cheka [Secret Police]) and as white-collar workers. For more on Jewish life under Soviet rule, see Salo Baron, *The Russian Jew under Tsars and Soviets* (New York: Macmillan, 1987); Zvi Gitelman, *A Century of Ambivalence* (Bloomington: Indiana University Press, 2001); Zvi Gitelman, *Jewish Nationality and Soviet Politics* (Princeton, N.J.: Princeton University Press, 1972); Nora Levin, *The Jews in the Soviet Union since 1917*, 2 vols. (New York: New York University Press, 1987); Jeffrey Veidlinger, *The Moscow State Yiddish Theater: Jewish Culture on the Soviet Stage* (Bloomington: Indiana University Press, 2000). Jews were also highly integrated into Polish society. See, for example Celia Heller, *On the Edge of Destruction: Jews of Poland between the Two World Wars* (New York: Columbia University Press, 1977) and "Poles of Jewish Background: The Case of Assimilation without Integration in Interwar Poland," in *Studies on Polish Jewry, 1919–1939: The Interplay of Social, Economic, and Political Factors in the Struggle of a Minority for Its Existence*, ed. Joshua Fishman (New York: YIVO Institute, 1974); Ezra Mendelsohn, "From Assimilation to Zionism in Lvov: The Case of Alfred Nossig," *The Slavonic and East European*

Review 49, no. 117 (1971); and "Jewish Assimilation in Lvov: The Case of Wilhelm Feldman," *Slavic Review* 28, no. 4 (1969). For a discussion of prominent Jews in Republican Turkey, see Bali, *Bir Türklestirme Serüveni;* Levi, *Turkiye Cümhuriyeti'nde Yahudiler.*

3. Particularly compelling first-hand accounts of the devastation in war-torn Jewish Eastern Europe are offered by S. An-sky, "The Destruction of Galicia: Excerpts from a Diary, 1914–1917," in *The Dybbuk and Other Writings,* ed. David Roskies (New York: Random House, 1986); Isaac Babel, *1920 Diary,* ed. Carol J. Avins, trans. H. T. Willetts (New Haven, Conn.: Yale University Press, 1995). See also Piotr Wrobel, "The First World War: The Twilight of Jewish Warsaw," in *The Jews in Warsaw: A History,* ed. Wladyslaw Bartoszewski and Antony Polonsky (Oxford: Basil Blackwell, 1991); Mark Von Hagen, *Soldiers in the Proletarian Dictatorship: The Red Army and the Soviet Socialist State, 1917–1930* (Ithaca, N.Y.: Cornell University Press, 1990); Shaw, *Jews of the Ottoman Empire,* 229–43. On Jews in the Balkan Wars, see Eyal Ginio, "Mobilizing the Ottoman Nation during the Balkan Wars (1912–1913): Awakening from the Ottoman Dream," in *Coexistence and Conflict in Ottoman Society,* ed. Reşat Kasaba and Sarah Abrevaya Stein (forthcoming).

4. The question of how secure was Jewish life and culture in the states of interwar Eastern Europe is a subject of much scholarly debate. For a discussion of this historiographic issue in relation to Poland, see Ezra Mendelsohn, "Interwar Poland: Good for the Jews or Bad for the Jews," in *The Jews in Poland,* ed. Chimen Abramsky, Maciej Jachimczyk, and Antony Polonsky (Oxford: Oxford University Press, 1986). See also Chimen Abramsky, Maciej Jachimczyk, and Antony Polonsky, eds., *The Jews in Poland* (Oxford: Oxford University Press, 1986); Henry Abramson, *A Prayer for the Government: Ukrainians and Jews in Revolutionary Times, 1917–1920* (Cambridge, Mass.: Harvard University Press for the Ukrainian Research Institute and Center for Jewish Studies, Harvard University, 1999); Joshua Fishman, ed., *Studies on Polish Jewry, 1919–1939: The Interplay of Social, Economic, and Political Factors in the Struggle of a Minority for Its Existence* (New York: YIVO Institute, 1974); Yisrael Gutman et al., eds., *The Jews of Poland between Two World Wars* (Hanover, N.H.: Brandeis University Press, 1989); Raphael Mahler, *Yehude polin ben shete milhamot olam: historya kalkalitsotsialit leor hastatistika* (Tel Aviv: Devir, 1968); Ezra Mendelsohn, *The Jews of East Central Europe between the Wars* (Bloomington: Indiana University Press, 1983); Antony Polonsky, Ezra Mendelsohn, and Jerzy Tomaszewski, eds., *Jews in Independent Poland, 1918–1939,* Polin: Studies in Polish Jewry, vol. 8 (London: Littman Library of Jewish Civilization, 1994). For more on Jewish life under Soviet rule, see Gitelman, *A Century of Ambivalence;* Gitelman, *Jewish Nationality and Soviet Politics;* Levin, *The Jews in the Soviet Union;* Veidlinger, *The Moscow State Yiddish Theater.* For further discussion of early Soviet policies toward culture and national particularism, see Brooks, *Thank You, Comrade Stalin;* James Mace, *Communism and the Dilemma of National Liberation: National Communism in Soviet Ukraine, 1918–1933* (Cambridge, Mass.: Harvard University Press, 1983); Gerhard Simon, *Nationalism and Policy toward the Nationalities in the Soviet Union: From Totalitarian Dictatorship to Post-Stalinist Society* (Boulder, Colo.: Westview Press, 1991); Yuri Slezkine, "The USSR as a Communal Apartment; or, How a Socialist State Promoted Ethnic Particularism," *Slavic Review* 53, no. 2 (1994). On the Southeastern European setting, see Adanir, "Armenian Deportations and Massacres"; Brubaker, "Aftermaths of Empire"; Davison, "The Armenian Crisis"; Ginio, "Aspects of Muslim Culture"; Reşat Kasaba, "Izmir 1922: A Port City Unravels," in *Modernity and Culture from the Mediterranean to the Indian Ocean,* ed. Leila Tarazi Fawaz and C. A. Bayly (New York: Columbia University Press, 2002); Stephen Ladas, *The Exchange of Minorities: Bulgaria, Greece, and Turkey* (New York: Macmillan, 1932).

5. These issues are explored in a comparative manner by the contributions to

Birnbaum and Katznelson, *Paths to Emancipation.* Todd Endelman, *The Jews of Georgian England, 1714–1830* (Philadelphia: Jewish Publication Society of America, 1979); Paula Hyman, *The Jews of Modern France* (Berkeley: University of California Press, 1998); David Sorkin, *The Transformation of German Jewry, 1780–1840* (New York: Oxford University Press, 1987).

6. Druk, *Tsu der geshikhte,* 98–102; Weiser, "The Politics of Yiddish."

7. *Der bezem,* no. 61 (12 March 1908).

8. *Yubileyem baylage der fraynd, tsenter yorgang,* vol. 13 (January) (Warsaw: *Der fraynd,* 1913).

9. *El tiempo,* no. 47 (27 March 1930).

10. It is possible that Fresco's support for the notion of Jewish self-defense was modeled on analogous efforts in Imperial Russia and interwar Poland, where the Bund and various factions of the Zionist movement organized similar movements. Leonard Rowe, "Jewish Self Defense: A Response to Violence," in Fishman, *Studies on Polish Jewry.*

11. With the outbreak of the First World War, official acquiescence to the pressure of the right gave way to policy. Hundreds of thousands of Jews from Russia and Galicia became subject to expulsions, pogroms, and dislocation, hapless victims of a war waged in the territory of Russia most densely populated by Jews. The Beilis trial was by no means a rehearsal for these events, but it did seem to presage the vulnerability of Russian Jewry in the interwar period. Rogger, *Jewish Policies,* 40–55. On the sensationalism of the Beilis trial in an international context, see Joel Berkowitz, "The 'Mendel Beilis Epidemic' on the Yiddish Stage," *Jewish Social Studies* 8, no. 1 (2002).

12. Among the many studies of Yiddish and Ladino publishing in the interwar era are the following: Benbassa, "Presse d'Istanbul et de Salonique"; Benbassa, *Une diaspora sépharade;* Bunis, *Voices from Jewish Salonika;* Paul Dumont, "Un organe Sioniste a Istanbul, La Nation (1919–1920)," in *Türkiye'de yabanci dilde basin* (Istanbul: Istanbul Universitesi Yayinlari, 1985); David Flinker and Moshe Ron, "Di yidishe prese in poyln tsvishn beyde velt-milkhomes," in *Yorbukh,* ed. Arye Tartakover (New York: Velt federatsye fun Poylishe-Yidn, 1967). Galanté, *La presse judéo-espagnole mondiale;* Selim Kaneti, "La presse en ladino sous la republique en Turquie," in *Türkiye'de yabanci dilde basin;* Mayzel, *Geven a mol;* Mayzes, "Di ershte yorn"; Nahum, *Juifs de Smyrne;* Nassi, "Synoptic List"; Sena, " 'Haynt' —A nehtn un a morgn"; Shmuelevitz, "Two Hebrew-Language Weeklies"; Shloyme Shreberk, "Zikhroynes fun a yidishn bukhhandler," in *Pinkes far der geshikhte fun vilna in di yorn fun milhoma un okupatsya,* ed. Zalman Reisen (Vilna: Aroisgegebn fun der historish-etnografisher gezelshaft oifn nomen fun S. An-ski, 1922); Steinlauf, "The Polish-Jewish Daily Press"; Weiser, "The Politics of Yiddish"; Shmuel Werses, "The Hebrew Press and Its Readership in Interwar Poland," in Gutman, *The Jews of Poland.*

13. See, for example, the photographs in Juhasz, *Sephardi Jews;* Lucjan Dobroszycki and Barbara Kirshenblatt-Gimblett, *Image before My Eyes: A Photographic History of Jewish Life in Poland, 1864–1939* (New York: Schocken Books, 1977).

14. Bal Makhshoves, "Notitsn fun a kritik."

15. Gitelman, *Jewish Nationality and Soviet Politics;* Rakhmiel Peltz and Mark Kiel, "Di yiddish-imperye: The Dashed Hopes for a Yiddish Cultural Empire in the Soviet Union," in *Sociolinguistic Perspectives on Soviet National Languages: Their Past, Present, and Future,* ed. Isabelle T. Kreindler (Berlin and New York: Mouton, 1985).

16. Reference to Jewish rates of fluency and literacy in Yiddish and Ladino in the interwar period may be found in Fishman, *Turning to Life,* table 9, 396–98; Freidenreich, *The Jews of Yugoslavia;* Ginio, "Language of Homer"; Gitelman, *Jewish Nationality and Soviet Politics,* 321; Astruc, "Bulgarian Jews"; Jacob Lestchinsky, "Di shprakhn bay yidn in umophengikn poyln," *YIVO bleter* 22 (1943); Mezán, "Les Juifs

Espagnols"; Mendelsohn, *Jews of East Central Europe;* Rivlin, *Pinkas hakehilot — Greece;* Chone Shmeruk, "Hebrew-Yiddish-Polish: A Trilingual Jewish Culture," in Gutman, *The Jews of Poland;* Weiker, *The Jewish Polity.* For a more modest estimation of the number of Ladino speakers in Turkey, see Shaw, *Jews of the Ottoman Empire,* 266.

17. Evidence of these divergent trends has not, to my knowledge, been studied in a systematic manner. Two studies of East European Jewish reading patterns do confirm one side of this hypothesis; that is, that the age of Yiddish readers was growing younger. One of these studies, conducted in 1908, suggests that an astonishing 26 percent of the members of one Russian Jewish lending library were under the age of 13. A second study, conducted in interwar Poland, documents that out of 420 readers of a left-wing Jewish library in interwar Poland, 321 members (76.5 percent) were younger than 20 years of age. Goldenberg, "Ha'yesh korim evrim?" Mayzel, *Geven a mol.* Readers of the Yiddish press in the United States were also strikingly young: one study of 1925 suggests that roughly 35 percent were under 26 years of age and, significantly, were patrons of the English press as well as the Yiddish. Mordecai Soltes, *The Yiddish Press: An Americanizing Agency* (New York: Teachers College, Columbia University, 1925), 33, 39–42. Evidence pertaining to the Ottoman setting is somewhat more anecdotal. A range of primary and secondary sources describe young readers increasingly turning away from Ladino and toward French, and, in time, Turkish, Bulgarian, Greek, and other regional languages. As chapter 2 documented, this process began at the turn of the century but gained momentum in the interwar period. Altabe, "The Romanso"; Franco, *Essai sur l'histoire des Israélites;* Rodrigue, *French Jews, Turkish Jews;* Benbassa, *Une diaspora sépharade;* Shaw, *Jews of the Ottoman Empire,* 248.

18. Joshua Fishman, citing Mayzel, documents that in 1923, 13.5 percent of all Yiddish books published were designed for young readers, while 11 percent were textbooks. Fishman, *Turning to Life,* table 2, 386. See also Dina Abramowicz, "On the Beginnings of Yiddish Children's Literature," *Judaica-Librarianship* 3, no. 1–2 (1986); Chone Shmeruk, "Yiddish Adaptations of Children's Stories from World Literature," in *Studies in Contemporary Jewry: An Annual,* ed. Ezra Mendelsohn and Richard I. Cohen (Oxford: Oxford University Press, 1990).

19. On the proliferation of autobiographical writing in interwar Poland, see: Moseley, "Life, Literature"; Shandler, *Awakening Lives.* On the absence of memoiristic literature in the Ladino world, see the introductory comments to Benbassa and Rodrigue, *A Sephardi Life.* On the more recent development of the French- and English-language Sephardi autobiography, see Stein, "Sephardi and Middle Eastern Jewries."

20. Fishman, *Turning to Life,* table 4, 388–90.

21. Lowenthal, *Elia Carmona's Autobiography,* 66–67, 221, especially footnote 36.

22. Kahan, *Jewish Social and Economic History;* Kuznets, "Immigration of Russian Jews"; Lestchinsky, *Dos yidishe folk in tsifern* and "Di antviklung fun yidishn folk."

23. A related point is that while most Jews in Eastern Europe tended to leave their home regions in search of opportunities, by the twentieth century, Jews in Southeastern Europe tended to be fleeing political events at home. From this we can infer that to many young Eastern European Jews, Imperial Russia seemed to afford fewer opportunities than did Poland or the Soviet Union (at least in the 1920s), while for many young Jews in Southeastern Europe, the Ottoman Empire was more hospitable than the nation-states that succeeded it. Kahan, *Jewish Social and Economic History;* Kemal Karpat, "The Migratory Movements of Jews in the Ottoman Empire" (in Hebrew), *Cathedra* 51 (1989); Ben-Ur, *Where Diasporas Met;* Rodrigue and Benbassa, *The Jews of the Balkans,* 184–91.

24. The Ottoman Jewish population figure is taken from official Ottoman census reports, and most likely underestimates the Jewish population in the region as it

excludes Jewish residents of the empire with European or Russian passports. It also excludes the Jewish residents of the independent or conquered regions, including Macedonia, Bulgaria, Serbia, and Austro-Hungarian controlled Bosnia-Herzegovina. Shaw, *Jews of the Ottoman Empire*, 273.

25. Lucjan Dobroszycki, "The Fertility of Modern Polish Jewry," in *Modern Jewish Fertility*, ed. Paul Ritterband (Leiden: E. J. Brill, 1981); Shaul Stampfer, "Marital Patterns in Interwar Poland," in *The Jews of Poland between Two World Wars*, ed. Yisrael Gutman et al. (Hanover, N.H.: Brandeis University Press, 1989); Freidenreich, *Jews of Yugoslavia*.

26. Gershon Bacon, *The Politics of Tradition: Agudat Yisrael in Poland, 1916–1939* (Jerusalem: Magnes Press, 1996); Nathan Eck, "The Educational Institutions of Polish Jewry (1921–1939)," *Jewish Social Studies* IX, no. I (1947); Miriam Epstein, *Jewish Schools in Poland 1919–1939* (New York: King's Crown Press, 1950); Shimon Frost, *Schooling as a Socio-Political Expression: Jewish Education in Interwar Poland* (Jerusalem: Magnes Press, 1998); Kh. Sh. Kazdan, *Di geshikhte fun yidishn shulvezn in umophengikn poyln* (Mexico City: Gezelshaft 'kultur un hilf,' 1947). See also Bernard Johnpoll, *The Politics of Futility: The General Jewish Workers Bund of Poland, 1917–1943* (Ithaca, N.Y.: Cornell University Press, 1967); Mark Kiel, "The Ideology of the Folks-Partey," *Soviet Jewish Affairs* 5, no. 2 (1975).

27. Levin, *Jews in the Soviet Union*, 168–93; Gitelman, *Jewish Nationality and Soviet Politics*, 321–79.

28. Weiser, "The Politics of Yiddish."

29. For a detailed history of YIVO, see Cecile Kuznits, "The Origins of Yiddish Scholarship and the YIVO Institute for Jewish Research" (Ph.D. dissertation, Stanford University, 2000).

See also Lucjan Dobroszycki, "YIVO in Interwar Poland: Work in the Historical Sciences," in Gutman, *The Jews of Poland;* Phillip Friedman, "Polish Jewish Historiography between the Two World Wars (1919–1939)," *Jewish Social Studies* 11, no. 4 (1949). On the fate of Yiddish in this period (and in the post–World War II era), see Harshav, *The Meaning of Yiddish;* Fishman, *Turning to Life.*

30. Examples of this phenomenon are discussed by Anthony Michels, " 'Speaking to Moyshe': The Early Socialist Yiddish Press and Its Readers," *Jewish History* 14, no. 1 (2000); Sarah Abrevaya Stein, "Illustrating Chicago's Jewish Left: Todros Geller and the L. M. Shteyn *Farlag,*" *Jewish Social Studies* 3, no. 3 (1997).

31. In Salonika, for example, the AIU managed to attain supervision of the reform of the Talmud Torah in only ten years. As a result, by 1912, the language of instruction of a majority of Salonika's youth was French. Mazower, "Salonica between East and West," 112. See also *Saloniki, ir veam bisrael,* 57–98; Benbassa, "L'education feminine en Orient"; Ginio, "Language of Homer"; Rodrigue, *French Jews, Turkish Jews.*

32. Marc Angel, *La America: The Sephardic Experience in the United States,* (Philadelphia: Jewish Publication Society of America, 1982) and *The Sephardim of the United States: An Exploratory Study* (New York: Union of Sephardic Congregations, 1974); Aviva Ben-Ur, "The Ladino (Judeo-Spanish) Press in the United States, 1910–1948," in *Multilingual America: Transnationalism, Ethnicity, and the Languages of American Literature,* ed. Werner Sollors (New York: New York University Press, 1998) and "Where Diasporas Met" and "The Ladino (Judeo-Spanish) Press."

33. Harris, *Death of a Language,* 213–14.

34. Ibid., Lewis, "Ataturk's Language Reform."

35. Of course, this was not true of Jews who lived in nation-states that seceded from the empire prior to the interwar period. In their political posture, the Jews of Bulgaria, for example, diverged greatly from Ottoman Jewry. Bulgaria had become independent in 1878 and in the ensuing years, Zionism was met with great popu-

larity by Jews in the region. By the first decade of the twentieth century, the movement had gained a vast public following. Esther Benbassa and Aron Rodrigue, *Sephardi Jewry: A History of the Judeo-Spanish Community, 14th–20th Centuries* (Berkeley: University of California Press, 2000).

36. As was suggested in the introduction to this work, Ottoman Jews' positive experience of empire invites comparison with Habsburg Jewry (and the Jews of Galicia, in particular). In the Habsburg setting, as in the Ottoman, a legacy of political tolerance bred a vibrant and distinct Jewish culture and lasting Jewish affinities toward empire that outlasted the imperial structure itself. For more on this comparison, see the introduction to this work, especially note 1. On Habsburg Jewry, see Deák, *Beyond Nationalism;* Dubin, *The Port Jews of Habsburg Trieste;* McCagg, *A History of Habsburg Jews;* Rozenblit, *Reconstructing a National Identity;* Wistrich, *The Jews of Vienna.*

37. To my knowledge, there exists no study of the symbol of the fez in photographs of Ottoman Jewish émigrés, nor are there many works that reproduce the kind of photographs I describe. To truly understand the cultural meaning of the wearing of the fez, one would have to compare its use by Jewish and non-Jewish émigrés. Anecdotal evidence seems to suggest that ethnic Turkish émigrés did not harbor such an affinity. Surely Armenians, Greeks, and other non-Muslims would not be expected to do so, either. A great deal of fine examples of photographs documenting Sephardim posing with the fez are contained within the University of Washington Libraries' Special Collections' "Jewish History Project" archives, at the University of Washington, Seattle. For a popular history of the fez, see Seal, *A Fez of the Heart.*

38. A discussion of Jews' declining status in the wake of empire may be found in Rodrigue, "From *Millet* to Minority." For a discussion of the history of anti-semitism in the region, see Bernard Lewis, *Semites and Anti-Semites: An Inquiry into Conflict and Prejudice* (New York: Norton, 1986). Nation building in North Africa and the Middle East was also widely accompanied by invented memories of Jewish betrayal under the rule of empire. On this, see Michel Ansky, *Les Juifs d'Algérie du décret Crémieux a la libération* (Paris: Éditions du Centre, 1950); H. Z. Hirschberg, *A History of the Jews in North Africa,* 2 vols. (Leiden: E. J. Brill, 1974–81); Simon Schwarzfuchs, *Les Juifs d'Algérie et la France (1830–1855)* (Jerusalem: Institute Ben-Zvi, 1981).

39. These words appeared in 1940 in the pages of a Salonikan weekly humor journal associated with the daily *Mesajero.* They are spoken during a rant against the Frenchified style of the Ladino press voiced by the fictional "Uncle Bohor" to his wife "Djamila." *Mesagjero* 5, 1480 (1940), cited in Bunis, *Voices from Jewish Salonika,* 103, 119.

40. Shohat, *Mosad harabanut mitaam berusya;* Lederhendler, *Modern Jewish Politics;* Weeks, *Nation and State;* Zipperstein, *The Jews of Odessa.*

41. Klier and Lambrozo, *Pogroms;* Rogger, *Jewish Policies;* Kahan, *Jewish Social and Economic History.*

42. On the theme of nostalgia and the shtetl, see David Roskies, *The Jewish Search for a Usable Past* (Bloomington: Indiana University Press, 1999); Steven J. Zipperstein, *Imagining Russian Jewry: Memory, History, Identity* (Seattle: University of Washington Press, 1999).

WORKS CITED

NEWSPAPERS AND PERIODICALS

El amigo de la familia, Constantinople
El amigo del puevlo, Belgrade, Sofia, Ruschuk
Anchar, St. Petersburg
L'Aurore, Constantinople, Cairo
El avenir, Salonika
Bikher velt, Warsaw
Di blutige teg, St. Petersburg
Boclikaya, St. Petersburg
Bomby, St. Petersburg
La boz de turkia, Constantinople
La boz del oriente, Constantinople
La boz del puevlo, Izmir
La buena esperansa, Izmir
Bulepom, St. Petersburg
Bureval, St. Petersburg
El burlon, Salonika
Burya, St. Petersburg
La epoka, Salonika
La epoka literatura, Salonika
La esperansa, Salonika
Dos folk, Kiev
Fornar, St. Petersburg
Der forverts, New York
Der fraynd, St. Petersburg / Warsaw
Der fraynd baylage, St. Petersburg
El givlis, Salonika
El grasiozo, Constantinople
Hamagid, Luck, Krakow, Vienna
Hamelits, Odessa
Hashiloah, Berlin
Hatsefira, Warsaw
Hatsofe, Warsaw

Haynt, Warsaw
Hayom, Warsaw
Hazman, St. Petersburg, Vilna
Der hoyz-fraynd, Warsaw
El imparsyal, Salonika
El instruktor, Constantinople
Le Journal d'Oriente, Constantinople
Le Journal de Salonique, Salonika
El jugeton, Salonika
K svimu, St. Petersburg
Kol mevaser, Odessa
Kosa, St. Petersburg
Kunst un lebn, Warsaw
Dos lebn, St. Petersburg
Leshii, St. Petersburg
Literarishe bleter, Warsaw
Der lodzer togblat, Lodz
El luzero, New York
Maskii, St. Petersburg
Mefistofel, St. Petersburg
Moi pulement, St. Petersburg
Der moment, Warsaw
Der morgen zhurnal, New York
Der morgenblat, Warsaw
Moskovskii listok, Moscow
Dos naye lebn, New York
Di naye tsayt, St. Petersburg
Di naye tsaytung, Warsaw
Niva, St. Petersburg
Nov, St. Petersburg
Novelista, Izmir
Novoe vremia, St. Petersburg
La nueva el avenir, Salonika
La nueva epoka, Salonika
Ovod, St. Petersburg
Pchela, St. Petersburg
Peterburgskii listok, St. Petersburg
Piatnitsa, St. Petersburg
Piatsii, St. Petersburg
Puertas del oriente, Izmir
Razsvet, St. Petersburg
Rech, St. Petersburg
La revista popular, Salonika
El rizon, Salonika
Russkoe slovo, St. Petersburg
Satira, St. Petersburg
Sekira, St. Petersburg
Serii volk, St. Petersburg
Der sheygets, St. Petersburg
Dos shtik, St. Petersburg
Shuta, St. Petersburg
Signal, St. Petersburg
El sol, Constantinople

Sotziale demokrat, Lemberg
Sprut, St. Petersburg
Svet, St. Petersburg
Svitaet, St. Petersburg
Svoboda, Warsaw
Teater velt, Warsaw
Der telegraf, Warsaw
El telegrafo, Constantinople
El tiempo, Constantinople
Der tog, St. Petersburg, New York
Der togblat, Lemberg
La tribuna libra, Salonika
Udav, St. Petersburg
Unzer lebn, Warsaw
Unzer tsayt, Warsaw
La vara, Cairo
Der veg, Warsaw
Der veker, Vilna
La verdad, Salonika
Vogaborot, St. Petersburg
Dos vokhenblat, Warsaw
Voskhod, St. Petersburg
Dos yidishe folksblat, St. Petersburg
Dos yidishe togblat, Warsaw
Di yidishe velt, Warsaw
Der yidisher arbayter, Vilna
Yontev bletlekh, Warsaw
Der yud, Warsaw
Zabiyaka, St. Petersburg
Zhurnal Zhurnalov, St. Petersburg

LIBRARIES AND ARCHIVAL COLLECTIONS

Ben Zvi Institute, Jerusalem
Hoover Library, Stanford University
National and University Library, Jerusalem
New York Public Library, Judaica Collection
Stanford University Libraries
Weidner Library, Harvard University
YIVO Institute for Jewish Research, New York

SECONDARY SOURCES CONSULTED

Abramowicz, Dina. "On the Beginnings of Yiddish Children's Literature." *Judaica-Librarianship* 3, no. 1–2 (1986): 68–70.
Abramsky, Chimen, Maciej Jachimczyk, and Antony Polonsky, eds. *The Jews in Poland.* Oxford: Oxford University Press, 1986.
Abramson, Henry. *A Prayer for the Government: Ukrainians and Jews in Revolutionary Times, 1917–1920.* Cambridge, Mass.: Harvard University Press for the Ukrainian Research Institute and Center for Jewish Studies, Harvard University, 1999.
Abu-Lughod, Janet Lippman. "The World System in the Thirteenth Century: Dead-

End or Precursor?" In *Islamic and European Expansion: The Forging of a Global Order,* edited by Michael Adas, 75–102. Philadelphia: Temple University Press, 1993.

Adanir, Fikret. "Armenian Deportations and Massacres in 1915." In *Ethnopolitical Warfare: Causes, Consequences, and Possible Solutions,* edited by D. Chirot and M. Seligman, 71–82. Washington, D.C.: Psychological Association, 2001.

Adas, Michael. "Bringing Ideas and Agency Back In: Representation and the Comparative Approach to World History." In *World History: Ideologies, Structures, and Identities,* edited by Richard H. Elphick, Philip Pomper, and Richard T. Vann, 81–104. Oxford: Blackwell Publishers, 1998.

Afanas'ev, A. N. [Aleksandr Nikolaevich]. *Russkie satiricheskie zhurnaly 1769–1774.* Kazan: Molodyia sily, 1920.

Agulhon, Maurice. *Marianne into Battle: Republican Imagery and Symbolism in France, 1870–1880.* Cambridge: Cambridge University Press, 1981.

Ahmad, Feroz. *The Making of Modern Turkey.* London and New York: Routledge, 1993.

———. "Unionist Relations with the Greek, Armenian, and Jewish Communities of the Ottoman Empire, 1908–1914." In *Christians and Jews in the Ottoman Empire: The Functioning of a Plural Society,* edited by Benjamin Braude and Bernard Lewis, 425–28. New York: Holmes & Meier, 1982.

Aivazian, Gia. "The Role of the Armenian Press in Istanbul, 1908–1915 in the Shaping of the Armenian National Identity." Paper presented at the Middle East Studies Association, San Francisco, 1997.

Akarli, Engin Deniz. *The Long Peace: Ottoman Lebanon, 1861–1920.* Berkeley: University of California Press, 1993.

Aksan, Virginia. "Locating the Ottomans among Early Modern Empires." *Journal of Early Modern History* 3, no. 2 (1999): 103–34.

Alcalay, Ammiel. *After Jews and Arabs: Remaking Levantine Culture.* Minneapolis: University of Minnesota Press, 1993.

Alloula, Malek. *The Colonial Harem.* Minneapolis: University of Minnesota Press, 1986.

Altabe, David. "The Romanso, 1900–1932: A Bibliographical Survey." *The Sephardic Scholar* 3 (1977–78): 96–106.

Anderson, Benedict. *Imagined Communities: Reflections on the Origin and Spread of Nationalism.* New York: Verso Press, 1983.

Angas, George French. *The Kafirs illustrated in a series of drawings taken among the Amazulu, Amaponda, and Amakosa tribes: also, portraits of the Hottentot, Malay, Fingo, and other races inhabiting southern Africa: together with sketches of landscape scenery in the Zulu country, Natal, and the Cape Colony.* London: J. Hogarth, 1849.

Angel, Marc. *La America: The Sephardic Experience in the United States.* 1st ed. Philadelphia: Jewish Publication Society of America, 1982.

———. *The Sephardim of the United States: An Exploratory Study.* New York: Union of Sephardic Congregations, 1974.

Ansky, Michel. *Les Juifs d'Algerie du décret Crémieux à la libération.* Paris: Éditions du Centre, 1950.

An-sky, S. "The Destruction of Galicia: Excerpts from a Diary, 1914–1917." In *The Dybbuk and Other Writings,* edited by David Roskies, 169–208. New York: Random House, 1986.

———. "Mendl Turk." In *The Dybbuk and Other Writings,* edited by David Roskies, 93–117. New York: Random House, 1986.

———. "Pogromnye vpechatleniia." In *Sobranie sochinenii,* 221–45. St. Petersburg: T-vo prosviashchenie, 1911.

Ascher, Abraham. *The Revolution of 1905.* 2 vols. Stanford, Calif.: Stanford University Press, 1988.

Astruc, Kalev. "Data Concerning the Demographic Situation of the Bulgarian Jews, 1887–1949." *Annual* 16 (1981): 85–96.

Ayalon, Ami. *The Press in the Arab Middle East: A History.* Oxford: Oxford University Press, 1995.

Babel, Isaac. *1920 Diary.* Translated by H. T. Willetts. Edited by Carol J. Avins. New Haven, Conn.: Yale University Press, 1995.

Bacon, Gershon. *The Politics of Tradition: Agudat Yisrael in Poland, 1916–1939.* Jerusalem: Magnes Press, 1996.

Bader, Gershom. "Dray momentn in der antviklung fun der yidisher prese in poyln." *Polish Jew, Eleventh Year Book* (1944): 60–62.

Bahloul, Jöelle. "The Sephardi Family and the Challenge of Assimilation: Family Ritual and Ethnic Reproduction." In *Sephardi and Middle Eastern Jewries: History and Culture in the Modern Era,* edited by Harvey E. Goldberg, 312–24. Bloomington: Indiana University Press, 1996.

Baigell, Matthew, and Milly Heyd, eds. *Complex Identities: Jewish Consciousness and Modern Art.* New Brunswick, N.J.: Rutgers University Press, 2001.

Baker, Mark. "The Voice of the Deserted Jewish Women, 1867–1870." *Jewish Social Studies* 2, no. 1 (1995): 98–124.

Bal Makhshoves [Isador Eliashev]. "Notitsn fun a kritik." *Kunst un lebn,* no. 1 (June 1908): 49–54.

———. "Pogrom Literature." In *Geklibene shriftn,* 167–74. Vilna: S. Sreberk, 1910.

Bali, Rifat N. "A Bibliography of Works on Journalism and Book Printing in the Ottoman Empire." In *Jewish Journalism and Printing Houses in the Ottoman Empire and Modern Turkey,* edited by Gad Nassi, 115–31. Istanbul: Isis Press, 2001.

———. *Cumhuriyet yillarinda Türkiye Yahudileri: bir Türklestirme serüveni (1923–1945).* Istanbul: Iletisim, 1999.

Balin, Carole B. *To Reveal Our Hearts: Jewish Women Writers in Tsarist Russia.* Cincinnati: HUC Press, 2000.

Barkey, Karen, and Mark Von Hagen. *After Empire: Multiethnic Societies and Nation-Building, the Soviet Union and the Russian, Ottoman, and Habsburg Empires.* Boulder, Colo.: Westview Press, 1997.

Barkhatova, Elena. "Pictorialism: Photography as Art." In *Photography in Russia 1840–1940,* edited by David Elliott, 51–61. London: Thames and Hudson, 1992.

———. "Realism and Document: Photography as Fact." In *Photography in Russia 1840–1940,* edited by David Elliott. London: Thames and Hudson, 1992.

Barnai, Jacob. "On the History of the Jews in the Ottoman Empire." In *Sephardi Jews in the Ottoman Empire: Aspects of Material Culture,* edited by Esther Juhasz, 18–35. Jerusalem: Israel Museum, 1990.

Baron, Salo. *The Russian Jew under Tsars and Soviets.* New York: Macmillan, 1987.

Barsoumian, Hagop. "The Dual Role of the Armenian *Amira* Class within the Ottoman Government and the Armenian *Millet* (1750–1850)." In *Christians and Jews in the Ottoman Empire: The Functioning of a Plural Society,* edited by Benjamin Braude and Bernard Lewis, 171–84. New York: Holmes & Meier, 1982.

Barth, Gunther. "Metropolitan Press." In *City People: The Rise of Modern City Culture in Nineteenth-Century America.* New York: Oxford University Press, 1980.

Bartoszewski, Wladyslaw, and Antony Polonsky, eds. *The Jews in Warsaw: A History.* Oxford: Basil Blackwell, 1991.

Bass, Hyman, ed. *Pinkes far der forshung fun der yidisher literatur un prese.* 3 vols. New York: Alveltlekher yidisher kultur-kongres, 1965–72.

Bassin, Mark. *Imperial Visions: Nationalist Imagination and Geographical Expansion in the Russian Far East, 1840–1865.* Cambridge: Cambridge University Press, 1999.

Bayrak, M. Orhan. *Türkiye'de gazeteler ve dergiler sözlügü, 1831–1993.* Istanbul: KUll Yayinlari, 1994.

Beinin, Joel. *The Dispersion of Egyptian Jewry: Culture, Politics, and the Formation of a Modern Diaspora.* Berkeley: University of California Press, 1997.

Benbanaste, Nesim. *Örneklerle Türk Musevi basininin tarihçesi.* Istanbul: N. Benbanaste, 1988.

Benbassa, Esther. "Comment Être non-musulman en terre d'islam." *l'Histoire* 134 (June 1990): 86–91.

———. *Une diaspora sépharade en transition. Istanbul XIXᵉ–XXᵉ siècles.* Paris: Cerf, 1993.

———. "L'éducation féminine en Orient: l'école des filles de l'alliance Israélite universelle à Galata, Istanbul (1879–1912)." *Histoire, économie, et société* 4 (1991): 529–59.

———. "Education for Jewish Girls in the East: A Portrait of the Galata School in Istanbul, 1879–1912." *Studies in Contemporary Jewry* 9 (1993): 163–73.

———. *Haim Nahum: A Sephardic Chief Rabbi in Politics, 1892–1923.* Tuscaloosa: University of Alabama Press, 1995.

———. "Modernization of Eastern Sephardi Communities." In *Sephardi and Middle Eastern Jewries: History and Culture in the Modern Era,* edited by Harvey E. Goldberg, 89–99. Bloomington: Indiana University Press, 1996.

———. "Presse d'Istanbul et de Salonique au service du sionisme, les motifs d'une allégeance (1908–1914)." *Revue historique* 560 (1986): 337–67.

———, and Aron Rodrigue. "L'artisanat juif en Turquie à la fin du XIXᵉ siècle: l'Alliance Israélite universelle et ses oeuvres d'apprentissage." *Turcica* 17 (1985): 113–26.

———. *Jews of the Balkans: The Judeo-Spanish Community, Fifteenth to Twentieth Century.* Oxford: Blackwell, 1995.

———. *Sephardi Jewry: A History of the Judeo-Spanish Community, 14th–20th Centuries.* Berkeley: University of California Press, 2000.

———. *A Sephardi Life in Southeastern Europe: The Autobiography and Journal of Gabriel Arié, 1863–1939.* Seattle: University of Washington Press, 1998.

Ben-Naeh, Yaron. "Hebrew Printing Houses in the Ottoman Empire." In *Jewish Journalism and Printing Houses in the Ottoman Empire and Modern Turkey,* edited by Gad Nassi, 73–96. Istanbul: Isis Press, 2001.

Ben-Ur, Aviva. "Ladino in Print: Towards a Comprehensive Bibliography." *Jewish History* 6, no. 3 (2002): 309–26.

———. "The Ladino (Judeo-Spanish) Press in the United States, 1910–1948." In *Multilingual America: Transnationalism, Ethnicity, and the Languages of American Literature,* edited by Werner Sollors, 64–77. New York: New York University Press, 1998.

———. "Where Diasporas Met: Sephardic and Ashkenazic Jews in the City of New York—A Study in Intra-ethnic Relations, 1880–1950." Ph.D. dissertation, Brandeis University, 1998.

Benvenisti, David. " 'El Pueblo,' the First Jewish Marxist Newspaper in Bulgaria (1902–1903)." *Annual, Social, Cultural and Educational Organization of the Jews in the People's Republic of Bulgaria* VIII (1978): 209–33.

Berkowitz, Joel. "The 'Mendel Beilis Epidemic' on the Yiddish Stage." *Jewish Social Studies* 8, no. 1 (2002): 199–225.

Berkowitz, Michael. "Art in Zionist Popular Culture and Jewish National Self-Consciousness, 1897–1914." In *Studies in Contemporary Jewry, an Annual,* edited by Ezra Mendelsohn and Richard I. Cohen, 9–42. Oxford: Oxford University Press, 1990.

————. *The Jewish Self-Image in the West.* New York: New York University Press, 2000.

Betz, Margaret Bridget. "The Caricatures and Cartoons of the 1905 Revolution: Images of the Opposition." Ph.D. dissertation, City University of New York, 1984.

Bhabha, Homi. "Of Mimicry and Man: The Ambivalence of Colonial Discourse." *October* 28 (1984): 125–33.

————. "Signs Taken for Wonders: Questions of Ambivalence and Authority under a Tree Outside Delhi, May 1817." In *The Location of Culture*, 102–23. New York: Routledge, 1994.

Biale, David. "Childhood, Marriage and the Family in the Eastern European Jewish Enlightenment." In *The Jewish Family: Myths and Reality*, edited by Steven Cohen and Paula Hyman, 45–61. New York: Holmes & Meier, 1986.

Bildiriler, Türk Kütüphaneciler Dernegi basim ve yayinciligimizin 250, no. 2. Ankara: Türk Kütüphaneciler Dernegi, 1979.

Birnbaum, Pierre, and Ira Katznelson, eds. *Paths of Emancipation: Jews, States, and Citizenship.* Princeton, N.J.: Princeton University Press, 1995.

Blackwell, William L. *The Beginnings of Russian Industrialization, 1800–1860.* Princeton, N.J.: Princeton University Press, 1968.

Blobaum, Robert E. *Rewolucja: Russian Poland, 1904–1907.* Ithaca, N.Y.: Cornell University Press, 1995.

Bonnell, Victoria. *Roots of Rebellion: Workers' Politics and Organizations in St. Petersburg and Moscow, 1900–1914.* Berkeley: University of California Press, 1983.

Bornes-Varol, Marie-Christine. "The Balat Quarter and Its Image: A Study of a Jewish Neighborhood in Istanbul." In *The Jews of the Ottoman Empire*, edited by Avigdor Levy, 633–46. Princeton, N.J.: Darwin Press, 1994.

Borovaia, Olga V. "The Role of Translation in Shaping the Ladino Novel at the Time of Westernization in the Ottoman Empire." *Jewish History* 16, no. 3 (2002): 263–82.

————. "Translation and Westernization: *Gulliver's Travels* in Ladino." *Jewish Social Studies* 7, no. 2 (2001): 149–68.

Bosworth, C. E. "The Concept of Dhimma in Early Islam." In *Christians and Jews in the Ottoman Empire: The Functioning of a Plural Society*, edited by Benjamin Braude and Bernard Lewis, 37–55. New York: Holmes & Meier, 1982.

Botsiavnovskii, Vladimir, and E. F. Gollerbakh, eds. *Russkaia satira pervoi revoliutsii 1905–1906.* Leningrad: Gosudarstvennoe izdatel'stvo, 1925.

Bowlt, John E. "Jewish Artists and the Russian Silver Age." In *Russian Jewish Artists in a Century of Change*, edited by Susan Tumarkin Goodman. New York: Prestel, 1995.

————. *The Silver Age: Russian Art of the Early Twentieth Century and the "World of Art" Group.* Newtonville, Mass.: Oriental Research Partners, 1979.

Bozdogan, Sibel, and Reşat Kasaba, eds. *Rethinking Modernity and National Identity in Turkey.* Seattle: University of Washington Press, 1997.

Brantlinger, Patrick. *Bread and Circuses: Theories of Mass Culture as Social Decay.* Ithaca, N.Y.: Cornell University Press, 1983.

Braude, Benjamin. "The Cloth Industry of Salonika in the Mediterranean Economy." *Pe'amim* 15 (1983): 82–95.

————. "International Competition and Domestic Cloth in the Ottoman Empire, 1500–1650: A Study in Underdevelopment." *Review* 2 (1979): 437–51.

————. "The Rise and Fall of Salonika Woollens, 1500–1650: Technology Transfer and Western Competition." *Mediterranean Historical Review* 6, no. 2 (1991): 519–42.

Braude, Benjamin, and Bernard Lewis, eds. *Christians and Jews in the Ottoman Empire: The Functioning of a Plural Society.* 2 vols. New York: Holmes & Meier, 1982.

Bronner, Simon. "Reading Consumer Culture." In *Consuming Visions: Accumulation and Display of Goods in America 1880–1920,* edited by Simon Bronner, 13–55. New York: Norton, 1989.

Brooks, Jeffrey. *Thank You, Comrade Stalin! Soviet Public Culture from Revolution to Cold War.* Princeton, N.J.: Princeton University Press, 2000.

———. *When Russia Learned to Read: Literacy and Popular Literature, 1861–1917.* Princeton, N.J.: Princeton University Press, 1985.

Brower, Daniel R., and Edward Lazzerini, eds. *Russia's Orient: Imperial Borderlands and Peoples, 1700–1917.* Bloomington: Indiana University Press, 1997.

Brubaker, Rogers. "Aftermaths of Empire and the Unmixing of Peoples." In *After Empire: Multiethnic Societies and Nation-Building — The Soviet Union and Russian, Ottoman, and Habsburg Empires,* edited by Mark Von Hagen and Karen Barkey, 155–80. Oxford: Westview Press, 1997.

Brummett, Palmira. "Dogs, Women, Cholera, and Other Menaces in the Streets: Cartoon Satire in the Ottoman Revolutionary Press, 1908–11." *International Journal of Middle East Studies* 27 (1995): 433–60.

———. *Image and Imperialism in the Ottoman Revolutionary Press, 1908–1911.* Albany: State University of New York Press, 2000.

Buloff, Joseph. *In the Old Marketplace.* Cambridge, Mass.: Harvard University Press, 1991.

Bunis, David M. "Modernization and the Language Question among Judezmo-Speaking Sephardim of the Ottoman Empire." In *Sephardi and Middle Eastern Jewries: History and Culture in the Modern Era,* edited by Harvey E. Goldberg, 226–39. Bloomington: Indiana University Press, 1996.

———. *Sephardic Studies: A Research Bibliography Incorporating Judezmo Language, Literature, and Folklore, and Historical Background.* Vol. 174. New York: Garland Publishers, 1981.

———. *Voices from Jewish Salonika: Selections from the Judezmo Satirical Series Tio Ezrá I Su Mujer Benuta and Tio Bohor I Su Mujer Djamila.* Jerusalem: Misgav Yerushalayim, 1999.

Burke, Timothy. *Lifebuoy Men, Lux Women: Commodification, Consumption, and Cleanliness in Modern Zimbabwe.* Durham, N.C., and London: Duke University Press, 1996.

Bushnell, John. *Mutiny amid Repression: Russian Soldiers in the Revolution of 1905–1906.* Bloomington: Indiana University Press, 1985.

Busse, Winfried. "Le Judeo-Espagnol — Un Jargon?" In *Hommage à Haim Vidal Sephiha,* edited by Winfried Busse and Marie-Christine Varol-Bornes, 239–46. Berne: Peter Lang, 1996.

Campos, Michelle. "A 'Shared Homeland' and Its Boundaries: Late Ottoman Palestine between Imperial Commitment and Communal Identification, 1908–1914." Ph.D. dissertation, Stanford University, 2003.

Canetti, Elias. *The Tongue Set Free: Remembrance of a European Childhood.* Translated by Joachim Neugroschel. New York: Seabury Press, 1979.

Çelik, Zeynep. *The Remaking of Istanbul: Portrait of an Ottoman City in the Nineteenth Century.* Seattle: University of Washington Press, 1986.

Çetin, A. Alâaddin. *Basbakanlik Arsivi Kilavuzu.* Istanbul: Enderun Kitabevi, 1979.

Clogg, Richard. "The Greek *Millet* in the Ottoman Empire." In *Christians and Jews in the Ottoman Empire: The Functioning of a Plural Society,* edited by Benjamin Braude and Bernard Lewis, 185–208. New York: Holmes & Meier, 1982.

Cohen, Amnon, and Elisheva Pikali. *Jews in the Moslem Religious Court: Society, Economy, and Communal Organization in the XVIth Century.* Jerusalem: Ben-Zvi Institute, 1993.

Cohen, Israel. *Vilna.* Philadelphia: Jewish Publication Society, 1992.

Cohen, Mark R. "Islam and the Jews: Myth, Counter-Myth, History." *Jerusalem Quarterly*, no. 38 (1986): 125–37.

———. "The Neo-Lachrymose Conception of Jewish-Arab History." *Tikkun* 6 (May–June 1991): 55–60.

———. *Under Crescent and Cross*. Princeton, N.J.: Princeton University Press, 1994.

Cohen, Richard. *Jewish Icons: Art and Society in Modern Europe*. Berkeley: University of California Press, 1998.

Corbin, Alain. *The Foul and the Fragrant: Odor and the French Social Imagination*. Cambridge, Mass.: Harvard University Press, 1986.

Corrsin, Stephen D. "Aspects of Population Change and Acculturation in Jewish Warsaw at the End of the Nineteenth Century: The Censuses of 1882 and 1897." In *The Jews in Warsaw: A History*, edited by Wladyslaw Bartoszewski and Antony Polonsky, 212–31. Oxford: Basil Blackwell, 1991.

———. "Language Use in Cultural and Political Change in Pre-1914 Warsaw: Poles, Jews, and Russification." *Slavonic and East European Review* 68, no. 1 (1990): 69–90.

———. *Warsaw before the First World War: Poles and Jews in the Third City of the Russian Empire 1880–1914*. Boulder: East European Monographs, Distributed by Columbia University Press, 1989.

Crisp, Olga. *Studies in Russian Economy before 1914*. Studies in Russian and East European History. New York: Barnes & Noble Books, 1976.

———, and Linda Edmondson, eds. *Civil Rights in Imperial Russia*. Oxford and New York: Clarendon Press, Oxford University Press, 1989.

Csergo, Julia. *Liberté, égalité, propreté: la morale de l'hygiène au XIXᵉ Siècle*. Paris: Albin Michel, 1988.

Davey, Richard. *The Sultan and His People*. London: Chapman and Hall, 1897.

Davis, Natalie Zemon. "Printing and the People." In *Society and Culture in Early Modern France*, 189–227. Stanford, Calif.: Stanford University Press, 1975.

Davison, Roderic. "The Armenian Crisis, 1912–1914." *American Historical Review* 53, no. 3 (1948): 481–505.

———. "Nationalism as an Ottoman Problem and the Ottoman Response." In *Nationalism in a Non-National State, the Dissolution of the Ottoman Empire*, edited by William Haddad and W. Ochsenwald, 25–56. Columbus: Ohio State University Press, 1977.

———. *Reform in the Ottoman Empire 1856–1876*. Princeton, N.J.: Princeton University Press, 1963.

Dawn, C. Ernest. *From Ottomanism to Arabism: Essays on the Origins of Arab Nationalism*. Urbana and Chicago: University of Illinois Press, 1973.

Deák, Istvan. *Beyond Nationalism: A Social and Political History of the Habsburg Officer Corps 1848–1918*. New York: Oxford University Press, 1990.

Demchenko, E. P. [Evgeniia Petrovna]. *Politicheskaia grafika Kieva, perioda revoliutsii, 1905–1907*. Kiev: Haukova dumka, 1976.

———. *Politicheskaia grafika v pechati Ukrainy, 1905–1907*. Kiev: Naukova dumka, 1984.

Diaz Mas, Paloma. *Sephardim: The Jews from Spain*. Chicago: University of Chicago Press, 1992.

Dimakis, John. "The Greek Press." In *Greece in Transition: Essays in the History of Modern Greece, 1821–1974*, edited by John T. A. Koumoulides. London: Zeno, 1977.

Dobroszycki, Lucjan. "The Fertility of Modern Polish Jewry." In *Modern Jewish Fertility*, edited by Paul Ritterband, 64–77. Leiden: E. J. Brill, 1981.

———. "YIVO in Interwar Poland: Work in the Historical Sciences." In *The Jews of Poland between Two World Wars*, edited by Yisrael Gutman, Ezra Mendelsohn,

Jehuda Reinharz, and Chone Shmeruk, 494–518. Hanover, N.H.: University Press of New England, 1989.

———, and Barbara Kirshenblatt-Gimblett. *Image before My Eyes: A Photographic History of Jewish Life in Poland, 1864–1939.* New York: Schocken Books, 1977.

Doumani, Beshara. *Rediscovering Palestine.* Berkeley: University of California Press, 1995.

Doyle, Michael. *Empires.* Ithaca, N.Y.: Cornell University Press, 1986.

Druk, Dovid. *Tsu der geshikhte fun der yidisher prese in rusland un poylen.* Varshe: Farlag zikhroynes, 1920.

Dubin, Lois. *The Port Jews of Habsburg Trieste: Absolutist Politics and Enlightenment Culture.* Stanford, Calif.: Stanford University Press, 2000.

Dubnov, Shimen. *Fun "zhargon" tsu yidish: un andere artiklen: literarishe zikhroynes.* Vilna: B. Kletskin, 1929.

———, Baron David Ginzburg, Albert Harkavy, and Lev Katznelson, eds. *Evreiskaia entsiklopediia.* 16 vols. St. Petersburg: Obshchestva dlia nauchnykh evreiskikh izdanii, 1908–13.

Dubnov-Erlich, Sophie. *The Life and Works of S. M. Dubnov: Diaspora Nationalism and Jewish History.* Bloomington: Indiana University Press, 1991.

Duls'kii, P. M. *Grafika satiricheskikh zhurnalov 1905–1906.* Kazan: Izdanie Tatgosizdata, 1922.

Duman, Hasan. *Istanbul kütüphaneleri arap harfli süreli yayinlari toplu katalogu, 1828–1928, Bibliographical Series/Research Centre for Islamic History, Art, and Culture; 3.* Besiktas, Istanbul: Islâm Tarih, Sanat, ve Kültür Arastirma Merkezi, Islâm Konferansi Teskilâti, 1986.

Dumont, Paul. "Le Français d'abord." In *Salonique, 1850–1918: La 'ville des juifs' et le revéil des Balkans,* edited by Gilles Veinstein, 208–27. Paris: Editions Autrement, 1992.

———. "Jewish Communities in Turkey during the Last Decades of the Nineteenth Century in Light of the Archives of the Alliance Israélite Universelle." In *Christians and Jews in the Ottoman Empire: The Functioning of a Plural Society,* edited by Benjamin Braude and Bernard Lewis, 209–42. New York: Holmes & Meier, 1982.

———. "Jews, Muslims, and Cholera: Intercommunal Relations in Baghdad at the End of the Nineteenth Century." In *The Jews of the Ottoman Empire,* edited by Avigdor Levy, 353–72. Princeton, N.J.: Darwin Press, 1994.

———. "Un organe sioniste à Istanbul, la nation (1919–1920)." In *Türkiye'de yabanci dilde basin,* 189–225. Istanbul: Istanbul Universitesi, 1985.

———. "La structure sociale de la communauté juive de Salonique à la fin du XIXe siècle." *Revue historique* 263 (April–June 1980): 351–410.

Eck, Nathan. "The Educational Institutions of Polish Jewry (1921–1939)." *Jewish Social Studies* IX, no. I (1947): 3–32.

Edmondson, Linda, and Peter Waldron, eds. *Economy and Society in Russia and the Soviet Union, 1860–1930: Essays for Olga Crisp.* Edited by Linda Edmondson and Peter Waldron. New York: St. Martin's Press; Basingstoke: Macmillan, 1992.

Efron, John. *Defenders of the Race: Jewish Doctors and Race Science in Fin-de-Siècle Europe.* New Haven, Conn.: Yale University Press, 1994.

Eldem, Edhem, Daniel Goffman, and Bruce Masters, eds. *The Ottoman City between East and West: Aleppo, Izmir, and Istanbul.* Cambridge: Cambridge University Press, 1999.

Eliashevich, D. A. *Evrei v Rossii: istoriia i kultura: sbornik nauchnykh trudov. Istoriia i etnografiia.* St. Petersburg: Peterburgskii evreiskii un-t, 1998.

———. *Pravitel'stvennaia politika i evreiskaia pechat' v Rossii, 1797–1917: Ocherki istorii tsenzury.* St. Petersburg and Jerusalem: Mosty kultury, Gesharim, 1999.

Elliott, David. *Photography in Russia, 1840–1940.* London: Thames and Hudson, 1992.

Elmaleh, Abraham. "Hasifrut veha'itonut haespanoliot." *Hashiloah* 26, no. 1 (1912): 67–73, 253–60.

Engelstein, Laura. *The Keys to Happiness: Sex and the Search for Modernity in Fin-de-Siècle Russia.* Ithaca, N.Y.: Cornell University Press, 1992.

———. *Moscow, 1905: Working-Class Organization and Political Conflict.* Stanford, Calif.: Stanford University Press, 1982.

Epstein, Miriam. *Jewish Schools in Poland 1919–1939.* New York: King's Crown Press, 1950.

Etkes, Imanuel, ed. *Hadat vehahayim: tenuat hahaskala hayehudit bemizrah eropa.* Jerusalem: Merkaz Zalman Shazar le-toldot Yisra'el, 1993.

Faroqhi, Suraiya, Bruce McGowan, Donald Quataert, and Sevket Pamuk. *An Economic and Social History of the Ottoman Empire.* 2 vols. Cambridge: Cambridge University Press, 1994.

Fawaz, Leila Tarazi, and C. A. Bayly, eds. *Modernity and Culture from the Mediterranean to the Indian Ocean.* New York: Columbia University Press, 2002.

Feiwel, Berthold, ed. *Die Judenmassacres in Kischinew.* Berlin: Jüdischer Verlag, 1903.

Feldman, Eliyahu. *Yehude rusya biyeme hamapekha harishona vehapogromim.* Jerusalem: Magnes Press, Hebrew University, 1999.

Fesch, Paul. "La presse et la censure." In *Constantinople aux derniers jours d'Abdul-Hamid,* 29–70. Paris: M Rivière, 1907.

Findley, Carter V. "The Acid Test of Ottomanism: The Acceptance of Non-Muslims in the Late Ottoman Bureaucracy." In *Christians and Jews in the Ottoman Empire: The Functioning of a Plural Society,* edited by Benjamin Braude and Bernard Lewis, 339–68. New York: Holmes & Meier, 1982.

Finkelstein, Haim. "Haynt'-a tsaytung bay yidn." In *Di yidishe prese vos iz geven,* edited by Dovid Flinker, Mordechai Tsanin, and Sholem Rosenfeld, 34–52. Tel Aviv: Veltfarband fun di yidishe zhurnalistn, 1975.

Fishman, David E. "The Politics of Yiddish in Tsarist Russia." In *From Ancient Israel to Modern Judaism: Intellect in Quest of Understanding — Essays in Honor of Marvin Fox,* vol. 4: *The Modern Age: Theology, Literature, History,* edited by Jacob Neusner, Ernest Frerichs, and Nahum Sarna, 155–73. Atlanta: Scholars Press, 1989.

———. *Russia's First Modern Jews: The Jews of Shklov.* New York: New York University Press, 1995.

Fishman, Joshua. "The First World Conference for Yiddish, 85 Years Later." In *The Earliest Stage of Language Planning: The "First Congress" Phenomenon,* edited by Joshua Fishman, 321–32. New York: Mouton de Gruyter, 1993.

———. *Never Say Die! A Thousand Years of Yiddish in Jewish Life and Letters.* New York: Mouton Press, 1981.

———, ed. *Studies on Polish Jewry, 1919–1939: The Interplay of Social, Economic, and Political Factors in the Struggle of a Minority for Its Existence.* New York: YIVO Institute, 1974.

———. *Yiddish: Turning to Life.* New York: John Benjamin's Publishing Co., 1991.

FitzLyon, Kyril, and Tatiana Browning. *Before the Revolution: A View of Russia under the Last Tsar.* London: Allen Lane, 1977.

Fitzpatrick, Anne Lincoln. *The Great Russian Fair: Nizhnii Novgorod, 1840–90.* New York: St. Martin's Press, 1990.

Flinker, David, and Moshe Ron. "Di yidishe prese in poyln tsvishn beyde velt-milkhomes." In *Yorbukh,* edited by Arye Tartakover, 266–325. New York: Velt federatskye fun Poylishe-Yidn, 1967.

Franco, Moïse. *Essai sur l'histoire des Israélites de l'Empire ottoman depuis les origines jusqu'à nos jours.* Hildesheim and New York: Georg Olms Verlag, 1897 (reissued 1973).

Frank, Stephen P. *Crime, Cultural Conflict, and Justice in Rural Russia.* Berkeley: University of California Press, 1999.

Frankel, Jonathan. *The Damascus Affair: "Ritual Murder," Politics, and the Jews in 1840.* Cambridge: Cambridge University Press, 1997.

———. *Prophecy and Politics: Socialism, Nationalism, and the Russian Jews, 1862–1917.* Cambridge: Cambridge University Press, 1981.

Freeze, ChaeRan Y. *Jewish Marriage and Divorce in Imperial Russia.* Hanover, N.H.: University Press of New England for Brandeis University Press, 2002.

Freeze, Gregory. "The *Soslovie* (Estate) Paradigm and Russian Social History." *American Historical Review* 91, no. 1 (1986): 11–36.

Freidenreich, Harriet Pass. *The Jews of Yugoslavia: A Quest for Community.* Philadelphia: Jewish Publication Society, 1979.

Fresco, David. "Cinquante cinq années de journalisme juif." *Hamenora* XI, no. 5 (1930): 16–24.

———, ed. *Numéro spécial, à l'occasion du 50me anniversaire de journalisme de Monsieur David Fresco, El tiempo.* Constantinople: El tiempo, 1925.

Friedman, Phillip. "Polish Jewish Historiography between the Two World Wars (1919–1939)." *Jewish Social Studies* 11, no. 4 (1949): 373–408.

Frierson, Elizabeth Brown. "Unimagined Communities: State, Press, and Gender in the Hamidian Era." Ph.D. dissertation, Princeton University, 1996.

Fritzsche, Peter. *Reading Berlin, 1900.* Cambridge, Mass.: Harvard University Press, 1996.

"From Kishineff to Bialystok: A Tale of Pogroms from 1903–1906." In *American Jewish Year Book,* 34–69. Philadelphia: American Jewish Committee, 1906–1907.

Frost, Shimon. *Schooling as a Socio-political Expression: Jewish Education in Interwar Poland.* Jerusalem: Magnes Press, 1998.

Fuller, William C. "Civil–Military Conflict in the Russian Revolution, 1905–1907." In *Civil–Military Conflict in Imperial Russia, 1881–1914,* 129–68. Princeton, N.J.: Princeton University Press, 1985.

Galanté, Abraham. *Histoire des juifs de Turquie.* 9 vols. Istanbul: Isis, 1985.

———. *Histoire des juifs d'Istanbul depuis la prise de cette ville, en 1453.* Istanbul: Isis, 1935.

———. *La presse judéo-espagnole mondiale.* Istanbul: Société anonyme de papeterie et d'imprimerie (Fratelli Haim), 1935.

Gaon, Moshe David. *Haitonut beladino: bibliografia.* Jerusalem: Ben Zvi, 1965.

Garnett, Lucy. *Home Life in Turkey.* New York: Macmillan, 1909.

Garrett, Leah. "Trains and Train Travel in Modern Yiddish Literature." *Jewish Social Studies* 7, no. 2 (2001): 67–88.

Gassenschmidt, Cristoph. *Jewish Liberal Politics in Tsarist Russia, 1900–1914: The Modernization of Russian Jewry.* Oxford: Macmillan, 1995.

Gatrell, Peter. *The Tsarist Economy, 1850–1917.* London: Batsford, 1986.

Gelbart, Nina Rattner. *Feminine and Opposition Journalism in Old Regime France.* Berkeley: University of California Press, 1987.

Gelber, N. M. "An Attempt to Internationalize Salonika, 1912–1913." *Jewish Social Studies* 17, no. 2 (1955): 105–20.

Gellner, Ernest. *Nationalism.* New York: New York University Press, 1997.

Gerçek, Selim Nüzet. *Türk matbaaciligi.* Istanbul: Istanbul Devlet Basimevi, 1939.

Gilbert, Martin. *The Jews of Arab Lands: Their History in Maps.* London: Martin Gilbert and WOJAC (World Organization of Jews from Arab Countries), 1976.

Gilroy, Paul. *The Black Atlantic: Modernity and Double Consciousness.* Boston: Harvard University Press, 1993.

Ginio, Eyal. "Aspects of Muslim Culture in the Ottoman Balkans during the XVIII Century: A View from Salonika." Ph.D. dissertation (in Hebrew), Hebrew University, 1999.

———. "'Learning the Beautiful Language of Homer': Judeo-Spanish Speaking Jews and the Greek Language and Culture between the Wars." *Jewish History* 16, no. 3 (2002): 235–62.

———. "Mobilizing the Ottoman Nation during the Balkan Wars (1912–1913): Awakening from the Ottoman Dream." In *Coexistence and Conflict in Ottoman Society,* edited by Reşat Kasaba and Sarah Abrevaya Stein, forthcoming.

Ginzburg, Shoyl. *Historishe verk, fun yidishen leben un shafen in tsarishen rusland.* 3 vols. New York: Shoyl ginzburg shriftn-komitet, 1937.

Gitelman, Zvi. *A Century of Ambivalence: The Jews of Russia and the Soviet Union, 1881 to the Present.* Bloomington: Indiana University Press, 2001.

———. *Jewish Nationality and Soviet Politics.* Princeton, N.J.: Princeton University Press, 1972.

Goffman, Daniel. "Izmir: From Village to Colonial Port City." In *The Ottoman City between East and West,* edited by Daniel Goffman, Edhem Eldem, and Bruce Masters, 79–134. Cambridge: Cambridge University Press, 1999.

———. *Izmir and the Levantine World.* Seattle: University of Washington Press, 1990.

———. *The Ottoman Empire and Early Modern Europe.* Cambridge: Cambridge University Press, 2002.

Goldberg, Harvey E., ed. *Sephardi and Middle Eastern Jewries: History and Culture in the Modern Era.* Bloomington: Indiana University Press, 1996.

Goldberg, Sylvie Anne. *Crossing the Jabbok: Illness and Death in Ashkenazi Judaism in Sixteenth-through-Nineteenth-Century Prague.* Berkeley: University of California Press, 1996.

Goldenberg, Shlomo. "Hayesh korim 'evrim?" *Hashiloah* 17 (1907): 417–22.

Goldscheider, Calvin, and Alan S. Zuckerman. *The Transformation of the Jews.* Chicago: University of Chicago Press, 1984.

Goldshmidt, A. I. "Di yidishe prese in vilne tsayt der milkhome." In *Pinkes far der geshikhte fun vilne in di yorn fun milkhome un okupatsye,* edited by Zalman Reisen, 571–613. Vilna: Aroysgegebn fun der historish-etnografisher gezelshaft oyfn nomen fun sh. an-sky, 1922.

Goldsmith, Emanuel. *Modern Yiddish Culture: The Story of the Modern Yiddish Language Movement.* New York: Shapolsky Publishers, 1987.

Gomberg-Verzhbinskaia, E. P. [Eleonora Petrovna]. *Russkoe iskusstvo i revoliutsiia 1905 g. grafika, zhivopis'.* Leningrad: Izdatel'stvo Leningradskogo Universiteta, 1960.

Goodman, Susan Tumarkin, ed. *Russian Jewish Artists in a Century of Change, 1890–1990.* Munich and New York: Prestel, 1995.

Gothelf, Yehuda. "Di umgebrakhte yidishe prese." In *Di yidishe prese vos iz geven,* edited by Dovid Flinker, Mordechai Tsanin, and Sholem Rosenfeld, 15–16. Tel Aviv: Veltfarband fun di yidishe zhurnalistn, 1975.

Goubert, Jean-Pierre. *The Conquest of Water.* Translated by Andrew Wilson. Oxford: Polity Press, 1986.

"Gramotnost' evreev v Rossii." In *Evreiskaia entsiklopediia,* edited by Lev Izrailevich Katsnelson, David Baron Gunzburg, Shimen Dubnov, and Albert Harkavy, 756–59. St. Petersburg: Obshchestva dlia nauchnykh evreiskikh izdanii, 1908–13.

Greenblatt, Stephan. *Marvelous Possessions: The Wonder of the New World.* Chicago: University of Chicago Press, 1991.

Greenboym, Yitzhak. "Zikhroynes vegn 'haynt'." In *Di yidishe prese vos iz geven,* edited by Dovid Flinker, Mordechai Tsanin, and Sholem Rosenfeld, 17–33. Tel Aviv: Veltfarband fun di yidishe zhurnalistn, 1975.

Gross, Nachum, ed. *Economic History of the Jews.* New York: Schocken Books, 1975.

Gulalp, Haldun. "Modernization Policies and Islamist Politics in Turkey." In *Rethink-*

ing Modernity and National Identity in Turkey, edited by Sibel Bozdogan and Reşat Kasaba, 52–63. Seattle: University of Washington Press, 1997.

Gutman, Yisrael, Ezra Mendelsohn, Jehuda Reinharz, and Chone Shmeruk, eds. *The Jews of Poland between Two World Wars.* Hanover, N.H.: University Press of New England for Brandeis University Press, 1989.

Haberer, Erich. "Cosmopolitanism, Antisemitism, and Populism: A Reappraisal of the Russian and Jewish Socialist Response to the Pogroms of 1881–1882." In *Pogroms: Anti-Jewish Violence in Modern Russian History,* edited by John D. Klier and Shlomo Lambroza, 62–97. Cambridge: Cambridge University Press, 1992.

Habermas, Jurgen. *The Structural Transformation of the Public Sphere: An Inquiry into a Category of Bourgeois Society.* Translated by Thomas Burger. Cambridge, Mass.: MIT Press, 1992.

HaCohen, Dov. "Hadafus haivri beizmir." *Kiryat hasefer* 64, no. 4 (1992): 1403–23.

Haddad, William. "Nationalism in the Ottoman Empire." In *Nationalism in a Non-National State: The Dissolution of the Ottoman Empire,* edited by William Haddad and W. Ochsenwald, 3–24. Columbus: Ohio State University Press, 1977.

———, and W. Ochsenwald. *Nationalism in a Non-National State: The Dissolution of the Ottoman Empire.* Columbus: Ohio State University Press, 1977.

Halkin, Hillel, ed. *Tevye the Dairyman and the Railroad Stories.* New York: Schocken Books, 1987.

Hanioglu, M. Sukru. "Jews in the Young Turk Movement to the 1908 Revolution." In *The Jews of the Ottoman Empire,* edited by Avigdor Levy, 519–26. Princeton, N.J.: Darwin Press, 1994.

———. *The Young Turks in Opposition.* New York: Oxford University Press, 1995.

Harris, Tracy K. *Death of a Language: The History of Judeo-Spanish.* Newark, N.J.: Associated University Press, 1994.

Harshav, Benjamin. *Language in Time of Revolution.* Berkeley: University of California Press, 1993.

———. *The Meaning of Yiddish.* Berkeley: University of California Press, 1990.

Hart, Mitchell. "Moses the Microbiologist: Judaism and Social Hygiene in the Work of Alfred Nossig." *Journal of Jewish Social Studies* 11, no. 2 (1995): 72–99.

———. *Social Science and the Politics of Modern Jewish Identity.* Stanford, Calif.: Stanford University Press, 2000.

Hassan, Iacob. "El estudio del periodismo sefard." *Sefarad* 26 (1988): 229–36.

———. "La literatura sefardi culta: sus principales escritores, obras y generos." In *Judios, Sefarditas, Conversos,* edited by Angel Alcala. Valladolid, Spain: Ambito, 1995.

Haynt yoyvl-bukh. Warsaw: Haynt Publishers, 1938.

Heller, Celia. *On the Edge of Destruction: Jews of Poland between the Two World Wars.* New York: Columbia University Press, 1977.

———. "Poles of Jewish Background: The Case of Assimilation without Integration in Interwar Poland." In *Studies on Polish Jewry, 1919–1939: The Interplay of Social, Economic, and Political Factors in the Struggle of a Minority for Its Existence,* edited by Joshua Fishman, 243–76. New York: YIVO Institute, 1974.

Henkin, David. *City Reading: Written Words and Public Spaces in Antebellum New York.* New York: Columbia University Press, 1998.

Heper, Metin. *The State Tradition in Turkey.* Atlantic Highlands, N.J.: Eothen Press, 1985.

Hershberg, Avrohm Shmuel. *Pinkes bialystok.* Vol. 2. New York: Bialystok Jewish Historical Association, 1950.

Hertz, Y. S. "Di umlegale prese un literatur fun bund." In *Pinkes far der forshung fun der yidisher literatur yn prese,* edited by Khaym Bas, 294–366. New York: Alveltlekher yidisher kultur-kongres, 1972.

———, ed. *Doyres bundistn.* 3 vols. New York: Unzer tsayt farlag, 1958–68.

Hesse, Carla. *Publishing and Cultural Politics in Revolutionary Paris, 1789–1810.* Berkeley: University of California Press, 1991.

Hirschberg, H. Z. *A History of the Jews in North Africa.* 2 vols. Leiden: E. J. Brill, 1974–81.

Hobsbawm, Eric J. *Nations and Nationalism since 1870.* Cambridge: Cambridge University Press, 1992.

Holmgren, Beth. *Rewriting Capitalism: Literature and the Market in Late Tsarist Russia and the Kingdom of Poland.* Pittsburgh: University of Pittsburgh Press, 1998.

Holquist, Peter. "Information Is the Alpha and Omega of Our Work': Bolshevik Surveillance in Its Pan-European Context." *Journal of Modern History* 69, no. 3 (1997): 415–50.

Horovits, H. D. "Unzer ershte teglikhe tsaytung (tsu der tsen-yoriger geshikhte fun'm fraynd)." In *Der pinkes, yorbukh fun der geshikhte fun der yidisher literatur un shprakh, far folklor, kritik un bibliographye,* edited by Shmuel Niger, 244–65. Vilna: B. A. Kletzkin, 1912.

Hosking, Geoffrey. *Russia, People and Empire.* Cambridge, Mass.: Harvard University Press, 1997.

Hroch, Miroslav. *Social Preconditions of National Revival in Europe: A Comparative Analysis of the Social Composition of Patriotic Groups among the Smaller European Nations.* New York: Cambridge University Press, 1985.

Hunt, Lynn. *Politics, Culture, and Class in the French Revolution.* Berkeley: University of California Press, 1984.

Hyman, Paula A. *Gender and Assimilation in Modern Jewish History: The Roles and Representation of Women.* Seattle: University of Washington Press, 1995.

———. *The Jews of Modern France.* Berkeley: University of California Press, 1998.

Inalcik, Hanil, and Donald Quartaert, eds. *An Economic and Social History of the Ottoman Empire, 1300–1914.* Cambridge: Cambridge University Press, 1994.

Isakov, S. *1905 God v satire i karikature.* Leningrad: Priboi, 1928.

Iskit, Server. *Türkiyede matbuat idareleri ve politikalari: 2.* Istanbul, Turkey: Tan basimev, 1943.

———. *Türkiyede matbuat rejimleri,* Istanbul: Ülkü matbaasi, 1939.

———. *Türkiyede nesriyat hareketleri tarihine bir bakis.* Istanbul: Devlet Basimevi, 1939.

Islamoglu-Inan, Huri, ed. *The Ottoman Empire and the World-Economy.* Cambridge: Cambridge University Press, 2003.

Islamoglu-Inan, Huri, and Çaglar Keyder. "Agenda for Ottoman History." In *The Ottoman Empire and the World-Economy,* edited by Huri Islamoglu-Inan, 42–43. Cambridge: Cambridge University Press, 2003.

Israel, Jonathan I. *European Jewry in the Age of Mercantilism, 1550–1750.* New York: Oxford University Press, 1989.

Issawi, Charles. *The Economic History of Turkey, 1800–1914.* Chicago: University of Chicago Press, 1980.

———. "The Transformation of the Economic Position of the *Millets* in the Nineteenth Century." In *Christians and Jews in the Ottoman Empire, the Functioning of a Plural Society,* edited by Benjamin Braude and Bernard Lewis, 261–86. New York: Holmes & Meier, 1982.

Jerusalmi, Isaac. *From Ottoman Turkish to Ladino.* Cincinnati: Isaac Jerusalmi, 1990.

Johnpoll, Bernard. *The Politics of Futility: The General Jewish Workers Bund of Poland, 1917–1943.* Ithaca, N.Y.: Cornell University Press, 1967.

Juhasz, Esther, ed. *Sephardi Jews in the Ottoman Empire: Aspects of Material Culture.* Jerusalem: Israel Museum, 1990.

Kabacali, Alpay. *Baslangiçtan günümüze Türkiye'de basin sansürü.* Istanbul: Gazeteciler Cemiyeti Yayinlari, 1990.

Kahan, Arcadius. *Essays in Jewish Social and Economic History.* Edited by Roger Weiss. Chicago: University of Chicago Press, 1986.

———, and Roger Weiss. *Russian Economic History: The Nineteenth Century.* Chicago: University of Chicago Press, 1989.

Kalderon, Albert E. *Abraham Galanté: A Biography.* New York: Sepher-Hermon Press, 1983.

Kamenskii, Alesander, and Vsevolod Petrov. *The World of Art Movement in Early 20th-Century Russia.* Leningrad: Aurora Art Publishers, 1991.

Kaminsky, Andrzej Sulima. *Republic vs. Autocracy: Poland-Lithuania and Russia 1686–1697.* Boston: Harvard University Press, 1993.

Kaneti, Selim. "La presse en ladino sous la republique en Turquie." In *Türkiye'de yabanci dilde basin,* 9–27. Istanbul: Istanbul Universitesi Yayinlari, 1985.

Kansu, Aykut. *The Revolution of 1908 in Turkey.* Leiden and New York: Brill, 1997.

Kaplan, Marion. *The Making of the Jewish Middle Class: Women, Family, and Identity in Imperial Germany.* Oxford: Oxford University Press, 1991.

Kappeler, Andreas. *The Russian Empire: A Multiethnic History.* New York: Pearson Education, 2001.

Karmi, Ilan. *The Jewish Community of Istanbul in the Nineteenth Century: Social, Legal and Administrative Transformations.* Istanbul: Isis, 1996.

Karpat, Kemal. "The Migratory Movements of Jews in the Ottoman Empire" (in Hebrew). *Cathedra* 51 (1989): 78–92.

———. "*Millets* and Nationality: The Roots of the Incongruity of Nation and State in the Post-Ottoman Era." In *Christians and Jews in the Ottoman Empire: The Functioning of a Plural Society,* edited by Benjamin Braude and Bernard Lewis, 141–69. New York: Holmes & Meier, 1982.

Karpat, Kemal H. *Ottoman Population, 1830–1914: Demographic and Social Characteristics.* Madison: University of Wisconsin Press, 1985.

Kasaba, Reşat. "Economic Foundations of a Civil Society: Greeks in the Trade of Western Anatolia, 1840–1876." In *Ottoman Greeks in the Age of Nationalism: Politics, Economy, and Society in the Nineteenth Century,* edited by Dimitri Gondicas and Charles Issawi, 77–88. Princeton, N.J.: Princeton University Press, 1999.

———. "Izmir 1922: A Port City Unravels." In *Modernity and Culture from the Mediterranean to the Indian Ocean,* edited by Leila Tarazi Fawaz and C. A. Bayly, 204–29. New York: Columbia University Press, 2002.

———. "Kemalist Certainties and Modern Ambiguities." In *Rethinking Modernity and National Identity in Turkey,* edited by Sibel Bozdogan and Reşat Kasaba, 15–36. Seattle: University of Washington Press, 1997.

———. *The Ottoman Empire and the World Economy in the Nineteenth Century.* New York: University of New York Press, 1988.

———, and Sarah Abrevaya Stein, eds. *Coexistence and Conflict in Ottoman Society.* Forthcoming.

Kats, Ben Tsien. *Zihronot: hamishim shana behistorya shel yehude rusya.* Tel Aviv: Hotsaot sefarim n. tevarski, 1963.

Katz, Jacob. "Orthodoxy in Historical Perspective." *Studies in Contemporary Jewry* 2 (1986): 3–17.

Katz, Moyshe. *A dor, vos hot farloyrn di moyre, bleter zikhroynes fun arum 1905.* New York: Moyshe kats yubiley-komitet, 1956.

Katznelson, Lev, David Baron Ginsburg, Shimen Dubnov, and Albert Harkavy. "Periodicheskaia pechat'." In *Evreiskaia entsiklopediia, svod znanii evreistva i ego kul'tury v proshlom i nastoiashchem,* 402–39. St. Petersburg: Obshchestva dlia nauchnykh evreiskikh izdanii, 1906–13.

Kayali, Hasan. *Arabs and Young Turks: Ottomanism, Arabism and Islamism in the Ottoman Empire, 1908–1918.* Berkeley: University of California Press, 1997.

———. "Jewish Representation in the Ottoman Parliaments." In *The Jews of the Ottoman Empire,* edited by Avigdor Levy, 507–19. Princeton, N.J.: Darwin Press, 1994.

Kazdan, Kh. Sh. *Di geshikhte fun yidishn shulvezn in umophengikn poyln.* Mexico City: Gezelshaft 'kultur un hilf', 1947.

Kel'ner, Viktor Efimovich, and D. A. Eliashevich. *Literatura o evreiakh na russkom iazyke, 1890–1947: Knigi, broshiury, ottiski statei, organy periodicheskoi pechati.* St. Petersburg: Gumanitarnoe agentstvo "Akademicheskii proekt," 1995.

Kendall, Elizabeth. "Between Politics and Literature: Journals in Alexandria and Istanbul at the End of the Nineteenth Century." In *Modernity and Culture from the Mediterranean to the Indian Ocean,* edited by Leila Tarazi Fawaz and C. A. Bayly, 330–43. New York: Columbia University Press, 2002.

Kennedy, Janet. *The "Mir iskusstva" Group and Russian Art, 1898–1912.* New York: Garland Publishers, 1977.

Keyder, Çaglar. "The Ottoman Empire." In *After Empire: Multiethnic Societies and Nation-Building,* edited by Karen Barkley and Mark Von Hagen, 30–45. Boulder, Colo.: Westview Press, 1997.

———. *State and Class in Turkey: A Study in Capitalist Development.* London and New York: Verso, 1987.

Khiterer, Viktoriia. *Dokumenty sobrannye Evreiskoi istoriko-arkheograficheskoi komissiei.* Kiev and Jerusalem: Instytut Iudaiki: Gesharim, 1999.

Kiel, Mark. "The Ideology of the Folks-Partey." *Soviet Jewish Affairs* 5, no. 2 (1975): 75–89.

King, David. *The Commissar Vanishes: The Falsification of Photographs and Art in Stalin's Russia.* New York: Metropolitan Books, 1997.

———, and Cathy Porter. *Images of Revolution: Graphic Art from 1905 Russia.* New York: Pantheon Books, 1983.

Kingston-Mann, Esther, and Timothy Mixter, eds. *Peasant Economy, Culture, and the Politics of European Russia.* Princeton, N.J.: Princeton University Press, 1991.

Kirzhnits, A. *Di yidishe prese in der gevezener rusisher imperye (1823–1916).* Moscow: Tsentraler felker-farlag fun fssr, 1930.

Klier, John D. *Imperial Russia's Jewish Question, 1855–1881.* Cambridge: Cambridge University Press, 1995.

———. "The Jewish Question in the Reform Era Russian Press, 1855–1865." *The Russian Review* 39, no. 3 (1980): 301–20.

———. *Russia Gathers Her Jews: The Origins of the "Jewish Question" in Russia, 1772–1825.* DeKalb: Northern Illinois University Press, 1986.

———. "Russification and the Polish Revolt of 1863: Bad for the Jews?" *Polin* I (1989): 91–106.

Kornberg, Jacques. *Theodor Herzl: From Assimilation to Zionism.* Bloomington: Indiana University Press, 1993.

Kosover, M. "Geshikhte fun der hebreyisher prese." In *Algemeyne entsiklopedye,* 285–351. New York: TSIKO, 1942.

Koven, Seth. "Dr. Barnardo's 'Artistic Fictions': Photography, Sexuality, and the Ragged Child in Victorian London." *Radical History Review* 69 (Fall 1997): 6–45.

Krämer, Gudrun. *The Jews in Modern Egypt, 1914–1952.* Seattle: University of Washington Press, 1989.

Kutsher, Ber. *Geven amol varshe: zikhroynes.* Paris: n.p., 1955.

Kuznets, Simon. "Immigration of Russian Jews to the United States: Nature and Background and Structure." *Perspectives in American History* 9 (1975): 35–126.

Kuznits, Cecile. "The Origins of Yiddish Scholarship and the YIVO Institute for Jewish Research." Ph.D. dissertation, Stanford University, 2000.

LaBerge, Ann. "Medicalization and Moralization: The Creches of Nineteenth-Century Paris." *Journal of Social History* 24, no. 1 (1991): 65–88.

———. "Nurses and Nursing: Alfred Donné and the Medicalization of Child Care in Nineteenth-Century France." *Journal of the History of Medicine and Allied Sciences* 46, no. 1 (1991): 20–43.

Ladas, Stephen. *The Exchange of Minorities: Bulgaria, Greece, and Turkey.* New York: Macmillan, 1932.

Lambroza, Shlomo. "The Pogrom Movement in Russia, 1903–1905." Ph.D. dissertation, Rutgers University, 1981.

———. "The Pogroms of 1903–1906." In *Pogroms: Anti-Jewish Violence in Modern Russian History,* edited by John D. Klier and Shlomo Lambroza, 195–248. Cambridge: Cambridge University Press, 1992.

Landau, H. *Der onteyl fun yidn in der rusish-ukraynisher tsuker-industrye, shriftn far ekonomik un statistik.* Vilna: YIVO Institute for Jewish Research, 1929.

Landau, Jacob M. *Abdul-Hamid's Palestine.* Jerusalem: Carta, 1979.

———, ed. *Ataturk and the Modernization of Turkey.* Boulder, Colo.: Westview Press, 1984.

Laskier, Michael M. *The Alliance Israélite Universelle and the Jewish Communities of Morocco, 1862–1962.* Albany: State University of New York Press, 1983.

Leach, William. *Land of Desire: Merchants, Power, and the Rise of a New American Culture.* New York: Vintage Books, 1994.

Lears, Jackson. "Beyond Vebler: Rethinking Consumer Culture in America." In *Consuming Visions: Accumulation and Display of Goods in America 1880–1920,* edited by Simon Bronner, 75–97. New York: Norton, 1989.

———. *Fables of Abundance: A Cultural History of Advertising in America.* New York: Basic Books, 1994.

Lederhendler, Eli. *Jewish Responses to Modernity: New Voices in America and Eastern Europe.* New York: New York University Press, 1984.

———. *The Road to Modern Jewish Politics: Political Tradition and Political Reconstruction in the Jewish Community of Tsarist Russia.* Oxford: Oxford University Press, 1989.

Lefebvre, Henri. *Everyday Life in the Modern World.* New York: Harper and Row, 1971.

Lehmann, Matthias. "The Intended Reader of Ladino Rabbinic Literature and Judeo-Spanish Reading Culture." *Jewish History* 16, no. 3 (2002): 283–307.

———. "Judeo-Spanish Musar Literature and the Transformation of Ottoman-Sephardic Society (Eighteenth through Nineteenth Centuries)." Ph.D. dissertation, Freie Universität, 2001.

Lestchinsky, Jacob. "Di antviklung fun yidishn folk far di letste 100 yor." *Shriftn far ekonomik un statistik* 1 (1928): 1–64.

———. *Erev khurbn fun yidishn lebn in poyln: 1935–1937.* Buenos Aires: Tsentralfarband fun poylishe yidn in argentina, 1951.

———. "Di shprakhn bay yidn in umophengikn poyln." *YIVO bleter* 22 (1943): 147–62.

———. *Dos yidishe folk in tsifern.* Berlin: Klal-farlag, 1922.

Levi, Avner. "Alexander Ben Ghiat and His Contribution to Journalism and Belles-Lettres in Ladino" (in Hebrew). In *The Heritage of Sephardi and Oriental Jews,* edited by Issachar Ben-Ami. Jerusalem: Magnes Press, 1982.

————. "The Ladino 'El Tiempo' of Istanbul during 1882–83." *Qesher*, no. 13 (May 1993): 22e–24e.

————. *Turkiye Cümhuriyeti'nde Yahudiler, hukuki ve siyasi durumlari.* Istanbul: Iletisim, 1992.

Levin, Nora. *The Jews in the Soviet Union since 1917.* 2 vols. New York: New York University Press, 1987.

Levy, Avigdor. *The Sephardim in the Ottoman Empire.* Princeton, N.J.: Darwin Press, 1992.

Levy, Avner. "Jewish Journals in Izmir." *Pea'mim* 12 (1982): 87–104.

————. "The Jewish Press in Turkey." In *Jewish Journalism and Printing Houses in the Ottoman Empire and Modern Turkey*, edited by Gad Nassi, 13–28. Istanbul: Isis Press, 2001.

Levy, Rebecca Amato. *I Remember Rhodes . . .* New York: Sepher-Hermon Press for Sephardic House at Congregation Shearith Israel, 1987.

Levy, Sam. "Mes memoires: Salonique à la fin du XIXe Siècle." In *Tesoro de los Judios Sefardies: estudios sobre la historia de los judios sefardies y su cultura.* Paris: Archives of the Alliance Israélite Universelle, 1961. Reprinted as *Salonique à la fin du XIXe Siècle.* Istanbul: Isis, 2000.

Lewis, Bernard. *The Emergence of Modern Turkey.* London: Oxford University Press, 1961.

————. *The Jews of Islam.* Princeton, N.J.: Princeton University Press, 1984.

————. "The Ottoman Legacy to Contemporary Political Arabic." In *Imperial Legacy: The Ottoman Imprint on the Balkans and Middle East*, edited by L. Carl Brown, 203–13. New York: Columbia University Press, 1996.

————. *Semites and Anti-Semites: An Inquiry into Conflict and Prejudice.* New York: Norton, 1986.

Lewis, G. L. "Ataturk's Language Reform as an Aspect of Modernization in the Republic of Turkey." In *Ataturk and the Modernization of Turkey*, edited by Jacob Landau, 195–214. Boulder, Colo., and Leiden: Westview Press and E. J. Brill, 1984.

Lieven, Dominic. *Empire: The Russian Empire and Its Rivals.* New Haven, Conn.: Yale University Press, 2000.

Lifshits, Ya'akov. *Zikhron ya'akov.* 3 vols. Frankfurt and Kovno: N. H. Lifshits, 1924–30.

Lifshitz, I. "Di varshaver yidishe tsaytung." *YIVO bleter* XLIV (1873): 107–38.

Lindisfarne-Tapper, Nancy, and Bruce Ingham, eds. *Languages of Dress in the Middle East.* Surrey: Curzon, 1997.

Loeb, Lori Anne. *Consuming Angels: Advertising and Victorian Women.* Oxford: Oxford University Press, 1994.

Lowenthal, Robyn. "Elia Carmona's Autobiography: Judeo-Spanish Popular Press and Novel Publishing Milieu in Constantinople, Ottoman Empire, Circa 1860–1932." Ph.D. dissertation, University of Nebraska, 1984.

Lunacharsky, A. V. [Anatoly Vasilievich]. *Stat'i o literature.* Moscow: Gos. izd-vo khudozh. lit-ry, 1957.

Luz, Ehud. *Parallels Meet: Religion and Nationalism in the Early Zionist Movement (1882–1904).* Philadelphia: Jewish Publication Society, 1988.

Lyons, Marvin. *Nicholas II: The Last Tsar.* New York: Routledge & Kegan Paul, 1974.

Mace, James. *Communism and the Dilemma of National Liberation: National Communism in Soviet Ukraine, 1918–1933.* Cambridge, Mass.: Harvard University Press, 1983.

Mahler, Raphael. *Yehude polin ben shete milhamot 'olam: Historya kalkalit-sotsialit leor hastatistika.* Tel Aviv: Devir, 1968.

Makdisi, George. "Corrupting the Sublime Sultanate." *Comparative Studies in Society and History* 42 (2000): 180–208.

Makdisi, Ussama. *The Culture of Sectarianism: Community, History, and Violence in Nineteenth-Century Lebanon.* Berkeley: University of California Press, 2000.

Malino, Frances, and David Sorkin, eds. *From East and West: Jews in a Changing Europe, 1750–1870.* Oxford: Basil Blackwell, 1990.

Manekin, Rachel. "The New Convenant: Orthodox Jews and Polish Catholics in Galicia (1879–1883)" (in Hebrew). *Zion* LXIV, no. 2 (1999): 157–86.

Ma'Or, Yitzhak. *Hatenuah hatsiyonit berusyah.* Jerusalem: Hasifriya hatsionit, 1986.

Mardin, Serif. "Power, Civil Society and Culture in the Ottoman Empire." *Comparative Studies in Society and History,* no. 11 (1969): 258–81.

Mark, Yudel. "Yidishe periodishe oysgabes in lite." In *Zamlbukh lekoved dem tsvey hundert un fuftsikstn yoyvl fun der yidisher prese, 1686–1936,* edited by Jacob Shatzky, 250–99. New York: YIVO Publishers, 1937.

Markovits, Andrei S., and Frank E. Sysyn. *Nationbuilding and the Politics of Nationalism: Essays on Austrian Galicia.* Cambridge, Mass.: Distributed by Harvard University Press for the Harvard Ukrainian Research Institute, 1982.

Masters, Bruce. *Christians and Jews in the Ottoman Arab World: The Roots of Sectarianism.* Cambridge: Cambridge University Press, 2001.

Mayzel, Nahman. *Geven a mol a lebn, dos yidishe kultur-lebn in poyln tsvishn bayde velt-milkhomes, bikher serye, dos poylishe yidntum.* Buenos Aires: Tsentral farband fun poyleshe yidn in argentina, 1951.

Mayzes, Mendel. "Di ershte yorn fun'm varshaver 'moment.' " In *Di yidishe prese vos iz geven,* edited by Dovid Flinker, Mordechai Tsanin, and Sholem Rosenfeld, 71–82. Tel Aviv: Veltfarband fun di yidishe zhurnalistn, 1975.

Mazower, Mark. "Salonica between East and West, 1860–1912." *Diagolos Hellenic Studies Review,* no. 1 (1989): 104–27.

McCagg, William. *A History of Habsburg Jews, 1670–1918.* Bloomington: Indiana University Press, 1989.

McCarthy, Justin. *Muslims and Minorities: The Population of Ottoman Anatolia and the End of the Empire.* New York: New York University Press, 1983.

McClintock, Anne. *Imperial Leather: Race, Gender and Sexuality in the Colonial Contest.* London: Routledge, 1995.

McKay, John P. *Pioneers for Profit: Foreign Entrepreneurship and Russian Industrialization, 1885–1913.* Chicago: University of Chicago Press, 1970.

McReynolds, Louise. "Imperial Russia's Newspaper Reporters: Profile of a Society in Transition, 1865–1914." *The Slavonic and East European Review* 68, no. 2 (1990): 277–93.

———. *The News under Russia's Old Regime: The Development of a Mass-Circulating Press.* Princeton, N.J.: Princeton University Press, 1991.

Mehlman, Israel. "Prakim betoldot hadafus besalonika." *Sefunot* 13 (1971–78): 215–72.

Mendelsohn, Ezra. *Class Struggle in the Pale: The Formative Years of the Jewish Workers' Movement in Tsarist Russia.* Oxford: Oxford University Press, 1970.

———. "From Assimilation to Zionism in Lvov: The Case of Alfred Nossig." *The Slavonic and East European Review* 49, no. 117 (1971): 521–34.

———. "German and Jewish Minorities in the European Successor States between the World Wars: Some Comparative Remarks." In *Studies on Polish Jewry: Paul Glikson Memorial Volume,* edited by Ezra Mendelsohn and Chone Shmeruk, li–lxv. Jerusalem: Hebrew University, 1987.

———. "Interwar Poland: Good for the Jews or Bad for the Jews?" In *The Jews in Poland,* edited by Chimen Abramsky, Maciej Jachimczyk, and Antony Polonsky, 130–39. Oxford: Oxford University Press, 1986.

————. "Jewish Assimilation in Lvov: The Case of Wilhelm Feldman." *Slavic Review* 28, no. 4 (1969): 155–90.

————. "Jewish Politics in Interwar Poland: An Overview." In *The Jews of Poland between Two World Wars,* edited by Yisrael Gutman, Ezra Mendelsohn, Jehuda Reinharz, and Chone Shmeruk, 9–19. Hanover, N.H.: University Press of New England, 1989.

————. *The Jews of East Central Europe Between the Wars.* Bloomington: Indiana University Press, 1983.

————. *On Modern Jewish Politics.* New York: Oxford University Press, 1993.

————. "The Politics of Agudas Yisroel in Inter-war Poland." *Soviet Jewish Affairs* 2, no. 2 (1972): 47–60.

————. *Zionism in Poland: The Formative Years, 1915–1926.* New Haven, Conn.: Yale University Press, 1981.

————, and Richard I. Cohen, eds. *Art and Its Uses: The Visual Image and Modern Jewish Society. Studies in Contemporary Jewry* 6 (1990).

Mevorah, B. "Effects of the Damascus Affair upon the Development of the Jewish Press, 1840–1846." *Zion,* no. 1–2 (1958–59): 46–65.

Mézan, Saul. *Les juifs espagnols en Bulgarie.* Sofia: "Hamishpat" Publishers, 1925.

Michels, Anthony. " 'Speaking to Moyshe': The Early Socialist Yiddish Press and Its Readers." *Jewish History* 14, no. 1 (2000): 51–82.

Milner, John. *A Dictionary of Russian and Soviet Artists, 1420–1970.* Woodbridge, Suffolk: Antique Collectors Club, 1933.

Mintz, Alan. *Hurban: Responses to Catastrophe in Hebrew Literature.* New York: Columbia University Press, 1984.

Miron, Dan. *Bodedim bemoadam.* Tel Aviv: Am oved, 1987.

————. *A Traveler Disguised: A Study in the Rise of Modern Yiddish Fiction in the Nineteenth Century.* New York: Schocken Books, 1973.

Mitchell, Timothy. *Colonizing Egypt.* Berkeley: University of California Press, 1988.

Mlachi, A. R. "Yidishe vokhenblat." In *Zamlbukh lekoved dem tsvey hundert un fuftsikstn yoyvl fun der yidisher prese, 1686–1936,* edited by Jacob Shatzky, 175–96. New York: YIVO Publishers, 1937.

Molho, Michael. "Haitonut espanyolit besaloniki." In *Saloniki, ir veam beyisrael,* 103–109. Jerusalem: hamakhon leheker yahadut saloniki, 1967.

————. *Literatura séfardita de Oriente.* Madrid and Barcelona: CSIC and Instituto Arias Montano, 1960.

————. *Le Meam loez: enclopédie popularire du sépharadisme levantin.* Thessalonica: n.p., 1945.

Molho, Rena. "Popular Antisemitism and State Policy in Salonika during the City's Annexation to Greece." *Jewish Social Studies* 50, no. 3–4 (1988–93): 253–64.

————. "Le Renouveau . . ." In *Salonique, 1850–1918: la 'ville des juifs' et le reveil des Balkans,* edited by Gilles Veinstein, 64–78. Paris: Editions Autrement, 1992.

Morrissey, Susan K. *Heralds of Revolution: Russian Students and the Mythologies of Radicalism.* Oxford: Oxford University Press, 1998.

Moseley, Marcus. "Life, Literature: Autobiographies of Jewish Youth in Interwar Poland." *Jewish Social Studies* 7, no. 3 (2001): 1–52.

Moss, Kenneth. "Jewish Culture between Renaissance and Decadence: *Di literarishe monatsshriften* and Its Critical Reception." *Jewish Social Studies* 8, no. 1 (2002): 153–98.

Motzkin, Leo[n], ed. *Die Judenpogrome in Russland.* Berlin: World Zionist Organization, Jüdischer verlag, 1909.

Nahum, Henri. *Juifs de Smyrne, XIXe–XXe siècle.* Paris: Aubier, 1997.

Nassi, Gad, ed. *Jewish Journalism and Printing Houses in the Ottoman Empire and Modern Turkey.* Istanbul: Isis Press, 2001.

————. "Synoptic List of Ottoman-Turkish-Jewish and Other Sephardic Journals." In *Jewish Journalism and Printing Houses in the Ottoman Empire and Modern Turkey*, edited by Gad Nassi, 29–72. Istanbul: Isis Press, 2001.

Nathans, Benjamin. *Beyond the Pale: The Jewish Encounter with Late Imperial Russia.* Berkeley: University of California Press, 2002.

Nehama, Joseph. *Histoire des Israélites de Salonique.* Salonique: Molho, 1978.

Nemirovskii, E. L. [Evgenii Lvovich], ed. *Russkaia satiricheskaia periodika, 1905–1907.* Moscow: Gosudarstvennaia biblioteka SSSR im. V.I. Lenina, 1980.

Netzer, Amnon. *The Jews of Persia and the Alliánce in the Late Nineteenth Century: Some Aspects.* Jerusalem: Hebrew University and Ben-Zvi Institute, 1974.

Neuberger, Joan. *Hooliganism: Crime, Culture, and Power in St. Petersburg, 1900–1914.* Berkeley: University of California Press, 1993.

Norton, John. "Faith and Fashion in Turkey." In *Languages of Dress in the Middle East*, edited by Nancy Lindisfarne-Tapper and Bruce Ingham, 149–77. Surrey: Curzon, 1997.

Obolensky, Chloe. *The Russian Empire: A Portrait in Photographs.* New York: Random House, 1979.

Ochs, Michael Jerry. "St. Petersburg and the Jews of Russian Poland, 1862–1905." Ph.D. dissertation, Harvard University, 1986.

Oral, Fuat Süreyya. *Türk basin tarihi.* 2 vols. Ankara: Yeni Adim Matbaasi, 1967.

Orbach, Alexander. *New Voices of Russian Jewry.* Leiden: E. J. Brill, 1980.

Owen, Roger. *The Middle East in the World Economy.* London and New York: Methuen, 1981.

Pamuk, Sevket. *The Ottoman Empire and European Capitalism, 1820–1913: Trade, Investment, and Production.* Cambridge: Cambridge University Press, 1987.

Panova, Snezhka. "The Development of the Textile Industry in the Balkan Countries and the Role of the Jewish Population in the XVI–XVII Centuries." *Annual: Social, Cultural and Educational Organization of the Jews in the People's Republic of Bulgaria*, no. 11 (1976): 123–40.

Parshin, Sergei. *Mir iskusstva.* Moscow: Izobrazitel'noe iskusstvo, 1993.

Pavlovskii, Boris, and Vladimir Cherepov. "Rossiiskaiia provintsiia." In *Revoliutsiia 1905–1907 goda i izobrazitel'noe iskusstvo*, edited by V. V. [Vladimir Vasil'evich] Shleev. Moscow: Izobrazitel'noe iskusstvo, 1987.

Pearson, Raymond. "Privileges, Rights, and Russification." In *Civil Rights in Imperial Russia*, edited by Olga Crisp and Linda Edmondson, 85–102. Oxford: Clarendon Press, 1989.

Peltz, Rakhmiel, and Mark Kiel. "Di Yiddish-Imperye: The Dashed Hopes for a Yiddish Cultural Empire in the Soviet Union." In *Sociolinguistic Perspectives on Soviet National Languages: Their Past, Present, and Future*, edited by Isabelle T. Kreindler, 277–309. Berlin and New York: Mouton, 1985.

Penslar, Derek. *Shylock's Children: Economics and Jewish Identity in Modern Europe.* Berkeley: University of California Press, 2001.

Pinney, Christopher. *Camera Indica: The Social Life of Indian Photographers.* Chicago: University of Chicago Press, 1997.

Pintner, Walter McKenzie. *Russian Economic Policy under Nicholas I.* Ithaca, N.Y.: Cornell University Press, 1967.

Pipes, Richard. "Catherine II and the Jews: The Origins of the Pale of Settlement." *Soviet Jewish Affairs*, no. 5 (1975): 3–20.

Polonsky, Antony, Ezra Mendelsohn, and Jerzy Tomaszewski, eds. *Jews in Independent Poland, 1918–1939.* Polin: Studies in Polish Jewry, vol. 8. London: Littman Library of Jewish Civilization, 1994.

Pomper, Philip, Richard H. Elphick, and Richard T. Vann, eds. *World History: Ideologies, Structures, and Identities.* Oxford: Blackwell Publishers, 1998.

Portnoy, Edward. "Exploiting Tradition: Religious Iconography in Cartoons of the Polish Yiddish Press." *Polin* 16 (forthcoming, November 2003).

Poshchupkin, Stanislav. "Moskva." In *Revoliutsiia 1905–1907 goda i izobrazitel'noe iskusstvo,* edited by V. V. Shleev, 4–16. Moscow: Izobrazitel'noe iskusstvo, 1978.

Prager, Leonard. *Yiddish Literary and Linguistic Periodicals and Miscellanies.* New York: Norward Editions, 1982.

Pratt, Mary Louise. *Imperial Eyes: Travel Writing and Transculturation.* London: Routledge, 1992.

Quataert, Donald. *Ottoman Manufacturing in the Age of the Industrial Revolution.* Cambridge: Cambridge University Press, 1993.

Raeff, Marc. "In the Imperial Manner." In *Catherine the Great: A Profile,* edited by Marc Raeff, 197–246. New York: Hill & Wang, 1972.

———. "Patterns of Russian Imperial Policy toward the Nationalities." In *Soviet Nationality Problems,* edited by Edward Allworth, 22–42. New York: Columbia University Press, 1972.

Rapoport, Shabsay. "Der onheyb fun 'fraynd.'" *Yubileum-baylage fraynd, tsenter yorgang,* no. 12 (1913): 2–5.

Reichman, Henry. *Railwaymen and Revolution: Russia, 1905.* Berkeley: University of California Press, 1987.

Reinharz, Jehuda, and Anita Shapira, eds. *Essential Papers on Zionism.* New York: New York University Press, 1995.

Renard, Raymond Robert. *Sépharad, le monde et la langue judéoespagnole des Séphardim.* Mons: Annales universitaires de Mons, 1966.

Reyzen, Zalman. *Leksikon fun der yidisher literatur, prese, un filologye.* Vilna: Tsentral, 1926.

Richards, Thomas. *The Commodity Culture of Victorian England: Advertising and Spectacle, 1851–1914.* Stanford, Calif.: Stanford University Press, 1990.

Rieber, Alfred J. *Merchants and Entreprenuers in Imperial Russia.* Chapel Hill: University of North Carolina Press, 1982.

Rivlin, Bracha, ed. *Pinkas hakehilot— Greece.* Jerusalem: Yad Vashem, 1998.

Roden, Claudia. "Jewish Food in the Middle East." In *Culinary Cultures of the Middle East,* edited by Sami Zubaida and Richard Tapper, 153–58. London: I. B. Tauris, 1994.

Rodrigue, Aron. "Abraham De Camondo of Istanbul: The Transformation of Jewish Philanthropy." In *From East and West: Jews in a Changing Europe, 1750–1870,* edited by Frances Malino and David Sorkin, 46–56. Oxford: Basil Blackwell, 1990.

———. "Eastern Sephardi Jewry and New Nation-States in the Balkans in the Nineteenth and Twentieth Centuries." In *Sephardi and Middle Eastern Jewries: History and Culture in the Modern Era,* edited by Harvey E. Goldberg, 81–89. Bloomington: Indiana University Press, 1996.

———. *French Jews, Turkish Jews: The Alliance Israélite Universelle and the Politics of Jewish Schooling in Turkey, 1860–1925.* Bloomington: Indiana University Press, 1990.

———. "From *Millet* to Minority: Turkish Jewry." In *Paths of Emancipation: Jews, States, and Citizenship,* edited by Pierre Birnbaum and Ira Katznelson, 238–61. Princeton, N.J.: Princeton University Press, 1995.

———. *Guide to the Ladino Materials in Harvard College Library.* Cambridge, Mass.: Harvard College Library, 1992.

———. *Images of Sephardi and Eastern Jewries in Transition: The Teachers of the Alliance Israélite Universelle, 1860–1939.* Seattle: University of Washington Press, 1993.

———. "The Ottoman Diaspora: The Rise and Fall of Ladino Literary Culture." In

Cultures of the Jews, A New History, edited by David Biale, 863–86. New York: Knopf, 2002.

———, and Nancy Reynolds. " 'Difference' and Tolerance in the Ottoman Empire." *Stanford Humanities Review* 5 (Fall 1995): 81–92.

Rodrigue, Aron, ed. *Ottoman and Turkish Jewry: Community and Leadership.* Bloomington: Indiana University Turkish Studies, 1992.

Rogger, Hans. *Jewish Policies and Right-Wing Politics in Imperial Russia.* Berkeley: University of California Press, 1986.

———. "Nationalism and the State: A Russian Dilemma." *Comparative Studies in Society and History* IV, no. 3 (1962): 253–64.

Romero, Elena. *La creación literaria en lengua sefardí.* Madrid: Editorial MAPRFRE, 1992.

Roskies, David. *Against the Apocalypse: Responses to Catastrophe in Modern Jewish Culture.* Cambridge, Mass.: Harvard University Press, 1984.

———. *The Jewish Search for a Usable Past.* Bloomington: Indiana University Press, 1999.

———, ed. *The Dybbuk and Other Writings.* New York: Schocken Books, 1992.

———, ed. *The Literature of Destruction: Jewish Responses to Catastrophe.* Philadelphia: Jewish Publication Society, 1989.

Rowe, Leonard. "Jewish Self Defense: A Response to Violence." In *Studies on Polish Jewry, 1919–1939: The Interplay of Social, Economic, and Political Factors in the Struggle of a Minority for Its Existence,* edited by Joshua Fishman, 105–49. New York: YIVO Institute, 1974.

Rozen, Minna. "Contest and Rivalry in Mediterranean Maritime Commerce in the First Half of the Eighteenth Century: The Jews of Salonika and the European Presence." *Revue des études juives,* no. 147 (1988): 309–52.

Rozenblit, Marsha. *Reconstructing a National Identity: The Jews of Habsburg Austria during World War I.* Oxford: Oxford University Press, 2001.

Rubinow, I. M. *Economic Conditions of the Jews in Russia.* Vol. 15. New York: U.S. Bureau of Labor Bulletin, 1907. Reprint, Ayer Company Publishers, New York, 1975.

Ruud, Charles A. *Fighting Words: Imperial Censorship and the Russian Press, 1804–1906.* Toronto and Buffalo: University of Toronto Press, 1982.

———. "The Printing Press as an Agent of Political Change in Early-Twentieth Century Russia." *The Russian Review* 40, no. 4 (1981): 378–96.

Ryan, James R. *Picturing Empire: Photography and the Visualization of the British Empire.* Chicago: University of Chicago Press, 1997.

Sablinsky, Walter. *The Road to Bloody Sunday: Father Gapon and the St. Petersburg Massacre of 1905.* Princeton, N.J.: Princeton University Press, 1976.

Safran, Gabriella. *Rewriting the Jew: Assimilation Narratives in the Russian Empire.* Stanford, Calif.: Stanford University Press, 2000.

Saloniki, ir veam beyisrael. Jerusalem: Hamahon leheker yahadut Salonik, 1967.

Sanders, Thomas, ed. *Historiography of Imperial Russia: The Profession and Writing of History in a Multinational State.* Armonk, N.Y.: M. E. Sharpe, 1999.

Saul, Samir. *La France et l'Égypte de 1882 à 1914: intérêts économiques et implications politiques.* Paris: Comité pour l'histoire économique et financière de la France, 1997.

Sbornik materialov ob ekonomicheskom polozhenii evreev v Rossii. St. Petersburg: Jewish Colonization Association, 1904.

Schudson, Michael. *Discovering the News: A Social History of American Newspapers.* New York: Basic Books, 1967.

Schwarzfuchs, Simon. *Les juifs d'Algérie et la France (1830–1855).* Jerusalem: Institut Ben-Zvi, 1981.

———. "Quand commença le déclin de l'industrie textiles des juifs de Salonique?"

In *The Mediterranean and the Jews: Banking, Financing and International Trade (XVI–XVIII Centuries)*, edited by Ariel Toaff and Simon Schwarzfuchs. Ramat Gan: Bar-Elan University Press, 1989.

Sciaky, Leon. *Farewell to Salonica: Portrait of an Era.* New York: Current Books, 1946.

Seal, Jeremy. *A Fez of the Heart: Travels around Turkey in Search of a Hat.* San Diego, New York, and London: Harcourt Brace & Co., 1995.

Seidman, Naomi. *A Marriage Made in Heaven: The Sexual Politics of Hebrew and Yiddish.* Berkeley: University of California Press, 1997.

Sekula, Allan. "The Body and the Archive." *October* 39 (Winter 1986): 3–64.

Sena, Moshe. "Haynt'-a nekhtn un a morgn." In *Di yidishe prese vos iz geven,* edited by Dovid Flinker, Mordechai Tsanin, and Sholem Rosenfeld, 53–63. Tel Aviv: Veltfarband fun di yidishe zhurnalistn, 1975.

Sephiah, Vidal. *Le judéo-espagnol.* Paris: Entente, 1986.

Sertel, Yildiz. *Annem: sabiha sertel kimdi, neler yazdi: yasanti.* Istanbul: Yapi Kredi Yayinlari, 1994.

Shandler, Jeffrey. *Awakening Lives, Autobiographies of Jewish Youth in Poland before the Holocaust.* New Haven: Yale University Press, 2002.

Shapiro, Ann-Louise. *Housing the Poor of Paris, 1850–1902.* Madison: University of Wisconsin Press, 1985.

Shaten, Morris. "Interview with Morris Shaten by His Son, Dr. Haim F. Shaten." YIVO Institute for Jewish Research, 1965.

Shatzky, Yakov. "Geshikhte fun der yidisher prese." In *Algemeyne entsiklopedye,* 199–285. New York: TSIKO, 1942.

———. *Geshikhte fun yidn in varshe, 1863–1896.* 3 vols. New York: YIVO Publishers, 1953.

———. "Yidn in dem poylishn ufshtand fun 1863." *YIVO historishe shriftn,* no. I (1929): 423–68.

———, ed. *Zamlbukh lekoved dem tsvey hundert un fuftsikstn yoyvl fun der yidisher prese, 1686–1936.* New York: YIVO Publishers, 1937.

Shaw, Stanford. *The Jews of the Ottoman Empire and the Turkish Republic.* New York: New York University Press, 1991.

———. "The Population of Istanbul in the Nineteenth Century." *Turk Tarih Dergisis* 32 (1979): 412.

Shayn, Y. "Materialn tsu a bibliografye fun yidisher periodike in poyln, 1918–1939." In *Shtudyes vegn yidn in poyln, 1919–1939,* edited by Joshua Fishman, 422–38. New York: YIVO Institute, 1963.

Shilo-Cohen, Nurit, ed. *Betsalel 1906–1929.* Jerusalem: Israel Museum, 1983.

Shleev, V. V. (Vladimir Vasil'evich). "Peterburg." In *Revoliutsiia 1905–1907 goda i izobrazitel'noe iskusstvo,* edited by V. V. Shleev. Moscow: Izobrazitel'noe iskusstvo, 1977.

———, ed. *Revoliutsiia 1905–1907 goda i izobrazitel'noe iskusstvo.* 3 vols. Moscow: Izobrazitel'noe iskusstvo, 1977.

Shmeruk, Chone. "Aspects of the History of Warsaw as a Yiddish Literary Center." In *The Jews in Warsaw, a History,* edited by Wladyslay T. Bartoszewski and Antony Polonsky, 232–46. Oxford: Basil Blackwell, 1991.

———. "Hebrew-Yiddish-Polish: A Trilingual Jewish Culture." In *The Jews of Poland between Two World Wars,* edited by Yisrael Gutman, Ezra Mendelsohn, Jehuda Reinharz, and Chone Shmeruk, 285–311. Hanover, N.H.: University Press of New England for Brandeis University Press, 1989.

———. "Yiddish Adaptations of Children's Stories from World Literature." In *Studies in Contemporary Jewry: An Annual,* edited by Ezra Mendelsohn and Richard I. Cohen, 186–200. Oxford: Oxford University Press, 1990.

Shmuelevitz, Aryeh. "Two Hebrew-Language Weeklies in Turkey: An Appeal to Revive Concept of a National Culture." In *Türkiye'de yabanci dilde basin*, 109–27. Istanbul: Istanbul Universitesi Yayinlari, 1985.

Shohat, Azriel. "The King's Cloth in Salonika." *Sefunot*, no. 12 (1971–78): 169–88.

———. *Mosad harabanut mitaam berusya: parasha bamaavak hatarbut ben haredim leven maskilim*. Haifa: University of Haifa, 1975.

Shreberk, Shloyme. "Zikhroynes fun a yidishn bukhhandler." In *Pinkes far der ge-shikhte fun vilna in di yorn fun milhoma un okupatsya*, edited by Zalman Reisen, 558–70. Vilna: Aroisgegebn fun der historish-etnografisher gezelshaft oifn nomen fun S. An-ski, 1922.

Shtif, Nahum. "Autobiographia fun nahum shtif." *YIVO bleter, hoydesh-shrift fun yi-dishn visenshaft institute* 5, no. 3–5 (1933): 195–226.

Simon, Gerhard. *Nationalism and Policy toward the Nationalities in the Soviet Union: From Totalitarian Dictatorship to Post-Stalinist Society*. Boulder, Colo.: Westview Press, 1991.

Simon, Rachel. "Between the Family and the Outside World: Jewish Girls in the Modern Middle East and North Africa." *Jewish Social Studies* 7, no. 1 (2000): 81–108.

———. "Language Change and Sociopolitical Transformations: The Case of Nine-teenth- and Twentieth-Century Libyan Jews." *Jewish History* 4, no. 1 (1989): 101–21.

Slezkine, Yuri. "The USSR as a Communal Apartment; or, How a Socialist State Pro-moted Ethnic Particularism." *Slavic Review* 53, no. 2 (1994): 414–52.

Slutzky, Yehuda. *Haitonut hayehudit-rusit bemea haesrim (1900–1918)*. Tel Aviv: Ha'agu-dah leheker toldot hayahadut, hamakhon leheher hatefutsot, 1978.

Smith, Anthony. *The Ethnic Origins of Nations*. Oxford: Blackwell Press, 1986.

Soltes, Mordecai. *The Yiddish Press: An Americanizing Agency*. New York: Teachers College, Columbia University, 1925.

Spivak, Gayatri Chakravorty. "Can the Subaltern Speak?" In *Marxism and the Inter-pretation of Culture*, edited by Cary Nelson and Lawrence Grossberg. Urbana: University of Illinois Press, 1988.

———. "Who Claims Alterity?" In *Remaking History*, edited by Barbara Kruger and Phil Mariani, 269–94. Seattle: Bay Press, 1989.

Stampfer, Shaul. "Gender Differentiation and Education of the Jewish Woman in Nineteenth-Century Eastern Europe." *Polin* 7 (1994): 63–87.

———. "*Heder* Study, Knowledge of Torah, and the Maintenance of Social Stratifica-tion in Traditional East European Jewish Society." *Studies in Jewish Education* 3 (1988): 271–89.

———. "Marital Patterns in Interwar Poland." In *The Jews of Poland between Two World Wars*, edited by Yisrael Gutman, Ezra Mendelsohn, Jehuda Reinharz, and Chone Shmeruk, 173–97. Hanover, N.H.: University Press of New En-gland for Brandeis University Press, 1989.

———. "What Did 'Knowing Hebrew' Mean in Eastern Europe?" In *Hebrew in Ashkenaz*, edited by Lewis Gilnert, 129–40. New York: Oxford University Press, 1993.

Stanislawski, Michael. *For Whom Do I Toil? Judah Leib Gordon and the Crisis of Russian Jewry*. New York: Oxford University Press, 1988.

———. "Russian Jewry, the Russian State, and the Dynamics of Russian Jewish Emancipation." In *Paths of Emancipation: Jews, States, and Citizenship*, edited by Pierre Birnbaum and Ira Katznelson, 262–85. Princeton, N.J.: Princeton Uni-versity Press, 1995.

———. *Tsar Nicholas I and the Jews: The Transformation of Jewish Society in Russia, 1825–1855*. Philadelphia: Jewish Publication Society of America, 1983.

———. *Zionism and the Fin de Siècle: Cosmopolitanism and Nationalism from Nordau to Jabotinsky*. Berkeley: University of California Press, 2001.

Starobinski, Jean. *1789, the Emblems of Reason.* Cambridge, Mass.: MIT Press, 1988.

Starr, S. Frederick. "Tsarist Government: The Imperial Dimension." In *Soviet Nationality Policies and Practices,* edited by Jeremy Azrael, 3–38. New York: Praeger, 1978.

Stein, Sarah Abrevaya. "Creating a Taste for the News: Historicizing Judeo-Spanish Periodicals of the Ottoman Empire." *Jewish History* 14, no. 1 (2000): 9–28.

———. "Divining the Secular in the Yiddish Popular Press." In *Sacred Stories: Religion and Culture in Russia,* edited by Mark Steinberg. Forthcoming.

———. "Faces of Protest: Yiddish Cartoons of the 1905 Revolution." *Slavic Review* (Winter 2002): 732–61.

———. "Illustrating Chicago's Jewish Left: Todros Geller and the L. M. Shteyn Farlag." *Jewish Social Studies* 3, no. 3 (1997): 74–110.

———. "Sephardi and Middle Eastern Jewries since 1492." In *The Oxford Handbook of Jewish Studies,* edited by Martin Goodman, 327–62. Oxford: Oxford University Press, 2002.

Steinberg, Mark D. *Moral Communities: The Culture of Class Relations in the Russian Printing Industry, 1867–1907.* Berkeley: University of California Press, 1992.

Steinlauf, Michael C. "The Polish-Jewish Daily Press." *Polin* 2 (1987): 219–45.

Stillman, Norman A. *The Jews of Arab Lands.* Philadelphia: Jewish Publication Society, 1991.

———. *The Jews of Arab Lands in Modern Times.* Philadelphia: Jewish Publication Society, 1984.

———. *Sephardi Religious Responses to Modernity.* London: Harwood, 1996.

Strelkov, Aleksandr. *Mir iskusstva.* Moscow: Aleksandr Strelkov, 1923.

Suny, Ronald. *The Revenge of the Past.* Stanford, Calif.: Stanford University Press, 1993.

Surh, Gerald. *1905 in St. Petersburg: Labor, Society, and Revolution.* Stanford, Calif.: Stanford University Press, 1989.

Swift, Anthony. "Fighting the Germs of Disorder: The Censorship of Russian Popular Theater, 1888–1917." *Russian History/Histoire Russe* 18, no. 1 (1991): 1–49.

Szeintuch, Yechiel. *Preliminary Inventory of Yiddish Dailies and Periodicals Published in Poland between the Two World Wars.* Jerusalem: Hebrew University of Jerusalem Center for Research on the History and Culture of Polish Jews, 1986.

Sztokfisz, David. *Sefer kutnah vehasevivah.* Tel Aviv: Irgun yotse kutnah, 1968.

Terdiman, Richard. *Discourse/Counter-Discourse: The Theory and Practice of Symbolic Resistance in Nineteenth-Century France.* Ithaca, N.Y.: Cornell University Press, 1985.

Thaden, Edward. *Russification in the Baltic Provinces and Finland, 1855–1914.* Princeton, N.J.: Princeton University Press, 1982.

Thomas, Julia. "Photography, National Identity, and the 'Cataract of Times': Wartime Images and the Case of Japan." *The American Historical Review* 103, no. 5 (1998): 1475–1501.

Tobias, Henry J. *The Jewish Bund in Russia from Its Origins to 1905.* Stanford, Calif.: Stanford University Press, 1972.

Toledano, Ehud. "The Emergence of Ottoman-Local Elites (1700–1900): A Framework for Research." In *Middle East Politics and Ideas: A History from Within,* edited by Ilan Pappe and Mose Ma'oz, 145–62. London: I. B. Tauris, 1997.

Toprak, Zafer. "Fikir dergiciliginin yuzyili." In *Türkiye'de dergiler, ansiklopediler, (1849–1984).* Istanbul: Gelisim Yayinlari, 1984.

Trommer, Elbert Aidline (Khaym eliezer ben mordkhe-dov). "Far vos ikh bin avek fun der alter heym un vos ikh hob dergreykht in amerike." New York: YIVO Institute, American Autobiography, Folder 182.

Tsinberg, S. L. *Istoriia evreiskoi pechati v Rossii v sviazi s obshchestvennymi techeniiami.* Petrograd: Tip. I. Fleitmana, 1915.

Tsitron, Shmuel Leyb. *Di geshikhte fun der yidisher prese fun yorn 1863–1889, fareyn fun yidishe literatn un zhurnalistn in vilne.* Vilna: Aygner farlag, 1923.

Tsur, Yaron. "Haskalah in a Sectional Colonial Society Mahdia (Tunisia) 1884." In *Sephardi and Middle Eastern Jewries: History and Culture in the Modern Era,* edited by Harvey E. Goldberg, 146–67. Bloomington: Indiana University Press, 1996.

Turgay, A. Uner. "Trade and Merchants in Nineteenth-Century Trabzon: Elements of Ethnic Conflict." In *Christians and Jews in the Ottoman Empire: The Functioning of a Plural Society,* edited by Benjamin Braude and Bernard Lewis, 287–318. New York: Holmes & Meier, 1982.

Turner, Brian. *Weber and Islam.* London and New York: Routledge & Kegan Paul, 1974.

Veidlinger, Jeffrey. *The Moscow State Yiddish Theater: Jewish Culture on the Soviet Stage.* Bloomington: Indiana University Press, 2000.

Veinstein, Gilles, ed. *Salonique, 1850–1918: la 'ville des juifs' et le réveil des Balkans.* Paris: Editions Autrement, 1992.

Verner, Andrew M. *The Crisis of Russian Autocracy: Nicholas II and the 1905 Revolution.* Princeton, N.J.: Princeton University Press, 1990.

Vigarello, Georges. *Concepts of Cleanliness: Changing Attitudes in France since the Middle Ages.* Cambridge: Cambridge University Press, 1988.

Vital, David. *Zionism: The Crucial Phase.* Oxford: Clarendon Press, 1987.

———. *Zionism: The Formative Years.* Oxford: Oxford University Press, 1982.

Vol'tke, Gr. "Prosveshchenie." In *Evreiskaia entsiklopediia,* edited by Lev Izrailevich Katsnelson, David Baron Gunzburg, Shimen Dubnov, and Albert Harkavy, 49–58. St. Petersburg: Brokhaus-Efron, 1906.

Von Hagen, Mark. *Soldiers in the Proletarian Dictatorship: The Red Army and the Soviet Socialist State, 1917–1930.* Ithaca, N.Y.: Cornell University Press, 1990.

———. "Writing the History of Russia as Empire: The Perspective of Federalism." In *Kazan, Moscow, St. Petersburg: Multiple Faces of the Russian Empire,* edited by Catherine Evtuhov, 393–410. Moscow: O. G. I., 1997.

Von Laue, Theodore H. *Sergei Witte and the Industrialization of Russia.* Studies of the Russian Institute, Columbia University. New York: Columbia University Press, 1963.

Wagner, Max Leopold. *Espigueo judeo-español.* Madrid: S. A. Torre, 1950.

Waldron, Peter. "Religious Toleration in Late Imperial Russia." In *Civil Rights in Imperial Russia,* edited by Olga Crisp and Linda Edmondson, 103–19. Oxford: Clarendon Press, 1989.

Walkowitz, Judith. *City of Dreadful Delight.* Chicago: University of Chicago Press, 1992.

Wallerstein, Immanuel. "The Ottoman Empire and the Capitalist World-Economy: Some Questions for Research." *Review* II, no. 3 (Winter 1979): 389–98.

Wasserstein, Bernard. *Vanishing Diaspora: The Jews in Europe since 1945.* Cambridge, Mass.: Harvard University Press, 1996.

Weeks, Theodore. *Nation and State in Late Imperial Russia: Nationalism and Russification on the Western Frontier, 1863–1914.* DeKalb: Northern Illinois University Press, 1996.

Weiker, Walter F. *Ottomans, Turks, and the Jewish Polity.* New York and London: University Press of America, 1992.

Weill, Georges. "The Alliance Israélite Universelle and the Emancipation of the Jewish Communities of the Mediterranean." *The Jewish Journal of Sociology* 24, no. 2 (1982): 117–34.

Weinberg, Robert. "The Pogrom of 1905 in Odessa: A Case Study." In *Pogroms: Anti-Jewish Violence in Modern Russian History,* edited by John D. Klier and Shlomo Lambroza, 195–247. Cambridge: Cambridge University Press, 1992.

———. *The Revolution of 1905 in Odessa: Blood on the Steps*. Bloomington: Indiana University Press, 1993.

Weinreich, Max. *Geshikhte fun der yidisher shprakh: bagrifn, faktn, metodn*. New York: YIVO Publishers, 1973.

———. *History of the Yiddish Language*. Translated with the assistance of Joshua A. Fishman and Shlomo Noble. Chicago: University of Chicago Press, 1980.

Weinstock, Nathan, Haim-Vidal Sephiha, and Anita Barrera-Schoonheere. "Yiddish and Judeo-Spanish: A European Heritage." *European Languages*, no. 6 (1997).

Weiser, Keith Ian. "The Politics of Yiddish: Noyekh Prilutski and the Folkspartey in Poland, 1900–1926." Ph.D. dissertation, Columbia University, 2001.

Welters, Linda. "Ethnicity in Greek Dress." In *Dress and Ethnicity: Change across Space and Time*, edited by Joanne B. Eicher, 53–78. Oxford and Washington, D.C.: Berg, 1995.

Werses, Shmuel. "The Hebrew Press and Its Readership in Interwar Poland." In *The Jews of Poland between Two World Wars*, edited by Yisrael Gutman, Ezra Mendelsohn, Jehuda Reinharz, and Chone Shmeruk, 312–33. Hanover, N.H.: University Press of New England for Brandeis University Press, 1989.

West, Sally. "Constructing Consumer Culture: Advertising in Imperial Russia to 1914." Ph.D. dissertation, University of Illinois at Urbana-Champaign, 1987.

Williams, Raymond. "Advertising: The Magical System." In *Problems in Materialism and Culture*, 170–96. London: Verso, 1980.

Wisse, Ruth. *I. L. Peretz and the Making of Modern Jewish Culture*. Seattle: University of Washington Press, 1991.

———. "Not the 'Pintele Yid' but the Full-Fledged Jew." *Prooftexts* 15 (January 1995): 33–61.

Wistrich, Robert S. *The Jews of Vienna in the Age of Franz Joseph*. Oxford: Oxford University Press, 1989.

Wrobel, Piotr. "The First World War: The Twilight of Jewish Warsaw." In *The Jews in Warsaw: A History*, edited by Wladyslaw Bartoszewski and Antony Polonsky, 278–90. Oxford: Basil Blackwell, 1991.

Wynot, Edward D. "Jews in the Society and Politics of Inter-war Warsaw." In *The Jews in Warsaw: A History*, edited by Wladyslay T. Bartoszewski and Antony Polonsky, 291–311. Oxford: Basil Blackwell, 1991.

Yaari, Avraham. *Hadefus haivri bekushta*. Jerusalem: Hotsaat sefarim al shem Y. L. Magnes, 1967.

———. *Reshimat sifrei ladino hanimtsaim bevethasefarim haleumi vehauniversitai biyerushalayim*. Jerusalem: Hevrah lehotsaat sefarim al yad hauniversitah haivrit, 1934.

Yakhinson, Y. *Sotsial-ekonomisher shteyger bay yidn in ruslan in 19tn y.h.* Kharkov: Tsentraler farlag far di felker fun F.S.S.R., 1929.

Yehuda, Zvi. "Iraqi Jewry and Cultural Change in the Educational Activity of the Alliance Israélite Universelle." In *Sephardi and Middle Eastern Jewries: History and Culture in the Modern Era*, edited by Harvey E. Goldberg, 134–45. Bloomington: Indiana University Press, 1996.

Ye'or, Bat. *The Dhimmi: Jews and Christians under Islam*. London: Associated University Press, 1985.

Yerushalmi, Yosef Hayim. *Zakhor: Jewish History and Jewish Memory*. New York: Schocken Books, 1989.

YIVO, ed. *Di ershte yidishe shprakhe-konferents, baricten, dokumenten, un apklangen fun der tshernovitser konferents, 1908*. New York: YIVO Publishers, 1931.

Yubileyem baylage der fraynd, tsenter yorgang. Vol. 13 (January). Warsaw: Der fraynd, 1913.

Yuditsky, A. *Der veg tsu oktober, revbavegung in rusland (1895–1917)*. Kiev: Kultur lige, 1925.

Zeine, Zeine N. *The Emergence of Arab Nationalism*. Beirut: Khayats, 1966.

Zheltiakov, A. D. *Matbaaciligin 250. kurulus yildönümüne armagan — türkiye'nin sosyo-politik ve kültürel hayatinda basin*. Ankara and Leningrad: Basin Yayin Genel Müdürlügü, 1979.

Zhitlovsky, Chaim. *Gezamlte shriften*. New York: Yubileyum oysgabe, 1912–19.

Zipperstein, Steven J. *Elusive Prophet: Ahad Ha'am and the Origins of Zionism*. Berkeley: University of California Press, 1993.

―――. *Imagining Russian Jewry: Memory, History, Identity*. Seattle: University of Washington Press, 1999.

―――. *The Jews of Odessa: A Cultural History, 1794–1881*. Stanford, Calif.: Stanford University Press, 1985.

―――. "Representations of Leadership in Russian Zionism: Picturing Leon Pinsker." In *Essential Papers on Zionism*, edited by Jehuda Reinharz and Anita Shapira, 191–209. New York: New York University Press, 1996.

Zohar, Zvi. "Halakhic Responses of Syrian and Egyptian Rabbinical Authorities to Social and Technological Change." *Studies in Contemporary Judaism* 2 (1986): 18–51.

―――. *Masoret u-temurah*. Jerusalem: Ben-Zvi Press, 1993.

―――. "New Horizons: A Major Nineteenth-Century Baghdadi Posek's Heightened Awareness of Socio-cultural Variety and Change" (in Hebrew). *Pe'amim* 36 (1988): 89–107.

―――. "Traditional Flexibility and Modern Strictness: Two Halakhic Positions on Women's Suffrage." In *Sephardi and Middle Eastern Jewries: History and Culture in the Modern Era*, edited by Harvey Goldberg, 134–45. Bloomington: Indiana University Press, 1996.

Zubaida, Sami, and Richard Tapper, eds. *Culinary Cultures of the Middle East*. London: I. B. Tauris, 1994.

INDEX

SARAH ABREVAYA STEIN

is Assistant Professor in the Department of History and
the Henry M. Jackson School of International Studies at
the University of Washington, Seattle.